THE IMPERIAL ROMAN ARMY

THE IMPERIAL ROMAN ARMY

YANN LE BOHEC

Translated by
RAPHAEL BATE

London and New York

First published in French 1989 as *L'Armée Romaine, sous le Haut-Empire*
by Les Editions Picard

First published in English 1994
by B. T. Batsford Ltd

First published in paperback 2000
Reprinted 2000, 2001
by Routledge
11 New Fetter Lane, London EC4P 4EE

Simultaneously published in the USA and Canada
by Routledge
29 West 35th Street, New York, NY 10001

Routledge is an imprint of the Taylor & Francis Group

Typeset by J. & L. Composition Ltd, Filey, North Yorkshire

Printed and bound in Great Britain at the University Press, Cambridge

British Library Cataloguing in Publication Data
A catalogue record for this book is available from the British Library

Library of Congress Cataloguing in Publication Data
A catalogue record for this book is available from the Library of Congress

ISBN 0–415–22295–8

CONTENTS

PLATES

INTRODUCTION

In AD 9 three legions with their accompanying auxiliaries, under the orders of Publius Quinctilius Varus, were annihilated in the Teutoburgwald by the Germans of Arminius. When he heard the news of the disaster Augustus went into mourning, and according to Suetonius he was prone to fits of rage for several months during which he would shout: 'Varus, give me back my legions!'[1] The emperor certainly considered that the army played an important role within the state, but was his point of view unbiased? Must we accept it without qualifications?

HISTORIANS AND THE ROMAN ARMY

Historians' views on the subject have evolved. In the nineteenth century they considered events to be of prime importance, writing 'battle-history'. From this perspective it would be necessary to relate the Teutoburgwald affair in minute detail. On the other hand, in the mid-twentieth century the Annales school of historians focused on the quantitative and social aspects. From this angle, Varus' army should be described without virtually any mention of the ambush in which it was destroyed. Today we consider that the 'structures' (recruitment, tactics, etc) are of fundamental importance, of course, but evolution is not neglected, while every effort is made to situate events, major conflicts and even battles exactly.

Moreover, two recent works[2] have shown the importance of war in ancient times. According to Y. Garlan war is the expression of a society: thus at Teutoburgwald, senators and equestrians perished, as well as plebeians, both citizens and foreigners. J. Hamand goes even further: he thinks that war expresses a civilization in its entirety; it is not related merely to social history, but also to political, economic, religious and cultural factors.

Furthermore, the Roman state is a complex structure, formed by three major interconnected elements – central administration, provincial administration and the army – modification to any one of these three instruments of power inevitably entailed a reshaping of the other two, precisely because of the close links that existed between them. Yet no synthesis about the third of these areas of study has been published recently; there is therefore a gap to be filled. While the organs of government, economic and social life, religion and culture in the Early Empire are becoming more familiar, the army still holds certain mysteries. There are, of course, many accounts of excavations describing numerous fortresses; two books[3] have concentrated on the Roman army and the Roman soldier, but their contents, far from overlapping, complement each other, and there is a need for an overall picture of the subject. This lacuna can probably be explained by the risks involved in such a venture (the fear of narrating 'battle-history' or the history of events) and by the discredit that has been heaped on military questions. Is it necessary to say that this lack of esteem seems totally unjustified?

CERTAIN PARADOXES AND PROBLEMS

Rome's military history comprises many points of interest, some of which are paradoxical. Before discussing them it must be specified that this book will deal only with the first three centuries AD, that is the Early Empire: the vast movement of conquests that left its mark on the Republic drew to a close with Augustus, while a new order was being installed, both in strategy and organization of the army. On the other hand, Constantine and Diocletian laid the foundations for a new era in these fields. They modified significantly the process of recruitment of soldiers and the distribution of the forces in charge of maintaining security within the Empire.[4]

To return to the paradoxes mentioned above, the most important one is of the greatest interest to historians. Rome certainly built for itself a vast and long-lasting Empire, and this, of course was thanks to its troops. But these conquerors suffered disasters like that of the Teutoburgwald; their weaponry was heterogeneous, the different elements having often been taken from the losers the previous day,[5] and their sense of discipline would certainly have shocked many a twentieth-century officer. What, then, is the true value of the Roman army?

But this is not all, and at least four more questions need to be asked. Firstly, were these soldiers even capable of maintaining law and order? If certain specialists like P. Petit[6] believed in the 'Roman peace', this concept is largely a myth for others like Y. Garlan.[7] The Empire would have been attacked at the same time by barbarians from the outside and brigands from the inside.

Secondly, what was the social composition of this army? This problem, of fundamental importance to the contemporary historian, is very complex; many questions have been asked to try to determine both the social backgrounds and the nationalities of recruits. M. Rostovtzeff wrote that in 238 the urban civilians were opposed to the peasant soldiers during particularly violent riots, but this theory has since been criticized. What is more, we now know that certain values helped to form the collective mentalities, and P. Veyne[8] has shown how power, prestige and honours all play their part along with money, in fact, all that goes to make up 'appearances' (though it is true to say that in the case studied by Veyne the military are not involved).

But there is in addition a technical problem; it is clear that types of unit, command, strategy and tactics have not been examined thoroughly, or even at all, for a long time now. Research is often based on erroneous information: some authors copy others when they are ignorant of the realities involved, and use in any context – normally, of course, the wrong one – Latin terms such as *vexillatio*, *castra* or the surprising *castrum*, the precise meaning of which they are unfamiliar with.

Finally, an effort must be made to answer the last question: 'what was the precise role of the Roman army in the world at its particular time?'. What was stated above must be repeated here, namely that it was one of the component elements of central power, a 'structure' of the state. Its importance will then be better understood if it is remembered that it was also linked to civilian society. The army had a certain influence on the provinces it was situated in, for example when spending salaries, while in its turn it was subject, through recruitment, to the influence of the background in which it evolved. There are, then, three areas of concern: politics, economics and spirituality (i.e. Romanization and religion).

If some new insight is to be brought to a general history of the Roman army it is essential to stick to a principle which is here called a global principle. While it would be somewhat pretentious to wish to say everything there is to be said in one book – and this is not my intention – nevertheless, it seems evident that many questions will go unanswered if only one aspect of the subject, one method[9] or one type of source is adopted; a synthesis must provoke confrontations within each of these categories. Everything is interconnected and one cannot hope to understand what the Roman army really was if one studies recruitment without also studying strategy; aerial photography without excavation reports; inscriptions without literary sources.

THE SOURCES

Literary sources

The ancient authors have not received their due attention from historians who have been attracted by the new information to be gleaned from excavations, while Latinists have often ignored what archaeology and inscriptions have to offer. Yet the former could have avoided many errors and the latter many misinterpretations if this were not so.

These authors can be put into two broad categories – one for whom military matters are not of major concern, but who nevertheless shed much light on the subject: Polybius and Julius Caesar for the Republican period, Josephus, Pliny the Younger, Suetonius, Tacitus, Aelius Aristides, Cassius Dio and the *Historia Augusta* for the following period. Further details can be obtained from the *Talmud* of Jerusalem and that of Babylonia, treatises on religious matters based on real events, compiled by Rabbis between the second and fifth centuries. Until now nobody had thought of reading them with this intention. Unfortunately the facts they relate are at worst late, at best misdated. The same is true of the legal documents, the *Theodosian Code* and the *Institutes* of Justinian.

However, better material exists, for certain ancient theoreticians wrote exclusively on the art of war.[10] Essentially they are tacticians and include specialists on sieges or stratagems: Onesandros, Vitruvius (in Book IX of *De Architectura*), Frontinus, Aelian, Pseudo-Hyginus, Arrian, Polyaenus, Modestus, and especially Vegetius, who interpreted the Early Empire to the best of his ability from his fourth-century standpoint. In addition, the possibility that Augustus and Hadrian instituted regulations for the army has been raised,[11] but it is above all Arrius Menander who is to be read on this subject. Whatever their individual merits, these works often contribute to a better understanding of inscriptions.

Inscriptions

The Romans often engraved texts on hard materials, and this mania or fashion, which the army shared, has left us a heritage of several hundreds of thousands of inscriptions.[12] They can be classified into three groups. 'Military diplomas' are certified true copies of imperial documents granting citizenship to soldiers at the time of their demobilization or to their children or to the mothers of these children. Secondly, there are epitaphs. Finally, there are dedications, which are termed honorific when written to celebrate the merits of a mortal, religious when addressed to one or more gods, commemorative when their aim is to immortalize some event or other (a victory, the construction of a building etc.); moreover, they are termed individual if requested by one person only and collective if several people have contributed, as is the case when clubs, called colleges, are formed at the time of demobilization of soldiers of the same age group, or in some other circumstances. These collective dedications are usually composed of two parts: the dedication itself and the list of sponsors. Very often the two parts have become separated with the subsequent loss of the first, the second being called 'military lists' (in Latin *latercula* which is preferable to *laterculi* the form universally accepted since Th. Mommsen). This has given rise to a fairly widespread misinterpretation since many historians wrongly believe that these lists are independent – archives established by the authorities to know how many men were at their disposal or how many were to be demobilized. In fact, these are private, not official, documents.

One major problem is that these documents rarely carry any clear date. To obtain some notion of their chronology, both the archaeological context, when known, and especially the formula used, must be examined. For example an epitaph found at Mainz[13] says: '(Here lies) Cneius Musius, son of Titus, of the tribe Galeria, (born in) Veleia, aged thirty-two years, having completed fifteen years service, eagle-bearer of the XIV legion Gemina. His brother, Marcus Musius, centurion, has set up (this epitaph).' A specialist would date this burial in the first half of the first century AD, based on the three following criteria: the names of the individuals; indications of civilian nature (age etc.); indications of military nature (length of service etc.). What follows is a brief look at those factors which the specialist bases a judgement on. To be sure, 'there is only local epigraphy'.[14] To study, and above all date, an inscription, only the criteria established for the region or city of that inscription must be taken into consideration. Nevertheless, as long as a too precise date is not put forward, a few major invariables can be established.

The name of a Roman citizen may comprise several elements: the *praenomen* (Caius), the *gentile nomen* (Claudius), at least one *cognomen* (Saturninus), the filiation (son of Lucius), the tribe (Galeria), the homeland (a city) and the *signum* (Antacius):

praenomen	*gen. nomen*	filiation	tribe	*cognomen*	homeland	*signum*
Caius	Claudius	Caii f.	Galeria	Saturninus	Abella	Antacius

Table 1: The names of a Roman citizen in the second century AD.

It is tempting to translate *praenomen* as 'first name', *cognomen* as 'familiar name' and *signum* as 'nickname', but this would be absurd. The *gentile nomen*, common to anyone whose ancestors received citizenship from the same magistrate or emperor (Julius, Claudius, etc.) presents a collective aspect, whereas the *praenomen*, the *cognomen* and *signum* individualize their bearer. The interest of onomastics here lies in its variation according to date, social class and geographical origin. Thus the *tria nomina* (*praenomen* – *gentile nomen* – *cognomen*) characterize the Roman citizen of the second century AD; before the Flavians the *cognomen* is often missing, whereas in the third century the habit of mentioning the *praenomen* is lost. When there is also the filiation, the tribe and the homeland, then the text dates from the first century AD. The *signum*, which appears at the end of the second century, was vulgar at that time but developed a certain cachet in the Late Empire. The *cognomen* carries a lot of information: it can indicate when the homeland is not mentioned, and if it is not of Latin origin, a person's province (a Hasdrubal will necessarily be an African); if it comes from the Greek (Cleitomachus, Epagathus, etc.) it corresponds to an oriental or servile origin, or possibly to a fashion – that of Hadrian's era; if it is found without *gentile nomen* and particularly if it comes from a barbarian dialect (for instance from Thracian like Bithus or Phoenician like Hiddibal) it indicates a *peregrinus*, a lower-class citizen, even a slave. The presence of several *cognomina* indicates nobles and social climbers.

The information of a civilian nature yielded by an inscription can be of different sorts. The use of 'vulgar' Latin forms (for instance Elius for Aelius) is considered 'late'. The mention of two emperors ruling together (e.g. the abbreviation Augg. for *Augusti duo*) cannot be earlier than AD161, the year in which Marcus Aurelius took Lucius as his co-ruler. When it is a question of the price of a monument the word 'sesterces' is written 'HS' in the second century, 'SS' in the third and 'I-S' in between. For epitaphs[15] the use of the nominative case would point to the first century, but a text beginning with the invocation 'To the Spirits of the dead' could not be before the end of the first century, while one beginning 'Memoria of X . . .' could not be earlier than the end of the second century.

Information of a military nature[16] also sheds much light on the subject. Inscriptions relating to auxiliary troops are considered early (first century AD) if the number of the corps follows the name of the unit (*ala Pannoniorum I* instead of *ala I Pannoniorum*), if the unit is designated in the ablative case with or without preposition (*miles ala Pannoniorum* or *ex* or *in ala Pannoniorum*) or if an officer indicates his rank only by *praefectus equitum* without any further precision. On the other hand, honorific epithets bestowed on wings and cohorts (*torquata, felix* etc.) do not appear before the Flavians.

Soldiers on the whole rarely mention the century to which they belong except in the first century, and the same is true of their length of service if they use the verb *militavit*: 'X of Rufus' century, served Y years'. However, when their length of service is expressed by the noun *stipendiorum* the text is probably from the third century. The use of *aerum* was a fashion largely but not exclusively restricted to Spain. The indication of ranks, and notably successive ranks corresponding to a career, is largely a third-century fashion. On the other hand, contrary to what was once received wisdom, the mention of comrades-in-arms as dedicators of a tomb has no special significance. Finally, it should be noted that a closely-argued study[17] has shown that the expression *centuria Rufi* indicates that the centurion Rufus still occupies his post, whereas the formula *centuria rufiana* indicates that he has left his unit and has not yet been replaced.

Coins and papyri

Numerous mintings of coins[18a] also shed light on the history of the Roman army. Some coin inscriptions glorify legions or even whole armies whose emperor (or a pretender) sought their support, as did Macer and his *legio I Macriana*, Hadrian and the various provincial *exercitus*. Others disseminate the military themes of imperial propaganda, the loyalty of armies (*fides exercituum*), particularly when the emperor is not very confident of it. Discipline is another theme thus treated. In the third century some mints were operating solely to satisfy military needs.

Egypt and especially Dura-Europos have yielded a large number of papyri, either official archives or private documents, which are of the greatest interest.[18b]

Archaeology

Excavations do not only yield inscriptions.[19] For some time now we have been aware of coins commemorating victories or else minted in honour of units that had distinguished themselves in action. But a more immediate interest can be found in the study of funerary monuments and military constructions. It is known that burial was practised at a later date than cremation, although cremation experienced a return to favour from time to time. With the African army it has been possible to chart an evolution: in the first century the soldiers' corpses were placed under *stelae* or flat stones; in the second century under cube-shaped altars, and in the third under 'cupules', half-cylinders resting on their flat section (pl.I,1). Some of these tombs were decorated with reliefs, especially those of officers and centurions. There is evidence of busts, some in simple relief, some within a niche, some in a temple (pl.I,2a). Sepultures depicting horsemen have also been found; these may be depicted dismounted and facing the onlooker or in the act of riding away or killing a fallen enemy (pl.I,2b). Another sort represents a standing figure sacrificing, or at a funeral banquet or facing onlookers (pl.II,2c). These sepultures were generally grouped together along roads leaving the camp or placed in a semicircle, at first around the fortresses and later around the civilian agglomeration that grew up alongside the fortress (pl.II,3).

However, it is military archaeology that provides the most information.

To begin with, several hundred fortresses and 'defensive lines' around the Mediterranean basin are known, the most famous of the latter is Hadrian's Wall in Britain. The existence of such ruins has sometimes been discovered by aerial photography, but these discoveries must always be checked on the ground. This technique has been used with particularly good results for the study of the Roman army in Syria by A. Poidebard and in south Algeria by J. Baradez;[20] and there is nothing to exclude the idea that one day artificial satellites will replace the aeroplane.[21]

Archaeology also provides some large monuments. Trajan's Column in Rome represents in fact a *volumen*, that is a book upon which has been depicted through sculptures and not words the Roman victories over the Dacians at the beginning of the second century AD; moreover, it was erected between two libraries. (It is 29.78m (98ft) high on a 10.05m (33ft) base). The more damaged reliefs of the Column of Marcus Aurelius, also in Rome, recount the wars waged by him against the Germans and Sarmatians (it was sculpted in AD180 on a shaft measuring 29.6m (97ft)). Finally the Adamklissi monument in Romania has an enormous circular base which supports a *tropaeum*, commemorating one of Trajan's victories.[22]

THE DUTIES OF THE ROMAN ARMY

After establishing a list of the sources that can be used to study the Roman soldiers, and before describing this army and its evolution, it would be useful to give a brief but precise account of its missions. An initial reflection of this sort will provide a better understanding of some of the analyses developed later in the book.

Main function: war abroad

When dealing with military matters historians sometimes have a tendency to forget a basic truth (for fear of telling 'battle-history'); to quote the words of an unfortunately little-known specialist, Ch. Ardant du Picq, 'combat is the ultimate aim of armies'.[23] A soldier's job is to wage war against a foreign enemy. His main task therefore is to kill without being killed. Legionaries were also duty-bound to ensure the protection of Roman citizens, wheatfields and temples, the last being of prime importance in ancient mentality. As a result they had to undergo preparation by exercises and manoeuvres; they also had to ensure the upkeep and guarding of fortresses, while also going on patrol to survey the enemy.

Secondary function: policing

As they represented a reliable force and as the Roman state had never thought of organizing the maintenance of law and order within its boundaries, it was the soldiers who performed this task.

They could act in a preventative manner, but in such a case their role was limited to one of surveillance of potential trouble-makers. *Stationarii* and *burgarii* patrolled the streets and market-places while the navy endeavoured to prevent the ever-possible return of pirates. In Judaea decurions were posted in the towns, centurions in the cities. Other officers were responsible for monitoring what was said in the schools.[24]

Their main task, however, was repressive. Runaway slaves had to be caught, and Pliny the Younger writes of a *stationarius* doing just that.[25] During the persecutions of the third century it was often the soldiers who arrested, interrogated and executed Christians. In fact, their principal task during peacetime was to eliminate banditry in general,[26] though it must be remembered that in times of civil war political enemies were also often called bandits (*latrones*). It is true that in any period these could be physically exterminated by a secret police specially formed for this task.[27] Finally, it is the army that acted as prison warders[28] and ensured the security of officials by means of ships and escorts.[29]

Subsidiary functions

Soldiers were also called upon to carry out duties that had nothing to do with the use of the force they represented. Some emperors saw in them no more than a relatively well-qualified workforce that cost the state nothing. Thus the army had to carry out administrative tasks,[30] carry official letters,[31] perhaps protect the collectors of a tax called the *portorium*,[32] and even, in some cases, take on civil engineering jobs.[33] On top of that it will be necessary to look again at what was the indirect role of the troops in the economy (spending of salaries), religion (cults of certain gods) and culture (spread of Romanization).[34]

I

ORGANIZATION OF THE ARMY

1

THE DIVISIONS
OF THE ARMY

For the uninitiated the expression 'Roman Army' evokes on the one hand the insufferable praetorians, capable of imposing their law even on the ruler, available at all times for a coup, and on the other legions keeping guard over the frontiers of the Empire with as much steadfastness as discipline. Needless to say, the reality appears in a slightly different light. In fact, the most essential features are to be found elsewhere, and more precisely in the double choice that Augustus made; having been left in command of the troops unwisely by the Senate in 27 BC, he stationed a large majority of them on the frontiers, but left about 5 per cent in the vicinity of Rome. Then he decided that several criteria would allow a distinction between units that were not of the same type. He acted in this way for military reasons (the main enemy was to be found beyond the frontiers) and political (it was not unwise to be able to exert pressure on plebeians and senators alike). This organization resulted in an army whose troop corps were arranged in a hierarchy, some subordinate to others, in which there were to be found elite troops as well as first-, and second- and third-line soldiers.

A text by the Latin historian Tacitus, who in his *Annals*[1] describes the forces Tiberius had at his disposal in AD 23, is a good demonstration of the complexity of the Roman army:

> He [Tiberius] made on that occasion a quick tally of the legions and the provinces they had to defend. It is also, I feel, a point I need to expound by stating what military force Rome disposed of at this time . . . Both coasts of Italy were protected by two fleets, one at Misenum, the other at Ravenna, and close at hand the coast of Gaul was guarded by warships Augustus had seized on his Victory at Actium and dispatched to Fréjus with quite considerable crews. But the main force was by the banks of the Rhine, where it served as a reserve against the Germans and also the Gauls; it consisted of eight legions. The two Spains, recently brought under total subjugation, were occupied by three legions. As for the Mauretanians, King Juba had received them as a present from the Roman people. The other parts of Africa were manned by two legions, as was Egypt, and the immense territory that spans the distance

from the borders of Syria to the Euphrates had only four legions to rule over it and the border peoples, Iberians and Albanians . . . The shoreline of the Danube [was held] by two legions in Pannonia and two in Moesia; two others had been stationed in Dalmatia where the geographical position allowed these to be placed behind those in Moesia but close enough to Italy to be called up promptly when danger threatened. Besides, Rome had its own soldiers living there, three Urban and nine Praetorian cohorts, levied mostly in Etruria and Umbria or in the old territory of Latium, as well as in long-standing Roman colonies. In the provinces moreover, and depending on needs, allied triremes, auxiliary cavalry and infantry had been posted, forces scarcely inferior to the others.

This text shows the existence of a navy, a frontier army of legions and auxiliaries, and finally troops stationed at Rome.

THE GARRISON AT ROME

To begin with the capital of the Empire: the ten thousand men who made up what is called 'the garrison of Rome' were not stationed at first in the very heart of the city. In particular, most of the praetorians were distributed by Augustus throughout the cities of Latium until the inhabitants became accustomed to seeing armed men in the streets, a situation contrary to the political and religious traditions of the Republic. Afterwards the troops were regrouped, mainly in the outlying districts, and true barracks were finally created between the Viminal, the Caelian and the Esquiline hills (pl. III, 4).

The Praetorian cohorts

The most famous of these units, the Praetorian cohorts,[2] owe their name and origin to the small group of men who accompanied the Republican magistrates, the Praetors, when they embarked upon a campaign. Adopting this practice Augustus created the Imperial Guard; there can be no doubt that essentially the primary duty of these men was to ensure the ruler's security. It was therefore logical that he should choose the best soldiers in peacetime as well as in time of war;[3] it was this that made A. Passerini see them as the elite of the fighting men. As the place they were garrisoned meant that they watched over public life, M. Durry quite rightly thought that they played a political role and that they had to ensure peace in Rome. Both interpretations complement rather than contradict each other.

These cohorts were under the orders of one of two prefects from the *praetorium*, men of equestrian rank directly answerable to the Emperor. Each cohort was individually led by one tribune and six centurions. The latter were generally of equal status, with the exception of the *trecenarius*, the chief centurion, whose name is derived from the fact that he also commanded the 300 *speculatores* (another of the ruler's guards), and his second, the *princeps castrorum*. The Praetorian cohorts were said to be *equitatae*, that is they contained a certain proportion of cavalry (one-fifth?) alongside a majority of footsoldiers (four-fifths?).

These nine cohorts were created by Augustus in 27 or 26 BC; they were numbered I to IX and given the scorpion as an emblem. In 2 BC the two Praetorian prefects were appointed primarily to supervise them. Tiberius (14–37) appointed only one commander, the notorious Sejanus; it was these two, emperor and officer, who set up the nine Praetorian and three Urban cohorts (see below) in Rome itself towards AD 20/3, more precisely on the Esquiline plateau, beyond the Servian wall, in what could be called the suburbs.[4]

The twelve units were billeted in a camp 440 × 380m (1445 × 1245ft), a total of 16.72ha (40 acres), to the west of which was installed a training ground or *campus*. Experts disagree on how many men each cohort contained – 1000 from their beginning according to Th. Mommsen, A. Passerini and, more recently, D.L. Kennedy;[5] only 500 for M. Durry and H.G. Pflaum until the time of Septimius Severus when they were made up to 1000. On this point the literary and epigraphical sources are not very helpful, whereas the archaeological evidence is decisive: the legionary camps, which housed about 5000 soldiers, measured between 18 and 20 ha (45 and 50 acres); each of the twelve Roman cohorts must have contained only 500 men as together they occupied just 16.72ha (40 acres); they were thus five-hundred and not one-thousand strong.

The rest of their history seems more simple. Before AD 47 they were increased to twelve, then sixteen in AD 69, during the civil war, by Vitellius, who made them all up to 1000 strong. Vespasian returned to the Augustan system of nine cohorts of 500, and Domitian added a tenth. During the strife following the assassination of Commodus in AD 192 the Praetorians sold off the Empire by auction; they gave the Empire to the highest bidder. To punish them Septimius Severus[6] replaced the rebels by soldiers from his own legions, but organized the new *praetorium* into units of 1000. In 312 they backed Maxentius; after their defeat at the Milvian bridge they were dissolved by the victor, Constantine.

The Urban cohorts

The Praetorian cohorts were very prestigious because they were intimately linked to the ruler and normally escorted him. But there existed in Rome itself another corps created by Augustus, in *c.* 13 BC, whose functions and unit-numbers were smaller. These were the Urban cohorts,[7] whose numbering followed on from the Praetorians, (X to XII), and whose organization was established on the same basis. Two others, were set up later, one stationed in Lyon, the other in Carthage. The task of the first three is defined by Suetonius[8] – they had to be 'the guard of the city' just as the Praetorians were the 'Emperor's guard'. They were basically a police force. In the first century AD they were answerable to the city prefect, a person of senatorial rank, i.e. noble, but in the second century they passed into the control of the prefects of the *praetorium*, and so were more closely linked to the ruler. Each of these Urban cohorts was commanded by a tribune and six centurions; it is quite possible that they included a few mounted soldiers in their ranks, as did the Praetorians, but there is only evidence for horsemen in the garrison at Carthage.[9] It seems reasonable, for the same reasons adduced earlier, to attribute to them an initial strength of 500, raised to 1000 by Vitellius and reduced again to 500 by Vespasian, before possibly being raised to 1500 by Septimius Severus.

Towards 20–3 they were housed in the same camp as the Praetorian cohorts, where they remained until 270, though it is possible that some of them lived in 'police stations' throughout the city. Their history later becomes one of variable unit-numbers: between 41 and 47 the three became six, then seven under Claudius, down to four in 69 under Vitellius, and back to three at Rome under Antoninus Pius. Septimius Severus increased their strength but not their unit-numbers. In 270 Aurelian had a special camp built for them, the *castra urbana* on the Campus Martius. They survived the 312 episode, but during the fourth century they lost their military role to become a workforce employed by the administration.

The *Vigiles*

There also existed in Rome a much humbler corps than the Praetorians and the *urbaniciani*; these were the seven cohorts of *Vigiles*,[10] created by Augustus in AD 6, and possibly 1000 strong right from the beginning. They grouped together men who had two functions – policing Rome at night and full-time fire-fighting. Each unit was assigned two of the fourteen districts into which the city was divided; they occupied 'emergency stations' everywhere. Equipped with lanterns for night patrol, siphons, buckets and brooms for fire-fighting, the *vigiles* do not seem to have been considered as real soldiers to start with. However, as Ulpian shows, they were militarized by the beginning of the third century AD at the latest. In their hierarchy a *princeps* came between the seven ordinary centurions and the tribune in each cohort. At their head was an equestrian officer, the prefect of the *Vigiles*, assisted by a sub-prefect from Trajan onwards. At first these 'firemen' were recruited from the lowest classes of society; in 24 Tiberius granted Roman citizenship to those of them who had completed six years of military service (afterwards the period was reduced to three years). Claudius[11] had one cohort of *Vigiles* stationed at Puteoli and another at Ostia, the two large ports through which supplies went to Rome. At the beginning of the third century AD these units were unquestionably 1000 strong.

Other units of the garrison at Rome

The list does not end with the preceding cohorts; Rome was home for more and more soldiers. First of all, the emperors seem to have thought very soon that the Praetorians were not sufficiently strong to ensure their safety, and various other corps were also assigned to this task. The 'German bodyguards' or 'Batavians'[12] (*corporis custodes*), numbering from 100 to 500, were recruited by Augustus, who seemed to use them as a private militia. This unit was disbanded after the Varus disaster but reformed before 14, and it was Caligula who militarized them completely. Once more disbanded under Galba, they were reformed yet again, probably under Trajan.. As they were cavalrymen, these soldiers were organized in squadrons (*turmae*), commanded by decurions and a tribune; their corps was what was called a *numerus*, that is a unit of irregular troops. Alongside them the 300 'scouts' (*speculatores*)[13] also acted as bodyguards; stationed at the same camp as the Praetorians they were also answerable to the prefect of the *praetorium*. However, the close security of the ruler was only really assured by the 'emperor's personal cavalry', the *equites singulares Augusti*,[14] not to be confused with the *equites singulares* of the provinces, attached to the legates of the legions and the governors. They were created by Trajan, or possibly the Flavians, and by the early second century were also organized into a *numerus* of 1000 (or possibly 500) men. They were commanded by decurions, a decurion *princeps*, and a tribune (two after Septimius Severus) who was himself subordinate to the prefect of the *praetorium*. They occupied two sites, first the 'old camp', then the 'new camp', both located near the Lateran.

Mention must also be made of the darker history of the Roman Empire: its assassins ready to obey the ruler. Barracks built in the first century near the Piazza della Navicella, on the Caelian Hill, housed two corps of similar functions, both commanded by the praetorian prefect. The *peregrini*[15] acted more or less like a secret police, responsible for putting into operation the ruler's orders anywhere in the empire. They were under the command of centurions, themselves subordinate to a *subprinceps* and a *princeps*. The *frumentarii*,[16] set up as a unit and stationed at Rome perhaps under Trajan, at the latest under Hadrian, acted as couriers; from time to time they discreetly executed opponents of the regime and were considered to be spies. Attempts have been made to see in them the ancestors of the infamous *agentes in rebus* of the Late Empire, but their small numbers – they functioned as a *numerus* of 90 to 100 soldiers – must have limited their misdeeds. It is uncertain if they were stationed on the Caelian from the start, but it is attested from Septimius Severus onwards. Whatever the case, they recognized the leader of the *peregrini* as their commander.

But that is not the whole story; the *numerus* of the *statores Augusti*, in the same camp as the Praetorians and consequently subordinate to the same superior, were used as military police. General-staff advisors were recruited from the *primipilares*, ex-chief centurions. Sailors[18] were used as couriers; those from the Ravenna fleet had been stationed near Augustus' naumachia on the right bank of the Tiber; those in Misenum, who were responsible among other things for the awnings that shielded the amphitheatre from the sun, were on the Esquiline, near the Colosseum. Finally, all sorts of soldiers,[19] either going from one garrison to another or mobilized for some exceptional circumstance, cluttered up the streets of the city. In 68 there were soldiers from Illyria and Germania, under Caracalla there were Germans and Scythians, etc.

Nevertheless, the Praetorian cohorts remained the most important units and it is possible to see how rapidly this situation evolved. The emperors of the first century quickly forgot the caution of Augustus who dared station only a few soldiers in Rome, but the new regime was a real monarchy that relied upon the support of the army.

THE PROVINCIAL ARMIES

From the political point of view the garrison at Rome was the most important, but the military nature and weight of numbers gave the leading position to the border troops. At times conflicts and jealousies arose from this contrast of situation.[20] Every province that bordered the barbarians was allocated an army comprised of one or more legions with their auxiliaries, or else just an auxiliary force. Here another hierarchy is discernible.

The legions

To begin with the units that commanded the most prestige means dealing first with the legions,[21] whose emblem was the eagle and who represented an elite. Each legion numbered about 5000 men, for the most part foot-soldiers, organized into ten cohorts of three maniples or six centuries each, except for the first cohort which had only five centuries but of twice the manpower of the others (pl. IV, 5). At the start of the Principate a detachment (*vexillum*) of veterans was added,[22] under the command of a curator or a prefect or a centurion called a *triarius ordo*, and a permanent group of mounted soldiers. The legionary cavalry, perhaps axed under Trajan, but quickly reinstated, comprised 120 men from the time of its origin up to the time of Gallienus (or earlier), who increased the number to 726. The legionary cavalry was peculiar in being placed under the command of centurions and not decurions. The command structure, from bottom to top was as follows: 59 centurions, the most highly graded of whom is called the *primipilus*; one (or several?) 'six-month' tribunes (*sexmenstris*), who probably commanded the cavalry; five tribunes called 'narrow-striped' because of the narrow purple stripe on their dress which indicated that they were of equestrian rank, each responsible for two cohorts; the prefect of the camp; a tribune called 'broad-striped' because of a broad purple stripe on his tunic, indicating that he belonged to the senatorial aristocracy; finally the legate of the legion, from the same aristocracy, and above him, in provinces which had more than one legion, an army legate. The units stationed in Egypt by Augustus, as well as those created by Septimius Severus, had equestrian prefects as commanders. The former inspired Gallienus to generalize the system. This emperor merely abolished the command positions reserved for senators which left the old camp prefect in charge of his corps in the absence of his two former superiors, the legate and the broad-striped tribune.

Each legion is designated by a number and a name, for instance First Minervian, Second Augustan, Third Cyrenaican. The variable nicknames will be discussed later. The creation of a legion corresponds to a preparation for a conquest,[23] while the loss of one reflects a defeat and the disbanding of one a revolt.

The evolution of the legions after the death of Augustus in AD 14 can be summarized in **Table 2**.

The auxiliaries

The legions never travelled alone. They were accompanied by less prestigious units[25] who were there to assist them, but who could also be used independently. These auxiliary corps were made up of 500 or 1000 men,[26] and were consequently called *quingenaria* or *milliaria*, but it is obvious that they were never perfectly round numbers. Experts conclude that the total number of soldiers in this category present in any province was more or less equal to that of the legionaries there. Thus Britain with its three legions was defended by 15,000 elite infantrymen and 15,000 soldiers of lesser importance. A text from Tacitus[27] describing Vitellius' entry into Rome in 69 gives a good picture of the hierarchy that existed within the Roman army. Here is how the military parade was organized:

> In front advanced the eagles from four legions, on the sides the standards belonging to the detachments of four other legions followed by the ensigns of twelve wings of cavalry; after the lines of infantry came the cavalry, then thirty-four cohorts of auxiliary infantry recognizable by their national names or their type of weapons.

This passage also reveals a certain degree of diversity existing within these types of units, for the documents speak of 'wings', (*alae*) 'cohorts' and *numeri*.

DATE	CREATED	DISAPPEARED
39	XVa Primigenia XXIIa Primigenia	
67	Ia Italica	
Galba (68–9)	Ia Adiutrix VIIa Gemina	
70		Ia (Germanica) IVa Macedonica XVa Primigenia XVIa (Gallica)
Vespasian	IIa Adiutrix IVa Flavia XVa Flavia	
83	Ia Minervia	
86–7		Va Alaudae
92		XXI Rapax
Trajan	IIa Traiana XXa Ulpia	
132–5(?)		XXIIa Deioteriana (or earlier)
c. 165(?)	IIa Italica IIIa Italica	IXa Hispana
c. 197	Ia Parthica IIa Parthica IIIa Parthica	

Table 2: Creation[24] and disappearance of legions

Among these less prestigious troops the wings represented a relative elite. Made up of cavalrymen they were divided into 16 squadrons (*turmae*) of 500[28] or 24 of 1000, a number that seems rarely to have been reached before the Flavian era.[29] In the first case they were commanded by a prefect, in the second by a tribune: this officer, assisted by a sub-prefect at the beginning of the Empire, was of equestrian rank. He was assisted by a decurion *princeps* and by other decurions, one for each squadron.

After the wings in hierarchical order came the cohorts, units of infantrymen made up of six centuries when numbering 500 men or ten of 1000,[30] a number which similarly does not seem to have been reached before the crisis of 68–9. Some of them enjoyed more prestige than others and must therefore be considered separately; they are the ones recruited from Roman citizens, a few of them having notably been levied from volunteers. Soldiers of these units enjoyed the same status as legionaries.[31] The command was entrusted to centurions under the leadership of one of their number, the centurion *princeps*, who was himself under the orders of a prefect in the 500-strong units, or a tribune in the Roman-citizen or 1000-strong units; the presence of a sub-prefect is again known only from the beginning of the imperial era.

But the situation is even more complex than it appears and mention must be made of another debate among historians. A few auxiliary cohorts, some of which are known to have existed from the beginning of the Empire,[32] were called *equitatae*,[33] an adjective simply translatable by 'mounted' but which leads to a certain ambiguity. The fact is that these units were mixed, made up of six or ten centuries and between three and six squadrons, depending on whether they were 500 or 1000 strong (here it is difficult to give exact numbers). Their command was entrusted to centurions and decurions, as well as to a prefect or a tribune according to whether they were 500 or 1000 men respectively. The question to be answered is the role of the cavalrymen.[34] According to G.L. Cheesman their horses were used only for moving around; they fought on foot and were therefore mounted infantry. But R.W. Davies thought differently, that they formed a cavalry, albeit second-line, but cavalry none the less. It is this second view that appears to be the correct one, confirmed by certain passages from the speeches of Hadrian in Africa,[35] and above all by bas-reliefs depicting cohort cavalrymen killing enemies on the ground. On one of these can be seen one such soldier, seated on his horse, sticking his lance into a man lying on his back (pl. IV, 6).[36] As for dromedaries, also used by the Roman army, they served as pack animals; but it has also been noted that camels frightened the horses.

At the very bottom of the ladder were the *numeri*.[37] In fact the term *numerus* has two different connotations. In its general meaning it designates any unit that is neither legion, wing nor cohort: thus there are the bodyguards of the imperial legates, known as *singulares legati*,[38] who form a *numerus* commanded by a centurion called *praepositus* or *curam agens* (these soldiers, cavalry and infantry alike, recruited exclusively from the wings and cohorts, are in addition to the *stratores*, legionary infantrymen assigned to the same task). The *singulares*, who constituted a reserve and an academy of officers, appeared on the scene next to the governors of the provinces in the Flavian era, and next to the legion commanders at the beginning of the second century at the latest.[39]

They disappeared in the second half of the third century to give way to the *protectores* although these are possibly attested earlier. In its restricted meaning the word *numerus* was applied to a unit of non-Roman soldiers who kept their ethnic characteristics of language, uniform or weaponry. This second category appears at the end of the first century or at the beginning of the second.[40] It was institutionalized by Hadrian but had been originated under Domitian, Nerva or, more probably, Trajan. The Mauretanian horsemen of Lusius Quietus and the *symmachiarii* mentioned by pseudo-Hyginus could have served as models. In this area a wide diversity prevails: there are units of 1000 men, others of 500, and others smaller still (the first are commanded by tribunes, the second by prefects, the others by 'officers' (*praepositi*) who are often seconded legionary centurions, or by curators (*curam agentes*[41]); there are also cavalrymen and infantrymen, of whom the subaltern command is assured respectively by decurions and centurions, as for the other auxiliaries.

When speaking of these soldiers the Romans used the term 'barbarians' (*nationes*) or designate them by their ethnic names (Mauri, Palmyrani) or their title (the Mauretanian *numerus*, the Palmyranian *numerus* etc.). The appearance of this type of unit can be explained: at the beginning of the Empire the subjugated peoples supplied men to the wings and the cohorts, but little by little, attracted by relatively high wages, Roman citizens and Romanized natives joined the units. As it was still desirable to use barbarians, something new had to be created for them: the *numeri* are for the second century what the other auxiliaries were for the first.

The latter, as a whole, follow the same pattern as the legions as regards nomenclature; more often than not there are three basic elements – type, number and name, for instance *cohors I Afrorum, ala I Asturum, numerus Palmyrenorum* – based on the model *legio I Augusta* etc. The third element normally designates the people from whom the soldiers were initially recruited, but it can be derived from the nomenclature of an individual, referring in that case to the person who was the first to have the honour of commanding the unit,[42] for instance *ala Indiana* recalls a certain Indus, not the Indians. After the number is sometimes found the name of the emperor who created the unit, for instance *cohors I Ulpia Brittonum*; for the first and second centuries there are *Augusta, Claudia, Flavia, Ulpia* and *Aelia*. In certain cases further precisions follow, such as distinctions and laudatory adjectives, such as 'pious', 'faithful', 'of Roman citizens', etc., or descriptive titles such as '1000-strong', *equitata, veterana* ('the most ancient'), *scutata* ('of shieldbearers'), *contariorum* ('of pikemen'), *sagittariorum* ('of archers'), or even an indication of the province in which it was garrisoned, for instance *cohors I Gallorum Dacica* was formed in Gaul and sent to Dacia. As for the 'variable' nicknames and those derived from noble imperial families, they will be examined later.

However, this organization of the army was modified during the third century. Auxiliaries were used more often, both in large concentrations and alone, independently of the legions. The origins of this evolution must perhaps be sought in Septimius Severus' creation of a corps of Osrhoenian archers.[43] But it was under Severus Alexander that this new tactic was experimented with on a larger scale; breastplated cavalrymen called cataphracts (*clibanarii*) and archers recruited in Osrhoena again, in

Mauretania and among Parthian deserters.[44] Gallienus provided himself with a mounted reserve force of Dalmatians and Mauretanians that was still operational under Claudius II[45] and Aurelian. The latter entrusted to each governor his own rapid intervention group, the *equites stablesiani*; he had a very mobile army, the *promoti* ('elite') and the *scutarii* ('shieldbearers'); he used Dalmatians and Germans against the Palmyranians and immediately after their defeat he then incorporated them into the Roman ranks as a heavy cavalry.[46] In spite of all of this, during the early Empire the legions still represented the most solid element of the frontier army.

THE NAVY

The navy,[47] on the other hand, has always suffered from a poor image in depictions of the Roman army, but a recent thesis[48] by M. Reddé has gone some way in rehabilitating it by showing its usefulness. In fact, the constitution of a permanent navy was one of the preoccupations of the victor at Actium: already in 31 BC Octavius, later to become Augustus, stationed most of his ships at Fréjus. Shortly afterwards he transferred them to Italy, to Misenum and Ravenna.[49] It is said that their mission was to control the Western and the Eastern Mediterranean from these two ports. Subsequently, small fleets were responsible for demonstrating Roman presence on the peripheral seas and the large rivers, for instance fleets of Britain, Germany, Pannonia, Moesia, Pontus, Syria and Alexandria.

The command of each Italian squadron was undertaken by a prefect of equestrian rank, except under Claudius and Nero when this post was sometimes entrusted to a freedman, although, of course, the admiral at Misenum had the last word over his counterpart at Ravenna. From Nero's time each was assisted by a sub-prefect. We also know of the existence of an officer called *praepositus reliquationi*, who must have been the chief of the depot or the reserve. Then come the *navarchus* (commander of one division?) and the centurion in charge of one ship, who can probably be identified with the *trierarchus*, since each ship, whatever its size, was considered as a century. Finally, the provincial fleets were entrusted to legionary centurions, seconded to the posts, and to equestrian prefects. The latest research on the Roman navy (see n. 48) estimates the number of men to have served in this force at between forty and forty-five thousand, a seemingly huge, but by no means improbable figure.

The squadrons at Misenum and Ravenna were called *praetoria*, probably under Domitian, a title they were to lose in 312. Generally speaking, a fleet was simply designated by two words, indicating its nature and the name of the geographical sector where it was to be found, for instance, fleet of Misenum, of Ravenna, of Germany, of Pannonia, etc.

THE DETACHMENTS

This organization, which was more varied in normal circumstances than might have been thought, was even more complicated in exceptional circumstances. For a particular mission such as fighting a war, engaging in work or occupying posts, even at a great distance, the garrison at Rome, the frontier army or the fleets could send detachments of varying size, sometimes called 'vexillations' (*vexillationes*), sometimes *numeri collati*.

Vexillations

The name 'vexillation' is derived from *vexillum*, which designates the standard around which soldiers, who had left their original unit for a particular task, rallied. The members of such a task force are called *vexillarii*, the same name as that of the cavalry standard-bearers.[51] This term should not be applied to any mobile unit, as has sometimes been the case; it is to be used only if it is explicitly mentioned in a text or if we are sure that a *vexillum* was present, as individual or collective movements might take place for numerous reasons without the men being grouped around this symbol. In some respects, therefore, the definition of a vexillation is an official or juridical one; a single tomb mentioning a soldier killed far from the unit's base is not sufficient to prove its existence.[52] As soon as they arrived at their new theatre of action the men passed under the control of the sector commander (thus we find soldiers from the *legio VI Ferrata* receiving orders from the legate of the *legio III Augusta*[53]); but as he was not known by his new subordinates he had difficulty in getting them to obey him.[54] Vexillations can be classified into two large groups according to the missions they were entrusted with.

War

A provincial army could send to the scene of operations a whole legion and a detachment from each of its legions, or only send the equivalent of two or four cohorts per unit, i.e. 1000 or 2000 men each time.[55] In the case of auxiliaries the army could proceed in the same way, sending all its troops or a fraction of each of them. In principle the command of Roman citizens could only be entrusted to an officer of senatorial rank, and that of barbarian soldiers only to someone of equestrian rank, but exceptions can be found, particularly for the first century when this rule is less strictly applied than was previously thought. An ex-first centurion (*primipilaris*)[56] or a camp prefect[57] could be given the responsibility. The rule was more strictly applied in the second century; right up to the time of Marcus Aurelius (161–80) the head of the legionaries, whether a tribune or a legate, was a noble, normally with the title 'imperial legate of the vexillations', exceptionally with that of *praepositus* or *praefectus*; the wing, cohort or fleet soldiers were then entrusted to an equestrian.

From Marcus Aurelius onwards the soldiers were assembled and indiscriminately placed under the orders of several senatorial or equestrian *praepositi*, who were themselves subordinate to a general (*dux*) who was an aristocrat. Finally, between the Augustan era and the middle of the third century we find commanders called *prolegato*, and Septimius Severus, when driven by the needs of the situation, organized large expeditionary forces under senators with equestrian subordinates.[58]

Other

But war was not the only mission (see n. 52): vexillations could be assembled for building-work, such as the construction of a fort, or for the occupation of a post, tasks which required fewer men. If they were legionaries most of them came from one cohort, or else a few were taken from each century; the command was assured by a centurion or a simple *principalis*, a soldier exempt from fatigues. In the case of auxiliaries, each century or *turma* detailed men subordinate to a *principalis*; sailors were entrusted to a centurion. In each case the head of the detachment carried the title *praepositus* or else the unit was said to be *sub cura* X (under the responsibility of X).

Numeri collati

Movements of troops far from their units of origin did not conform to regulationary practices in some cases, or were effected as a vexillation in others, but a third possibility has still to be mentioned. On four African inscriptions from the third century can be found the words *numerus collatus*.[59] Three interpretations have been proposed: firstly, that this was an ordinary *numerus*, analogous to the barbarian corps of the same name; secondly, that it was a unit assigned to another to reinforce it;[60] and thirdly it was a sort of vexillation. To understand the significance of this expression, each of the two words that compose it must be defined. The term *numerus* designates either non-Roman soldiers or any types of troop that are not legions, wings or cohorts. The past participle *collatus* signifies 'collected' or 'gathered together'. In Maghreban epigraphy are very often found the words *aere collato*, meaning 'money having been gathered' or 'having made a collection'.

In none of the four texts are the soldiers or the officers presented as belonging to the unit in question (nowhere is there mention of a *miles* or *centurio* or *praefectus numeri collati*). The command is assured by detached officers, a legionary centurion, an auxiliary centurion and a wing decurion with the title of *praepositus*. What is more, the inscriptions are dispersed geographically from Numidia to Tripolitania, yet the auxiliaries of this region seem only to have operated in a restricted sector in the third century. It seems reasonable therefore to reject the first hypothesis; the whole context suggests that it is not a permanent unit. Furthermore, these *numeri collati* sometimes accompanied other detachments, but they could also act independently, so the second hypothesis must be rejected (it will be noted besides that an 'assigned' unit is nothing more than a vexillation). This leaves the third interpretation. The *numeri collati* were detachments that were not entitled to a *vexillum*; they were made up of men (126 in one text) taken from several camps or from several units with a special task in mind, and could be permanent.

THE QUESTION OF 'LOCAL MILITIAS'

The Roman army seems therefore to have been constituted of many types of units. Should even more be added? Some historians believe in the existence of 'local militias', on a municipal or provincial level.[61] This expression presents a problem because it is ambiguous. Municipal authorities certainly disposed of armed men to maintain law and order on land under their jurisdiction. But it was the army, as has been said, that had as its principal duty the protection of the Empire from all external threat. Did these other men join up with the legions and the auxiliaries in times of war abroad, *bellum externum*? That is another question altogether. In any case, many errors have been made by historians who have based their opinions on two types of argument. First, they thought they had found trace of these units in the famous 'frontier soldier-farmers' the *limitanei* of the *Historia Augusta*,[62] as well as in other corps called 'lance-bearers' (*hastiferi*), 'allies' (*symmachiarii*), 'young men' (*iuvenes*), 'Mauretanians', or 'explorers of Pomaria' (Pomaria was in Caesarean Mauretania). Then they drew up a list of officers that had commanded this type of combatant, peace-officers (*irenarches*) in the east and military tribunes *a populo* in the west, coastline prefects (*ora maritima*), national prefects (*gentes*) and city prefects.

Unfortunately, there is not much solid evidence for this. The *limitanei* are mentioned for this era only in two suspect passages of the *Historia Augusta*, which are confirmed by no other writer. The *hastiferi* were worshippers of the goddess Bellona.[63] The *symmachiarii*, Mauretanians and Pomarian explorers served very regularly in the Roman army and were organized in *numeri*. Only the organization of the *iuvenes*[64] could effectively resemble a sort of local militia; these associations grouped together sons of nobles and young men of humbler origin[65] who were given a physical education with a military flavour (the *lusus iuvenum* made them do physical exercise, and they particularly esteemed Mars). As for the so-called 'officers', we now have more precise knowledge of them. The military tribunes described as *a populo*[66] were carrying out a normal service, simply after having been recommended to the emperor by the plebeians of their homeland. The national prefects, city prefects and peace-officers, all regular municipal magistrates, had the same means as their counterparts for fulfilling police functions. As for the *praefectus orae maritimae*, he was someone carrying out an equestrian task for the state with regular troops at his disposal.

It is certain, nevertheless, that each city disposed of units whose charge it was to maintain law and order on its territory.[67] Moreover, it is possible that an inscription from Tripolitania[68] describes an intermediate stage during which certain local authorities would have had to organize a defence against the barbarians. This text, dating from the reign of Philip, indicates that a small fort 15m (50ft) square was built by a tribune under the orders of a *praepositus limitis*, and without mention of the name of any wing or cohort whatsoever. As it is difficult to imagine that the commander of a 1000-man unit was placed at the head of such a small post, it is possible to conceive that this is the ancestor of the Late Empire tribune, the head of a local militia.

CONCLUSION

With its garrison at Rome, its provincial troops and its fleet, the Roman army presented a great diversity.[69] Consequently it is possible to attempt only a relatively accurate estimate of the number of men who constituted it. An auxiliary soldier cannot replace a legionary; furthermore, the rare figures there are must be treated with caution. Nevertheless, some calculations can be made, using Tacitus' figures of about 60 men per century and auxiliary numbers equal to those of the legionaries.

If we consider the length of the border to be defended, even the most optimistic numbers suggested by J. Carcopino indicate just how under-manned the army was. To make up for the lack in quantity the Romans had only one recourse, that is to quality. The diversity described above implies the existence of a certain hierarchy among the different types of

DATE	NUMBER OF LEGIONS	TOTAL NUMBER OF MEN	REFERENCES
31 BC	15	160,000	*Res Gestae Divi Augusti*, ed. J. Gagé, 1977
AD 14	25 (23?)	240,000	idem
23	25	240,000	Tacitus, *Annals IV, 5*
c. 161	28 (+5)	315,000	CIL, VI, 3492
211	33	456,000 (estimate probably too high)	*Historia Augusta, Sept. Sev, XXIII, 2* (see VIII, 5); J. Carcopino in *Mél. R. Dussaud* 1939

Table 3: Roman army numbers

units, elite troops and second-line troops. This raises the problem of recruitment. What criteria were used? Why was one man directed towards the auxiliaries, another to the legions? But the first point to be noted is that within a single unit there are two characteristics – diversity and hierarchy – something which should not come as a surprise when dealing with military matters.

Table 4 Organization of the Roman army in AD 23

PLACE OF GARRISON	UNITS	OFFICERS	TYPE OF UNITS	NUMBER OF UNITS	APPROXIMATE NUMBER OF MEN
Rome *garrison of Rome*	Praetorian Cohorts	1 or 2 Praetorian prefects (E) 1 tribune (E) × 9 6 centurions × 9	D foot-soldiers (+ some cavalry)	9	4500
	Urban Cohorts	1 Prefect of Rome (S) 1 tribune (E) × 3 6 centurions × 3	D foot-soldiers	3	1500
	Cohorts of *Vigiles*	1 Prefect of *Vigiles* (E) 1 tribune (E) × 7 7 centurions × 7	D (?) or M foot-soldiers	7	3500 7000
	German Bodyguards	1 tribune (E) some decurions	100–500	1	250
	Speculatores	Praetorian prefect	300	1	300
	Equites singulares Augusti	Praetorian prefect	M (D?) (formed after 23)	1	1000
	Peregrini	1 Princeps some centurions	(formed after 23)	1	?
	Frumentarii	Princeps of the *Peregrini*	100 (formed after 23)	1	100
	Statores	Praetorian prefect		1	
	Primipilares				
	Sailors				
TOTAL GARRISON AT ROME					10,000

... cont.

Frontiers *Provincial armies*	legions	(1 army legate) (S) 1 legion legate (S)*1 1 tribune (S)*2 1 camp prefect 5 tribunes (E) 1 (?) six-month tribune 59 centurions of whom 1 primuspilus	5000 men foot-soldiers except for 120 cavalry*3	25	125,000
	legions				
	auxiliaries • *alae* (wings) • cohorts • mixed cohorts	1 prefect (E)*4 16 decurions 1 prefect (E)*4 6 centurions 1 prefect (E)*4 3 decurions 6 centurions	D*5 cavalry D*5 foot-soldiers D*5 foot-soldiers +cavalry	250	125,000
	TOTAL FRONTIER ARMY				250,000
Misenum and Ravenna *navy*	fleets of Misenum and Ravenna	1 prefect per fleet (E) navarchi centurions trierarchi	sailors called soldiers		40,000
Provinces *navy*	fleets of Britain, Germany Pannonia Moesia, Pontus, Syria Alexandria	1 prefect per fleet (E) trierarchi	sailors called soldiers		
GENERAL TOTAL					300,000

D = 500 men; M = 1000 men; (E) = equestrian; (S) = senator

*1 The legion legate (S) was replaced by a prefect (E) in Egypt by Augustus. Septimius Severus appointed a prefect (E) to the three 'Parthian' units. Gallienus made this a general rule.

*2 The tribune (S) disappeared under Gallienus.

*3 Gallienus increased the cavalry to 726 men.

*4 These prefects replaced by tribunes (E) for 1000 strong units (see *5).

*5 Some auxiliary units were 1000 strong, generally from the Flavian era.

2

THE MEN

When talking of 'the praetorians', 'the legionaries' or 'the auxiliaries', this at best conjures up a picture of men capable of advancing in one line, at worst some sort of indescribable rabble. In fact almost every soldier occupied a specific position, fulfilled a well-defined function and could seldom be replaced by another: the range of activities possible ranged from artillery to cavalry, the signals corps to health services, exercise to music, and included a thousand other specialists. Despite existing already in the Republican era, this diversity seems to have reached its apogee only at the end of the second century AD.

Moreover, it must not be forgotten that the hierarchical nature of the Roman army meant that every social class, including the servile, was represented in it. There were noblemen: senators inscribed on the census list as possessing at least one million sesterces and enjoying the monopoly of the magistracies (quaestors, aediles, praetors and consuls) served as officers. There were also men of equestrian rank who possessed only 400,000 sesterces and who then worked for the emperor as procurators and prefects. They constituted a lower rank of officers. Sons of municipal worthies were appointed as centurions. Roman citizens of plebeian origin entered the legions, and the *peregrini* the auxiliary forces. In addition, some units used slaves for administrative tasks. Historians use the German term 'Rangordnung' to denote this double classification according to hierarchy and specialization.[1]

THE OFFICER CORPS

Following the method of the ancients, we start with the most highly-ranked people, the officers.[2] It should be noted that the term is used here to designate any man superior to a centurion.

36

General points

Membership of this corps, which was based on social and institutional criteria, could also vary according to circumstances and personality;[3] a brave man in a difficult war could occupy a more important post than he would in normal times.

It has been said too often that the quality of the Roman army was due to the efficiency of its soldiers and its centurions, in contrast to the mediocrity of their superior officers who were no more than incompetent amateurs: in effect, victories were won by the troops despite the presence of their superiors. This cliché should be rejected. Each son of a senator or equestrian had treatises on the art of war in his library and also regularly went on military exercises. Such reading and exercise formed part of the education generally given to a young man of good birth. As military techniques at the time were not of great complexity it required only a few weeks of actual command to assimilate the essentials; furthermore, many officers proved capable of notable exploits. The equestrian Caius Velius Rufus boasted of having carried out a sortie through Dacia, the kingdom of Decebalus, and later on of bringing to the emperor spoils and prisoners, including the two sons of the Parthian king.[4] With his own hands Marcus Valerius Maximianus killed Valaon, the king of a Germanic people called the Naristes.[5] In 238 senators still had good military experience. Some of them actually boasted of their love of the army;[6] they led an austere life, trained regularly, wore a sword at all times and were called the *viri militares*.[7] They do not, however, appear to have formed a caste and their community remained open.

In fact, every officer fulfilled practically the same functions, leading men to war, preparing them through exercise and administering justice. Moreover, the setting up of a closed group would have been made difficult by a prerogative the emperor accorded himself, that of deciding on promotions.[8]

The hierarchy

In this domain there existed a *de facto* head, the emperor himself. He was the one considered to be the victor of every battle, even if he was not present on the field of action. In the latter case it was his charisma that acted, his religious powers that were able to sway the gods in Rome's favour. Thus when an emperor assumed the title of 'conqueror of the Parthians', this in no way signifies that he had actually been to the East. Cassius Dio is the author who describes most clearly the powers exercised by the emperors over the army: 'They have the right to recruit the army, to levy taxes, to wage war and sign peace-treaties, to have the same command over foreign soldiers [i.e. auxiliaries] and legions'.[9]

The emperor appointed a general staff and in military matters was assisted by the praetorian prefect(s), who acted simultaneously as both prime minister and minister for war. This second function was highlighted by Pseudo-Hyginus for the beginning of the second century,[10] there is proof of it for Perennis,[11] and the same could be demonstrated for Paternus and Cleander,[12] the latter filling the post without actually having the title. (These three served under Commodus between 180 and 186.) At the time of Severus Alexander, Flavian and Chrestus were still carrying out these roles.[13]

At the head of each provincial army was the governor, an imperial legate who was a propraetor of senatorial (consular) rank where legions were based, but otherwise a procurator of equestrian rank. Until the time of Caligula, Africa was an exception: there the proconsul who governed it, normally for one year, also had troops at his disposal even though he was selected by the Senate (in general it was the emperor who chose the commanders). The basic duties of governors were to maintain public order, which entailed 'announcing the laws' (i.e. administering justice), to supervise religious life, to maintain the temples, to ensure, with the help of a quaester or procurator, that the collection of taxes was not interrupted, and finally to see to the safety of the territory. From the time of Gallienus only men of equestrian rank remained in the army and about AD 262 the title of *praeses perfectissimus* is used to designate the person responsible for the province. The word *praeses*, simply meaning 'chief', was already in use at the end of the second century, but only in a domestic context. The hypothetical 'senatorial reintroduction' under the Emperor Tacitus is still contested by some scholars, and even if it was a reality, it was very short-lived.

A legion was commanded by another imperial propraetor (praetorian) legate,[14] who was subordinate to his provincial governor of the same title. In the case of a single unit of this type in a district, the same person carried out both duties. During the two or three years of posting this officer ensured the smooth running of the units under his command, including the auxiliaries. Discipline and exercise were part of his remit,[15] as were financial and judicial matters.[16] From the time of Gallienus the camp prefect, who previously only ranked third in the unit, became the highest-ranking official due to the suppression of the legate and laticlavian tribune. His title changed to 'distinguished [*egregius*] prefect of the legion', and he answered directly to the *praeses*. His powers remained wholly military.[17] This organization of superior command entrusted to a prefect already existed in some legions, namely those stationed in Egypt, as since Augustus' time senators were not allowed to reside in this territory belonging to the emperor, and in those three units termed Parthian that were created by Septimius Severus.

The laticlavian tribune was ranked second;[18] the name came from the broad purple stripe decorating his toga that recalled his senatorial origins. He was assisted by a personal officer staff; his role was that of advisor, but he also held military and judicial powers.[19] He was responsible for physical training,[20] and despite his youth (he would be about 20) and his limited experience (his was a one-year post) he would replace the legate if the latter were to fail, with the title of *tribunus prolegato*. In any case, during the course of his career he would eventually reach this position for which he had been preparing himself for a long time.[21]

The camp prefect,[22] third in command in the unit, was in charge of rampart maintenance,[23] and consequently of directing sieges during expeditions.[24] He decided where posts should be built and supervised their construction. When the army was on the march he saw to the baggage, and in combat he commanded the artillery. At all times he took part in the deliberations of the legate's staff. The qualifications for this rank were to have been tribune at Rome three times[25] or a retired *primipilus*, which, according to B. Dobson, gave access to the equestrian order.

The five narrow-striped (angusticlavian) tribunes, next in rank, got their name from the narrow purple stripe sewn on their toga, indicating that they belonged to the equestrian order. During combat each was at the head of two cohorts, that is one thousand men.[26] They acted as advisors at meetings of the legion staff, and in peacetime[27] conducted physical training, supervised the security of the camp gates, the foodstores, the hospital as well as acting in a judicial capacity. After them came the 'six-month' (*sexmenstris*) tribune who probably commanded the legion's cavalry. He would have been alone in occupying this post.

The titles of other officers appear in inscriptions or literary texts. The term *dux*[28] generally means 'leader', i.e. *qui ducit*; in the first and second centuries, in a technical sense, it designates someone who is not of the senatorial order but who exercises a wide command; from the period of the Marcomannic wars of Marcus Aurelius, however, it designates senators who command detachments of legionaries and auxiliaries. Finally, in the middle of the third century appeared the *dux limitis*, the commander of a small section of border country. The term *praepositus* also refers in general to a leader, but of lesser status than the *dux*, for example an equestrian at the head of vexillations of either legionaries or auxiliaries. After Marcus Aurelius, however, a senator sometimes had this title. Furthermore, there is evidence of a unit comprised wholly of citizen-soldiers and formed for a precise mission being assigned to a *prolegato* in the period between the Augustan era and the mid-third century.[29] In combat, ex-prefects with the title of *primipilares*[30] were in charge of posts manned by soldiers; under their orders were wing and cohort commanders. Between 253 and 268 there is also evidence of *protectores divini lateris*,[31] an elite imperial guard recruited from among the officers; they constituted the reserve.

Little is known of the exact situation in units other than the legions. It is possible that the prefects of the garrison of Rome, and those of the auxiliaries, had powers over their men that were similar to those the propraetorian legates had over theirs. As for the tribunes of the urban corps, their roles must have approximated to those of their namesakes in the border armies.

Two studies have concentrated on naval officers and particularly on their annual salaries.[32] A prefect of the Italian fleet received 100,000 sesterces in the first century, 200,000 in the second, and was called 'distinguished' (egregius). In the third century he was called perfectissimus; a sub-prefect, also 'distinguished' and a head of depot or of the reserve (praepositus reliquationi) earned 60,000 sesterces, while a prefect of the fleet in Germany, Britain or on the Pontus Euxinus drew 100,000 sesterces from the time of Septimius Severus. From then on a ship's captain (trierarchus) could become squadron leader (navarchus), then first centurion of the fleet (princeps) before becoming primipilus in a legion.[33]

Careers

These posts have yet to be seen in the context of any career-structure. We know that during the Early Empire there were two categories among the social elite. The nobility, who belonged to the Senate, qualified for this privilege by their wealth, of course, but also by holding magistracies; apart from these duties they fulfilled preliminary functions (before), intermediate (between) and priesthoods.

1. Preliminary duties Vigintivir Laticlavian Tribune*	
2. Magistracies	3. Intermediate duties
Quaestor	Curator
Aedile or Tribune of the People	Legate*
Praetor	Proconsul
Consul	Various
4. Priesthoods	

Table 5: Senatorial career-structure
(Functions marked with an asterisk carried with them military powers)

An inscription throws light on the subject.[34]

> To Lucius Dasumius Tullius Tuscus, son of Publius, of the tribe Stellatina, consul, companion of the Emperor, augur, member of the Hadrian brotherhood, (imperial) propraetor legate of the provinces of Upper Germany and Upper Pannonia, prefect of the Treasury of Saturn, praetor, tribune of the people, legate of the province of Africa, quaestor to the Emperor Antoninus Pius, Augustus, military tribune of the Fourth Flavian legion, member of the committee of three responsible for the striking and engraving of bronze, silver and gold, Publius Tullius Callistio had (this inscription) placed.

This career is not given in forward, but in reverse, chronological order. Tuscus assumed these magistracies therefore at Rome (quaestor, tribune of the people, praetor, consul). Previously he had begun his state career as a money minter, then as laticlavian tribune in a legion. In between his high City functions he assisted the proconsul of Africa, administered the State Treasury (the Treasury of Saturn), governed two provinces where legions were to be found, supervised civil engineering and gave advice to the emperor. He also served the gods Hadrian and Antoninus who were deified after their death, and was augur. Normally members of the Senate occupied only a few military posts: they served as laticlavian tribunes, legates of legions (fifty candidates for twenty-five posts), army or vexillation commanders. Under Augustus and Tiberius they could also become prefects of wings. The equestrians represented a second-rank elite in the Empire, specializing both in military, and surprisingly, financial spheres.

1. *Equestrian militiae*   Prefect of a cohort*   Angusticlavian tribune of legion* or three tribunacies at Rome*   Prefect of a wing*

2. *Procuratorships*
 Procurator at 60,000 sesterces per annum
               100,000
               200,000
               300,000
 head of department in chancellery, or in finance or governor of a province*

3. *Prefectures*   Prefect of the fleet*   Prefect of the vigils*   Prefect of the corn-supply   Prefect of Egypt*   Prefect of the *praetorium*
4. *Priesthoods*

Table 6: Equestrian career-structure
(Functions marked with an asterisk carried with them military powers)

Equestrians began with 'three equestrian *militiae*', each of three years' duration.[35] At the beginning of the Empire *primipili* became commanders of cohorts and inexperienced senators commanders of cavalry regiments. All that was left for a young man of this second rank was to be a tribune, and from Claudius onwards the sequence was a cohort, a cavalry regiment and then a legion.[36] Under the Flavians the sequence was modified to cohort, legion, cavalry regiment and remained thus.[37] An inscription from Spain demonstrates this:[38]

To Lucius Pompeius Faventinus, son of Lucius, from the tribe Quirina, prefect of the VIth Asturian cohort, military tribune of the VIth Victorious Legion, prefect of the cavalry of the IInd Spanish Cavalry Regiment, decorated by the Emperor Vespasian, deified, with a golden crown, a pure spear and a cavalry standard, flamen of the province of Nearer Spain, priest of Rome and Augustus; Valeria Arabica, daughter of Caius, his spouse had [this honorary monument?] made.

Between 161 and 166 at the latest, perhaps as early as Hadrian, the state offered to those who wished it the possibility of a fourth military duty, while the command of auxiliary footsoldiers became optional. Septimius Severus enabled those who wished it to miss out the period in a legion. Nevertheless, in the third century it was the equestrians who made the best officers in the Roman army.[39]

An impressive list of the possibilities open to equestrians can be drawn up. At Rome they could be prefects or sub-prefects in the *praetorium* or with the *Vigiles*, tribunes in all the corps. In the legion they could be used as prefect commanders in Egypt, and as camp prefects and tribunes in the three Parthian units. In the navy all the posts of prefect and sub-prefect were reserved for them, while in the *auxilia* they occupied all the posts of prefect and tribune. It has been said that the 'coastal prefect' (*ora maritima*) commanded at least one cohort; up to the time of Hadrian this equestrian was stationed at Tarragona, but another equestrian with the same title carrying out his duties on the Black Sea did not have troops at his disposal and had to ask the governor of the province for an escort.[40]

The advantage of these equestrian positions lay in their social role; whether they were a culmination or the starting point for a career, they constituted an opening. At first this was an opening somewhere near the bottom; thus, under Augustus, one ordinary soldier became successively centurion then cohort prefect[41] while another was able to rise to be Praetorian prefect, admittedly during the crisis of 68–9.[42] Normally, the son of an equestrian started straightaway in the *militiae*, then moved on to the procuratorships (finance officers or provincial governors or heads of sections in Rome). The high-flier would go on to the main posts of prefect (*Vigiles*, corn-supply, Egypt, Praetorian). Some even moved up to be senators; in this case they followed a mixed career structure, thus demonstrating that this type of service could provide an opening towards the top.

Finally, mention must be made of the case of the 'six-month' (*sexmenstris*) tribune, who appears to be similar to the prefect of the workforce, a purely civilian appointment more or less equivalent to the head of a magistrate's cabinet. These two posts might have been bought by local dignitaries to enable them to join the equestrian order.[43]

To sum up, it seems that there is evidence of a significant change in the officer corps in the second half of the third century, with senators being replaced entirely by equestrians.

CENTURIONS AND DECURIONS

Moving one step downwards in the hierarchy of the Roman army are the centurions in the infantry and the decurions in the cavalry who were subalterns, but unlike the officer corps, career soldiers.

Centurions in the legions

The best-known organization is the legion,[44] whose ten cohorts were each subdivided into six centuries, apart from the first cohort which had five, but of double the number of men. Within each cohort in order of rank we find *pilus prior, princeps prior, hastatus prior, pilus posterior, princeps posterior, hastatus prior*. While there was no *pilus posterior* in the first cohort, there was the *primus pilus*, the leading officer of this rank for the whole legion.

FIRST COHORT			SECOND – TENTH COHORTS		
primus pilus	*princeps prior*	*hastatus prior*	*pilus prior*	*princeps prior*	*hastatus prior*
	princeps posterior	*hastatus posterior*	*pilus posterior*	*princeps posterior*	*hastatus posterior*

Table 7: Organization of the positions in the cohorts

The *primuspilus*, present at meetings of the legate's chief of staff, held authority over his century and his cohort like every *pilus prior*. Each centurion, assisted by an adjutant, led his men into battle and made them exercise. He spent on average three and a half years in each of his garrisons during his period of service, which lasted at least twenty years. However, there is a problem here. A legion should normally contain 59 centurions, but Tacitus says[45] that there were 60, while an African inscription lists 63,[46] of whom two had the title of *primuspilus*: the ninth cohort had only five but the first and the eighth had seven each, while the sixth had eight![46] A shortfall can always be explained as being due to a vacancy still unfilled, but there are several possible explanations for a surplus. Some writers have claimed that the oldest men fulfilled administrative tasks; the *triarius ordo*,[47] the commander of the veterans, can also be included, but this post existed only at the very beginning of the Empire; mention must be made of a more likely explanation: the commander of the 120 cavalrymen, the heads of the vexillations sent to posts some distance from the camp, the commandants of certain auxiliary units. On top of that we know of *primipili bis*, but the concern here is with careers.

It is generally believed that all the centurions of the second to the tenth cohorts were of equal rank and were assigned according to the number of their years of service.[47a] Assignment to the first cohort constituted real promotion, and within it its five positions represented a ladder of further promotion. These careers have received some study recently.[48] A fairly wide diversity has been noted, but two main channels were open to candidates. Roman equestrians or sons of dignitaries could in fact obtain the actual rank they wanted, straight from civilian life. In the first case they were said to be 'of equestrian rank' (*ex equite romano*), but more often than not this title was conferred on men already living in the army; sometimes these were ordinary soldiers (a normal situation among the auxiliaries), but mostly officers (it will be seen that certain adjutants normally went on to become centurions, but this was neither systematic nor obligatory). They could also be cavalrymen in a cavalry regiment or soldiers in the Praetorian cohorts, allowing them to be promoted in Rome itself as well as in the provincial armies. Promotion was determined by the initial appointment, a factor that may surprise the twentieth-century reader; the higher up the ladder one started, the higher one finished (someone who started as a centurion was more likely to become a *primuspilus* than an adjutant was). And it must be remembered that a soldier's first post was determined by his social status; an *ex equite romano* began his career at a higher level, rose through the ranks more quickly and to a higher level than the son of a dignitary.

When he became a centurion a soldier normally performed several successive commands at the same rank, as this text from Tarragona in Spain demonstrates:[49]

> To Marcus Aurelius Lucilius, son of Marcus, of the tribe Papiria, born in Poetovio [Pannonia], came from the Imperial Guard [*equites singulares Augusti*], centurion in the First Adiutrix Legion, in the Second Trajana Legion, in the Eighth Augusta Legion, in the Fourteenth Gemina Legion, in the Seventh Claudia Legion, *hastatus prior* in the Seventh Gemina Legion, [died] age 60 after forty years of service. His wife and heiress, Ulpia Iuventina, had [this sepulture] made for her husband who carried out all his duties and was full of kindness.

Lower down, several possibilities existed; a soldier could be *primuspilus* (a second post of this sort carried greater authority than that of a tribune) or a camp prefect and even a commandant of an auxiliary corps or a unit of the garrison at Rome. It is still a moot point whether the camp prefect was of equestrian class; the uncertainty regarding the *primuspilus* is even greater.[50] But let us turn our attention to a case of promotion: 'Lucius Alfenus Avitianus, *primuspilus*, tribune of the third cohort of Vigils, of the 12th Urban ...' (an inscription from Cadiz[51]). A very rare and privileged minority were appointed as procurators; the following case is exceptional: 'To Cneius Pompeius Proculus, centurion of several legions, *primuspilus* of the Fourth Flavian Felix Legion, tribune of the first Urban cohort, procurator of Bithynia-Pontus'. Proculus' career, known from a document from Rome,[52] is not a common occurrence. In fact, here we are dealing with an important aspect of the society and the mentality of the Early Empire. The position a man was appointed to varied according to his social background, and because of this, the higher it was at the beginning, the higher it would be at the end. Individual merit played only a secondary role, but it could have an important influence on a son's advancement. In those days a man worked with posterity in mind. Under Gallienus there appears a new type of career that is complicated by the use of the title *protector*.[53]

Some special cases remain. No one yet knows what an *adstatus* was;[54] unless it is a misreading of *hastatus*? We do not really know either what the terms *deputati* and *supernumerarii*, mentioned in several inscriptions, signify. For M. Durry, they could be part of the garrison at Rome.[55] For many historians *primi ordines* was the title given to the five centurions of the first cohort, but a passage in Tacitus is problematical.[56] The episode, which occurred during the civil war that followed the death of Nero, concerns the Seventh Galban Legion: 'six of his first-class centurions were killed'. 'First-class centurions' is the translation of *primi ordines*, and the text reveals that there were more than six *primi ordines* in a legion. *Ordo* means 'century',[57] and the question can therefore be asked whether we are not dealing with officers fighting in the front lines. What is more, an analogous meaning could easily be given to the title *ordinarius*,[58] which, according to the glossaries, implies a notion of ability, and for which Vegetius gives the following definition: 'those who lead the first centuries in battle'. In this definition 'first centuries' would mean those preceding the main body of the legion, and not those that constitute the first cohort. An American scholar had previously put forward another interpretation:[59] an *ordinarius* would have commanded an *ordo*, just as an *ordinatus* did. This second title remains obscure; for R.W. Davies it would refer to the first centurion of a mixed cohort, but the glossaries link this word to the notion of discipline.[60]

Decurions and centurions of units other than legions

In studying the legions something exceptional is evident, namely that the cavalrymen are commanded by centurions and not by decurions, as would normally be the case. For the other corps there are few peculiarities. In the Praetorian cohorts the centurions are of equal ranking except for the *trecenarius*, who takes precedence over all, and his deputy, the *princeps castrorum*. In his book on the Praetorians (see n. 55), M. Durry analyses a type of career he calls 'equestrian praetorians'. The soldier started with three officer appointments in the garrison at Rome, then became a centurion in a legion and in the three urban corps, then a *primuspilus* and returned once more to the capital for a triple tribuneship which could lead to procuratorships.

The auxiliaries were characterized by a fairly wide diversity. The cavalry regiments required sixteen decurions if they were 500-strong or twenty-four if they were 1000-strong. The chief decurion was called *princeps*; similarly, the infantry cohorts had six or ten centurions, the chief of whom was also called *princeps*. The mixed units had three to six decurions and six to ten centurions. Finally, the number of officers in the *numeri* varies. A cohort decurion was subordinate to a cavalry regiment decurion who in turn was subordinate to a centurion.

The navy also causes certain problems. For M. Reddé,[61] each ship, classed as a century, was commanded by a *trierarchus*, and several ships constituted a squadron under the leadership of a *navarchus*, but both these naval officers, as regards the provincial fleets at least, were inferior in rank to a centurion in a legion.

THE ORDINARY LEGIONARIES

The legions did not consist of masses of undifferentiated men; a reading of inscriptions gives quite the opposite impression. There is a surprising diversity of titles and functions, a high degree of specialization of a technical nature, with new posts constantly coming into existence. It might be asked why these same principles were not applied to industry and agriculture? It is probably a question of mentality, otherwise Rome would doubtless have experienced an extraordinary economic development. The fourth-century Vegetius described the situation under the Early Empire (see n. 62):

> The eagle bearers and the portrait carriers are those who carry the eagles and the images of the emperor; the adjutants are the lieutenants of higher-ranking officers, who adopt them in some sort to carry out their duties in case of illness or absence; the ensign bearers are those who carried the ensigns and whom we now call standard bearers. The officers of the password [*tesserarii*] are those who take the word or the command to the barracks while those who fight at the head of the legions still are designated by the name of *campigeni*, because they help to instil discipline and values in the field by the example they give. From the word *meta* [limit] is derived the name of the *metatores* who precede the army to mark out the limits of the camp. *Beneficiarii* are those who rise to this rank by the favour of the tribunes. From *liber* is derived the name of the *librarii* who record all the rations of the legion; from *tuba*, trumpet, from *buccina* [sic], horn, from *cornu*, cornet, the users of these different instruments are called *tubicines*, *buccinatores* [sic], *cornicines*. Soldiers who are good swordfighters and who receive double rations are called *armaturae duplares*; those who receive only single rations are called *armaturae simplares*. The *mensores* measure the space allotted to each group of soldiers for pitching their tent or mark out their quarters in town ... As regards rations, there were some who got double allowances, some single, and were

in line for promotion. These, then, are the leading soldiers or officers of the different classes who enjoy all the privileges that go with their rank. As for the others, they are called workers because they are forced to carry out tasks and all sorts of services in the army.

And yet Vegetius gives a very oversimplified version of the reality.

Criteria for classification

If we start with the legions it is because discoveries in the field allow greater knowledge of them than any other corps. The first difficulty is to classify the men. Faced with a plethora of names the Austrian scholar, A. von Domaszewski,[62] acted like a legal expert: he gave precedence to the study of each officer's personal staff. The drawback with this system is that it leads us to believe in the existence of a large number of administrative staff and a minority of combatants. The true situation seems to have been more satisfactorily perceived by English scholars like E. Birley, B. Dobson and D.J. Breeze.[63] They concentrate on salaries, some of which are three times as high as others, and on exemption from fatigues. A third criterion should be added: the honour that a post conferred. An eagle bearer who carried the emblem that represented the whole legion must have had more prestige than a bearer of the *signum* for a maniple. Furthermore, it is important to see clearly that what was essential for every soldier was preparation for war. Some titles probably were no more than temporary, e.g. *ad portam*, 'in charge of the gate' whereas others implied a more permanent position.

On joining the army a young man was first seen by the recruiting board (*probatio*); if satisfactory (*probatus*), he became a conscript (*tiro*) for a period of four months, then took the oath and served as a combatant. The term *miles* designates any serviceman, from the ordinary soldier (*gregalis*)[64] to the general,[65] as well as to the veteran, who kept the title until he died. But here an initial classification can be made; some enlisted men were exempt from fatigues, others received a higher salary.

Certain titles imply a particular honour. The 'candidate' was designated by an officer to fill some post or other; the *cornicularius* owed his name

TITLES		FATIGUES	SALARY
munifex[66]	*simplaris*	yes	1
immunis	*simplaris*	no	1
immunis = principalis[67]	*sesquiplicarius*	no	$1\frac{1}{2}$
	duplicarius[68]	no	2
	triplicarius[69]	no	3

Table 8: Elementary hierarchy

to a decoration consisting of two small horns hanging from his helmet. He presided over the personal staff of an officer. The *beneficarius* owed his title to the fact that he had been given a mission as an assistant, a 'benefit' by a tribune or a prefect.[70] Some served as major-domo, others as governors of prisons or state mail-staging posts (the *stationes* of the *cursus publicus*).

Other titles imply the exercise of authority. The curator was someone entrusted with a mission (*cura*); under Augustus the curator of the veterans commanded the detachment of veterans. A master (*magister*) directed the artillery, and from the time of Aurelian another directed the cavalry. In the third century this title gradually became synonymous with *optio*. The *optio* was the adjutant of someone who had a post, particularly a centurion (this is the ordinary adjutant), but some, called *ad spem ordinis* or *spei*, formed an elite who would one day become centurions themselves. In classical Latin *discere* meant 'to learn', but in military terms and during the Late Empire, the verb could mean 'to teach', and the *discentes* (similar to *doctores*) were instructors who initiated eagle-bearers, cavalry standard-bearers, architects and cavalrymen in their tasks. *Evocati* were soldiers of any rank still in service after the expiration of their legal contract. They might be officers,[71] but in practice they were more likely to be highly-qualified administrators, policemen, surveyors, architects, quartermasters and particularly physical training instructors. More often than not they came from the *praetorium* (*evocati Augusti*), sometimes from a legion, and were highly ranked, next in line to the last centurion of the unit.[72] Finally, even if they were no longer in the army, the veterans retained some prestige.

Military offices

Arms

The modern classification of infantry, cavalry and artillery in operation applies for the Romans too. Of course, the majority were foot-soldiers, called *antesignani* if they fought in the front line in front of the standards (*signa*), *postsignani* otherwise.[73]

The 120-strong cavalry was perhaps disbanded under Trajan, only to be reinstated afterwards, by Hadrian's time at the latest, and increased to 726 per legion under Gallienus. An exceptional feature was that the cavalry was not led by centurions but by decurions who were assisted by several officers, namely the standard bearer (*vexillarius*), the password officer (*tesserarius*), the adjutant, the foal-breeder(?) (*pollio*) and the groom (*mulio*). Training was under the control of the head of the training ground (*magister campi*), the person in charge of the actual training (*exercitator*) and the instructor (*discens*). Care and treatment of the horses was left to the groom, as already mentioned, the veterinary surgeon (*pequarius*), and also, perhaps, the *pollio*, if this term really does mean a foal-breeder and not the person responsible for seeing that weapons were kept clean.[74] Nor is it known what the *hastiliarius* actually did, though we know that his function was restricted to the cavalry; the word has been linked to *hastile*, 'javelin shaft'. Another mysterious figure was the quaestor of the cavalry;[75] he paid for something, most probably supplies. Finally, it is worth repeating that it was a tribune, probably the *sexmenstris*,[76] who commanded the mounted legionaries in combat.

As for the third class of arms, it is through epigraphy that we learn of artillerymen (*ballistarii*) and artillery experts (*doctores ballistarum*), under the command of the chief of the *ballista* or catapult. It seems unlikely that the architect of the legion had a considerable role to play in this field, whereas the *libratores*[77] actually launched missiles and projectiles, although it must be admitted that this was not their primary function.

But the infantry kept its reputation as 'the queen of the battlefield'. The legion had two advantages for Rome, namely that it could muster a large number of men, and these men could easily be deployed. Officers had two means of transmitting orders.[78]

Transmission of orders

First of all, soldiers had to keep their eyes on their standards. Each legion had an eagle, a cult object that was in the keeping of the eagle-bearer (*aquilifer*)[79] (pl. V, 7), an officer who shouldered a heavy responsibility. He was instructed in his duties by a *discens*. Each maniple (composed of two centuries) had a *signum* kept by the *signifer*[80] (pl. V, 8), who led the way on the march and in combat, and who supervised in camp the money deposited under the shrine of the ensigns and also the market where the soldiers bought their provisions. In these civilian activities he was helped by assistants (*adiutores*). *Signiferi* had a hierarchy: a *principalis*, adjutants and *discentes*. Moreover, the cavalry followed a *vexillum*-bearer, called a *vexillarius* and not a *vexillifer*, who should not be confused with the member of a vexillation, designated by the same term (pl. VI, 9). Here, too, *discentes* are attested. Even though it does not appear to have been a tactical function, mention must also be made of the *imaginifer* whose duty was to present the imperial bust or busts in ceremonials. It is not known whether there was one for each legion or one for each deified emperor. However, it has been established that one was registered with the third cohort, and this contradicts the view that they were necessarily attached to the first cohort.

Secondly, soldiers had to obey audible commands, both those spoken by their superiors and those transmitted by music. Music was used for reveille and the changing of the guard,[81] but its main function was tactical. In combat three instruments were used: the straight trumpet (*tuba*)[82] had to be obeyed by every soldier as it gave the signal to charge or retreat, as well as to leave camp. It was also used for sacred ceremonies. The horn (*cornu*), a curved *tuba* reinforced with a metal bar, was obviously different.[83] In combat it was blown for the bearers of the *signa*. Normally, trumpets and horns were played together to order the soldiers to advance on the enemy or engage in hand-to-hand combat[84] and during religious ceremonies such as the *suovetaurilia*, the sacrifice of a pig, a bull and a ram. The *bucina* was a rarely-used instrument and not much is known about its use. It was possibly a short *tuba* with a slight curve (pl. VII, 10). Trumpet players had to purify their instruments during the *tubilustrium*. There were 38 in each legion, i.e. 27 for the maniples of cohorts II to X, five for the centuries of the first cohort, three for the cavalry and three for the officers.[85] There were only 36 horn blowers, organized on the model of the *tubicines*, without any being assigned to the officers. Both categories had adjutants. It is with the *bucinatores* that difficulties arise. Their very limited presence in inscriptions, one mention in Vegetius and another in the Latin glossaries gives the impression that the *bucina* was a second instrument sometimes used by certain *tubicines* or by certain *cornicines*.[86]

Finally, although this office was not concerned with military tactics, came the *hydraularius*, who played the organ during certain rites.[87] On Trajan's Column we see flute players accompanying the purification of a camp (*lustratio*);[88] these must surely be civilians or perhaps even slaves.

	VEGETIUS			GLOSSARIES		
TITLES	*tubicen*		*cornicen*	*tubicen*		*cornicen*
Instruments	*tuba*	*cornu*	*cornu* + *bucina*	*tuba*	*tuba* + *bucina*	*cornu*

Table 9: Musicians

Security

The same meticulous desire to distribute responsibilities also played a role in the organization of security in the camp. To achieve this, dogs were used to warn of spies and deserters and to waken men on watch who might fall asleep, but most faith was put in humans. Among the sentinels (*excubitores*), some had specific tasks; there were those who watched over the shrine of the ensigns (*aedituus*), and especially over the *signa* (*ad signa*), others kept watch over the exercise room (*custos basilicae*), over the armoury (*custos armorum*), the baths (*ad balnea*), the grain stores (*horrearius*) and the camp-gate (*ad portam*) or one of its monuments. The *clavicularius* or 'keeper of the keys' (of the camp?) doubtlessly fulfilled a similar function to the last mentioned. Patrols were carried out by a *circitor*, and the watchmen received a password written on a tablet carried by the *tesserarius*. Each century had a *tesserarius*, and some of these were mounted. In connection with this must be mentioned the admirable attitude of Antoninus Pius when he felt he was near to death; to the soldier who asked him what was the password he should pass on to the sentinels he replied 'aequanimitas', 'peace of mind'. Finally, the *horologiarius* gave the signal for the musicians to sound the changing of the guard.

But the camp was not the only place, and officers in particular had to be protected and escorted according to their rank. At first this task was carried out by the ten *speculatores*,[90] but later these men were given different duties. They had previously served as scouts, but now they became couriers, law-enforcers, and sometimes policemen and executioners. The army legates, and at least from Trajan's time the legion legates, were allowed to have bodyguards (*singulares*) from among the *auxilia*. The *secutor* was a *singularis* of inferior rank according to some authors, yet we know of one who received double pay. A few officers were allowed at least one equerry (*strator*) or one major-domo (*domicurius*).

When the army was on the march the high command needed to be told about enemy movements. This job was normally carried out by the *proculcatores*, or exceptionally by the *mensores*, after the former scouts, *speculatores*, had abandoned it. Finally, the *explorator* kept watch on the enemy's movements.[91]

Exercise

To all these responsibilities must be added some others that were of fundamental importance. Historians have been too prone to neglect the preparation for combat. Training took place under a decorated 'veteran',[92] an *evocatus* or instructor, in a special area under the control of the *campidoctor*,[93] his subordinate the *doctor cohortis* and an *optio campi*. Cavalrymen were trained by a *magister campi* and an *exercitator*; swordsmen by a *doctor armorum* or *armatura*. We even hear of a *discens armaturarum*, a sort of 'trainers' trainer'. Men on manoeuvres were called *quintanari*. Thus a soldier's principal function was to fight in battle for which he had to be prepared. In order to be totally free to do this, the soldiers were relieved of certain material worries by their officers who handed these over to specialized services.

The services

Provisions

Roman legionaries received plenty to eat and the food was much more varied than has been suggested. The embryo of a supply corps was put under the control of an *evocatus* and the bearers of the *signa*,[94] assisted by the *quaestor*, who made payments and an *actarius* or *actuarius* who kept the books.[95] We know of the existence of a victualler (*cibariator*), but even in this field specialization gradually developed. The staple diet was always wheat-based. On campaign it was the job of the *frumentarii* to find wheat (in peacetime these soldiers acted as couriers or perhaps took care of the *annona*); in camp grain was bought by a quartermaster (*dispensator*), given to the storekeeper (*horrearius*), ground by a miller (*molendarius*) and distributed by the *mensor frumenti*. At each stage of the proceedings the *librarius horreorum* kept the accounts. During war, meat was supplied by hunters (*venatores*), otherwise it was bought by the butcher (*lanius*) who was also responsible for the market. Firewood for heating the baths was the job of the *ad lignum balnei*. That part of the food provided by the state from the time of Septimius Severus was organized by the *salariarius*.[96] Finally, transport of these goods was the job of carters or cartwrights (*ascitae* and *carrarii*).

The engineers and the workshops

It is not difficult to see that some of these activities could be left to civilians, but the army tended to live in a state of self-sufficiency and the engineering corps developed to the point of being in charge of a veritable industry. In the beginning the objective was to be able to build a sturdy camp each night on campaign. The *metator* went on ahead of the troops to find a suitable location and then divide up the units;[97] the *librator* made sure everything was level (his skills were used to help the artillerymen and to dig canals, for example);[98] the surveyor or *mensor*[99] marked out the sites for the individual barrack-rooms and the limits of a legion's territory, and he could stand in for the architect. The latter, whose exact rank has still to be established, was responsible for the construction of buildings and the repair of war machines;[100] he fulfilled more or less the same functions as the *librator*. In the permanent fortresses there was a workshop (*fabrica*) managed by a master (*magister*), producing both weapons and bricks.[101] He was assisted by an *optio* and a *doctor*. Elsewhere, a long list of titles corresponding to the activities of this veritable factory can be found, though the two scholars who have drawn up these lists made use of many documents that do not seem to be strictly military.[102]

The health services

The health services were placed under the control of the camp prefect at a late date;[103] they were staffed by a numerous, very specialized personnel. The doctors (*medici*) were mere *immunes*, *sesquiplicarii*, *duplicarii* and even centurions. Some were said to be 'ordinaries' but it is uncertain whether these were civilians attached to the army, general practitioners or, on the contrary specialists with the rank of centurion. They can also be thought of as surgeons accompanying the front-line soldiers in combat (see n. 58); one such person can be seen on Trajan's Column, carrying a helmet and a sword attending to a casualty.[104] The hospital had an adjutant, but it is not known if the box that gave the *capsarius* his name was used for storing documents or bandages. He could have been a pharmacist. There were also medical secretaries (*librarii*), and instructors (*discentes*) for the last two functions. The *marsus* would have been both magician and herpetology specialist.[105] Finally, the livestock would have been entrusted to a veterinary doctor (*pequarius*); foals were perhaps allotted to a specialist called the *pollio*, and camels to an *ad* or *cum camellos* (*sic*). But the Roman army did not cater only for men and animals; it endeavoured to satisfy the gods too.

The priesthoods

Each legion had a *haruspex* responsible for reading the omens in the entrails of animals which had been prepared for sacrifice by the *victimarius*, probably a similar office to the *ad hostias*. The sacred chickens were looked after by the *pullarius*.

All these offices distance us more and more from the tactical functions which we should not forget remained essential. However, it is necessary also to consider the administrative personnel.

The administration

Personnel

Documentation in general was the responsibility of the *exacti*, one of whom, designated by the title *actarius* or *actuarius* noted the details of daily service and of the corn-supply from the time of Septimius Severus onwards.[106] The *commentariensis*, also called a *a commentariis*, under the orders of a head curator (*summus curator*), was in charge of the purely military archives, while the *librarius*[107] specialized in accountancy, sometimes actually referred to as *librarius a rationibus*, 'archivist for the accounts'. He also worked for the state mail. When the legate gave orders, these were at once taken down by a stenographer, the *notarius* or *exceptor*; it is difficult to see any difference between these two offices. Finally, the army used its own interpreters,[108] for instance *interpres Dacorum, interpres Germanorum*. Information had to be obtained at all costs, and men could even be despatched to the barbarians; one such soldier was sent to the Garamantes. Then come certain functions, the exact nature of which eludes us: the *cerarius* wrote on wax tablets,[109] and the *canalicularius* was employed as a writer, and not as a water engineer.[110] Some officers had a secretariat: *immunis legionis, legati* and *consularis* entered into this category. Finally, all of these soldiers were assisted by helpers (*adiutores*).

Bureaux

Some more or less important figures, like the African proconsul or the Black Sea Coast prefect, were granted helpers in the form of officers (*cornicularii, beneficiarii*, etc.) sent from the nearest army.

Each of the legates, prefects and tribunes was assisted by a particular administration (*officium*), normally under the orders of a *cornicularius*; the *cornicularii* were then grouped in their turn in a bureau, also called an *officium*, as was the accountancy bureau (*officium rationum*). The soldiers attached to the service of the legion commander were subordinate to the praetorian adjutant and to a centurion. A. von Domaszewski has drawn up several tables of these bureaux which can be updated and schematized as follows:

| | ROME | | | | FRONTIERS | | | | | | | | |
| | | | | | LEGIONS | | | | | | AUXILIARIES | | |
	PREFECT OF ROME	URBAN TRIBUNE	PRAETORIAN PREFECT	PRAETORIAN TRIBUNE	LEGATE GOVERNOR	LEGION LEGATE	LATICLAVIAN TRIBUNE	PREFECT	ANGUSTICLAVIAN TRIBUNE	SEXMENSTRIS TRIBUNE	WING PREFECT	COHORT PREFECT	PRAEPOSITUS NUMERI
actarius						x					x	x	x
adiutor:													
cornicularii			x										
librarii						x							
principis					x								
officii corni-													
culariorum					x								
tabularii													
stratorum					x								
beneficiarius	x	x	x	x	x	x	x	x	x	x	x	x	
commentariensis	x				x					x			
cornicularius	x	x	x	x	x	x	x	x			x	x	x
discens								x					
domicurius					x								
eques						x							
exactus			x		x	x							
exceptor					x								
frumentarius					x								
haruspex					x								
immunis					x			x					
immunis cera-													
rius						x							

	ROME				FRONTIERS								
					LEGIONS						AUXILIARIES		
	PREFECT OF ROME	URBAN TRIBUNE	PRAETORIAN PREFECT	PRAETORIAN TRIBUNE	LEGATE GOVERNOR	LEGION LEGATE	LATICLAVIAN TRIBUNE	PREFECT	ANGUSTICLAVIAN TRIBUNE	SEXMENSTRIS TRIBUNE	WING PREFECT	COHORT PREFECT	PRAEPOSITUS NUMERI
interpres					X								
librarius				X	X	X		X			X	X	X
optio	X										X		
pullarius													
a quaestionibus	X		X		X								
quaestionarius					X								
secutor		X		X					X				
singularis		X	X	X	X	X	X				X		
speculator					X								
stator						X					X		
strator					X	X					X		
uexillarius											X		
uictimarius					X								

Table 10: Officers' staffs (according to A. Domaszewski and B. Dobson)

Each archive holding (*tabularia*), which also served as a cash register, was also entrusted to a *cornicularius*; there were at least three: that 'of the camp', that of the *centurio princeps* and that of the *stratores*, or squires, who also had therefore administrative functions. The differences between these three services have yet to be clarified. Finally, the unit's money was managed by the quaestor and his office, not to be confused with his namesake in the colleges – officer associations of a religious nature. The quaestor was assisted by slaves and freedmen attached to the finance department of a legion or a province, who acted as surrogates for certain soldiers in the same way that imperial slaves and freedmen did for pro-curators. Thus we know of the existence of a cashier (*arkarius*), the account-ant (*tabularius*), the paymaster (*dispensator*) and the assistant (*vikarius*). As for the soldier called *ad anuam* in cursive script documents, it is possible that he should be identified as an *ad annua*,[111] responsible for paying pensions to veterans, but this is only a hypothesis. There remains one final point to discuss, on which a great deal of nonsense has been written.

Justice and policing

Since any legionary, acting on orders, could sometimes arrest a trouble-maker, interrogate him and execute him if necessary, some authors have pictured soldiers spending all their time in the pursuit of suspects. The reality was simpler. Inside the camp order was maintained by a police station (*statio*) under the orders of a tribune;[112] the prison cells were guarded by an adjutant, while torture was administered by a *quaestionarius*. The *stator*, not to be confused with the *strator*, arrested and condemned soldiers guilty of minor offences. Outside the fortress, the army could despatch men to ensure the guard of municipal and civilian prisons, and to arrest guilty people. In general it sent *beneficiarii* and *frumentarii*, *speculatores* and *commentarienses*. Finally, small garrisons of *burgarii* and *stationarii* were used to watch over the roads and the travellers that used them.

It is evident therefore that a legion contained a wide range of specialization. Some specializations remain a mystery; is the *ad fiscum* a tax-collector? Is the *ad praepositum* a guard assigned to the chief officer of a small-sized camp? Is the *conductor* a finance officer responsible for leasing supplies? These are no more than hypotheses.

Promotions and transfers

During their period of service soldiers left one post to take up another. For instance there is the case of an inhabitant of Verona known by the epitaph he had set up for his wife:[113] 'Lucius Sertorius Firmus, son of Lucius, of the tribe Publilia, *signum*-bearer, eagle-bearer for the XIth Claudian legion, pious and loyal, freed, curator of the veterans of the same legion, [had this inscription engraved] for his wife, Domitia Prisca, daughter of Lucius'. In some cases the change of position does not appear to have been associated with any substantial advantage, such as an increase in salary, but in others there is no doubt that a promotion is involved. Plotius Firmus, a mere legionary, became prefect of the *praetorium*, admittedly during the civil war of 69.[114] Normally, any rise up the hierarchy was in the purview of the superiors, in theory the emperor. Sometimes change was brought about *ex suffragio*; this practice, which is characteristic of the Roman army, clearly shows the importance given to the men who were part of it, who were always considered as Roman citizens. In any assembly, such as at the end of a parade, the soldiers could ask by acclamation that one of their number be promoted to a certain rank. The perverse use this could be put to is demonstrated by Tacitus:[115] 'In order to accustom the soldiers to lawlessness, the bad general would offer legions the posts of centurions who had been killed. Their votes [*suffragia*] ensured that the most turbulent were elected.' The movements of personnel known to us at present can be schematized as follows:

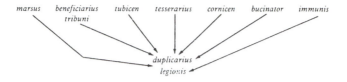

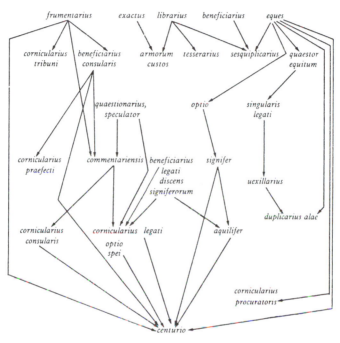

Table 11: Movements of personnel in the hierarchy

ORDINARY SOLDIERS IN UNITS OTHER THAN LEGIONS

In units other than legions, more or less the same titles are encountered, but as they are less well documented, certain functions have not yet been attested in the *auxilia*, the navy or at Rome. However, this does not mean that these functions did not exist. On the other hand, some specializations are characteristic of the *Vigiles*, for example, who sometimes acted as firemen. These remarks will therefore be limited to general points, with a few concrete examples. Firstly it must be remembered that as only the legions had an eagle, there is no *aquilifer* found elsewhere.

Excellent careers were possible within the *praetorium*: Lucius Pompeius Reburrus,[117] a Spaniard, entered the VIIth cohort after passing before the recruiting board; subsequently he was *beneficiarius* of the tribune, *tesserarius*, adjutant, *signum*-bearer, finance curator, *cornicularius* of the tribune, and finally *evocatus*, or more precisely, imperial *evocatus*, for the adjective 'imperial' was reserved for the praetorians and not given to other *evocati*. For the military duties, the absence of the *imaginifer* is explained by the fact that the *signa* in the praetorian corps carried the portrait of the emperor. Security was probably tighter; we know of the existence of a (camp?) guard, the *ostiarius*, and a topographer (*chorographiarius*), no doubt to help the general find his bearings during operations.

The exact functions of the *tector*[117] are unknown, but he was probably linked with the imperial guard of the *equites singulares Augusti*. A 'doctor of archery' took part in training. A *caelator*, engraver or inciser (of arms?), is attested, as are priests with differentiated titles (*sacerdos* and *antistes*). But it is the administration that seems huge, perhaps not surprising when it is remembered that the prefect of the *praetorium* was also the Prime Minister and the War Minister. The *scriniarius*, and his superior, the *primoscriniarius*, were office workers, as was the *laterculensis*, who drew up lists of soldiers, and the *fisci curator*, who managed the sums of money paid to the cohorts by the imperial treasury. The cohorts were called upon to prepare the bouts in the amphitheatres, and as part of the preparations they paid a 'zoo-keeper' (*custos vivarii*).

The Urban cohorts do not differ in any way from this (they also had a *fisci curator*), but the *Vigiles* did show variations because of their specific function of fire-fighting. The *sifonarius*, helped by the *aquarius*, activated the pump, the *uncinarius* used a hook to clear away the rubble, and the *falciarius* a tool similar to a scythe. Unfortunately we do not know what the *emitularius* did. Moreover, there was a *codicillarius* who fulfilled some sort of administrative functions.

As for the other units of the garrison at Rome, the bodyguards (*equites singulares Augusti*) included the *tablifer* (standard-bearer) and the *turarius*, priest of the Thracian cult, as well as the *aedilis* in the *peregrini*, keeping watch over the markets or the temples.

The *auxilia* closely resembled the legions except that the horsemen were organized in squadrons (*turmae*). In the ranks of the *numeri* were to be found couriers (*veredarii*) and messengers (*baiuli*[118]), one to each squadron.

The navy presents more specialities because of certain functions that were peculiar to it. The sailors, called 'soldiers' (*milites*) and not 'seamen' (*nautae*), had officers who were navigation specialists: the helmsman (*gubernator*), the bows 'officer' (*proreta*), the sails master (*velarius*), the chief oarsman (*celeusta* or *pausarius*), and the officer in charge of setting the rhythm (*pitulus*). On shore the boats were maintained by arsenal workers (*fabri navales*), probably under the supervision of a *nauphylax*. Finally, in the religious sphere we know of a *coronarius*, whose title is linked in some way with the wreaths that were used in certain ceremonies.

Thus, units other than the legions display certain peculiarities and it is possible that future discoveries will provide evidence for functions that were hitherto attested only for some other unit. Be that as it may, three types of unit present some sort of peculiarity, the *praetorium* through its administrative functions, the *Vigiles* because of their fire-fighting activities, and the navy.

MILITARY LIFE

Daily activities

In all these types of units soldiers led more or less the same sort of life; they shared the same activities which brought them largely similar punishments and rewards.

In order to understand the daily life of a soldier, archaeologists look for the camp rubbish dumps, which, together with cemeteries, are their favourite hunting grounds. There they might find part of the post commandant's records if the climate has allowed them to survive. In this way papyrus leaves have been discovered, mostly in Egypt, but also some at Dura-Europos in Syria. There is also a collection of *ostraca* found at Bu-Njem in Libya;[119] these are clay fragments on which the day-to-day activities of the fort were recorded in note form. A daily report has been found, indicating how the number of men varied between 42 and 63, and giving a review of events of the day, comprising four incidents, and the notes sent by the soldiers who were on guard at the various tiny positions placed around the fortress. Yet, once again, the literary sources are most valuable. A passage in Tacitus shows that sometimes at least military life was not free from a certain degree of harshness.[120] The events in question happened shortly after the death of Augustus, when the legions defending the left bank of the Rhine rebelled, and their leader, Germanicus, returned post-haste to their camp: 'When he had entered the entrenchment, he began to hear confused grievances being uttered. Some soldiers took hold of his hand as if to kiss it, but put his fingers into their toothless mouths so that he could feel their gums, while others showed him their limbs bent with old age.'

This state of exhaustion among the soldiers could be explained by the length of their service, but it is due above all to the various duties they had to perform; they had to carry out administrative functions, transport official mail, collect certain taxes and work on civil engineering, in addition to their most important tasks of training and fighting. Nevertheless, certain armies, such as that in Spain in the second century, were known to be less exposed to external threat than others, for instance that in Germany, and this gave rise to a feeling of satisfaction among some soldiers, and aroused jealousy among others.[121]

Added to all this was the daily routine, beginning with the morning parade. The soldiers had to line up before their centurions, the centurions before their tribunes, and the officers before their legate, who gave them the password and the orders of the day.[122] Some were also sent off in detachments to fetch wood, wheat, fresh supplies and water,[123] or to occupy and defend small border posts. Others were sent out on patrol to reconnoitre the area around the fortress. Yet others were detailed to do the duties associated with communal life: there had to be sentries, particularly for the nightwatch,[124] the camp streets and different locales had to be cleaned, messages had to be carried. Certain soldiers, the *immunes*, were exempt from fatigues at all times, while others, suffering from laziness, could always buy their exemption from their centurion.[125] This practice will doubtless surprise many who thought that everyone in the Roman army was ruled with the same iron discipline.

In addition to all this the day might include particular ceremonies, among which were parades which were carried out at a measured pace. Tacitus' description of the entry of Vitellius into Rome in 69 has already been mentioned (p. 27); the legionaries were in front, followed by the cavalry wings and the auxiliary cohorts; officers preceded the ordinary ranks:

> In front of the eagles marched the camp prefects, tribunes and first-rank centurions, all dressed in white. The other officers each flanked their own centuries, resplendent in their weapons and decorations. As for the soldiers, they glistened with their *phalerae* and torcs. It was an awesome sight, an army worthy of an emperor other than Vitellius.[126]

Also, the emperor or his representative, the legate, could address the troops. Roman civilization was one of the word, and speech played a large role. This ceremony, the *adlocutio*, appears several times on coins (pl. VII, 11), on Trajan's Column and on that of Marcus Aurelius, alongside many other ceremonies of a religious nature, such as various sacrificial rites and purification of the army (*lustratio*). Religion also played an important part in influencing the collective mentality of the time (see Part III, chapter 9).

Punishments

Returning now to the harshness of military service, discipline, in the modern sense of the word (we shall see below that the meaning is different in Latin), can be seen in two forms, which may appear contradictory. On the one hand Roman soldiers, especially legionaries, who were always treated as citizens, took many liberties with their commanding officers and with their dress (in this respect they have more in common with the 'Tsahal', Israel's army, than with the army of Frederick II). On the other, particularly in combat, blind obedience was imposed on them and terrible punishment inflicted if they did wrong.

Augustus' severity is mentioned by Suetonius in order to praise its quality:[127]

He put up for auction a Roman *eques*, who had cut off the thumbs of his two young sons to get them exempted from military service, and all his goods, but seeing that the public farmers [also of equestrian rank] were ready to buy him, he sold him off to one of his emancipated slaves with orders to relegate him to the country, but to let him live as a free man. When the men of the tenth legion obeyed him, but in rebellious mood, he cashiered them all with ignominy, and when others were too insistent in demanding their leave, he demobilized them without giving them the rewards they were owed. When cohorts had given ground he had them decimated and fed on barley. If centurions deserted their posts they were put to death like ordinary soldiers. For other offences he imposed various ignominious sentences, for example ordering them to stand in front of the general's tent all day long, sometimes dressed in a plain tunic, without a belt, sometimes holding in their hand a ten-foot pole or a turf of grass.

This text shows the variety of punishments that existed, but it is not exhaustive. They can be classified into several groups. Some had essentially a moral impact: for a minor offence the soldier could find himself with extra watch duties, or he could be put in prison, or conversely made to spend the night outside the ramparts.[128] He might even be given inferior food to his colleagues, for instance barley,[129] or beaten with the vine stock, the centurion's baton that gave him the right to strike a Roman citizen. This right was so important that in inscriptions the schematized baton was used to denote the officer in question.

Other punishments had an economic impact in that they entailed a drop in salary. These included fines and the withholding of pay, demotion (a centurion was demoted to the rank of soldier, a *duplicarius* to the rank of *simplaris*), transfer from one unit to another (a legionary was sent to an auxiliary cohort). In the last two cases financial loss went hand in hand with deep humiliation. But there was worse. An entire unit could be disbanded, as happened to the tenth legion, according to Suetonius in the passage cited above, and also to the *legio III Gallica* under Elagabal and the *legio III Augusta* in 238. This last-named legion had sided against Gordian I and Gordian II in Africa, and so when Gordian III, the grandson of the first and the nephew of the second, was acknowledged as Emperor by the Senate in Rome, he decided to punish the unit that had caused the deaths of his grandfather and uncle. Finally, commanding officers could resort to individual or collective death penalties in extreme cases to punish deserters or cowards.[130] In the latter case, decimation was practised; soldiers were lined up and every tenth man had to step forward, whereupon he was summarily executed.

Rewards

On the other hand, officers could reward good soldiers, using the basic but nevertheless effective psychological approach of alternating severity and generosity. The latter took two forms: promotions and decorations.

A soldier could leave one post for another that was simply judged to bring more honour to him (a *signifer* becoming an *aquilifer*), or be exempted from fatigues on a temporary basis or for the duration of the service he then performed as an *immunis*. Better still, he could change unit, going from an auxiliary cohort to a legion, or be promoted to a *duplicarius* or even to a centurion. Sometimes he received a gift of precious metal; Augustus distributed gold and silver from time to time.[131]

Like other emperors, Augustus most frequently handed out medals (*dona militaria*), but even here he acted in a discerning fashion.[132]

> By way of military rewards [he] was much more inclined to give decorations, the collars and all the other insignia of gold and silver, rather than the siege and mural crowns whose value was purely honorary. The latter he gave extremely rarely, and then often to ordinary soldiers, not seeking to gain any popularity from this action. He presented M. [Marcus] Agrippa with an azure flag after his Sicilian naval victory.

The decorations came in a wide variety of forms.[133] A fundamental difference was between those given to ordinary soldiers and those given to officers. The former were in fact normally awarded in recognition of an exploit (*ob virtutem*) as we are informed by an inscription found near Turin in honour of 'Lucius Coelius, son of Quintus, soldier in the IXth legion, *signum*-bearer, rewarded for his courage [*ob virtutes*: *sic*] with *phalerae* [badges more or less equivalent to modern medals], collars and armlets'. Moreover, ordinary soldiers could as a rule only obtain the three awards listed in the above passage (pls VIII–IX, 12; pl. V, 7 shows an *aquilifer* flaunting nine *phalerae* and two collars on his breastplate). In exceptional circumstances they could receive crowns (*coronae*), distinctions reserved in principle for higher ranking persons. These are called 'mural' crowns or 'rampart' crowns (for those men who were first to reach the enemy ramparts), 'civic' (awarded for saving the life of a Roman citizen), 'naval' (for a victory at sea), 'siege' (for having lifted a siege) or 'golden' (for various exploits). In principle, with the exception of *primipili* who, in addition, could receive a spear shaft (*hasta pura*), centurions received only crowns.

Officers however were not normally rewarded for their courage, but for merely taking part in a campaign; even a civil war could bring them decorations in certain circumstances. They were eligible to receive crowns, spear shafts and cavalry standards (pls VIII–IX, 12), whose number was never rigorously regulated and varied for the most part according to three criteria. Firstly, the beneficiary's rank in the hierarchy was taken into account; the higher the rank the larger number of honours. Secondly, it seems possible to distinguish two levels of decorations for each rank, and here personal merit would appear to have played a role. Finally, certain chronological distinctions have to be made; some emperors, like Trajan, were more generous than others, like Marcus Aurelius.

RANK	CROWN(S)	SPEAR(S)	CAVALRY STANDARD(S)
cohort prefect	1	1	-
angusticlavian tribune = cohort tribune	1	1	1
cavalry prefect	2	1	1
fourth *militia* = laticlavian tribune	2	2	1
legion legate	2	2	2
army legate	3	3	3
	4	4	4

Table 12: Officers' decorations under Trajan[135]
(Note that each rank has a superior and an inferior level)

Under Marcus Aurelius, however, a legion legate received only 3 crowns, 2 spears and 2 standards, while another case recorded under Hadrian is of an even smaller amount, 1, 1, 0. On the other hand, the figures are 8, 8, 8, for Lucius Licinius Sura, a general under Trajan, and for Titus Pomponius Vitrasius Pollio, a general under Marcus Aurelius and Lucius Verus. Other similar cases of varying numbers could be adduced.

In general terms two remarks still need to be made. Firstly, the reiteration of a decoration is considered to represent an honour, a promotion within a rank, so to speak. Secondly, epigraphists have remarked that the habit of mentioning this sort of reward disappears at the beginning of the third century, and does not go beyond the reign of Caracalla. However, literary texts refer to it throughout that century, under Severus Alexander, Valerian, Tacitus and Probus.[136]

Length of military service

Military service consisted of a series of occupations that were time-consuming and monotonous, spent in the fear of punishment and the hope of reward. It lasted a very long time. How many years? That is a question that cannot easily be answered. In fact, the Romans did not have the same concept of time that we have. Thus, those for whom we have some sort of official record do not have precise ages; these were often rounded up or down to the nearest figure ending in 5 or 0.[137] Moreover, Roman soldiers in the second century were often discharged every two years, whereas levying took place every year, and there was always the risk of being kept in service beyond the legal duration if circumstances demanded, for instance a difficult war, or even of being discharged early if the army had financial problems.

Once all these caveats have been taken into account, it is possible to suggest a few figures that vary according to one essential principle – the only certitude in this area – namely that the higher the rank of the unit, the shorter the period of service in it. Thus, in the garrison at Rome from AD 6 onwards,[138] the praetorians served sixteen years while the soldiers in the urban cohorts served twenty. The bodyguards (*equites singulares Augusti*) served between twenty-seven and twenty-nine years up to the year 138, twenty-five after. The figures for legionaries show a wide variation. In 13 BC they served sixteen years, followed by four as veterans. In AD 5 the distinction was blurred and the period of service was counted as twenty years, but in the next year it was increased to twenty-two. At the end of Augustus' reign it was theoretically a minimum of twenty years,[139] but in reality some soldiers served as long as thirty or forty years.[140] This abuse of practice led to revolts, and shortly after AD 14 there was a temporary return to sixteen years. However, the period soon became twenty again. In the second century the figures vary between twenty-three and twenty-six.[141] The least prestigious units are also the least well-documented unfortunately. According to J. Carcopino,[142] the auxiliaries served twenty-five years under Augustus, twenty-six from the middle of the first century until the reign of Caracalla, who increased the duration to twenty-eight. Sailors served twenty-six years at the beginning of the first century, and twenty-eight in the second half of the second. But these figures which appear very straightforward should probably be looked at carefully to bring out any slight differences of interpretation.

In short, then, it can be seen that any man who embarked upon a military career gave up a large part of his life to the service of the state; the constraints which this entailed did not prevent him from having a private life, however, nor from playing a role in the economic and religious life of the province in which his garrison was stationed.

CONCLUSION

There was a wide diversity between the different types of unit, such as the garrison at Rome, the provincial armies and the fleets, and this diversity was based on hierarchy. The Praetorians were superior to the urban cohorts, the legionaries to the auxiliaries and the navy. Within an individual unit we also find diversity and hierarchy, linked to a very complex system; not only did a centurion find himself above a soldier, but also, if he was in an urban corps, he was superior to his opposite number who commanded a ship. A decurion would be held in greater esteem and find it more beneficial to belong to a cavalry wing than to a cohort. The primary hierarchy was therefore created by the nature of the unit the soldier served in, but the secondary hierarchy of specialization was added to this. The eagle-bearer, the artilleryman and the musician enjoyed a prestige that was unknown to the non-officer ranks. Such a hierarchical organization made heavy demands on the dedication of the officers; it implied that the aristocracy agreed to play its part and that the state operated a recruitment policy based on quality.

Table 13: Legion organization
This summary makes no effort to distinguish between the permanent and the temporary posts, especially as regards the soldiers, as it is sometimes impossible to do so.

I. *The officers* (by order of rank)
    1 imperial propraetor legate (senatorial rank)
    1 laticlavian tribune (senatorial rank)
    1 camp prefect
    5 angusticlavian prefects (equestrian rank)
    1(?) 'six-month' (*sexmenstris*) tribune
The legion legate is replaced by an equestrian prefect in Egypt, starting from Augustus' time and for the three units called 'Parthian' from the time of their creation by Septimius Severus. Gallienus made this practice general and at the same time did away with the laticlavian tribune.

II. *Non-commissioned officers*
    59 centurions headed by a *primipilus* and the other four centurions of the first cohort.

III. *Soldiers*

1. Hierarchy
Elementary hierarchy

		Honorific titles:	
	triplicarius	*candidatus*	*optio*
immunis	*duplicarius*	*cornicularius*	*discens*
= *principalis*	*sesquiplicarius*	*beneficiarius*	*euocatus*
immunis	= *simplaris*	*curator*	*ueteranus*
munifex	= *simplaris*	*magister*	

2. Purely military duties
(some titles may figure under more than one heading):

ARMS	TRANSMISSION	SECURITY	TRAINING
Infantry	**Standards**	**Sentries**	*campidoctor*
antesignanus	*aquilifer*	*excubitor*	*doctor cohortis*
postsignanus	*discens aq.*	*aedituus*	*optio campi*
	signifer	*ad signa*	*magister campi*
Cavalry	+ *audiutor*	*custos basilicae*	*exercitator*
eques	*discens sig.*	*custos armorum*	*doctor armorum*
discens eq.		*ad balnea*	*armatura*

ARMS	TRANSMISSION	SECURITY	TRAINING
uexillarius	principalis sig.	horrearius	discens arm.
tesserarius	optio sig.	ad portam	quintanarius
optio	uexillarius	clauicularius	
pollio	[imaginifer]	circitor	
mulio		tesserarius	
magister campi	**Music**	horologiarius	
exercitator	tubicen		
pequarius	cornicen	**Escorts**	
hastiliarius	bucinator	speculator	
quaestor	[hydraularius]	singularis	
		secutor	
Artillery		strator	
ballistarii		domicurius	
doctores			
ballistarum		**Information**	
magister		proculcator	
ballistarum		explorator	

3. Services

STORES	ENGINEERS AND WORKSHOPS	HEALTH SERVICE	PRIESTS
(signifer)	**Construction**	**Medicine**	haruspex
quaestor	metator	medicus (simple	uictimarius
act(u)arius	librator	or ordinarius)	ad hostias
cibariator	mensor	capsarius	pullarius
frumentarius	architectus	librarius	
dispensator		discens caps. and lib.	
horrearius	**Workshop**	marsus	
molendarius	magister		
mensor frumenti	optio	**Veterinary**	
librarius horreorum	doctor	**service**	
uenator		pequarius	
lanius		pollio	
ad ligna balnei		ad, cum camellis	
salariarius			
ascita			
carrariarius			

4. Administration

SOLDIERS	exactus act(u)arius commentariensis or a commentariis	summus curator librarius (a rationibus) notarius exceptor scriba	interpres cerarius canalicularius immunes adiutores ad anuam = ad annua (?)
BUREAUX SLAVES AND FREEDMEN	officia arkarius tabularius	tabularia dispensator	quaestura uikarius

5. Police and the law

optio	quaestionarius	stator	burgarius	stationarius

6. Unknown tasks

conductor	ad fiscum	ad praepositum

3

RECRUITMENT

From 235 to 238 the Roman Empire was governed by a giant of a man known as Maximinus. According to the *Historia Augusta* he had formerly been a shepherd who had subsequently spent most of his life in the camps, rising up through the ranks until he reached the top. Such a career profile is doubtlessly out of the ordinary and probably contains an element of fiction in it, but nevertheless it is clear that this man's destiny was fixed the day he joined the army. From this example we get our first sight of the importance of recruitment.

But this question has an even more fundamental importance for historians today, as it has social connotations: such as from which region or regions and from which social background or backgrounds did the soldiers come? These questions are more important than might be supposed, because a man's origins determined the role that would be given him. The collective mentality of antiquity worked in this way, namely that the son of a centurion would be more likely than the son of an ordinary soldier to be promoted. In view of what has been established in the preceding chapters, it goes without saying that distinctions must be made between different sorts of units and between officers and ordinary ranks.

It seems pointless and even impossible to study the recruitment of superior officers in the framework of this book. Indeed, in theory every senator had to progress through the rank of laticlavian tribune and legate of a legion, every equestrian had to start his career in the equestrian *militia* (though there are some exceptions). Such a study would therefore entail a complete examination of these two orders, which would fill more than one book.[1] Moreover, as these functions in the army were more or less compulsory for virtually everyone, this type of research would be unlikely to bring to light many original aspects.

In respect of the ordinary soldiers we are fortunate to have two good books, one on the auxiliaries by K. Kraft,[2] the other on the legionaries by G. Forni;[3] even if these two are now more than thirty years old, they have been brought up to date. Unfortunately, the other aspects of the subject have not always been treated so thoroughly.

GENERAL POINTS

These deficiencies in documentation create one difficulty, but there are others. Ideally recruitment should be studied on the basis of three essential distinctions. First of all, there is the fundamental point of evolution over three centuries; it is obvious that Augustus did not find himself organizing his army in the same circumstances as one of the short-lived emperors of the third century who experienced 'the crisis of the empire'. Secondly, it would be preferable to be able to observe each of the main types of unit for this period – the garrison at Rome, the frontier armies and the fleet – as it is obvious that things did not happen in exactly the same way in each. A final point, it would be desirable to differentiate between centurions, officers of all ranks and ordinary soldiers in each type of unit. However, the gaps in our documentation as well as in the secondary literature do not allow a complete picture to be drawn.

These are not the only difficulties. To take into account the developments regarding the units of citizens,[4] as well as the flanks and the cohorts[5] would require an attempt at synthesis, and yet it is about these soldiers that we have the most information at the present time. But that is not all. Some historians have found pleasure in complicating what was already not a simple reality by using a vocabulary that was too often imprecise, speaking of recruitment that was 'local', 'regional' or 'foreign'. Each of these three adjectives requires a precise definition. I propose to reserve the term 'local' for soldiers from the town built near the camp in which they serve, to equate 'regional' with 'provincial' and to define as 'foreign' those who do not fit into either of these categories. To be sure, this does not do away with all ambiguity, since under Septimius Severus Numidia was separated from Africa, Palestine from Syria and Brittany was divided into two parts. Accordingly I shall restrict myself to consideration of the Roman world as it was at the end of the second century, for example under Commodus.

This problem, created by modern writers, is added to another that has its origins in the reality of antiquity, the collective mentalities of the ancients. In fact, each inhabitant of the empire had three homelands, not one, that overlapped in varying degrees or else affected each other. Take the example of a legionary who mentions his *origo* in his onomastics: Marcus Aquilius Proculus, son of Marcus, of the Aniensis tribe, from *Ariminum* (present-day Rimini). It is also necessary to recall that some people who lived in the provinces kept the memory of the Italian town where their ancestors had once lived. Septimius Severus perhaps did not forget that his family came from over the sea,[6] but he was born in Lepcis Magna, in modern Libya, did not lose his appalling African accent, and his forebears bore all the marks of being half-castes. Every man therefore felt that he belonged to one city and sometimes maintained links with another. Secondly, each inhabitant of the empire was characterized by his legal status; he was, for a longer or shorter time, a slave or a free-man, Roman citizen or *peregrinus*. If he were in the last category and lived in a colony, he was considered to be a foreigner, and could take no part in the collective life of the city in which he lived, being debarred, for example, from voting in the elections for municipal magistrates. Finally, each belonged to one of the numerous cultures that not only rubbed shoulders with each other, but moreover influenced each other throughout the empire. Indigenous traditions found themselves side by side with Italian ones and intermingled. Thus a Parisian would say either in Latin or in the Gallic tongue that he lived in Lutetia but was a Roman citizen or *peregrinus*. In this case it is advisable to acknowledge the very real distinction that M. Benabou established between Romans, the 'partially Romanized' and the 'resistants'.[7]

Through failure to take these difficulties into account historians have often found clear, logical, coherent conclusions hard to come by. On the other hand, the problems raised by the question of recruitment are well-known, and both the evolution and also the differences between various types of units must not go unconsidered. Specialists have asked various questions: what were the geographical origins of the soldiers? What were their backgrounds, country or city, rich or poor, and at what age did they join the army? Finally, were the changes that are attested the consequence of a clear political will, or did they happen by force of circumstances, such as financial constraints?

In order to answer these large questions it is necessary to examine how recruitment was organized.

ORGANIZATION

The person in charge and contingency

Recruitment (*dilectus*) was always entrusted to a high-ranking member of society. In normal circumstances this task was part of the duty of the governor of a province, whatever his rank, procurator,[8] imperial propraetor legate or proconsul. The *Acts of Maximilian* show that at the time of the Tetrarchy, on 12 March, 295, the promagistrate in Carthage journeyed to Tebessa in order to recruit troops.[9] As Italy was not organized into provinces in the Early Empire, the emperor sent a person with the explicit title of *dilectator* to do the recruiting. When certain young men paid an enormous amount of money to buy their exemption from military service on grounds of being unfit, the recruiting officer was punished. Thus, in the reign of Nero 'Paedius Blaesus was excluded from the senate because of accusations by the Cyrenians that he had plundered the treasure of Aesculapius and allowed himself to be corrupted by intrigue and by gold during the raising of troops'.[10]

In times of crisis or some other difficulty, when the need for further reinforcements was felt to be urgent, special officials were called upon whose titles varied according to the juridical status of the region in which they were operating. In the peninsula they were *missi ad dilectum*, in the senatorial provinces *legati ad dilectum*, and in those provinces under imperial authority *dilectatores* and *inquisitatores*. Whatever the rank of the person in charge, he was always accompanied by an impressive escort, as we learn from an inscription in honour of a tribune by the 'centurions and soldiers of the *legio III Cyrenaica* and the *legio XXII Deiotariana* who were sent to the province of Cyrene to levy troops there [*dilectus caussa* (*sic*)]'.[11] The two units in question belonged to the army in Egypt and men serving under their standards were sent to the neighbouring territory for these operations.

The number of young men likely to be concerned, however, was small. According to the calculations of G. Forni each of the 25 legions needed only 240 new recruits per year, that is approximately 6000 for the 25 legions of the whole empire.[12] If we envisage a more or less similar number for the auxiliary forces and also for the garrison in Rome and the navy, we arrive at a total of 18,000 men for the whole of the Mediterranean basin. Whatever the global population of these territories, it should not have been difficult to muster numbers of this sort. However, this was not the case. The state therefore started by calling up volunteers, but as these did not suffice, their numbers were made up by conscripts; compulsory military service was maintained, in theory at least, during the whole of the period of empire.

The imperial finances always had trouble in bearing such a burden, thus in 69, according to Tacitus, 'Vitellius ordered a reduction in the numbers of legionaries and auxiliaries and banned any further recruitment, while offering leave to everyone'.[13] Finally, conscripts and volunteers sometimes failed to make up the numbers required, and then retired soldiers and veterans were recalled to action.[14] These difficulties can be surprising to understand; after all, 18,000 is not a large number of men for such a vast area. But in fact, not just anybody was recruited; the criterion of quality, chosen as a deliberate policy by the Roman state, meant that selection was seriously restricted.

The recruiting board

This requirement is all the more evident when considering the recruiting board, the *probatio*[15] (in fact, this examination concerns ordinary soldiers as much as officers, although the latter, like some centurions, are not affected by the *dilectus*). In Egypt this operation was associated with a sort of census, a local census called the *epikrisis*. The assessment had three main aspects; it began with a physical examination in which the examiner checked the general good shape of the young man, his masculinity, his eyesight, and then measured him to ensure that he was not below the minimum height required (1.65m (5ft 5in) for a legionary[16]). Then the authorities carried out an intellectual examination; in order to serve the recruit had to be able to understand Latin, since it was the language of commands in the whole empire. At least some were required to know how to read, write and count.

Finally came the legal aspect (which was not the simplest) which was always present in Roman civilization. A young man's origins needed to be checked. If he was the son of a notable he could hope for a centurionship, if a citizen he was sent to a legion, and if he was born to a family of *peregrini* he was directed towards the *auxilia*. Sometimes, if the need for legionaries was pressing, the corresponding status was given to a barbarian before enlistment. This well-attested practice has led some historians to describe the army as a machine for multiplying the number of citizens. But there are certain very rare cases in which *peregrini* kept their status after being enlisted to front-line units.

In certain very exceptional circumstances the emperor was forced to promote people of even lower station:

> Only twice did Augustus enlist emancipated slaves as soldiers, the first time to protect the colonies on the borders of Illyricum; the second to guard the [left] bank of the Rhine. The slaves were recruited from the households of rich men and women and immediately freed, whereupon they were placed in the front line, but kept separate from the freeborn and given different weapons.[17]

In normal circumstances access to a given unit was strictly forbidden to slaves, and Trajan proved uncompromising on this point. In answer to a question from the governor of Bithynia, the younger Pliny, who was asking for information about a case concerning two men of this status he said:

> It is important to know whether they are volunteers, conscripts or merely given as replacements. If they were called up then the recruiting board was at fault; if they were given as replacements those who gave them are guilty; if they came of their own accord, fully aware of their status, they must be punished by death.[18]

Trajan's attitude is not exceptional, but some historians have thought that the *origo verna* mentioned on some inscriptions meant that the bearer was not a free man. In fact, the term *verna* has two meanings; it can certainly designate a child born in slavery, but it can also apply to a person who

72

still lives where he first saw the light of day and then means 'native of this very place'.[19]

The legal examination covered other aspects too. Some professions, like slave merchants, were considered disgraceful and totally banned from the army, even if it was not the young man himself, but his father who was a member. Moral standards were also taken into consideration; a candidate could not have received any convictions, and Augustus was particularly careful not to allow men convicted of adultery into the army.[20]

At this point there is a problem that has not always been addressed satisfactorily, namely the age at which a young man became a soldier. Most historians who have studied the question have drawn up a list of epitaphs written in the following manner: 'N . . . , soldier [*miles*] of V unit, lived X years and served Y years.' They then subtracted Y from X to find the required number and drew up a list of the results obtained. However, problems did arise from this method, because men were found who enlisted at the age of 40 or even 50 and it is difficult to imagine a man of that age attacking a rampart or taking part in the very demanding daily training exercises.[21]

The error is due to the fact that even when a man returned to civilian life he kept the title of *miles* until his death. In the case of a citizen with this title, who has served twenty-five years and died at the age of 75, the interpretation should be that he was recruited around the age of 20 and discharged around 45, and he was not prevented from calling himself a soldier for the rest of his life. Only inscriptions which explicitly mention that a soldier died during his service should therefore be used, since in these cases subtraction does indeed give the age of enlistment. They should also be compared with literary evidence which shows that the rule was to enlist recruits between the ages of 18 and 21 in normal circumstances, but that in times of crisis the recruitment age could be extended to 30. These figures appear more plausible in view of the length of service and the hardships involved.

Admission to the army

Having a letter of recommendation from one's father or from some important person did one no harm. Pliny the Younger bombarded Trajan with this sort of reference:

> Sir, the *primuspilus* Nymphidius Lupus was my comrade in arms . . . I share all his feelings, especially those he has for his son Nymphidius Lupus, an honest, active young man, totally worthy of his distinguished father; he will know how to respond to your kindness, as you can judge by his preliminary trials, since in his role of cohort prefect he has deserved the unstinting praise of the very honourable Julius Ferox and Fuscus Salinator. Any promotion that you gave his son would be for me a cause for joy and gratitude.[23]

The person praised in this letter is an officer, but even ordinary soldiers were advantaged if they had references. It was obviously in the beneficiary's interest not to part with such letters of recommendation as they could be used each time there was a prospect of promotion.

When the young man had finished with the recruiting board he was promoted to the title of *tiro*, 'recruit', and enjoyed an intermediate status between that of civilian and soldier. Indeed, three formalities still had to be accomplished. As Roman society was strictly stratified, that is membership of a group or a class was subject to legal criteria, he had to be listed in the registers (*in numeros referri*). Next he received the *signaculum*, a piece of metal to hang around his neck to symbolize his belonging to the army, and was said to be *signatus*, 'marked'. Finally he swore by the gods and the emperor to serve well. Normally this ceremony occurred four months after the *probatio*, but we know of one case where it happened immediately afterwards.[24] This exception might be explained by the fact that the levy in question took place during the Civil War. This commitment, called *iusiurandum* or sometimes *sacramentum*, had a religious aspect, and in consequence some Christians believed that the oath-*sacramentum* was incompatible with the baptism-*sacramentum*.

The complexity of the steps that went to make up recruitment demonstrate that these formalities, which were not taken lightly, were aimed at maintaining a policy of quality.

RECRUITMENT OF CENTURIONS AND *PRIMIPILI*

Since we will not dwell on the question of senatorial or equestrian officers, the starting point will be the centurions and *primipili*, who had their own hierarchical structures. They were closer to the ordinary soldiers than to the aristocracy. It is necessary to note first that little attention has been paid to this subject, particularly in recent times, except for the *primipili*[25] and the *III Augusta* legion which was part of the African army,[26] and the *VII Gemina*, stationed in Spain.[27] In this last study, P. Le Roux has discounted one hypothesis, namely that in the course of a career no particular province or unit constituted a privilege, a fast track for promotion. Centurions stayed on average three and a half years in each garrison before being transferred where vacancies arose. Only the first cohort or the garrison in Rome represented promotion for an officer serving in a legion.

Primipili

The picture will be clearer if we start with the highest-ranking soldiers, the *primipili* (see n.25) and adopt a system of classifcation to be used extensively later on, that of geographical origins followed by social background.

In the first century AD the vast majority of *primipili* came from Italian towns, the rest coming from colonies in the west, that is those cities considered legally as part of Rome, established at a distance; their inhabitants were entitled to full citizenship rights and enjoyed the same privileges as citizens living in the capital. They were overseas Italians. In the second century, by the time of Trajan and Hadrian, a greater diversity is already apparent; people who lived in the provinces found it easier to be appointed *primipili*. These emperors did not practise a deliberate, conscious policy of exclusion of Italians: the impetus came from the Italians themselves who preferred to join the garrison at Rome rather than the legions, because this guaranteed them higher salaries and allowed them to enjoy the attractions of city life. Moreover, it is known that the peninsula had demographic problems after the end of the first century. Finally, in the third century it seems that there were no longer any Italians; the evolution that began in the second century would therefore have reached its conclusion.

From a social angle the situation appears to be both simpler and more stable. As far as we can ascertain from the disappointing sources at our disposal, the *primipili* came normally from families of note. Their fathers were landowners whose estates rarely stretched beyond the limits of a city and who exercised municipal functions in this narrow context. The numbers were completed by a few equestrian Romans (*ex equite romano*).

The centurions

The differences in recruitment between centurions and *primipili* ought not to be very great as the latter are really only the best of the former. While there are, however, some aspects that are peculiar to them, care must be taken as the small number of systematic studies on the subject has not generated sufficient information. And yet there is abundant documentation. Moreover, figures can be obtained for the two legions mentioned above (see nn.26, 27). It would seem preferable to present these tables (**Tables 14 and 15**) and then to discuss them.

Geographical recruitment

Generally speaking, in the first century the Italians dominated, though this rule is not completely valid for Spain and certainly not for Africa. Those from the long-standing colonies contributed significantly, but there were already a few easterners in the *legio III Augusta*, and the regional recruitment, although modest, certainly did exist; Josephus speaks of a Syrian centurion serving in a unit stationed in Syria in the time of Nero.[28]

Legio VII Gemina	CENTURIES			
	I	II	III	Total
Indigenous Spaniards	2	9	2	13
Westerners { Italians	7	7	2	16
{ Others	5	5	5	15
Easterners	0	0	1	1
Total	14	21	10	45

Legio III Augusta	I	II	III	Total
Indigenous Africans	1	9	2	12
Westerners { Italians	1	5	1	7
{ Others	1	6	2	9
Easterners	2	7	1	10
Total	5	27	6	38

Table 14: Centurions' birthplaces.

In the second century, as early as the Trajanic-Hadrianic period, there was a rapid increase in numbers from the provinces, but mainly from western colonies. There is a corresponding decrease in the number of Italians, though these still maintained a solid presence, especially in Spain. Although easterners were still absent from this region they henceforth played an important role in Africa, whereas locals everywhere remained few in number. This is no doubt explicable by the fairly large mobility that existed within the centurion corps.

In the third century a clear diversification as early as the reign of Septimius Severus is observable. Although officers who came from the peninsula had not yet disappeared from the lists, they were no longer in the majority and had definitively yielded to their colleagues from the provinces, especially the Romanized regions of the west and the plains of the Danube. If the easterners were henceforth present everywhere, their numbers were very small in Spain. Equally, the percentage of indigenous centurions does not give them an absolute majority; this group decidedly did continue to move around a lot.

Social origins

Although the mention of the homeland (*origo*) on a centurion's inscription is sometimes found, identification of the social origin remains difficult, as very few inscriptions give that sort of information. This necessitates an indirect approach to tackle the problem, and there are two elements which are of use. Firstly, we know that new citizens adopted their *gentile nomen* from the magistrate who granted them their naturalization. In the empire that means the emperor in the vast majority of cases, though not exclusively. Further, if we come across a Julius in the second century we know that we are dealing with a native whose family has been Romanized for some time, since Julius refers to Julius Caesar or Augustus. On the other hand, names which are not those of emperors probably belong to the descendant of an Italian immigrant. However, it is necessary to take into account the fact that provinces conquered during the Republic were subject to a policy of Romanization before Augustus.[29] Furthermore, governors always had the power to promote a few of their citizens (for further information see n.26). Secondly, the *cognomina* can be used even if some historians have claimed that some of them are in fact no more than Romanized indigenous names (Libyan, Iberian, etc.). Clearly the fact that a need was felt to give them a Latin form is significant. Here again more detailed lists exist elsewhere (see n.26).

Table 15 shows that there are very few imperial *gentilia nomina* in the first century; in the second century they seem to be more frequent, but in fact they refer to rulers of the Julio-Claudian or Flavian eras. On the

Legio VII Gemina		I	II	III	Total
Gentile Nomen	Imperial	1	10	4	15
	non-Imperial	12	14	6	32
	Total	13	24	10	47
Cognomina	Latin	14	20	9	43
	Greek	0	0	1	1
	other	0	0	0	0
	Total	14	20	10	44

Legio III Augusta

Gentile Nomen	Imperial	3	39	35	77
	non-Imperial	32	42	34	108
	Total	35	81	69	185
Cognomina	Latin	24	121	64	209
	Greek	1	6	2	9
	other	1	1	2	4
	Total	26	128	68	222

Table 15: Romanization of centurions

contrary, in the third century the two categories are more or less equally balanced; it is therefore at the beginning of this period that an evolution in the recruitment of centurions took place. In fact, these names reveal that we are dealing with people from families that have long since been granted Roman citizenship. More precise information can be found in another book (see n.26); it has been shown that only two emperors agreed to award the vinestock to recently naturalized men. These were Hadrian (Aelius) and Caracalla (Aurelius), and their recruitment policy was therefore less strict.

In examining the *cognomina* what is striking is the importance, or rather the overwhelming dominance, of the Latin; in the *legio VII Gemina* there is in fact only one Greek name, which is third-century, and none derived from a regional language. More important, the percentage of onomastics taken from Italy remained constant throughout the whole of the Early Empire, including the third century. We can deduce that to be a centurion one had to have attained a certain, not to say important, degree of Romanization.

From these and other studies it transpires that these officers normally came from families of note, and that they were sometimes appointed to their posts directly, without working their way up through the ranks.[30] Of these some could claim to be sons of soldiers, a category that seems to have increased during the third century. Finally, a very small minority was descended from the equestrian order (*ex equite romano*).

Thus *primipili* and centurions came from the oldest and most deeply Romanized sections of a middle class we know from other sources to have been very attached to the imperial regime. This selection reveals a clear desire of the authorities to maintain a policy of recruitment based on quality.

RECRUITMENT OF LEGIONARIES

Historiography

When studying the recruitment of legionaries it must be remembered that their social background is very close to that of the centurions, since the latter were sometimes chosen from the ranks of ordinary soldiers. Nevertheless, there can be slight, and sometimes even marked, differences. This question is also one of the best understood, due to the abundant documentation and the important studies over the years.

It was indeed the great Th. Mommsen who first inspired research by establishing lists of places of origin. He concluded that it was necessary to distinguish two areas of recruitment, the East and the West, and several periods, the main chronological divisions being the reigns of Vespasian,

Hadrian and Septimius Severus. This brilliant study seemed to discourage possible emulators for some time,[31] until M. Rostovtzeff's criticized, but still useful, work that concentrated on the social origins of legionaries.[32] He developed the theory of progressive ruralization of the Roman army from the beginning of the second century, a trend that reached its peak during the events in Africa in 238, when the *legio III Augusta* crushed the revolt of the nobles backing the proconsul Gordian who had been proclaimed emperor. Rostovtzeff saw in these events an episode in a civil war between soldier-peasants and urban-civilians.

But since Mommsen's time many discoveries have been made. Moreover, Rostovtzeff's theory did not earn the universal acclaim of critics, as for many historians the unrest of 238 was no more than an uprising caused by too heavy taxes that were considered to be no longer bearable.[33] In its turn this uprising had been put down by soldiers who were merely disciplined. It was left to G. Forni in two exemplary studies (nn.3, 4) to update the lists of known countries of origin and to produce a synthesis of the problems. Finally, two recent works have slightly modified the statistics and brought some more precision.[34] To present these results it seems simpler to adopt the distinction already used for the centurions.

The geographical aspect

The places of origin are well known but the major difficulty stems from the sources. When consulting literary writers it is important to beware of the excessive optimism of a few and the very fashionable pessimism of the many. Tacitus, like St Cyprian, for example, was always ready to think that things were better in the past. As for inscriptions, epitaphs or 'lists', they are sometimes damaged and often cannot be dated with any precision.

Nevertheless, they are of considerable interest to the subject. Here is a text found near Alexandria:[35]

> To the emperor Caesar Lucius Septimius Severus, Pertinax, Augustus, Supreme Pontiff, tribune for the second time [194], acclaimed *Imperator* three times, consul for the second time, proconsul, father of the homeland. The veterans of the *Legio II Trajana*, discharged with an honourable discharge, and who began their service in the consulship of Apronianus and Paulus [168] [lacuna] [offered this inscription].

There follows a fragmented list of names organized into cohorts and centuries, of which this is an example:

Vth cohort
Century of Celer:
Marcus Gabinius Ammonianus, son of Marcus, of the camp (*castris*);
Century of Flavius Philippianus:
Titus Aurelius Chaeremonianus, son of Titus, of the tribe Pollia, of the camp;

Caius Valerius Apollinaris, son of Caius, of the tribe Collina, from Hierapolis;
Century of Severus:
Marcus Aurelius Isidorus, of the tribe Pollia, from Alexandria;
Caius Pompeius Serenus, son of Caius, of the tribe Pollia, of the camp.

Still more names follow, but this extract is sufficient to illustrate the idea
that at the time of their discharge the soldiers had an inscription engraved
in honour of the emperor, whose honours they specify. They indicate the
reason for composing the text and finally those who shared in the cost of
the monument are listed.

Before outlining an assessment of this, two further remarks of a general
order have yet to be made. On the one hand it is hard to believe today in
sudden changes brought about by decisions of emperors. On the contrary,
it seems that Mommsen's view is wrong, and that evolution was slow and
continuous. On the other hand it is noticeable that some traditions were
established: during the whole of the first century the custom of Gaul was
to send young men to serve in Africa, despite the fact that there seems to
have been no special need for this migration.

The first century is that of the 'foreigners'; recruiting officers generally
found men hard to come by;[36] few provinces were capable of supplying their own defenders, and in any case it seemed normal to the
political powers to carry out a certain mixing of populations. However,
it is essential to make a distinction between the two halves of the
Mediterranean basin. In the west, where Latin was spoken, the Italians
were most numerous, with the exception of those from Latium, Etruria
and Umbria, as well as the old colonies, who preferred to join the
Praetorian and Urban cohorts to enjoy high salaries and the attractions
of the city. Nevertheless, there is a slow but inexorable reduction in the
number of soldiers originating from the peninsula. Towards the time of
Vespasian few were to be found in the legions, and yet no decision on this
point had been taken by the political powers. Today, opinion is therefore
in favour of G. Forni's arguments rather than Mommsen's. At the same
time, there is a progressive rise in the number of non-Italians coming from
the senatorial provinces, the richest, the most Romanized and the most
peaceful of the empire, namely Gallia Narbonensis, Baetica, Africa and
Macedonia.

In the eastern part of the empire where Greek was the language of
administration, the situation was different. In the first century soldiers
normally came from this part of the Mediterranean basin; they were called
'Orientals'. As early as the time of Augustus there was an infrequent,
but real, practice of local recruitment in operation; in a 'list' found at
Alexandria, mention is made of men born in the city and of others who
name the camp (*castris*) as their homeland.

The question of the *origo castris*[37] raises a problem. It should first
be noted that the expression is not '*ex castris*' as is sometimes said
to be the case, since the preposition is never found in inscriptions.

Some soldiers therefore do not give their place of birth as a city but rather the camp. For a long time the view of all historians was that they were sons of soldiers, conceived during the father's military service by women living in the *canabae*, that is the non-military buildings (houses, cabarets, shops etc.) built near forts to satisfy all the needs of the soldiers. As such unions were forbidden until 197 when Septimius Severus authorized them, any children born were illegitimate.[38] Also, from 212, the year of Caracalla's famous edict, every free man in the empire was granted Roman citizenship.

However, a different theory was advanced by the Hungarian, A. Mócsy.[39] According to him, the *origo castris* would have been given as a fictitious homeland for young men who were *peregrini* at the time of enlistment and who therefore did not have the necessary qualifications to join the legion. This explained the recruiting of country people important for M. Rostovtzeff. But, as has been said, the latter's theory had been contested, and so too was A. Mócsy's, particularly by F. Vittinghoff, a very skilful defender of the traditional interpretation.[40] Admittedly it has been possible to prove that in the time of Hadrian the *origo castris* was given to recently naturalized men,[41] but normally this indicates that the bearer was indeed born in the *canabae* near the camp.

If we look again at chronology we notice a steady evolution from the beginning of the second century, a slow transition from a regional recruitment to a local one via an intermediary phase during which the soldiers come from cities nearer and nearer to the fort. Thus the *legio III Augusta*, which was stationed to the north of the Aures, recruited initially in Africa, then in Numidia, and finally in Lambaesis itself, in the *canabae*.

However, for this period a distinction must be made between two types of possible circumstances. Firstly we need to look at what happens in normal situations. We know that Trajan devised a policy to try to increase the population in Italy, one of the aims of which was to start to supply men for the army again.[42] He created the *alimenta*, loans offered by the State to wealthy landowners in the peninsula on which it could then use the interest to help to raise poor children who were freeborn.[43] Apparently this initiative was a failure, since Hadrian is credited with important reforms that followed a radically opposite direction, namely making regional recruitment a more general practice and directing a solid impetus towards local recruitment. In fact he was forced to follow an evolution which perhaps accelerated in his reign from force of circumstances. At that time there were still 'foreigners' in the legions, Galatians in Egypt and Gauls in Africa. In both cases this represented a tradition that went back to the Triumvirate and is thus understandable.

Despite the difficulties facing the empire in his time, Marcus Aurelius still went to great lengths to choose the best men for the legions, while being far more lax when supplying the *auxilia*. At the end of the second century and at the beginning of the third, regional recruitment seems to have become standard practice, but there is a large percentage of men who mention the *origo castris*, and even the 'foreigners' and the Italians did not disappear completely from the lists, though they represent a very small contingent. However, we cannot be sure of what happened at the height of the great crisis of the third century. St Cyprian notes ruefully that at the worst time the camps were empty, and despite the fact that he was pessimistic by nature we cannot totally ignore his observation. In fact specialists believe that the Illyrians and the Thracians joined the legions in huge numbers at that time. In Africa, however, it seems that there was a general reliance on the children of soldiers.

Besides this normal recruitment we know of some exceptional practices, which came into being in times of war and therefore constitute a different case. During the whole of the Early Empire the principle of compulsory military service was maintained. Severus Alexander (222–35) called upon provincials and Italians,[47] and again it is from the peninsula that the State drew its troops to oppose Maximinus.[48] However, this mobilization across the whole of the empire was only practised in times of serious difficulties. Normally, before a campaign the recruits were drawn from the regions closest to the threatened border. For example Galatians and Cappadocians were called upon to defend Armenia.[49]

After the campaign, the army was initially brought back to the provinces situated in the vicinity of the theatre of operations, and there the competent authorities could put into effect one of two diverging principles, following the recommendations of the general. Firstly, losses sustained in the recent action might be made up on the spot; thus a detachment of a legion in Germany sent to fight the Parthians received a contingent of Syrian soldiers. The second principle consisted in incorporating the remnants of a vexillation into the local army. In both cases there is a mixing of populations. The presence of 'foreigners' in a 'list' of soldiers must therefore be interpreted with due caution. It may reflect either a regular flow of men or an exceptional movement. There is another possibility that must not be forgotten, even though it was a rare occurrence, namely the disbanding of a unit as a disciplinary sanction. In this situation it does indeed seem that the soldiers of the punished legion were not sent back to civilian life but were dispersed among various different garrisons.

Regions of origin

One aspect of this is often neglected: few researchers have asked why this or that region did or did not supply soldiers, and how many. Table 16 clearly shows that all the regions of the Empire supplied soldiers. It must, however, be interpreted with caution as the figures advanced do not always have the same implications. Thus the primacy of Italy in the Early

Table 16: Regions of origin (after G. Forni, see n.3 and 4)

	AUGUSTUS– CALIGULA	CLAUDIUS– NERO	FLAVIANS– TRAJAN	HADRIAN– END OF THE THIRD CENTURY
Italy	215	124	83	37
Provinces	134	136	299	2019
Spain (unspecified)	0	3	1	1
Tarraconensis	2	5	11	15
Baetica	3	13	3	1
Lusitania	3	1	4	3
Britain	0	1	0	4
Gaul (unspecified)	0	3	4	18
Narbonensis	31	58	34	6
Lugdunensis	4	4	12	5
Aquitania	0	2	6	0
Belgium	0	0	0	5
Alpes Maritimes	0	1	3	2
Appenines	0	1	1	0
Germany (unspecified)	0	0	0	12
Lower Germany	0	0	27	21
Upper Germany	0	0	2	15
Sardinia	0	0	0	1
Raetia	0	0	2	12
Noricum	0	9	21	31
Pannonia (unspecified)	0	0	0	8
Upper Pannonia	0	0	10	44
Lower Pannonia	0	0	4	55
Lower Moesia	0	0	1	22
Upper Moesia	0	0	1	128
Dacia	0	0	0	51
Dalmatia	3	6	5	19
Macedonia	14	10	7	10
Epirus	0	0	4	0
Achaia	0	0	0	1
Thrace	0	0	2	107

. . . cont.

	AUGUSTUS–CALIGULA	CLAUDIUS–NERO	FLAVIANS–TRAJAN	HADRIAN–END OF THE THIRD CENTURY
Asia	3	2	4	5
Bithynia	3	0	30	6
Galatia-Lycaonia Paphlagonia	30	5	6	5
Lycia	0	0	0	1
Pamphylia-Pisidia	10	1	2	1
Pontus-Cappadocia	4	4	2	0
Cilicia	1	0	0	11
Cyprus	1	0	0	0
Syria-Palestine	5	3	53	55
Egypt	9	0	11	45
Cyrenaica	1	0	1	1
Africa-Numidia	7	4	24	874
Mauretanias	0	0	0	5

Empire must be interpreted politically – it can be explained by the fact that the conquest and the Civil War which preceded the advent of the Empire were fought by soldiers who came from the peninsula. It was they who overcame all the other peoples of the Mediterranean basin, as Virgil said: 'Do not forget, Roman, it is your task to subjugate the nations'[50] (and by 'Roman' should be understood 'Roman citizen', which at the beginning of the Principate meant all the Italians). As a result it seemed normal that the conquerors should continue to maintain security in the occupied territories. Then, a demographic slowing down imposed a decline in this sort of recruitment, with the garrison at Rome managing to accommodate all volunteers.

On the other hand, the increase in the participation of certain regions reflects an increase in their population and the extension of Romanization. It is necessary only to consider the old proconsular provinces. From a very early date Africa supplied men and sent them to all types of units.[51] Asia, that is the western fringe of Anatolia, was also densely populated, and the protagonists of the conflict of 68–9 knew how to exploit this.[52] Similar observations could be made for Macedonia, Cyrenaica,[53] Baetica and Gallia

24 Vienne	6 Arles, Béziers, Nimes	1 Carcassonne, Antibes
18 Narbonne	5 Alba	Apt, Castelnau-de-Lèze
13 Fréjus	4 Valence	Cavaillon, Digne,
12 Luc-en-Diois	3 Aix	Tarascon, Uzès, Vaison
8 Saint-Remy	2 Riez	

Table 17: Recruitment of legionaries in Gallia Narbonensis

Narbonensis.[54] It is even possible to show which cities in southern Gaul provided soldiers and how many were chosen from each by the authorities.

Alongside these political and demographic considerations there are others of a more technical nature. The peaceful senatorial provinces were gradually replaced by border regions like Syria,[55] (but one could also cite Germania, Pannonia, Moesia and Dacia) because many sons of soldiers were to be found there, and these young men were far more inclined to join the army. But of course at one time or another every region of the Empire was required to provide soldiers.

The haphazard nature of our discoveries must also not be forgotten. If there are so many Africans in these lists it can be largely explained by the exceptional state of preservation of the site of Lambaesis, to the north of the Aures, the headquarters of the *legio III Augusta* in the second and third centuries. On the other hand, it must be due to bad luck that very few soldiers are known from Cyrenaica, when two separate documents (n.53) indicate that recruitment took place there.

The receiving armies

Having seen where the recruits came from, we should ask where they went. Because there are not many studies on this point we can do no more than take three sample soundings.

In Africa,[56] where only one legion, the *III Augusta*, was stationed for most of the time, the abundant documentation for the second century and the reigns of the Severi allows us to chart the evolution there. The first century is that of the 'foreigners', Italians and Gauls in particular; for the Gauls, as suggested earlier, it was no doubt a tradition dating back to the Triumvirate, when Lepidus is thought to have come to Africa accompanied by legionaries recruited from the other side of the Mediterranean. This would have been the start of the practice of some cities of Gaul of sending young men to serve abroad. At the beginning of the second century Africans joined the legions (some had already done so in the first century), but they were still inferior in number to the 'foreigners', now Bithynians, men from the Lower Danube, no doubt during Trajan's Dacian War, and especially Syrians from the time of his Parthian campaigns. For the end of the second century the percentages are reversed: Africans are in the majority, first from the north of the

	Italy	Spain					Gauls	Africa	Others	Total
		Lusitania	Baetica	Citerior	Not spec.	Total				
Augustus-68	14	7	19	11	0	(37)	10	0	0	61
68–99	5	14	4	22	0	(40)	4	0	0	49
Second century	1(?)	4	1	20	8	(33)	1	4	0	38
Third century	0	2	2	12	9	(25)	0	4	2	31
Total	19(20?)	27	26	65	17	(135)	15	8	2	179

Table 18: Recruitment of legionaries for the Roman army in Spain

	Total number of men	Percentage by origin								Refs
		Italy	Galatia, Paphlagonia	Pamphylia	Bithynia	Syria	Africa	Egypt	Various	
Augustus	36		44.4	8.3				25	22.2	CIL III 6627
Pre 41	14	14.2	35.7			21.4	14.2		7.1	BGU IV 1083 pap.
157 (joined in 131–2)	132	11.3			2.2	13.6	67.4		5.3	Ann. Epig 1955 238 = 1969 –70 633
194 (joined in 168)	40				2.5	15	5	77.5		CIL III 6580

Table 19: Recruitment of legionaries for the Roman army in Egypt

Maghreb, then from Numidia. For the beginning of the third century the percentage of 'foreigners' remains stable, whereas the *origo castris* is very strongly represented even if it falls short of being in the majority. The legion was disbanded sometime between 238 and 253 and probably reformed later from local recruits, but by this time the practice of mentioning the soldier's homeland has been dropped.

The situation in Spain, can usefully be summarized with a table (**Table

18).[57] In the case of the army in Spain the initial importance of Italians and Gauls is also noticeable, as is their steady decline, followed by the appearance of small numbers of Africans in the second and third centuries. On the other hand there is one unusual feature, namely the permanent presence, clear from the very beginning, of a strong contingent of indigenous soldiers.

The origins of legionaries who served in Egypt are less well known as there exist very few 'lists'. Despite the relatively small numbers, **Table 19** allows certain points to be made. Firstly the presence of an Italian contingent even in the Roman east should be noted. The peculiarity of the army in Egypt is twofold; firstly it is characterized by the presence of many soldiers born in Asia Minor in general, and from Galatia in particular (in the latter case it seems also to be a tradition dating back to the Triumvirate); secondly, local recruitment, even that of *castris*, is vouched for as early as Augustus, though this was not the norm. On the other hand, the presence of Syrians is less surprising in view of the proximity of their homeland, while the increase in the local recruitment, even though it started earlier, is nothing if not normal. Finally the very high percentage of Africans noted on one of the inscriptions is probably explicable by the fact that a vexillation of the *legio III Augusta* had just been attached to the *II Trajana*.

The social aspect

The question of the geographical origins of the soldiers is complex; the evolution from the provinces they left to the armies they joined needs to be brought out. But since a certain number of soldiers mention their homeland the problem does not appear to be impossible to solve. On the other hand, not one of them indicates his father's profession, nor the one he himself was perhaps practising when he was recruited. No soldier mentions his social background, so indirect methods of research have to be used, as for centurions, but fortunately this time the documentation is much greater.

The law

As mentioned above, the recruiting process (*probatio*) contained a legal examination. Slaves were not allowed to join a legion, nor were freedmen nor *peregrini*. The last mentioned could sometimes be admitted into these types of units but had to keep their original status. Such a situation is attested, but seems to have been a very rare occurrence. Exceptional and serious circumstances could mean resorting to one or other of these inferior categories, but normally the officer in charge of the *dilectus* would have had to have given the candidates their freedom, if necessary, and then citizenship; only then could he enlist them. Indeed, it was the rule that legionaries had to have all the rights associated with being a Roman, and a recent study on the legal status of soldiers strongly emphasizes two requirements, 'selection and elitism', in the recruitment process.[59] But a passage from the *Sentences* attributed to the famous third-century jurist Paulus, tells us that soldiers were liable to capital punishment for certain crimes,[60] though capital punishment was only applicable to the lower classes of society, the *humiliores*. Of course, it may be that this was a new law, ratifying a state of affairs that had begun to develop some time previously, or perhaps the text only repeats a legal decision of long standing. The first interpretation (see n.59) seems more plausible, but the legal aspect is not the only path of enquiry.

Social backgrounds

A second observation reinforces one already made; contrary to what certain writers have thought, the results of a very detailed study have shown that legionaries did not come from the urban notable class.[61] Few, if any at all, came from those families that dominated the municipal councils (*curiae*), at least in Africa. In this respect there is a real difference between centurions and ordinary soldiers.

When looking at the lowest levels of society is it necessary to agree with M. Rostovtzeff that there was an influx of barbarian peasants into the lines? Certainly not, since Rostovtzeff was taken in by the myth of the excellent soldier from the countryside and the mediocrity of the soldier from the city, a myth already propagated by ancient literary sources.[62] However, this goes back to the time before Augustus set up a professional army. Another misconception of Rostovtzeff's was that the mention of an *origo* means that the soldier actually lived in that town.

This question of city dweller or country dweller is a very good example of a non-existent problem. Each *origo* refers to a city, that is a town together with its territories. Furthermore, many sites which we class as urban were in fact no more than large villages, where everyone lived off the land. It is necessary only to think of the numerous sites in Asia or Africa, like Dougga; only a few important centres like Ephesus or Carthage had secondary or tertiary activities. In any case, the ancient way of thinking did not allow such a dichotomy since the inhabitants of large cities lived closer to nature than a Londoner, a Parisian or a New Yorker in the twentieth century, adapting to the rhythm of the seasons and the harvests. The richest businessman had but one goal in mind, to invest the money he earned by commerce or his craft in land. Besides, as a soldier joined up at the age of twenty for a 25-year period of service it is probable that he felt that he belonged to the camp rather than to the town or the country.

The argument can be taken further. We know that provinces under the rule of the Senate were richer, more peaceful and more Romanized than those under the emperor's jurisdiction, and that naturally Italy was more heavily represented. A study of this situation has been carried out for the legion *III Augusta*:[63]

	Italy	Senatorial Provinces	Imperial Provinces
First century	19	23	56
Second century	1	54	44
Third century (start)	0	62	37

Table 20: Regional Origins of soldiers of *III Augusta* in per cent

Admittedly Italy's percentage decreases, but so does that of the imperial provinces, with the senatorial provinces gaining. A different impression therefore emerges from this table, namely that legionaries came from a higher-class milieu than was previously imagined. This impression is reinforced by another means of verification since we know that colonies, parts of Rome separated from the mother-city, and the *municipia*, cities that shared the burden of the inhabitants of the metropolis, represented an elite in the hierarchy of urban status, at the bottom of which were the foreign cities. Calculations based on the African legion show 615 men or 92 per cent came from the first category and 53 men at most or 8 per cent from the second.[64]

Another aspect of the origins of legionaries has been neglected: the background of their childhood and adolescence. Whether a future soldier spent his early years in a port, a rural village or near a fort is not without significance, and it has been possible to establish some figures on this for the *legio III Augusta*.[65]

	Coastal Towns	Inland Towns	Lambaesis and camps
117–61	46	30	23
161–92	33	43	25
193–238	16	44	39

Table 21: Backgrounds of soldiers in *III Augusta* in per cent

This table shows two sharp falls in the number of men from harbour towns born of families of sailors, from tradesmen and craftsmen, with correlating rises first in the number of young men from rural villages in the second century, and then of sons of soldiers at the beginning of the third.

The lessons of onomastics

The above tables took into account the important feature of mentions of homelands. Yet another factor, onomastics, can be used, which is all the more interesting because it involves greater numbers. It has already been demonstrated that this technique can be of great help to researchers and all that needs to be done is to adopt the two principal points examined in the section on centurions (pp. 81–4).

Gentilia nomina

Taking these as the starting point: if they belonged to known people like emperors or governors, they indicate Romanized natives, but this is not the only information they give, as they also show how recent the naturalization was. A Claudius was newly promoted if he lived in the middle of the first century, since his name refers to the emperors Claudius and Nero, whereas if he were living in the third century he would have been considered a Roman of long date. As for rare *gentilia nomina* which do not correspond to any known emperor or magistrate, they strongly suggest an Italian immigrant transmission. The following table once again takes its information from the *legio III Augusta*.[66]

	First century	Second century	Third century	Second to third century	Average
emperors	21	39	35	35	35
governors (republic)	21	17	18	25	19
governors (empire)	14	12	13	14	13
Italian immigrants	29	23	24	19	24
from *cognomina*	3	3	3	2	3
various *gentilia*	11	7	7	6	7

Table 22: *Gentilia nomina* of soldiers in *III Augusta* in per cent

The figures show that the Roman army in Africa had in its ranks about 25 per cent Italian immigrant descendants (nearly a third in the first century) and 65 per cent Romanized Africans. However, the importance of *gentilia nomina* referring to governors of the Republican period leads us to believe that these soldiers came from families Romanized long before. Finally, although it is not evident from the table, there does not appear to have been any great evolution in the era of the Severi compared with the second century. The figures for imperial names can be broken down further by distinguishing between the different emperors, here by also comparing it with the army of Spain, essentially the *legio VII Gemina*.[67]

Gentilia nomina	Emperors	III Augusta	Spanish legions
Iulii	(Caesar) Augustus Tiberius, Caligula	49	59
Claudii	Claudius, Nero	8	3
Flavii	Vespasian, Titus, Domitian	13	10
Ulpii	Trajan	5	3
Aelii	Hadrian, Antoninus Pius, Marcus Aurelius, Commodus	14	3
Aurelii	Marcus Aurelius, Commodus, Caracalla	12	22

Table 23: Imperial names of legionaries in per cent

In order fully to understand this table it should be made clear that Marcus Aurelius and Commodus changed their onomastic in the course of their reigns and that in 212 Caracalla gave Roman citizenship to all free men in the Empire who had not yet received it, thus completing an evolution begun a long time previously. The importance of the work of the Julii (essentially Julius Caesar and Augustus) is very noticeable; far behind them come the Flavii and the Aurelii, the latter being above all represented by Caracalla. If the army in Spain followed more or less that of Africa in its evolution, it nevertheless presents some original features, with a higher percentage of Julii and Aurelii.

Cognomina

In studying these, both different and complementary information is obtained to that from the *gentilia*. For a start, it is possible to see which languages are behind the names of the soldiers of the *legio III Augusta* and of the army in Spain, and to compare them (**Table 24**).

Two essential lessons can be learned from these tables. Firstly, the differences that exist between the legions of Africa and Spain seem fairly

	III Augusta				Spanish legions			
	Latins	Greeks	Natives	others	Latins	Greeks	Natives	others
First century	96	1	1	2	94	0	4	2
Second century	91	7	0.5	2	95	3	0	2
Third century	95	2	2	1	97	0	2	0
Average	94	3	1	2	95	1	2	1

Table 24: Language of the *cognomina* of the soldiers in per cent (see n.67)

insignificant. Secondly, the Latin language predominates. Admittedly it could be argued that the documents are largely inscriptions, and that as the custom of engraving texts on stone is Italian, this predominance is hardly surprising. A comparison will therefore help us to estimate more precisely the importance of these figures. In the province of Britain P. Salway noted only 50 per cent of Latin names for the whole of the region in which soldiers were stationed.[68]

Furthermore, it has been established that some *cognomina* were more frequently used by nobles, others by ordinary citizens and yet others by slaves,[69] without any group having any complete monopoly in this area. Different fashions existed in the different social groups. Research carried out for the *legio III Augusta* shows a mixture of names, some up-market, others more common, and it is possible to suggest that these soldiers belonged to a middle class that drew its onomastics sometimes from the upper classes, sometimes from the lower.[70]

However, one line of research must be abandoned. Many epigraphists thought that some Latin *cognomina* belonged to a certain part of the Empire, either because they were translations of native names or else reflected a local fashion. This theory has recently been questioned by Sir Ronald Syme who doubts the 'African' nature of Donatus, Fortunatus, Optatus and Rogatus.[71] Before him J.-J. Hatt had shown that Saturninus was to be found with equal frequency in Gaul and in Proconsular regions.[72] The views of these two scholars should probably be adopted;[73] indeed, the *cognomina* Felix, Secundus, Maximus, Primus and Rufus are to be found in virtually all the provinces. Only two special cases are to be noted in the Empire: in Rome the very high percentage of Greek names may seem surprising but it can be explained by the large numbers of slaves living there as well as the ethnic mixes in the capital of the Empire. Secondly, inhabitants of military regions understandably seem to have had a strong liking for calling their children Victor. Consequently the expression 'native names' should be reserved for those that were not translated, like Baricio and Namphano in Africa, and Andergus and Clutamus in Spain. It should also be noted that these are very rare during the whole of the period of the Early Empire.

The question of Greek *cognomina* has been the subject of debate, with three theories established. For H. Solin such onomastics have a social significance: they indicate that we are dealing with a slave or an emancipated slave.[74] Secondly, Ph. Leveau has envisaged the possibility of the role of fashion, in particular during the era of the great Philhellene Hadrian (117–38).[75] Finally, in answer to Solin, P. Huttunen considers a wider spectrum of explanations.[76] In any case, this type of nomenclature is only rarely met with in legionaries, and insofar as any conclusions can be drawn from such a small number of examples, we can say that they fall into three categories;[77] some soldiers did indeed come from the east, others from the camp (*castris*), and others lived at the beginning of the second century, around the time of Hadrian.

It would be possible to push this type of analysis even further, but it seems necessary at this point to highlight some important characteristics in the recruitment of legionaries. These soldiers undoubtedly belonged to the plebeian *humiliores*, but they constituted an elite within it, the upper echelon, the earliest to be Romanized. This choice of the best can be explained by a deliberate policy, consciously pursued by the imperial power.[78] During the third century especially, however, the wishes of the State had to be compromised because of force of circumstances. It was becoming more and more difficult to find men and then to pay them attractive wages, and the crisis broke when the barbarians in the north and in the east were moving to attack the Empire.

RECRUITMENT OF AUXILIARIES

There are two reasons why historians are almost as familiar with the recruitment of auxiliaries as they are with that of legionaries. Firstly, they have at their disposal a fairly large quantity of documents, funeral inscriptions, 'lists', 'military diplomas' and papyri. Secondly, the question has been very thoroughly studied, in particular in K. Kraft's superb work on the provinces of the Rhine and the Danube.[79] But many other works of no less merit could be cited. The sum of all this research has brought scholars to almost total agreement on two conclusions. The first rule is — that there is no rule, at least no firm rule, with individual regions and armies evolving in their own ways. However, the second point of consensus is that there is a general tendency which runs counter to what was observed in the case of legions. Whereas legions were enlisting young men from progressively humbler backgrounds, the auxiliary corps were generally enlisting more and more Roman citizens. As a result there is a gradual convergence of the two types of unit.

Geographical aspect

Starting with the geographical aspect, that is the homelands, we know that the name of a people that was incorporated into the name of an auxiliary unit indicates the area where it was formed and carried out its first recruitment. The *ala I Thracum* originated in Thrace, the province where its longest-serving soldiers came from. It was possible to continue to choose new soldiers in the region of origin for a certain time, insofar as traditions and links between the province and its army became established. When a unit has two ethnic names, for instance *ala Gallorum et Pannoniorum*, it signifies that there has been a fusion of the remains of two different corps, in this case the Gauls and the a *North-west Europe*

Regions	*Alae*	Units Cohorts	Total	Denominations Nations	Tribes
Britain[83]	2	16	18	Brittones	
Tarraconensis[84]	12	49	61	Hispani (+ H. Compagones et Vettones)	Arauaci, Astures (+ Callaeci), Ausetani, Bracaraugustani, Cantabri, Carietes (+ Veniaeses), Celtiberi, Lucenses (Hispani, + Callaeci), Vardulli, Vascones.
Lusitania	0	9	9	Lusitani	
Belgium	6	41 + x	47 + x	Belgae[85] Germani	Bataui, Canninefates, Cugerni, Lingones, Mattiaci, Menapii, Morini, Nemetes, Neruii,[86] Sequani et Rauraci, Sugambri, Sunuci, Treueri, Tungri,[87] Vangiones, Vbii, Vsipi.[87]
Lugdunensis	11 (+ 14?)	21	32 (+ 14?)	Gali (+ Bosporani, + Pannonii)	
Aquitania	0	7	7	Aquitani	Bituriges
Narbonensis	2	0	2		Vocontii
Corsica	0	3	3	Corsi (+ Sardi and Ligures)	
Sardinia	0	3	3	Sardi (+ Corsi)	
Alps[88]	1	12	13	Alpini	Ligures (+ Corsi), Montani, Trumplini, Vallenses.
Raetia	0	19	19	Raeti	Heluetti Vindelici; gaesati
Noricum	1	1	2	Norici	

b *North-east Europe*

Regions	Alae	Units Cohorts	Total	Denominations	
				Nations	Tribes
Pannonia	8	18	26	Pannonii (+ Dalmatae)	Breuci, Illyrici, Sarmatae, Varciani
Dalmatia	0	11	11	Dalmatae	
Moesia	2	5	7		Bosporani, Dardani
Dacia[89]	1	6	7	Daci	
Thrace[90]	9	22	31	Thraces	
Macedonia	0	3	3	Macedones	Cyrrhestici
Crete (see Cyrenaica)	0	1	1	Cretes	

Asia

Galatia	1	6	7	Galatae	Paflagones, Phryges[91]
Cilicia	0	4	4	Cilices	
Cyprus	0	4	4	Cypri	
Syria[92]	2 + 2)	22 (+ 5)	24 (+ 7)	Syri	Antiochenses, Apameni, Canatheni, Chalcideni, Commageni, Damasceni, Hamii, Hemeseni, Tyrii + Parthi,[93] sagittarii
Palestine	2	10	12		Ascalonitani, Ituraei, Sebasteni
Arabia	0 (+ 1)	6	6 (+ 1)		Petraei + dromedarii

Africa

Egypt[94]	0	2	2		Thebaei
Cyrenaica (see also Crete)	0	4	4	Cyrenaici	

Africa[95] + Mauretania	5	14	19	Numidae, Mauri Musulamii.	Afri,[96] Cirtenses, Cisipadenses, Gaetuli,

Table 25: Initial Recruitment of auxiliaries according to G.L. Cheesman.

Pannonians. This type of name has been attested so far only for the second century.

The peoples that supplied these men have not been studied recently, but we can turn to the lists given by G.L. Cheesman,[80] which admittedly date from 1914,[81] but which enable us to get a general picture of the situation (**Table 25**).[82] Some updating of these will be provided in the notes (*infra*,[83–96]).

Even though their chronological significance is limited, insofar as they are of interest only for the moment of their coming into existence, these lists allow some illuminating observations to be made. Europe supplied more than three-quarters of the auxiliaries (301 units out of 383, i.e. 78.5 per cent), while the western part of the continent provided more than a half (215, i.e. 56 per cent). Far behind come Asia (57, i.e. 15 per cent) and Africa (25, i.e. 6.5 per cent). The cavalry were recruited in Celticized regions (Tarraconensis and Lugdunensis), later in Thrace and Pannonia. The poor representation of bowmen in these lists can be explained by the fact that many were to be found in the *numeri* which Cheesman excluded from his enquiry.

The following tables show the evolution by simplifying the results obtained from recent studies of the military zones of the Rhine, the Danube and Mauretania.

	'FOREIGNERS'	NATIVE
Flavians-Trajan		
Rhine	13	28
Danube	30	25
Total	43	53
Hadrian *c.* 170		
Rhine	1	3
Danube	18	24
Total	19	27
End second-third century		
Rhine	6	8
Danube	25	29
Total	31	37

Table 26: Recruitment of *alae* and cohorts on the Rhine and the Danube (after K. Kraft).[97]

Flavians-Trajan	16	1
Second century	0	1
Second-third century	3	7
Third century	2	3

Table 27: Recruitment of auxiliaries in Caesarean Mauretania (after M. Benseddick).[98]

To yield any valuable observations these figures need to be linked with information obtained from other sources, particularly literary texts. For the first century many 'foreigners' were enlisted, recruited from Tarraconensis, Gaul and Germany. But from the time of Tiberius new types of recruitment appear – regional and even local mobilization – types that can also be observed in Nero's reign.[99] This situation is very characteristic of Mauretania and the Danube provinces, whereas on the Rhine indigenous recruitment is paramount.

Subsequently, contrary to what has often been maintained, it seems that a fairly widespread stability is observable; in general men born in the province are slightly more numerous than, or at least as numerous as those recruited from outside. The *origo castris* does not appear in the European garrisons at least before the beginning of the Antonine period.

In the second century a certain number of units were not influenced by local recruitment, in particular the *numeri*, who came into existence at the end of the first century, and were considered from the start as a barbarian unit, so it was important for them to keep their links with their original homelands. Furthermore, other units (though in practice often *numeri*) were constituted by specialist troops like bowmen;[100] the talents of the Easterners were put to good use in this field. This could be as specific as having confidence in a single city's reputation, such as that Palmyrania had for bowmen; the *numerus Palmyrenorum sagittariorum* always chose its men from the city itself. As regards the cavalry, however, westerners like Gauls, Germans and Spanish, were preferred. Some barbarians appear to have given Romans misgivings, and these were stationed far from their homelands. The Britons fall into this category, and they were never garrisoned in their island; similarly, leaving too many Mauretanians in Mauretania was avoided, if the findings of a recent study are to be trusted, though admittedly limited to a small sample.[101] Conversely, Syrians rarely emigrated. The second century is less well known, as documents are fewer, more difficult to date, and few studies have therefore been attempted. Nevertheless, particularly in the early stages, a not inconsiderable number of 'foreigners' has to be admitted.

The social aspect

The legal status of the auxiliaries has been carefully studied by K. Kraft, and reproduced here is a simplified version of the table he drew up.[102]

	ALAE		COHORTS	
	Peregrini	Roman citizens	*Peregrini*	Roman citizens
Julio-Claudians	48	7	44	0
Flavians-Trajan	32	19	27	17
Hadrian-*c*. 170	13	10	13	17
Second-third century	0	38	3	43

Table 28: Legal status of auxiliaries, after K. Kraft.

At the time of their formation, in most cases at the beginning of the Early Empire, auxiliary units were made up of soldiers of *peregrini* status, and of various barbaric cultures. This was more evident in cohorts than in *alae*. There was already one exception, however: some cohorts were not identified by the name of a nation but were said to be 'of Roman citizens'. Normally the soldiers serving in them held this legal status and were considered the equals of legionaries. Cohorts so-named from their very beginnings were designated as consisting of volunteers (*voluntarii*), or freemen (*ingenui*) or sailors (*classicae*); these last-named have been identified with certainty as the soldiers of the fleet who were naturalized in 28 BC after having taken part in Marcus Valerius Messala Corvinus' campaign in Aquitaine. Later on this dignity was conferred as a reward to cohorts that had similarly distinguished themselves in combat.

In the Julio-Claudian period the auxiliary corps generally comprised *peregrini*, in greater numbers in the infantry than in the cavalry, where the presence of Roman citizens is already discernible. Normally only barbarians were to be found among these soldiers.[103] Tacitus remarked that their appearance was strikingly strange and their languages incomprehensible, though it must be remembered that he was contemptuous of soldiers.[104] He described the Germans in the 68–9 crisis as 'naked, according to the custom of their country, advancing in undisciplined fashion to the sound of a savage hymn and waving their shields above their shoulders'.[105]

The beginnings of change can be seen between the reigns of Vespasian and Hadrian, when fully-fledged citizens joined the ranks of the *alae* and the cohorts, though not in any great number. However, for 82 and 83 Tacitus described units in this category as still being composed mainly of barbarians.[106] From Hadrian until about 170 Romans and *peregrini* are almost equal in number, while in the period *c*.170–*c*.210 there were only a few remnants of the latter, except in the *numeri* and units that were not specialized. Nevertheless, faced with a serious problem that needed urgent attention, Marcus Aurelius enlisted anyone into the auxiliaries – slaves promoted to 'volunteers', bandits and gladiators – while still choosing his legionaries with care.[107] However, exceptional circumstances demanded exceptional measures; a dangerous enemy was getting closer and closer.

If the different types of soldiers recruited for the frontier armies are compared, we note that those who were not born into Roman citizenship received it on enlisting or on discharge; in both cases military service was a means of spreading citizenship.

RECRUITMENT OF CORPS OTHER THAN LEGIONS AND *AUXILIA*

For each different unit of the garrison at Rome and the fleet, the situation is different. Sometimes the imperial power wanted to confer privilege on the soldiers, sometimes it did not.

The garrison at Rome

The Praetorian cohorts

The fact that the Praetorian cohorts constituted the cream of the Roman army can be seen in their recruitment, at least at the beginning of the Principate. Indeed, in the first century it was necessary to be Italian to be chosen, and until the time of Tiberius it was restricted to Italians from Latium, Etruria, Umbria and the oldest colonies.[108] Under Claudius, Cisalpine Gaul, that is the plains of the river Po, was added. At the beginning of the second century the peninsula still provided 89 per cent of these soldiers, a figure that was to fall only slightly by the end of the Antonines, to the advantage of a few Dalmatians and Pannonians. At the beginning of Septimius Severus' reign in 193 there was a radical change. The African emperor decided to punish the Praetorians who had auctioned off the Empire after the death of Commodus and so disbanded them. He reformed them with his own provincial troops that he wanted to reward, especially Illyrians. Their social origins are not known. According to M. Durry they were people of modest birth on the whole,[109] but A. Passerini argues that they came from families of note.[110] The following table showing the scale of the reform of 193 is based on the Italian scholar's figures.

	First–second century	Third century
Italians	86.3	0
Westerners	9.5	60.3
Easterners	4.2	39.7

Table 29: Praetorian recruitment in per cent (after Passerini)

Urban cohorts

When discussing the urban cohorts two cases must be distinguished. The first consists of those who never left Rome. Their recruitment was the same as that of the Praetorians at the beginning,[111] but a major difference is that they did not undergo any significant change later on. The question was studied by two epigraphists who differed in the methods they used, and thus found different results in absolute values but broadly similar percentage values. F.C. Mench found 85.5 per cent Italians and 14.5 per cent provincials,[112] while H. Freis found 88 per cent and 12 per cent respectively.[113] As there are only 15 per cent of imperial *gentilia nomina* (98 out of 640) in the lists it seems logical to construe that very few were citizens.

There is evidence elsewhere, however, to show that two urban cohorts were permanently stationed outside Rome, one in Lyon the other in Carthage. The latter has been the subject of recent research,[114] but the amount of data about homelands is too small to reach any significant conclusions. However, 25 per cent of the sample had imperial *gentilia nomina* and 28 per cent had names of governors of Proconsular colonies. This would mean that more than half were naturalized Africans and only 45 per cent were of Italian ancestry. The *cognomina* are 90 per cent Latin, 6.4 per cent Greek and 2.8 per cent based on indigenous languages. From the point of view of Romanization this cohort would be superior to the Numidian legion but inferior to the other urban cohorts in Rome.

Other units of the garrison at Rome

Less is known of the other units of the garrison at Rome. At first the cohorts of *Vigiles* were made up from emancipated slaves;[115] as these corps of firemen were later militarized it follows that the class of men recruited must have been higher, since ex-slaves were not generally considered to be fit to be soldiers. In fact, as early as 24, Roman citizenship was granted after six years of service, and soon men of free birth chose to enlist in these corps.

The imperial 'Police Force', the *statores Augusti*, was normally manned by retired soldiers from the emperor's personal mounted guard, the *equites singulares Augusti*, who have recently been studied.[116] They were horsemen recruited directly or taken from the *alae* of auxiliaries. In the second century there was a clear majority of westerners, particularly Germans. After 193 there is a large preponderance of Pannonians, Dacians and Thracians. However, 90 per cent of these soldiers have imperial *gentilia nomina*, and this is explained by F. Grosso in terms of the *equites singulares Augusti*, who were *peregrini*, being granted Latin citizenship upon entry into the army and full Roman citizenship on discharge.[117]

The fleet

The study of sailors also raises a legal problem of some nicety.[118] According to Th. Mommsen everyone, including officers, was either a slave or an ex-slave,[119] but S. Panciera had noted the presence of Roman citizens in the ranks as early as Augustus' reign.[120] Recently M. Reddé (see n.118) considered the situation to be more complex. A few slaves had been enlisted, but only after receiving their freedom, and they were to be considered as exceptions to the rule (in fact their presence is probably a legacy of the Civil War). Alongside these were emancipated slaves, *peregrini* and even Roman citizens, as early as Panciera had suggested. After Augustus, [121] sailors were essentially non-citizens who received the status of Latins at the end of their service.[122] *Peregrini* rubbed shoulders with a minority of emancipated slaves and a few men with the status of Egyptians, an even lower rung on the ladder of ancient value, near to the servile class. By the Flavian era (69–96) all these soldiers had the *tria nomina* and the 'diplomas' granted to them on discharge gave them Roman status. From Hadrian's time, according to V. Chapot,[123] Latin rights were required for entry into the navy. Of course, sailors were given the *civitas Romana* in 212 when Caracalla conferred this privilege on all free men living in the Empire. The geographical origins

	Misenum	Ravenna
Italy	6	1
(Western)		
Africa	11	2
Dalmatia	12	12
Pannonia	10	5
Corsica	4	3
Sardinia	22	3
Total	59	25
(Eastern)		
Asia	38	3
Syria	13	7
Egypt	54	7
Thrace	37	2
Greece	8	1
Total	150	20
Various	4	1
Overall total	219	47

Table 30: Recruitment of sailors according to M. Reddé.

are less of a problem. Admittedly we know nothing about provincial fleets, but M. Reddé (see n.118) has been able to compile new lists for the others.

Thus the sailors on ships based in Misenum came from Egypt, the province of Asia, Thrace and Sardinia;[124] the fleet at Ravenna recruited its sailors from Syria and Egypt, Pannonia, and particularly Dalmatia, as far as we can judge from the limited sources.

CONCLUSION

Both Roman tradition and collective mentalities considered certain types of unit more worthy of interest than others, and these attitudes were reflected in the sort of men called upon to serve in them. The elite units were composed of Roman citizens from Latium and Central Italy. The further from Rome and the lower down the scale of legal status, the less important the soldiers become for the security of the Empire. Thus, to the hierarchy of the troop corps is added a hierarchy of recruitment. Such choices testify clearly that the imperial power was intent on maintaining a policy of quality. But for these choices to remain possible the armies could not encounter too many difficulties, too many wars and, above all, too many defeats. The soldiers also had to have a certain degree of public respectability to enhance their prestige, as appearances remained important in society. To achieve these aims the State must have had at its disposal considerable financial resources.

II

THE ACTIVITIES OF THE ARMY

4

TRAINING

What is required of a soldier? Firstly, to obey his superiors; secondly, to die in combat if the occasion demands. At least that is what many of our contemporaries, and most of our historians, believe. For them training serves only as a part of the daily life of a soldier, to be written up in a section between the brothel and the baths. Hence the most prestigious encyclopaedias devoted to antiquity, *Pauly-Wissowa* and *Daremberg-Saglio*, did not think fit to include even a short article on the subject of training.

Obviously this attitude needs to be changed. Today certain military experts understand that this activity was far more important than we have been led to believe,[1] and some have even sensed the exceptional role that training played in the effectiveness of the Roman army. But nobody has faced the problem head-on, coming to it obliquely instead, A. Neumann through the study of regulations,[2] and R. Davies through the archaeological study of cavalry training grounds.[3] An important gap has therefore to be filled here.

Training should certainly not be ignored,[4] as it is this that largely explains the success of the Roman army. In the eyes of the ancients the art of warfare was akin to a science, a *disciplina* to be taught and learned like mathematics or literature. To denote this activity the Latin language had two terms, *exercitium* and *exercitatio*. In the *Thesaurus Linguae Latinae*, that huge dictionary in which all references to known authors are listed, each of these words occupies a four-column entry.[5] Their importance is thus manifest, which makes the lack of curiosity among modern scholars even more surprising. The Romans themselves attached a great deal of importance to training. In his etymological studies Varro did not hesitate to reverse what we would consider to be the normal order of things.[6] He went so far as to derive the word for 'army' (*exercitus*) from the verb 'to exercise' (*exercitare*). Cicero gave him the backing of his authority:[7] 'You see . . . what we consider as the meaning of the word "army" . . . ; and what can I say about the training of legions? . . . Put an equally brave, but untrained soldier in the front line, and he will look like a woman.'

Without claiming to present an exhaustive list of literary or epigraphical texts that mention the subject,[8] it is nevertheless right to quote several authors that mentioned this activity in more than a passing fashion. The mid-first-century author Onesandros reminded a general of his duties in this domain.[9] Not much later, Flavius Josephus, a Jewish officer defeated by Vespasian and Titus, put his failure down to the effectiveness that training gave to the legions.[10] Naturally Tacitus often spoke of it.

But it is in Hadrian's time that we find the most information. The emperor himself attached great importance to exercise, an attitude that enabled him to secure the obedience of the officers in the army who otherwise blamed him for a certain 'pacifism' or at least a reluctance to go on the offensive.[11] He personally went to Lambaesis, to the north of the Aures, to preside over some of the African army's manoeuvres, and in some famous speeches, preserved for the most part in an inscription, he gave his views on training. One of his generals, Arrian, effecting a tour of inspection of garrisons stationed around the Black Sea, made the soldiers do some training. A tribune in charge of an auxiliary force of 1000 Batavians in Lower Pannonia boasted of having swum across the Danube at the head of his fully-armed troops, claiming Hadrian's support for this exploit.[14] A little-known passage from Fronto can also be cited.[15] In fact, the most interesting source for this subject remains Vegetius, the fourth-century writer who gives information on earlier periods.[16] He took pains to name the authors he used, Cato the Elder, three great emperors (Augustus, Trajan, Hadrian), and finally Tarruntenus Paternus and Cornelius Celsus. The question to be asked here is exactly why training acquired such importance, and there will be more than one explanation.

THE IMPORTANCE OF TRAINING

Military uses

It is obvious that it is in the military field that training has the greatest role to play. The advantages of this activity were perceived as early as the Republican era; Cato the Elder, Varro and Cicero have already been mentioned, but other, earlier examples[17] could have been cited had they been relevant to the period covered in this book. The basic goal of training was to give the Roman army superiority over the barbarian in battle.

The legionary had to be physically stronger than his potential adversary, and it is easy to see where sport fits in to this aim.[18] But there is also the question of mental strength. Josephus noted: 'By their military exercises the Romans prepared not only robust bodies but also strong souls.'[19] Moreover, training helped men to cope better with wounds, to suppress fear and panic.[20] The psychological effect also played an important role in giving the Roman soldiers an advantage; if they were capable of carrying out their manoeuvres to perfection in front of the enemy, the latter might be discouraged and choose to avoid combat by flight.[21]

But that is not all. Training was linked to discipline, which was held in such esteem that it was deified and had altars set up to it in camps.[22] It did not encompass only blind obedience to orders; if anything this attitude came as a consequence. In fact, in *disciplina* is found the stem of *disco*, *discere*, meaning 'to learn'.[23] The soldier had to be formed for the military profession, to 'learn' all its mysteries. Obeying an order, even one that seemed absurd, and respecting one's superiors were part of the imperatives of the profession, and can be learned, just like the handling of arms or the building of defences.[24] The soldier who knew what to do in battle because he had practised it a thousand times on the training ground was confident in his own ability and that of his superiors.[25] The Roman army applied the principle of studying in order to conquer, an idea that has been taken up again today by many military academies, even if the level of knowledge they required was pretty low and very mechanical.

A passage in Tacitus demonstrates clearly the effectiveness of training.[26] Well-trained, and therefore very disciplined, Roman soldiers without qualms accepted an order that exposed them to the enemy weapons because they knew that a few losses would bring them a resounding victory.

> After a three-day march he [the general Cerialis] arrived in front of Rigodulum [Riol, near Trier] which was held by Valentinus with a strong band of Treveri. The position was naturally protected on one side by mountains and on another by the Moselle, and Valentinus had strengthened it even more with trenches and barricades of rocks. These defensive structures did not stop the Roman general from ordering his infantry to storm them and his cavalry to climb the hill in strict formation. He had contempt for an enemy army that had no fixed plan and whose territorial advantage was not enough to counter his resourceful and courageous legionaries. The ascent of the hill was somehwat slow as the cavalry passed through the enemy bombardment of projectiles but as soon as hand-to-hand combat ensued the enemy was dislodged and thrown down like an avalanche. Part of the cavalry rode over some less steep inclines to get around the back of the position where they captured the most noble of the Belgae with their chief Valentinus.

One consequence of this state of affairs was mentioned by Arrian: men who have not undergone training should not be led into battle.[27] That would mean giving up one's superiority, losing an important advantage and laying oneself open to defeat. To engage in hostilities in these circumstances would be absurd. Furthermore, the abandonment of training would mean condemning the soldiers to a life of inactivity and lethargy. The absence of things to do brings indiscipline and disobedience.[28]

The political role

Officers had to take part in training. To understand the significance of this obligation, it is essential to understand the meaning of *virtus* which is so often incorrectly translated as 'courage'. *Virtus* is what characterizes a man (*vir–tus*, *vir* has given 'virile' in English), that is to say service to the state in its two complementary functions of civil service (exercise of magistracies) and military service (command); to follow the career structure it was necessary to show evidence of this quality. A noble, therefore, had to carry out the functions of quaestor, aedile, plebeian tribune, praetor and consul, but not to restrict himself to these. He had also to prove his suitability for the army.

The importance assigned to training is attested throughout the whole of Roman history, and it is manifest during the Republican era. Plutarch[29] recalled that when Pompey was in the east, he was improving his horsemanship during the siege of Petra when messengers arrived, their laurel-decorated javelins signifying they were bringing good news. But the general made them wait and continued his manoeuvres in order to remind them that training was the most important obligation of all. It took all the insistence of his soldiers to make him interrupt his riding and hear the news of his victory because of Mithridates' suicide. A few decades later Tiberius wanted to show Augustus that he was wrong to suspect him of being over-ambitious, and in order to prove that he did not want the Empire for himself he withdrew to Rhodes and refrained from training.[30] In this way he manifested his intention of abandoning his *virtus*, of becoming politically harmless.

In the course of the Civil War, Vitellius neglected the preparation of the troops, an irreparable mistake that caused his downfall, according to Tacitus.[31] Trajan on the other hand paid full attention to these matters, and earned praise by mixing with his men to set a good example.[32] His successor, Hadrian, whose attitude we have already noted (see nn.11–14) was meticulously careful about training in order to calm the worries of the senators and equestrians who might think him too prudent, even a 'pacifist'. Later still, Severus Alexander was educated from his early childhood with the consulship in mind,[33] and military preparation was part of the education he underwent (it is the *Historia Augusta*, written at the very end of the fourth, or even at the beginning of the fifth, century that is the source of this anecdote). Finally, according to Herodian, Maximinus I became emperor in 235 because he showed an excellent aptitude for forming recruits.[34]

Training can be used in different ways, but still to political ends. After the battle of Actium in 31 BC when Augustus triumphed over Mark Antony, he wanted to spread the idea that peace for Rome had finally and definitively arrived. To achieve this piece of political propaganda he ceased training.[35] In other circumstances Tiberius used the same weapon; in order to frighten the Senators and make them accept his plans he invited them to watch the training of the Praetorian guard.[36] Thus during the whole of the Early Empire training was a double-edged sword, political and military.

THE CONTENT OF TRAINING

The implementation of a strategy defined by the commanding officers, the application of tactics to the battle-field and the building of a camp all show that a military science really did exist,[37] and that training was a part of it.[38] It was carried out by officers with the assistance of some other men with specialized technical knowledge (thus the *metator* plays a role in the construction of the camp). As the Romans had a legalistic turn of mind this education was codified, as Josephus clearly stated, and there is no reason to doubt his testimony.[39] Regulations were well and truly written down. Hadrian decreed a certain number of measures as regards training which were still in force at the beginning of the third century.[40] The military culture that had been in force since the beginning received a legal extension under Septimius Severus. Other regulations were retained even longer; the compendium of laws gathered together under Justinian recalls a point from an eternal law:[41] if a man is wounded on a training ground (*campus*) by a soldier who is training, the soldier is not at fault, but if the incident happens anywhere else the soldier is held responsible and legal proceedings arise. At every period it was axiomatic that training should be a daily activity.[42]

Activities

Training is a word that covers widely different activities, though they can be grouped under two main headings: individual and collective. The first objective was to ensure that a Roman soldier had superiority over a barbarian even in single combat or hand-to-hand fighting. Here again it is important to distinguish between purely physical activities and those of a military nature. The combatants started with gymnastics.[43] As all armies of the world do, they paraded in their gymnastic kit, or with their equipment or carrying extra weight.[44] They were also made to run and jump,[45] and when conditions permitted they practised swimming.[46] We have already mentioned the case of the 1000 Batavians (n.14) who swam fully-armed across the Danube behind their officer, but this exploit is presented as being absolutely exceptional.

Once his body had been toned up physically the soldier moved on to more professional activities of a military nature, which consisted mainly of weapon practice.[47] He practised fencing against a post, the *palus*,[48] the forerunner of the quintain. He practised throwing projectiles,[49] arrows and javelins, and stones, and being on the receiving end of them. He had therefore to learn how to handle a sling and use a bow (n.14). All the activities mentioned so far were common to soldiers and gladiators. In principle special weapons were given to soldiers for training; thus mounted soldiers wore a particular helmet.[50] In fact horse-riding was the final important element of the activities of an individual nature, and concerned not only the ordinary cavalrymen, but more importantly the officers.[51]

Once a soldier had acquired a minimum of physical strength and skill in the use of the sword and the javelin he could progress to another level of exercise. This was designed to ensure that the Romans would be superior in combats as collective units. Their first task was to take part in civil engineering exercises, as manhandling stones was thought to help in body-building. In this way the legionaries also supplied the emperor with a qualified, cheap workforce, thus allowing him to display his generosity at no great cost. In some cases the army put specialized technicians at the disposal of civilians. Under Antoninus Pius the town of Bejaia (Bougie) wanted to build an aqueduct, but as it could not find a competent engineer it ended up asking the governor of the province, who managed to obtain a *librator* from the legate of the *legio III Augusta*. Archaeologists have uncovered the canalizations which are 21km (13 miles) long, requiring the digging of a 428m (1400ft) tunnel at an altitude of 86m (280ft).[52]

These civil engineering feats are outstanding because of their diversity.[53] Sometimes the soldiers levelled the terrain or cleaned out ditches; sometimes they built monuments intended to testify to the emperor's benevolence. Some of these edifices, for instance the arches, were meant only to be decorative, while others, such as squares, streets, aqueducts, leisure complexes (theatres, amphitheatres, circuses), improved the attractions or the comforts of the city.

Others still had a more economic function. Soldiers worked in the mines and quarries; they could build markets or whole cities. In 100 the town of Timgad, to the north of the Aures, was consecrated on the orders of Trajan; it had been entirely built by military manpower. Timgad was built on virgin soil;[54] its centre was orginally a square (350m (1150ft) per side) surrounded by a wall with four gates and rounded corners. The streets at right-angles contained regular blocks of houses. Contrary to what has been written, this plan is not a copy of a fort; it was a colony designed to enhance the economy of the southern part of the high plains of the region of Constantine. Soldiers were capable of building more than just camps; they also erected temples and sanctuaries.

Above all, commanders wanted the soldiers to be able to construct all the parts of the different defensive systems. Some of these tasks had very fortunate economic implications – roads had to be built, boundary markers placed between tribes, jobs of quantity surveying and delineation of troops quarters carried out. The prime function of these different tasks was military, the easy movement of troops and the surveillance of potential enemies, and they were an integral part of training. Being able to see them through to their completion demonstrated 'discipline'. Frontinus stated that legionaries had to be able to build bridges faster than barbarians.[55] This speed and technical know-how were intended to remind the enemy of his inferiority and to discourage him from attacking. The aim was also to settle the semi-nomadic tribes who were a constant source of trouble. But the pacification of natives, the development of agriculture and the installation of a good road network were beneficial to the whole of a province. Finally, it was the job of the infantryman, under the protection of the cavalry, to build towers, forts, exercise grounds and defence lines.[56] Pseudo-Hyginus goes even further when he recommends that a ditch be dug around the temporary transit camp, even in friendly territories, 'for the sake of good discipline'.[57]

The participation of soldiers in these various tasks is attested by stamps on bricks, a type of document found in profusion throughout the Empire.[58] The fortress workshop, the *fabrica*, was in fact a brick factory. Before the earth was baked a mark was stamped on it with a seal; the short text gives in abbreviated form the name of the unit and sometimes that of the person in charge, the commander or the *magister fabricae*. At Mirebeau (Côte d'Or) a relatively lengthy inscription with more than usually explicit information has been found.[59]

LEG.VIII AVG. LAPPIO LEG. – *Leg(io) VIII Aug(usta)*, *Lappio leg(ato Augusti propraetore)*. It was therefore deduced that the *legio VIII Augusta*, normally stationed near Strasbourg, had sent a detachment more than 200km (125 miles) from its base (or perhaps instead, a more plausible explanation would be that the whole legion had come temporarily to Mirebeau), and had some monument or other built, apparently a camp and an exercise ground at least. Furthermore, the imperial legate Aulus Bucius Lappius Maximus is well known; he served under the Flavians. In certain cases, the plasticity of the clay allowed different names to be engraved on the bricks each time;[60] this then served to mark the spot for each individual soldier's bed and weapons, etc.

Unlike gymnastics and fencing, these jobs accustomed the men to working together collectively, and this is at the heart of the matter. The principal aim of training was to teach soldiers to manoeuvre in regular units. It was important that each man knew his place in the combat formation, where, when and how he must move without destroying the cohesion of his century.[61] The officers set up battle simulations, infantry against infantry or the cavalry. Even the navy was not exempt from this obligation; from time to time the ships were brought together for fighting in squadrons. As will be mentioned later, the soldiers trained in full battle dress.

INSPECTION

In view of the great importance attached to inspection, it was not left to just anyone. The troops' level of preparation had to be monitored by officers. Each morning they carried out an inspection, each centurion being responsible for his unit, a tribune for two cohorts and a legate for his legion. The result was a veritable cascade of reports. Furthermore, there is evidence of extraordinary inspections. Sometimes it was a general who toured the garrisons in a given sector; under Hadrian, Arrian conducted just such an inspection tour around the Black Sea (n.13). He examined the state of the fortifications, kept a tally of the foodstocks and checked the soldier lists, but he did not forget training. It is worth remembering that Hadrian himself went personally to Pannonia and also to Africa in 128 (nn.12, 14), and that his sole aim on the journey was to ensure that the parade ground was used regularly enough. Other circumstances, equally unusual, gave rise to additional inspections; a papyrus found at Dura-Europos reveals that inspection parades accompanied the paying of the soldiers' wages.

Lower in rank than the superior officers (legate, tribunes, centurions) were other officers specialized in the preparation of training. Normally the direction of this activity was entrusted to a decorated *evocatus* when the unit had one. His job was that of head instructor. Trajan himself was not above carrying out this job himself, which goes to show the importance attached to it. When an incompetent emperor or a slapdash legate left the job to a person who was not up to the task, 'a little Greek master' according to the younger Pliny's scornful phrase,[62] sensible people murmured their disapproval. But if the general's wife intervened, as did Plancina, the wife of Piso, the Commander in the East, then a scandal ensued.[63] Whatever else it was, Roman society was surely misogynistic.

The exercise ground was in the purview of a lower grade officer called a *campidoctor* and his subordinate a *doctor cohortis*; the stem *doct-* indicating that the person had received an education and had learned a science in which he was highly accomplished. He was an educated man who must transmit his knowledge to others. His position of responsibility allowed him to have a deputy who helped and eventually replaced him, the *optio campi*. Two other activities also required the services of specialists; fencing was supervised by the *armatura* or *doctor armorum*, and here again the title of *doctor* is not without significance. The presence of a *discens armaturarum*, a sort of instructor of instructors, is a clear indication that the art must be learned. Secondly, cavalry manoeuvres required the presence of particularly competent riding instructors, the *exercitator* and the *magister campi*. There was a whole hierarchy of training supervision to ensure that it was carried out properly.

PLACES

Some officers had responsibilities only on the parade ground, the *campus*, but some training activities took place elsewhere. Vegetius says: 'masters of the military art wanted training to be continuous, under cover when it rained or snowed, or on the parade ground the rest of the year.'[64] It is essential to clarify the content of this quotation to understand the exact functioning of these practices, and this clarification should in turn enable us to touch on certain aspects of military archaeology.

At the beginning of Rome's history soldiers prepared for war on the *Campus Martius*. As their conquests grew, and young men living farther and farther away from the city were integrated into the army, new solutions had to be found. Activities had to be organized either in the cities where recruitment was being carried out or near the camps. In the Early Empire different places were selected according to the type of activity to be practised. Firstly, of course, a part of the training, such as marching, was carried out in the countryside. Secondly, soldiers used monuments, like amphitheatres, that had been built for other purposes. Archaeologists have often noticed the presence of arenas near camps and have rightly explained this phenomenon by the soldiers' liking for violent spectacles. But another factor must be considered: military training was similar to that of the gladiators in several respects, and in good weather fencing could easily be practised where *retiarii* and *mirmillones* came to die at other times.

Nevertheless, some constructions were purpose-built for training, a factor that highlights its importance. Basilicas were built for training (*basilicae exercitatoriae*).[65] We know that the basilica or 'royal portico' was a large room protected by a roof. It was very simple in plan – a rectangle with one door, divided into three naves by a double colonnade. Sometimes there was an apse at one end. The Romans used these buildings to shelter from the rain or the heat of the sun. Several training basilicas have been located, notably in Britain, at Inchtuthil, a camp from the Flavian era,[66] at Netherby (222)[67] and at Lanchester (under Gordian III).[68] Another has been located in Dacia, at Turda (Potaissa), also from the time

113

of Gordian III. It seems that sometimes they were built inside the camp, sometimes outside, but this is not certain; the inscription in Britain dated to Gordian III was found 'to the east of the fort of Lanchester', but the stone had perhaps been moved. Historians have probably been right to think of them as arms rooms, and that fencing took place in them, but they could also be used as rings for horse riding, since the one in Netherby is called a *baselica (sic) equestris exercitatoria*.

The training ground par excellence was the *campus*. M. Rostovtzeff invented the phrase *campus exercitatorius* on analogy with *basilica exercitatoria*. This invention has been followed by several commentators since, but it is a pleonasm. The word can, however, be interpreted in different ways.[70] In general it designates a plain but by extension it can be applied to a public square, a battlefield or a training ground. Only the last interpretation can be maintained when employed in a military context,[71] and a paragraph from Justinian's manual (see n.71) clearly shows that it was the normal place for training.

Archaeologists studying the topography of Rome believe that they have located the *campus* of the Praetorian and Urban cohorts, to the west of their barracks, built in the time of Tiberius. As nothing much has been found there, it is considered that the sports ground was no more than a simple hard surface. The only well-known *campus*, that of Lambaesis, to the north of the Aures, (pl.X,13) has been excavated and studied (see n.4); moreover, the speech made by Hadrian in 128 on this spot proves that it was the *campus*.[72] It takes the form of a square, 200m (650ft) each side, delineated by a stone wall 60cm (24in) thick, with two gates set in it. The corners are rounded, and 14 semicircular shapes flank the enclosure; the presence of hydraulic cement means that these were probably used as watering places for the horses or washbasins for the soldiers. Several trials have indicated that nothing was built inside the walls except for the tribune (*tribunal*) in the centre, from which those in charge could supervise the movements of infantry and cavalry. This small stone construction was transformed into a commemorative monument for Hadrian's visit in 128, and soldiers fixed on to it plates on which the emperor's speech was engraved. At the same time, probably, a column was set up for aesthetic reasons. It is surrounded by a very narrow paved area.

Other training grounds are known from epigraphical evidence, and there can be no doubt that every fort had its own. However, the unsophisticated nature of these structures, with their thin walls around a floor of beaten earth, has meant that they have disappeared or have escaped the notice of scholars. Inscriptions mention one in Tebessa (Africa) for the Flavian era,[73] and three others in the East. In 183 at Palmyra a decurion of a *numerus*, on the orders of the centurion commander of the unit and the legate, had his men build a new *campus* with a platform.[74] At Dura-Europos in 208–9(?) a cohort built a temple after enlarging the training ground.[75] At *Colybrassos* in Cilicia in 288 a legion flattened a hill in order to have a space to train in.[76]

Epigraphy (see nn.72–6), for once fairly informative, allows us to define certain characteristics of the *campus*. First of all, it should be set up on flat terrain – it could then be enlarged if the unit using it received reinforcements, for example. There may have been several to a single fort. At Palmyra the soldiers built a 'new *campus*', which proves there must have been another older one. Finally, but hardly surprising in view of our knowledge of the Romans, it was placed under the protection of certain gods (see below). On the other hand, it is apparent that the particular characteristics of training grounds reserved for cavalry manoeuvres have yet to be defined.[77]

These vast, empty places must have tempted officers to use them for other purposes, like parades, not strictly related to training. They were ideal places for meetings. We know that Roman civilization set great store by language, and soldiers were no exception to this rule; the imperial speech and the ceremony of the *adlocutio* would naturally take place on the training ground. Coins bearing the inscription ADLOCVTIO, for instance those struck by Hadrian between 134 and 138,[78] and many literary passages describe this sort of ceremony,[79] which is also to be found on the columns of Trajan and Aurelius. Finally it was the place where soldiers gathered in times of trouble to initiate a debate or discuss some matter; the *campus* was to the soldiers what the forum was to the civilians.[80]

EMPERORS, TRAINING AND DISCIPLINE

When dealing with training and discipline it is obvious that the situation varied according to the character and attitude of each officer and, above all, of the emperor. Later on, the policies which were implemented by the different rulers who succeeded each other at the head of the state will be discussed. As some sort of preface it is essential to determine their attitudes towards training, which really means their attitudes towards soldiers. Since the Empire was a military monarchy whose power was dependent on the goodwill of the army, this is where the main chronological cleavages of history in general are found.

It is not surprising to find that the Julio-Claudian era starts well and ends badly. Augustus was considered a good general,[81] and Tiberius an even better one, according to Tacitus[82] (a remark that is all the more touching considering the lack of sympathy the author had for this ruler). Every emperor up to and including Claudius, who has always been criticized but is now being rehabilitated, received his share of praise; not only was he capable of maintaining discipline in the camps but he was also astute enough to have around him such energetic officers as Corbulo. On the other hand, Nero proved to be incapable of maintaining discipline among the troops.[85]

Historians in antiquity considered that discipline was a very important factor in the crisis of 68–9. Nero was too mediocre to be able to keep his title. His successor Galba was overzealous in his severity and this caused his downfall.[86] Vitellius failed also, but his failure was due to his ignorance of military matters and his lethargy.[87] Cerialis on the other hand is an interesting case: he neglected discipline because he thought the fact that he enjoyed the special protection of the goddess Fortuna meant that he had no need of it.[88] But this protection proved to be insufficient as Fortuna could do nothing without the assistance of another deity, Discipline, and Cerialis' venture came to grief.

After the confusion of this crisis, there was again a strong hand on the Empire in general, and on the army in particular. This movement from disorder to order was the work of the energetic Vespasian.[89] However, under the Flavians the general decline witnessed during the Julio-Claudian period repeated itself: the dynasty that came to power with the arrival of a person of authority foundered on the weakness of its ultimate representative. In fact, Domitian either could not or would not maintain discipline, and neglected the supervision of training. This inadequacy, that caused his failure as a leader and his departure, allowed Pliny the Younger to draw a splendid contrasting portrait of Trajan, the soldier-emperor, the true founder of the Antonine dynasty, if we disregard the ephemeral Nerva.[91]

Hadrian's personality is not so clear-cut. Admittedly it was noted earlier that he took a strong interest in the training of soldiers, even to the point of sending Arrian to the garrisons surrounding the Pontus, and going himself to take part in the manoeuvres in Africa and Pannonia. However, Fronto criticizes him for his shortcomings as regards discipline;[92] no doubt the philosophical emperor was more philosopher than emperor. If his military policies are compared with those of his predecessor Trajan, they seem to be both lacking in vigour and too defensive. It might well have seemed to at least some of his generals that he showed a regrettable lack of understanding of *disciplina*, the art of combat, which also included a rational, hence offensive, strategy.

During the civil war that broke out in 193 the importance of authority reappeared, in a situation not dissimilar to the crisis of 68–9. Pertinax was considered authoritarian,[93] and Pescennius Niger even more so.[94] But Septimius Severus poses a similar sort of problem as Hadrian did. He certainly demanded obedience from his soldiers,[95] and Herodian noted that he made sure that training was carried out on a regular basis.[96] However, the same Herodian accused him of being the first to weaken discipline, a reproach that presumably stemmed from the reform policies the African emperor attempted to introduce, increasing salaries and allowing soldiers to live with their women and officers to join together in colleges. Changes brought fears. Septimius Severus was reproached for his generosity, Hadrian for his relative pacifism. Among his immediate successors the short-lived Macrinus stands out as someone who supported tradition by asserting that Romans owed their superiority to their discipline.[98] Then came Severus Alexander, the final representative of the dynasty, who proved too energetic for his soldiers' liking.[99]

It was after the death of this emperor that the crisis which had been threatening for fifty years finally broke in all its seriousness. The Empire was attacked by the Germans in the north and the Persians in the east. A few important figures emerged from a series of short-lived rulers, for at the time the Empire was 'an absolute monarchy tempered by assassination'. They owed their relative longevity to their authority. Maximinus in particular, as we have seen, owed virtually everything to his talents on the training grounds, and he was considered to be extremely severe.[100] Among those emperors who managed to hold on to power for some little time despite the troubles was Gallienus, who was even said to have been cruel to his soldiers.[101] Admittedly this judgement was made in the *Historia Augusta*, whose author had no affection for this ruler because he judged, perhaps wrongly, that his policies were inimical to the Senate.

Among the emperors of the second half of the third century, called Illyrians because of their geographic origins, were several who have left behind them a reputation as efficient and energetic, though rather uneducated, soldiers. Those like Claudius II,[102] Aurelian[103] and Probus[104] in particular who appeared to be good officers, were sticklers for discipline and training.

TRAINING AND THE GODS

If emperors had their say on the subject of training, then our knowledge of Roman history tells us the gods could not remain indifferent to it.[105] We can distinguish three sacred poles towards which the veneration of soldiers was directed.

First came Discipline. Romans had a habit of deifying abstractions like Fortune, Honour, etc., so it is not surprising to find the cult of Discipline, particularly when the numerous links between this concept and training are recalled. In the camps altars were raised to it (ARA DISCIPLINAE, 'the Altar of Discipline'[106]), and as this practice goes back to the beginnings of Rome's history it enjoyed a very long life.

After this came the group of divinities associated with the *campus*, and called *campestres*. However, we must not fall into the error that has misled many an epigraphist, and fail to note that this adjective could also be used for the 'gods of the plain', in which case it had no military connotations. It is not impossible that such cults were celebrated in some parts of the Empire. Consequently it is essential to know where the inscriptions that mention them come from, as the meaning of the adjective will vary according to whether they are found in camps, on training grounds or in the countryside. So the names of the *Campestres*[107] of Germany and the *Matres Campestres*[108] of Britain perhaps do not relate to the same thing.

In Spain a *Mars Campester* is attested,[109] and in this case no ambiguity is possible:

> Consecration to Mars of the training ground. Titus Aurelius Decimus, centurion of the VII *Legio Gemina* Lucky, head [*praepositus*] of the bodyguard [*equites singulares*] and at the same time master of the exercise ground [*campidoctor*] (had this monument erected) to the health of the emperor Marcus Aurelius Commodus, Augustus, and to the safety of the bodyguards. The dedication took place on the Kalends of March in the consulship of Mamertinus and Rufus [1 March, 182].

Nemesis, the goddess who punished pride, was worshipped in the same way, as an inscription from Rome[110] informs us:

> To holy Nemesis of the training ground, for the safety of our two lords the emperors. Publius Aelius Pacatus, son of Publius, of the tribe Aelia, native of Scupi [a town in Moesia, now called Uskub], warned by a dream, has willingly placed (this dedication) he had promised when doctor of the cohort, now that he is doctor of the training ground in the Ist Praetorian cohort Pious and Vengeful.

We also know that powers called 'spirits' protected the men and their belongings, and more precisely each one of them individually. It does indeed seem that one inscription mentioned a spirit of the *campus* (see n. 73). For all these divinities there were special rituals. An annual procession in their honour (see n. 105) started from the platform of the parade ground; it seems that in Egypt gazelles were sacrificed to them. A temple was built on the training ground at Dura-Europos (see n. 75), and it does also appear that the same was true at Rome for Praetorian and Urban cohorts' training ground.

Finally, the group of associated gods must not be forgotten; indeed, when the ancients celebrated a cult, they addressed a particular main divinity but did not omit to address other related powers in order to be certain of the effect of their prayers. The task of the related powers was to reinforce the action of the main divinity (for example Demeter was readily associated with her daughter Persephone). On the training ground Jupiter was the main recipient of honours as protector of Rome and its army. A 'military Mars' and a deified abstraction, Victoria Augusta, are also attested. Training was thus supervised by the officers and protected by the gods.

CONCLUSION

It does not seem a waste of time to return to a point made earlier, namely that the importance of training has been overlooked by many historians. It is this training that goes a long way to explaining the success of the Roman army, as the ancient writers themselves recognized. They considered that a noble could not have a career if he did not train regularly, as an emperor could not rule if he did not ensure that the training grounds were regularly used.

Training, quantity surveying, tactics and strategy go together to form a discipline, a science[111] that evolved gradually from the time of Rome's origins to its position at the beginning of the third century when it was codified into a legal form. The word discipline encompasses two apparently different, but in fact related realities, a store of knowledge first, and only secondly obedience.

The acquisition of this military culture presupposes the existence of culture 'tout court'; to achieve this aim a policy of recruitment based on quality proved to be essential.

TACTICS

In the twentieth century soldiers like those of the United Nations are deployed to keep the peace. To the Romans such an idea would have appeared absurd, and their conception of war remained unchanged: 'man does not go to war in order to fight, but to win'.[1] This success, which is the aim of every military enterprise, depended to some degree on the use of tactics; first you had to move your army and then get it to fight.

Combat was the subject that many intellectuals reflected on and wrote about during the Empire. Nevertheless, despite the abundant material available, modern writers have hardly looked at the subject, for fear of writing 'battle history'. However, the progress of Hadrian's campaigns in Dacia, for example, was not without economic consequences:[2] huge quantities of gold were brought back.

One of the first observations to be made when studying the treatises is that many of the writers of the imperial period wrote in Greek and normally drew comparisons with the history of Sparta, Athens or the Hellenistic kingdoms, as though they thought the Romans had not invented anything in this domain.[3] But before deciding if this bizarre state of affairs was merely a fashion or a mistaken point of view, it will be useful to be clear about the means the combatants had to carry out their professional duties.

FIGHTING CONDITIONS: WEAPONS

Before reviewing what we know about warships, which is in fact relatively little, let us first pause for a moment to consider the weapons of the individual soldier. As more and more archaeological discoveries are made, there is a corresponding increase in the already abundant material at our disposal. However, for a very long time now we have had two marvellous 'picture-books': Trajan's Column (pl.XI–XXII) and the Aurelian Column, though the latter has been somewhat restored in modern times because it was more damaged than the former. In addition, excavations have yielded swords, helmets, hundreds of other items and also reliefs portraying soldiers (pl.XXIII–XXV, 14–17). Finally, literary sources furnish a certain number of indications. All this accounts for the fact that this has been the subject of several well-written studies while other subject-areas remain almost untouched.[4]

What is immediately striking is the enormous diversity of the weapons we know about. The same man can be represented in four different modes of dress, for instance: for a parade the soldier did his utmost to flaunt his wealth and his luxurious clothes; in combat his equipment was more functional, more effective; on the training ground, however, his equipment was not so shiny or dangerous as accidents had to be avoided if possible; on his tomb the sculptor he commissioned was free to indulge in flights of fantasy, reproducing Greek models, so that the artist assimilated the Roman warrior to a Hellenic hero in order to flatter him.[5]

The weapons had to be looked after by the soldier, since he owned them, but what then could have been the job of the *custos armorum*? We know that each camp had stores (*armamentaria*) for which this officer was responsible, and that these were situated in the middle of the fort (*principia*). Many historians have been of the opinion that the soldiers kept possession of their equipment as long as they had use of it, but otherwise they had to leave it in this arsenal in the care of the *custos armorum*. H. Russell Robinson has put forward the attractive hypothesis that the *custos armorum* would have been in charge only of spare weapons.[6] One might add that his remit might also have extended to the artillery, as someone had to look after collective armaments. It is significant that archaeologists have discovered stone projectiles in some *principia*.

Whatever the actual role of this officer, ancient writers attributed Rome's success largely to the superiority of their individual weapons. At the time of the Jewish War which started in 66, Josephus was unstinting in his admiration for his opponents:[7]

> The footsoldier is armed with a breastplate and helmet, and wears a sword at each side, but the one on the left is significantly longer, the one on the right being only a half a cubit in length. The best infantrymen, who constitute the general's guard, carry a spear and a round shield, the rest of the legion a javelin and an oblong shield as well as a saw, a basket, a spade and an axe, not to mention a belt, a scythe, a chain and rations for three days. In this way the infantryman is hardly less heavily laden than the pack mules. The horsemen carry a long cutlass by their side and a large javelin in their hand. A long shield rests diagonally across the horse's flank, and in the quiver hanging by their side they have three or more broad-headed javelins as long as spears. Their helmets and their breastplates are identical to those carried by all the infantrymen. The best horsemen, who constitute the general's personal guard, have the same weapons as the other horsemen.

Even as late as the third century Herodian still believed that Rome's military superiority was largely due to the quality of the soldiers' weapons.[8]

It would be wrong to imagine that there was some sort of uniformity in this area. Firstly, virtually each rank and each type of unit had their own individual features. Secondly, there was practically no such thing as 'Roman' weapons. From the Republican period onwards commanders took from the defeated enemy anything of use, with the result that in Augustus' time a legionary wore a Gallic helmet, was protected by a Greek breastplate and wielded a Spanish sword. However, in the ensuing three centuries a gradual change is visible based on the astonishing adaptability of the Romans in fighting techniques.

Weapons of the legionaries

In what follows defensive and offensive arms will be contrasted, while keeping in view the changes brought about by time. Legionaries are the starting point because they are the most well-known.

Under Augustus, the legionary's protection was as follows. He wore a helmet (*galea, cassis*) of fairly simple design, a skullcap with a neck-cover sometimes added. Next he had a cuirass (*lorica*) though here there was more scope for differences; the Greek type, normally for officers, is termed 'muscular' in that the contours of the muscles of the chest are reproduced on the bronze, and a rarer version of this has leather strips on the bottom. There is some variation too in the most Roman type; the coat of mail is much more common than the leather cuirass covered with metal discs. On his legs, the legionary wore greaves. Finally there was his shield (*scutum*), normally rectangular, and either flat (like a Gallic one) or concave (like that of a Samnite gladiator).

As offensive weapons he had a spear (*hasta*) and a javelin, short and thickish (*pilum*) for fighting at a distance. For close combat he used a short Spanish sword (*gladius*) as well as a dagger. It is the combination of sword and javelin that is most characteristic of the legionary in the first and second centuries.[9] Obviously he still used the spear and the dagger, but less frequently. The throwing weapon was given added length, and a belt (*cingulum*) allowed the support of a hand weapon, though this in turn gave way to a longer sword (*spatha*) which was quite widespread at the end of the second century.

Changes in the other parts of armour can also be recognized. The helmet of the first century was the 'Gallic' type, with cheek-pieces and neck-cover but no crest. This was superseded by the classic plumed model,[10] while under Marcus Aurelius a form resembling the Phrygian cap, with no crest or plume, became popular. Various types of breastplate are also encountered; the so-called 'muscular' version was adopted by non-officers, and it is possible that superior officers then started to wear a shorter version as a distinction. The version with metal strips, called 'segmented', is the most common, but we also have evidence of the scale armour[12] and chain mail.[13] There is no standard form of shield, either. As well as the concave or flat rectangular shields so much in evidence on Trajan's Column, there was the oval form,[14] sometimes hexagonal, and the cavalry's round shield. Greaves were a permanent part of the armour.

At the same time as the legal status of the soldiers was beginning to become more uniform (see above), their armour was also. Writing about the period at the beginning of the third century, especially the reign of Caracalla, Herodian felt inspired by a passage from Aeschylus' play *The Persians* to contrast the Western (Roman) infantrymen and lancers with the Eastern (Parthian) cavalrymen and archers.[15]

Throughout the major crises of the Empire the infantry remained supreme in battle, even if the mounted troops played an increasingly important role. Soldiers kept the original types of helmets, but abandoned the wearing of breastplates. Instead they relied more and more on their shields for protection, which were now of the oval type for the most part. For the offensive they had a long sword which had entirely replaced the Spanish sword, and a javelin that was lighter than the old *pilum*.

Weapons of the auxiliaries

If the legionary was characterized during the Empire by the combination of the Spanish sword and the javelin (*gladius* and *pilum*), the auxiliary could be defined by another pair of weapons, the sword and the spear (*spatha* and *hasta*).[16] However, too much emphasis cannot be laid on the diversity within these units, particularly as regards the contrast between foot-soldiers and mounted troops.

The foot-soldiers of the first century were poorly protected, but from Trajan onwards the situation changed. They wore helmets of various shapes,[17] and leather tunics sometimes covered with metal plates or chain mail. They carried large, flat, narrow shields. They attacked with a spear, the long sword and a dagger. During the course of the second century many new weapons made their appearance and in all probability these were used by the auxiliaries rather than by the legionaries.

The cavalry of the *alae* received better protection as early as the first century. Even at that time they had iron helmets, iron strips to protect their bodies and longish oval shields. They used the same weapons as the infantrymen in the cohorts. The best of these mounted troops came from the Celticized regions of the Empire.[18] From Trajan's time their protection was even more effective; on Trajan's Column they are shown wearing a coat of mail over their leather tunics. Their shields are fairly narrow, sometimes oval.[19] In the reign of Antoninus Pius they used wider swords and occasionally javelins.[20]

However, the greatest element of variety in the auxiliaries is found in the use of specialized units, particularly in the third century. Very early on the need was felt for troops who used missile-throwing weapons. Slingers are attested in the Flavian era;[21] of Syrian origin, they feature on Trajan's Column but were used most of all in the third century. Generals also used archers in the same way;[22] they too appear to come from Syria or Arabia. Osrhoeni were used first against the Parthians then against the Persians. Some, however, were Thracians. Recruitment of these took place in Nero's reign, and they can be seen on Trajan's Column and the Aurelian Column,[23] but the great expansion of these corps occurred at the beginning of the third century.[24] They used the composite bow;[25] some were mounted and constituted light cavalry units.[26]

For the first onslaught of close fighting the Romans used *contarii*, named after the heavy spear (*contus*) they used;[27] they normally wore a coat of mail, as can be seen from the fights depicted on the base of the Adamklissi trophy and on the Aurelian Column. The *Talmud of Jerusalem* describes their weapon as a club.[28] The Roman army also made use of *gaesati*, soldiers who got their name from their heavy spear (*gaesum*); these were recruited among the Celts, particularly of Raetia.[29] On Trajan's Column, too, Swabians can be seen fighting with clubs.[30]

All these troops, with the exception of a few units of archers, were made up of foot-soldiers. However, generals also wanted to be able to draw upon different sorts of mounted soldiers, both light and heavily armed. The Mauretanians, seen on Trajan's Column,[31] were used particularly in the third century, as their formidable mobility and dextrous use of the javelin gave generals two possible advantages over the enemy. Totally different to these were the *cataphractarii* whose horses even wore protective armour. Their existence is known in the time of Hadrian;[33] they are also to be found on the Aurelian Column, but again it is during the great crisis in the third century that there is most evidence for their use.

Weapons of other soldiers

There is less information about the weapons of the other soldiers with the possible exception of the Praetorians and the officers. M. Clauss wrote that scouts (*speculatores*) carried a sword and a spear, the *frumentarii* and *beneficiarii* also had a spear; this weapon may have characterized men serving in the administration of a governor, his *officium*. Furthermore, this superior officer had at his disposal a bodyguard, either mounted (*equites singulares*) or on foot (*pedites singulares*). The former were no different from the legionary cavalry, the latter may have had round shields and a *hasta*. The emperor's personal bodyguard (*equites singulares Augusti*) can be seen on Trajan's Column where they are recognizable by their oval shields, their javelins and their spears.

But, as has been said, the Praetorians were better-known,[36] especially in the second century. At first, like the legionaries, the infantry wore the segmented armour (*segmentata*) made of metal strips, but in the time of Marcus Aurelius they adopted the breastplate with scales, already worn by the cavalry. This type of armour was to be characteristic of, if not exclusive to, these units, and they were still wearing it in 312. Their helmet was of the 'ring' type for fighting and with a 'plume' for parades. The analogy with the legionaries can be pursued further; the Praetorians used the same weapons, the Spanish sword and javelin.

The equipment of the *Vigiles* was quite specific because of their main task of fire-fighting. For this they used pumps (*siphones*), hooks (*unci*), tools similar to scythes (*falces*), not to mention blankets (*centones*), brooms (*scopae*) and buckets (*amae*). They used ladders (*scalae*) for saving people trapped in upper storeys in Rome's many apartment blocks. Officers needed to be readily identifiable; up until the second century the centurions wore helmets with a sideways plume going from ear to ear, called the *crista transversa*.[37] These officers[38] also wore a 'muscular' breastplate at the beginning of the Empire, but this later changed to a shorter model. At their side they wore a short sword called a *parazonium*.

This survey serves to show the heterogeneous nature of the weapons used by Roman soldiers, from the Spanish sword to the Gallic shield, the Syrian bow to the Greek breastplate. This selection of what was best in the armoury of conquered nations was partly responsible for the effectiveness of the Roman legions and *auxilia*.

Soldiers' clothes

Finally, in considering the soldiers' appearance the question of their dress has to be discussed. The answer is not obvious, and specialists have varying views.[39] It is true to say that legionaries and Praetorians are often represented in civilian clothes, particularly on funeral reliefs. At the time of their death many had already left the army, and all were keen and proud to show off their togas, which identified them as Roman citizens, since this conferred much prestige on them.

On the other hand, a battle-dress, the *procinctus*, did exist. Soldiers wore it during operations, when mustered for an expedition and on certain missions as well as on manoeuvres, hence seemingly contradictory translations of the phrase *esse in procinctu*, as 'to be ready for battle', 'to be in the middle of a battle'. The phrase simply means 'to be in battle-dress',[40] and it does not prove that there is a conflict or a war going on. To describe this uniform some writers use the noun *sagum*, which signifies the soldier's 'cassock', a short coat worn on top of the tunic. Officers were distinguished by their boots (*calcei*); ordinary soldiers wore military boots like open sandals (*caligae*). The name of the emperor Caligula ('Little Boot') was an affectionate nickname given to him quite early in his life by the soldiers, when he followed his father, the general Germanicus, around the camps.

Opinions differ as to the existence of a particular parade uniform, but we do know that it was the custom for soldiers to wear their decorations, and that the right to dress in white (*albata decursio*) for march-pasts, which Septimius Severus gave to centurions, was later extended to all soldiers by Gallienus.

Auxiliaries dressed in the most diverse fashion, especially those in the barbarian *numeri* who preserved their national costumes. There is however some tendency towards increasing uniformity. This was most noticeable in the *ala* cavalry who often wore a cassock over a short tunic, and trousers, the latter probably being a fashion from Celtic areas. The military may well be the source for the spread of the wearing of this garment.[41]

Thus having already seen the astounding variety of corps and task-forces in the Roman army, the range of weapons and clothing increased this diversity.

COMBAT CONDITIONS: THE SHIP

In order to understand tactics and strategy it is necessary to know the individual soldier's weapons, but there is also some point in knowing what warships were like. The following description is taken from a study by M. Reddé:[42]

Underwater archaeology has uncovered many civilian boats which lay on the sand at the bottom of the sea, protected by their cargo of amphoras, but has not been so successful where warships are concerned because these did not carry similar cargoes and have been broken into thousands of pieces by the currents. We have recovered only one warship from antiquity, the famous Punic galley of Marsala which dates back to the third century BC. Studies in this subject cannot therefore be based on direct observation of the evidence, but must interpret literary texts and images on monuments, where perspective and detail have often had to be abandoned because of the difficulties of portraying a large ship in a small space.

Nevertheless, some solid conclusions can be drawn. The most important and surprising one reached by M. Reddé is that Italian shipyards made far better ships than their Greek counterparts. Three arguments support this view. Firstly, Roman ships were stronger because they were built by assembling the side panels (*virures*) one against the other, edge to edge. The carpenters started by assembling the bottom of the hull, then inserting the frames to stiffen it. They then erected the sidewalls, following the same technique. Only when this was completed did they add the other frames, finishing with the superstructure. Once the caulking and ballasting (with stones or sand) had been carried out they could deliver the boat to its users.

Secondly, Roman ships were more sophisticated. Helmsmen used a two-sided rudder, for mobility and speed was obtained by two methods of propulsion. A main square sail was attached to the large mast and a smaller one to a secondary mast. Moreover, all ships could be rowed, producing a speed of two or two and a half knots. The problem here is to determine how many banks of oars there were and in what formation. An epitaph from Misenum will provide an example of this:[43]

> (Consecration) to the spirits of the dead. To Titus Terentius Maximus, soldier of the triarch *Jupiter*, a Bessus by birth [Thracian tribe], he lived forty years and served twenty. Caius Julius Philo of the triarch *Mercury* and Quintus Domitius Optatus of the tetrarch *Minerva*, his heirs, took it upon themselves (to have this monument erected), when Sulpicius Priscus was adjutant of the triarch *Jupiter*.

This text mentions two triarchs (the *Jupiter* and the *Mercury*) and one tetrarch (the *Minerva*); in point of fact, the former do appear to have been more numerous and constituted the standard class of ship, with three banks of oars, one above the other but staggered. For boats with four or more banks of oars we have little idea of what formation was adopted by the complement of oarsmen.

There were other sorts of ships. The *liburna*, almost as well known as the triarch, was lighter and therefore more manoeuvreable.[44] Various sorts of transport boats were used for men and materials. The war fleet was composed of some two hundred and fifty ships, that is sixty for each of the two Italian fleets and one hundred and thirty for the provincial squadrons, according to M. Reddé.

Thirdly, Roman ships were better armed. Artillery pieces were able to strike from a distance so that the enemy was demoralized and decimated before they attacked with boarding parties. Each vessel had a bronze ram fixed to the keel. One or more towers were built on the deck to enable the marines to overwhelm the enemy from on high. Finally, the boarding party had to be formed; these soldiers could not only intervene with effect in sea battles, they could also disembark and provide a surprise attack on land where the enemy least expected, either on their flanks or from behind.

Thus the Roman army was not only outstanding by virtue of its armaments, it also excelled through the quality of the product of its shipyards.

THE ARMY ON THE MOVE

Combat is the primary purpose of any army. But a good general did not engage in hostilities on any terrain; he chose the one that best suited the troops at his disposal, while trying to take into account the enemy forces. His first problem was to get to know the troops under his orders, to ascertain how many horsemen, infantrymen, auxiliaries and legionaries he had at his command. He also needed to know what condition they were in; whether they were tired or rested, well-trained or not, battle tried and in good spirits.

Secondly, he needed to get information about the enemy forces so that he could decide on the battlefield. Finally, he had to organize his troops in such a way as to achieve his objectives. This step was of paramount importance because an enemy could take advantage of the fact that Romans were not organized in battle-formation on the march and could therefore attack them more easily. While on the march they were always at risk from an ambush, and it should not be forgotten that Publius Quinctilius Varus was not defeated in the course of a pitched battle. Moreover, any reorganization of troops was subject to the twin obligations of speed and safety. The general would wish to spend the least possible time in this position of weakness to avoid any unpleasant surprise. However, he had to expect even the unexpected, and act so as to minimize any potential losses if attacked while on the march. Roman strategists gave a lot of thought to the problem of choosing the right order of march for the infantry, cavalry, legionaries, auxiliaries, and the right place to put the baggage.

Order of march

Different answers have been given to these questions.[45] Nevertheless, the generals who showed some interest in the order of march were in agreement on some points (pl.XXVI,18). Firstly, the vanguard was normally made up of auxiliaries and cavalry to explore the terrain and to retreat rapidly if necessary. Similarly, the rearguard was formed by less important units. The baggage was normally placed in the middle to receive maximum protection as it was an army's weakspot when on the march. The loss of baggage risked a total disruption of the column of soldiers as they usually broke ranks in order to retrieve their belongings if they saw them being stolen. Protection of the baggage was therefore a constant obligation, but to do this one of two solutions imposed by the topography had to be adopted, according to the strategists.

If the army had to advance over a narrow terrain, either entering a gorge or following a valley, then it was virtually impossible to provide adequate cover for the flanks as the troops were drawn out into one long line. In 57 BC (during the Republic) Julius Caesar was faced with just such a situation while fighting against the Belgians.[46] He placed his auxiliaries, that is his cavalry, archers and slingers, in front. After them came the bulk of his army made up of his six best legions, followed by the baggage and two legions of recruits. Although Caesar does not say so, it is quite possible that a few cohorts of allies brought up the rear, as this is what other strategists did.

In the middle of the first century Onesandros devoted a treatise to the obligations of a general-in-chief. He recommended that he should preferably choose open terrain, but if that were not possible, because a gorge had to be entered, he ought to make occupation of the high ground his priority.[47]

In Samaria Titus followed almost the same pattern as Julius Caesar, as we learn from Josephus' detailed description of the organization of his troops:[48]

> During his advance into enemy territory Titus had in the vanguard his royal troops and all his auxiliaries. They were followed by his pioneers and camp surveyors, then the officers' baggage, the troops entrusted with its protection. After them came Titus himself with the elite of the soldiers, in particular the lancers; behind him the legionary cavalry who preceded the war machines, directly followed by the tribunes and the prefects of the cohorts with elite soldiers. After them came the insignia grouped around the eagle and preceded by the trumpets, then the bulk of the column in rows six wide. Behind them came the batmen of the legions preceded by their baggage. The rear was drawn up by mercenaries watched over by a rearguard.

The similarity between the marching order of Caesar and of Titus is striking, though there are some differences. Josephus does not say whether the vanguard included cavalry, which seems very likely, and on the contrary specifies that it is the auxiliaries who were to be found in the rearguard. The main difference between the two generals lies in the fact that the first placed the kit just behind the bulk of the legionaries whereas the second placed it just in front.

The advance of an army through a narrow defile had to be avoided at all costs, so this was an exceptional experience. Normally a general chose a flat, open terrain to avoid risk of ambush and be able to protect his flanks.

At the very beginning of Tiberius' reign Germanicus led the Rhine army against the Usipetes and the Bructeri:[49]

> the general . . . made arrangements for the march and the combat. Part of the cavalry and the auxiliary infantry were in front; then came the first legion, protecting the baggage; the left flank was formed by soldiers of the twenty-first, the right by those of the fifth. The twentieth legion, followed by the rest of the allies brought up the rear.

In this passage, too, we can see the importance attributed to the baggage; it is surrounded on all sides by the best soldiers.

Shortly afterwards, in the middle of the first century, Onesandros' treatise on the duties of a commanding general echoes the choices made by Germanicus; his advice not to enter narrow defiles but to keep to flat open land as far as possible has already been noted. In these conditions he argued for putting the troops in a tight square formation with the baggage protected in the middle.[50] Like all the strategists, he placed the cavalry in the vanguard. Moreover, he recommended that soldiers should be sent ahead to forage, at the same time acting as scouts to bring back information on any enemy presence in the vicinity.

This progress through dangerous terrain is so important that in the time of Antoninus Pius, Arrian devoted a whole treatise to it, 'Marching arrangements and battle-order against the Alans'. He recommended a plan of action that was very close to that adopted by Germanicus more than a century earlier. In front were mounted scouts, auxiliary *alae* and cohorts, followed successively by legions, allies and baggage. The rearguard was comprised of other auxiliaries, infantrymen and horsemen to protect the flanks. It is here, indeed, that the main difference between the two generals lies, since Germanicus detailed legionaries to protect the army's flanks while Arrian used auxiliaries.

In fact Arrian refers twice to the same question,[52] and in *Tactics* he gave advice that sometimes complements and sometimes contradicts that found in 'Marching order . . .'. Nevertheless the baggage is his main concern; it must be placed on the opposite side to where the enemy attack would occur, in the front, in the rear, on the right or the left, but could be placed in the middle if this was not known. In any case the cavalry need not have a fixed station, but the general should take into account the terrain and the position of the enemy in deploying it. The legions marched in front and behind or on the flanks, with the auxiliaries either following or flanking them.

This second text of Arrian is extremely valuable in making us realize yet again that Roman tactics, like their weaponry, changed with different situations, but nevertheless certain constants can be seen; a general must place the baggage in the centre, near his legionaries, with the cavalry up front and the auxiliary cohorts at the rear.

Engineering works

An army going through enemy territory did not always encounter the facilities to which the Roman world had accustomed it, and it had to develop the land it crossed by building roads, bridges and camps in order to ensure maximum security.

These tasks were just one of the many factors that brought success to the Roman army, and consequently were not undertaken haphazardly or by anybody. It was normally the infantry, particularly the legions, that supplied the labour, while the cavalry, including that of the *auxilia*, guarded and protected the building sites. It should be remembered that mounted soldiers enjoyed the privilege of being exempted from fatigues (*immunes*). This division of responsibilities has been well explained by G.Ch. Picard.[53] There is a text of Pseudo-Hyginus that shows a distribution of roles identical to that under Trajan; the navy's infantry built the roads, protected by the Mauretanian and Pannonian horsemen.[54]

Roads and bridges

Generals insisted on having good roads in order to advance quickly in enemy territory, but it should not be imagined that these were paved. In fact the infantry did little more than cut down trees when crossing a forest, clear boulders from gorges and drain a few small marshes on the plains when necessary. Apart from that they were content to level the ground, or easier still, erect a few landmarks to indicate the route to follow. We know in fact that the famous Roman roads were rarely paved,[55] except in the vicinity of towns and their main thoroughfares. Paving would otherwise have represented a colossal waste of time and energy.

Crossing rivers however presented a real difficulty, and one of three solutions could be chosen. The navy could be called upon to ferry the troops across,[56] or make a bridge by lashing their boats together and putting a flat surface over them.[57] The third solution was to build a permanent bridge in stone or wood.[58] During his campaign against the Dacians, Trajan had used the know-how of Apollodorus of Damascus. He is represented on Trajan's Column organizing the crossing of the Danube,[59] and even revealed his secrets in a treatise.[60]

Temporary camps

Whatever admiration these constructions might arouse, there was something even better. Every evening soldiers belonging to an expeditionary force had to be protected by a rampart. These temporary transit camps (*castra aestiva*) were sometimes built and dismantled daily.[61] They differed from the permanent camps (*castra hiberna* or *stativa*) which will be the subject of the next chapter, in their dimensions and the materials used to construct them. Because they were built quickly and dismantled immediately afterwards they have left few traces for archaeologists, and consequently have to be studied using literary sources,[62] and representations on the columns of Trajan and Marcus Aurelius.[63]

The origin of Roman fortifications remains a mystery. Frontinus says that in the beginning Romans gathered together in cohorts in huts. King Pyrrhus of Epirus probably gave them the idea of building an enclosure to protect them, when one of his camps was studied and copied by Italian soldiers who had overrun it. If this account is not totally true, at least the presence of Greek elements can be accepted. However, the influence of the Etruscans in the peninsula cannot be totally ruled out because of the art of the augurs and the techniques of cadastral surveyors. Moreover, King Philip V of Macedonia felt so much admiration in front of a Roman camp that he declared that men capable of erecting such an edifice should not be classed as barbarians.[66]

Before building a camp, the site had to be chosen with care. One type of slope is more suitable than another[67] for draining water, for ventilation and a possible sortie against an enemy.[68] Water must be available in sufficient quantity in case of a siege. Finally the officer must be certain that the position is defendable,[69] avoiding one that is overlooked by a hill from which an enemy could throw javelins, arrows and rocks on the garrison.

The soldiers started by levelling the ground.[70] Next they built a rampart, smaller for a temporary camp than for a permanent one. To obtain the simplest of fortifications[71] (pl.XXVI,19) they first dug a 'V'-shaped ditch (*fossa*) and then piled up behind it the earth that had been removed, this they flattened to form a sort of elevated walkway (*agger*). The *vallum* was a rampart mound, sometimes topped by a wooden palisade or occasionally a low stone or turf wall[72] flanked by towers or bastions supporting artillery pieces, scorpions, catapults and *ballistae*.[73] Behind this they always left a space (*intervallum*) into which arrows and javelins that managed to clear the wall fell and which also made possible rapid movement within the fortress.

The four entrances to the camp had to be carefully defended,[74] as they were obvious weakspots in the rampart. Two sorts of gates are known (pl.XXVI,20). Either the soldiers built a small obstacle (*titulum*) directly in front of the opening, parallel to the main perimeter,[75] so as to break the momentum of an attack, or else the rampart was continued towards the inside and the outside by two quarter-circle segments, called 'a little key' (*clavicula*) by the architects.[76]

In fact, because of the relative weakness of this type of construction, requiring only a few hours to build, it was particularly the impact caused by an assault that was feared, hence the desire to break any momentum of a potential assailant. In front of the fortress the legionaries therefore dug holes into which they placed as obstacles tree trunks with their branches still intact, called *cervoli* ('little stags').[77] Pseudo-Hyginus says that a camp had five protections, the ditch, the walkway, the rampart, the 'little stags' and the weapons of the soldiers within.

The plan of the camp evolved, if not through time at least in the opinions of individual writers. Writing in the time of the Republic, in the second half of the second century BC, Polybius (pl.XXVII,21)[79] indicates that the Romans of his time built square camps divided into thirds by the *quintana* road and the *principalis*. Beyond the *principalis* was the public square (*forum*), the tent of the quaestor, the officer responsible for the finances of the operation (*quaestorium*), and that of the general (*praetorium*). The other two thirds were divided down the middle by the *decumanus* road. Two centuries later Josephus was still talking of a square.[80]

On the other hand, writing some twenty or thirty years later, Pseudo-Hyginus recommended different proportions, namely a rectangle with a ratio of 2:3 between the sides[81] (pl.XXVII,22). The spatial organization also differs, although the *quintana* and the *principalis* still divided the whole into thirds, the *praetentura*, the *lateri Praetorii* and the *retentura*. But the part beyond the *principalis* was intersected by the praetorian road, the *praetorium* (the general's tent) was placed in the middle and the *quaestorium* was situated in the middle of the final third,[82] after the *quintana*.

Pseudo-Hyginus and Josephus provide a great deal of information about the space inside the fortress, as nothing should be left to chance. Once the ground had been levelled a surveyor set up in the middle (pl.xxvii,23) his *groma*,[83] an instrument made up of four plumb lines, which enabled him to mark out angles of 90° which determined the location of the roads and the rampart (it also gave its name to the centre-point of the camp). The roads created rectangles in which tents were pitched[84] (pl.xxvii,24), the most important being that of the general, considered as sacred as a temple.[85] Close by was the *auguratorium*, where the auspices were taken by the general who observed the flights of birds to determine the will of the gods.[86] Close at hand also was a platform from which the commander-in-chief dispensed justice and made speeches.[87]

Other accommodation was available for officers and ordinary soldiers. Some space had to be left for communal buildings such as the workshop where damaged weapons were repaired,[88] a hospital for treating the wounded and even an infirmary for the animals.[89] And of course, because we are dealing with Roman architecture, due emphasis must be placed on the inevitable public square (*forum*).[90]

When describing a camp, with its various constructions to ensure its protection and the extremely complex organization of its interior, all built in one evening on a new site and destroyed the following morning, the conclusion must be that every officer knew exactly what he had to do and every soldier was fully aware of his role to avoid any unnecessary waste of time. These demands imply that men were recruited on criteria of quality and trained very extensively.

The role of the fleet

The Romans used their fleet to move troops whenever possible.[91] It has often been said that the Roman navy served little purpose because Roman domination of the Mediterranean basin prevented the rise of any rival maritime power or the activities of any pirate bands; these would simply have had no landbase to build from. In fact the first, and probably the chief, reason for the building of warships, was that they ensured the logistics of any military operation.

They were used to move supplies and men;[92] the fleet at Ravenna was thus able to participate in the great expedition against the Parthians in 214–17.[93] In 231 the fleet at Misenum shipped money and equipment to the East in preparation for the war against the Persians.[94] Many other examples could be cited. Finally Roman officers were aware of the surprise effect of an unexpected landing and used the tactic on more than one occasion.

Thus a Roman general had to take a number of precautionary measures when moving his troops, in order to avoid being ambushed or forced to fight when his troops were resting. Obviously these practices required men to be competent and well-trained, but they did mean that they would arrive in the best possible fighting condition.

THE ARMY IN BATTLE

Ancient writers included many descriptions of battles as they saw in these accounts the possibility of glorifying such virtues as courage and condemning such vices as cowardice. It goes without saying that for a twentieth-century historian the perspective is different; the need is to highlight certain permanent defining features of the art of war, and this will have certain implications of a social nature, as we shall see. Roman tactics varied according to the situation. Three scenarios were possible, siege, open-terrain combat and sea battles.

Sea battles

Arrian mentions the existence of specific naval combat tactics, but failed to expound them.[95] The absence of any other maritime power in the Mediterranean and the lack of a landbase for any would-be pirates make any naval engagement on the high seas fairly hypothetical. Nevertheless, it was the duty of a good admiral to expect even the unexpected, and the fleets at Misenum and Ravenna were prepared for all eventualities. They possessed artillery, catapults and *ballistae*, as the missiles from these would damage enemy ships' rigging, kill or wound a few of the men and sap morale before hand-to-hand fighting. Sailors used hooks and grappling irons to fix their ship to the enemy ship for boarding. Soldiers then boarded the enemy ship and fought hand-to-hand battles as on land.

Sieges

These are often mentioned by ancient writers because ancient society lived under a city regime, that is a city and its dependent territory, and control of the enemy's nerve centre always seemed the best way of deciding a conflict. Ancient writers therefore wrote at length on the science of poliorcetics, which owed a lot to Greeks as its name suggests.[96] Historical accounts abound with these descriptions,[97] while Trajan's Column shows how the Romans went about capturing Sarmizegethusa, the capital of Dacia.[98] In this domain the technical side of the Roman army was again evident, with no mere siege by numbers, but one in which every man carried out a certain function. A wide variety of machines was used to overcome the resistance of even the thickest walls, and soldiers had to undertake major engineering works.

The besieged

Deployment of the Roman forces depended on what the besieged had at their disposal. But the legionaries themselves could be caught in a trap (Trajan's Column shows the Dacians being driven back from a fortress they wanted to capture),[99] so poliorcetics had also to include how to defend oneself when surrounded by barbarians. The city ramparts naturally represented the greatest obstacle. From their heights, behind the protection of bulwarks, *propugnacula*,[100] the city's defenders threw javelins, arrows and rocks on their attackers,[101] even before these had reached the bottom of the walls. When they did reach the walls the besieging troops faced a new ordeal of having boiling water or burning oil poured down on them.[102]

The second problem facing the Roman commanders was the defenders themselves, not only from their cover behind the bulwarks, but also when they made a mass sortie to engage the Romans in hand-to-hand combat.[103] The besieged had therefore to be confined within their city. If this was successful, it aggravated the problem of shortage of food and water,[104] and any defenders sent out to try and bring back food were subject to Roman attacks. Sometimes encouraging desertion was a more effective tactic, as Titus proved in his siege of Jerusalem, though he forgot about the greed of some of his auxiliary troops:[105]

> One of the Jewish deserters who was among the Syrians was seen in the act of removing gold coins from his excrement. He had swallowed these coins before leaving because the rebels carried out bodysearches and gold was so plentiful in the city that a coin that was worth twenty-five Attic drachmas could be bought for only twelve. From this one case rumour spread throughout the camp that deserters were arriving full of gold, and the Arab scum along with the Syrians slit open their stomachs to search in their intestines. In my opinion this was the worst calamity that ever happened to the Jews; in one night up to two thousand were gutted.

Above all, any communication with potential allies had to be prevented, so no messenger could be allowed to cross Roman lines. Romans relied greatly on the psychological effect caused by the uncertainty about food and water supplies, and this confinement also prevented reinforcements being called.

The besiegers

To overcome the twin difficulties of walls and defenders, the imperial siege experts had three modes of action at their disposal: well-trained soldiers, siegeworks and machines. Normally the supervision of a siege was the job of the prefect, the number three officer in the legion.[106] The siege camp was the most important element in the siege. It was built rapidly for temporary use, like that built on a march rather than a permanent fortress, and was protected by a wooden rampart, though occasionally stones or turves were used.

However, two distinctive features must be pointed out here. Firstly, the site under attack was surrounded by several fortified positions,[107] with a main one occupied by the chief of staff and a series of subsidiary operational bases to complete the system. This organizational set up was already used in the siege of Alesia at the end of the Republic.[108] During the siege of Jerusalem, Titus built one large camp,[109] but then moved it several times to where his men had achieved partial successes. He also built thirteen small forts which he abandoned as circumstances dictated. In 72 Flavius Silva had detachments of the *legio X Fretensis* and *auxilia* positioned around Masada. This siege offers a great deal of interest to a historian because of the availability of a written description from the hand of Josephus,[110] and the results of archaeological excavations[111] (pl.XXVIII,25). Eight enclosures, two large and six smaller, have been discovered on the site. One of the two larger enclosures was further extended during the course of the siege by the addition of a second rampart. All the gates were of the 'little key' (*clavicula*) type. The same practice was followed at the sieges of Piacenza[112] and Cremona[113] in the civil war of 68–9 and at the siege of Sarmizegethusa (see n. 98) during Trajan's campaigns against the Dacians from 101 to 107. Moreover, the plans of the camps varied according to the lie of the land. On flat terrain squares or rectangles were built, but in other circumstances any shape was possible. In the last years of the Republic Caesar had organized the siege of Alesia in the same way (see n. 108). At Masada (see nn. 110–111 and pl.XXVIII,25), at the beginning of Vespasian's reign, a square (E), a lozenge (H), and some indeterminate shapes (F2 and G particularly) are found. But the texts and the results of archaeology show the existence of considerable supplementary constructions. In describing the siege of Cremona (see n. 113) Tacitus uses three terms, *castra* (camp), *vallum* (mound plus rampart) and *munimenta* (fortifications in general). These other constructions have a threefold objective.

Firstly, the besieged had to be totally isolated from the outside. To do this they were surrounded by a rampart called a 'countervallation', probably no more than a simple earth embankment, an *agger*.[114] More often than not this fortification was reinforced by a ditch and a reed palisade,[115] thus providing the 'elementary fortification' already described. At Jerusalem, Titus had a complete wall built, starting and ending at the headquarters, 7.85km (5 miles) long.[116] The excavations at Masada, which confirm Josephus' account, have also brought about the discovery of a similar construction, over 3.65km (2¼ miles). If the Romans were afraid of a relief army arriving on the scene, as Caesar was at Alesia, an even longer second rampart, called a circumvallation, protected them from the outside.

Such efforts highlight the concern of generals to protect their men and keep losses to a minimum. This was their second objective. In order to achieve this, the Romans had fixed defences, wooden hurdles and palisades to shelter behind.[118] Mobile defences were also used for protection when approaching the enemy's walls; called the 'tortoise' (*testudo*) and 'little rat' (*musculus*) they were galleries,[119] with roofs considerably reinforced by metal plates and leather strips, often fitted with wheels.

But the Roman general's third, overriding objective remained the capture of the city. If surrender was not forthcoming, then an assault had to be launched, but before this could happen several problems had to be resolved. Normally a fortified city had a ditch around it which would take too long to be filled in by an assailant. Instead, the tactic was to build an approach platform, a narrow strip of stone and earth, as high as possible. At the siege of Jerusalem Titus had at least five built;[120] at Masada there was only one and its remains have been uncovered by archaeologists[121] (pl.XXVIII,25). In some cases when the platform was particularly narrow we can talk of an 'approach bridge'.[122]

Of course, the wall itself was the main obstacle. An attempt could be made to breach it, at least in one place. There were several ways of doing this; sappers could attack it under cover of a 'tortoise' with picks or a battering ram, or they could set fire to it with wood chippings and brushwood placed in holes bored into its surface,[123] or they could even undermine it.[124] The digging of a tunnel also provided a means of penetrating into the town while avoiding the obstacle. Rome's enemies could also use this tactic from time to time; at Dura-Europos the corpse of a soldier killed by the Persians in the mid-third century has been found several metres underground.[125] It was also possible to look over the obstacle by building towers, some of which were iron-barded and mounted on wheels.[126] They served both as observation and firing posts, and housed battering rams, support ladders and the flying bridges used in the final stage of the assault.

Finally, it is necessary to add a type of construction rarely mentioned and even more rarely studied, the 'arm' (*bracchium*).[127] Livy gives the most precise information about it. In 438 BC Ardea was besieged by the Volsci, who in turn were surrounded by the Roman relief army, which built two *bracchia* to gain access to the city.[128] We know of a construction to which this name had been given by the same author;[129] this was the three 'Long Walls' built after the Persian Wars to link Athens to its harbour. Frontinus also confirms this interpretation.[130] *Bracchium* is therefore translated here as a linear defence (wall) connected to a defence point such as a town or camp. A double 'arm' assures that communication can be maintained, while a single 'arm' was an impediment to any really efficient form of encirclement if it linked a camp to a river, for example. It is possible that this type of construction can be seen on a part of Trajan's Column.[131]

A final point is that Roman soldiers had a very great variety of 'tortoises' to shelter under while they worked or launched their attack.[132] These also served as protective covers for their machines, battering rams, etc. This stunning range of constructions confirms what has already been said about the Roman army's technical side. Ancient strategists were well aware of the importance of these. Quoting a leading general of the mid-first century, Frontinus states it unambiguously: 'According to Domitius Corbulo the enemy must be defeated by the pick, that is by hard work.'

The assault (pl.XXIX,26)

If such activities did not generate sufficient fear among the besieged to bring about their surrender, the only course of action left was combat. The Romans do not appear to have regularly practised a general assault from all directions, but to have preferred to attack the weakest spot of the rampart,[134] where they built their assault platform.

At this juncture an initial attack by the artillery was launched[135] with three objectives: to cause further damage to the rampart; casualties among the enemy; and loss of morale. There were machines called *tormenta*[136] that launched javelins and arrows,[137] some of them incendiary,[138] or rocks and beams (pl.XXIX,27). These machines were also used at sea for naval combat and for pitched battles on land. In sieges they were normally possessed by both sides; defenders of towns put them on ramparts and towers, the attackers put them on wheels, or on warships if attacking ports. This mobile artillery was essentially Greek in concept and was predicated on a principle of physics: a lever was inserted into a skein of twisted horsehair to increase torsion, and when the arm was released a considerable amount of energy was thus freed. When Kaiser Wilhelm II had some Roman machines copied in 1902, an arrow hit the centre of a target at 50m (160ft) and a second split the first in two! A 60cm (24in) arrow pierced a 2cm ($\frac{3}{4}$in) plank at 340m (1115ft).

However, Roman artillery still holds some problems as it is not easy to put a name to each machine, especially as research in this domain does not appear to have been exhaustive (see n. 135). At present historians seem to agree on some definitions. In the first century, every century (group of 100 men) had a catapult for hurling arrows and a *ballista* for stones; in the second century the term *ballista* is used to designate both types of machines while in the fourth the term 'catapult' is used for the stone-throwing machine and the *ballista* for the arrow launcher. A 'scorpion' was a small catapult, an 'onager' a small scorpion[139] and a *carroballista* was a machine mounted on wheels. According to Vegetius a legion possessed ten 'onagers' (one per cohort) and 55 *carroballistae* (one per century). Passing over the question of legions having 55 centuries, it is important however to stress that there is no differentiation in the designation of the artillerymen on inscriptions; they are all called *ballistarii*. Caesar talks of catapults that launch stones and *ballistae* that throw beams at the enemy.[140] Perhaps the explanation lies elsewhere, that some machines were used to achieve a direct trajectory (catapults) and others a curved trajectory (*ballistae*), unless the second acquired a generic value. While most of the machines used torsion, some used metal springs.

There are other machines that are classed under the heading *tormenta* and fired by legionary infantrymen.[141] The rampart was battered with 'helepoles'[142] or battering rams, the latter being also used to break open city gates.[143] Josephus describes a huge one used at the siege of Jotapata (see n. 143):

> It is an immense beam, similar to a ship's mast, with one end covered with iron shaped into a ram's head; hence its name. It is suspended from another beam like a balance arm by cables around its middle, and this in turn is supported at both ends by posts fixed in the ground. It is drawn back by a huge number of men who then push it forward in unison with all their might so that it hits the wall with its iron head. There is no tower strong enough nor any wall thick enough to withstand repeated blows of this kind, and many cannot resist the first shock.

While this was going on the general stationed his troops opposite what he considered the weakest spot. Josephus shows how Vespasian conducted the siege at Jotapata:

> In order to dislodge the defenders from the breaches he had the bravest horsemen dismount and form three assault columns in front of them. They were in full armour with their lances at the ready, determined to be the first to enter the town as soon as the assault ladders were in place. Behind them Vespasian placed the elite of the infantry. He deployed the rest of the cavalry facing the rampart the whole length of the area linked to the mountain to prevent any of the besieged escaping without being seen. Behind the cavalry cordon he deployed his archers, his slingers and his machines with orders to be ready to fire when needed.[144]

The attack could then begin. The legionaries protected themselves by forming a 'tortoise' with their shields.[145] Archers and artillerymen launched a final shower of projectiles and arrows while the infantrymen added their javelins. The assault ladders were placed against the wall,[146] or dropped from the tops of mobile towers. When the top of the rampart was reached a series of single combats ensued. If the Romans succeeded in gaining control of this position they could be pretty sure of having won the day.

Then the sack of the town began, with all its horrors, worse than during the siege. Traditionally the spoils were handed over to the officers when the enemy surrendered without a fight, but kept by the soldiers when an assault had proved necessary. The siege of Jotapata ended in massacre.[147] The capture of Cremona was the occasion for even worse cruelty, possibly because it happened during a civil war:[148]

> Forty thousand men at arms, as well as an even larger number of army servants and sutlers, who were far more versed in cruelty and debauchery, rushed towards the place. Neither age nor rank provided any protection; rape led to murder, murder to rape. Very old men and women at the end of their lifespan, who were not considered worthy of being spoils of war, were dragged off as mere playthings. When they came across a nubile virgin or a handsome man they fought among themselves so violently to carry them off that they ripped the victims to pieces and even killed each other in the attempt. While some were stripping the temples of their silver and heavy gold offerings, they were massacred by others arriving on the scene . . . For four days Cremona provided horrors of this sort.

And in Jerusalem massacres occurred every time a new district was captured.

Sieges therefore required the talents of numerous participants. Some officers at least needed to be familiar with poliorcetics and architecture, while many of the ordinary soldiers were expected to be specialists in particular fields of action, but all of them were expected to have become very efficient in their area through constant training.

Battle in open country

To win a battle in open country soldiers had to be well-trained, but the technical side of their job played a less important role than in sieges. Courage replaced machines, which were rarely used. Ancient writers provide many descriptions of battles,[149] and archaeology has uncovered some interesting reliefs,[150] but many problems have yet to be cleared up.[151]

Intelligence was certainly not absent from this type of battle, but was largely confined to strategies, claimed to be the highest level in the hierarchy of tactics. In particular two writers have left us interesting treatises on the topic. First is Frontinus, who attributed the elaboration of this study to the Greeks because he noted that the name used to designate it was Greek. He grouped his advice under four headings: before a battle; during a battle; during a siege; and virtues associated with discipline. In fact, rather than a reflection on the art of winning, his work is a series of formulas for achieving success whatever the circumstances. Hence he recommends lighting a delayed fire when being pursued.[152]

Before a battle it is sensible to let the enemy wear itself out, as Tiberius did,[153]

140

who, seeing the fierce hordes of Pannonians walking to do battle at daybreak, kept his troops in the camp and left the enemy to suffer the brunt of the heavy rain that fell all day long. When he saw that the barbarians were physically exhausted by the battering of the storm, low on courage and resolve, he gave the signal for attack and defeated them.

But above all, it was necessary to make the most of the circumstances prevailing, especially those that were least expected:[154] 'The divine Vespasian Augustus chose to attack the Jews on a Saturday as they were forbidden to do anything whatsoever on that day, and he defeated them.'

Secondly, Polyaenus also attributes the invention of stratagems to the Greeks, starting from mythical times. The examples he cites are listed by date and place, and Augustus is the only Roman he deigns to mention. These two writers did not go in for a profound analysis of tactics; this science was enlightened by the Romans and by real-life situations. That is what we now need to look at.

Battle order

The first thing to happen was a meeting of the commanders to decide on a battle formation to suit the situation on the ground.[155] The training of the soldiers and the adaptability of the cohorts enabled them to build some obstacles which would hamper the enemy but be easily negotiated by the legions; ditches were dug and stakes driven into the ground.[156] The troops were marshalled on the terrain as space permitted. Roman generals usually considered that the manoeuvreability of their men went towards giving them superiority over the barbarian rabble. For an encirclement or an outflanking to be possible it was necessary to have a centre and two flanks.[157] This tripartite division did not involve the light infantry, particularly the archers and slingers who kill from a distance, and who were stationed in front, behind or on the flanks.[158]

At the end of the first century Agricola provides an example of simple tactics on a narrow battlefield:[159] (pl.xxx,28a)

> he organized his men as follows; the 8000 auxiliary infantrymen in the centre, 3000 horsemen on the flanks, the legions in front of the retrenchment. The victory would be famously glorious if it were obtained without the shedding of any Roman blood, while if a retreat had to be sounded there would be a reserve force in waiting there.

In addition to these the Roman general had 'four cavalry units set aside in case of unexpected emergencies'. Thus Agricola placed the auxiliaries in the front line, 8000 footsoldiers in the middle and 1500 horsemen on each flank; in the second line he put the 12,000 legionaries with their backs against the camp, and some 2000 mounted soldiers to act as a mobile reserve force.

In the middle of the second century Arrian showed how the troops could be deployed when space was not an issue[160] (pl.xxx,28b). His distribution presents a far more complex picture, and while it is a possibility that progress had been made in the meantime in this field, it may well be that Arrian was simply a shrewder tactician than Agricola. Legionaries formed the main part of his forces, deployed in eight rows with the most experienced on the right. On both flanks of this phalanx foot-soldiers, archers and artillery pieces were stationed in equal numbers on two hillocks, at the foot of which a few auxiliary cohorts were placed. Behind the elite infantrymen there was a line of archers, some mounted, some on foot, followed by more cavalry and artillerymen, who would move to reinforce the flanks as soon as hostilities began. In addition, the general had in reserve a force made up of the elite of the cavalry, the officers' bodyguard and two hundred legionaries.

A third possibility is mentioned by Tacitus.[161] When the army entered barbarian country it had to be ready to withstand an attack and to react at any moment, even if it had no previous knowledge of the whereabouts of the enemy. To achieve this the soldiers were organized in battle formation every morning in front of their camp, and they marched in that order until they met the enemy, so marching order and battle order were synonymous.

One final point remains to be considered, that of the structure of the legion in battle.[162] Caesar's tactics are familiar to us; his soldiers were arranged in three rows (*triplex acies*). By Arrian's time, however, they were grouped together in a solid phalanx, elbow to elbow, shield to shield. To the enemy they appeared as a wall of iron, bristling with javelins. In fact, generals could choose between several possible tactics, and the final decision depended on the enemy and the terrain. But the legion remained the principal element of any organization, and its internal structure of cohorts, maniples and centuries (pl.IV,5) gave it a great deal of flexibility. Historians do not agree on the role of each of these groups in the battle proper, but it seems to us that the most important tactical unit was the maniple, individualized by its *signum*. The deployment of the cavalry did not lack organization either; they formed a square or a wedge, according to the general's orders.

The battle proper

In order to maintain its superiority the Roman army was not to engage in hostilities until it had found the best possible formation. As soon as this had been done, battle could begin, but here again, a certain number of instructions had to be followed. In Mediterranean societies whose civilization is based on the word, everything, including war, began with a speech. With every soldier in place the general made a speech to encourage them;[163] Tacitus in particular obviously derived pleasure in 'rewriting' these speeches.

The actual fighting then began. The first objectives were achieved by an initial artillery salvo that sought to kill some enemy and bring some measure of demoralization and disorder in their ranks.[164] This softening up by the artillery was accompanied by the shots of the archers and slingers, and in a case where the enemy was within distance, by the launch of javelins.[165] Then a huge shout would rise from the Roman lines.[166] According to ancient writers the importance of this should not be underestimated, since it strengthened the courage of the Romans and put fear into their enemies.

The manoeuvring now began. Three scenarios were possible.[167] First the enemy might run away immediately because they were frightened by the Roman battle formation, having been weakened by the first salvo of missiles they had suffered. In this case the phalanx split up into several parts, allowing the cavalry to pass through it, the leading riders pursuing at full speed to make sure that the retreat was not merely tactical, while the rest advanced carefully in formation. The infantry then came down from the elevated positions it had occupied in order to have an overview of the battle theatre.

In a second scenario, the enemy not only did not run away, but actually took the initiative and attempted an outflanking operation. In this situation Arrian recommended self-control with no widening of the front line to counter it; instead, the general should send in his cavalry to meet the attackers.

The third scenario was the one the Romans preferred, in which they kept the initiative and made the moves. As in the attack on a town wall they must choose the weakest spot in the enemy line.[168] The honour of starting the fighting fell to the auxiliary infantrymen who were directed to the area the general felt was the least well defended.[169] In all these scenarios one constant feature can be singled out: even if the role of the cavalry became more important in the third century, it was the infantry, especially the legions, that remained 'the queen of the battlefield' throughout the Early Empire.[170] There were several advantages: one was the shock effect of a mass of men,[171] as the younger ones in front were pushed on by the veterans in the rear.[172] This pressure was lethal as the front line bristled with spears, and the training of the Romans allowed them to navigate an obstacle like a small mound without breaking their phalanx. Furthermore, they were well protected as they would have been in the 'tortoise' formation, with those in the front line making a protective wall with their shields and those behind holding their shields over their heads to prevent enemy arrows from hitting them. While this was happening the light infantry, archers and slingers, would be moving in all directions to complement the actions of the heavy infantry. During this advance the Roman soldiers had to make sure they never lost sight of their standards (eagles, *signa*, *vexilla*),[174] and listened for any orders conveyed by trumpet or horn.

In such conditions the cavalry played a secondary role;[175] the light units harassed the enemy by a constant shower of arrows and javelins. The *cataphractarii* did not produce the same shock effect as the legionaries because their armour was only protective and not designed to add to their weight in clashes with the enemy troops. The mounted soldier has only the advantage of dominating the foot-soldier from the height of his mount. Whatever the situation his actions resulted in a duel that could bring him some sort of glory. Thus, during Titus' war against the Jews,

> when the Jews were routed and already being pushed back down the ravine in total disarray, one of the cohorts' cavalrymen, named Pedanius, galloped his horse at full speed on their flank and captured one of the fleeing enemy, a tall, well-built young man, armed from head to toe. He seized him by the ankle while leaning forward the full length of his horse, displaying an extraordinary strength of arm and body as well as an extraordinary agility as a rider. Spiritedly carrying off his prisoner as a valuable object he brought him to Caesar. Titus expressed his admiration for the strength of the man who had made the capture.[176]

To return to the infantry. Having completed the move that was ordered, they engaged in man-to-man combat, which would be most effective if the enemy line had been broken at the moment of impact. During the battle in Jerusalem

> arrows and spears were useless to both Romans and Jews. Drawing their swords they fought hand-to-hand and in the engagements it was impossible to see to which side each group belonged, as the narrowness of the place caused them to be thoroughly mixed up. The cries were heard in a confused manner in all the din.[177]

All of the above descriptions are united in concise form in a battle narrative that owes much of its value to the wonderfully taut style of Tacitus;[178] for instance the battle that took place in Britain in 83:

> At the beginning of the engagement fighting occurred at a distance; with steadfastness and skill the Britons used their long spears and their short shields to parry or turn aside our soldiers' javelins while pouring down a shower of arrows. Then Agricola gave the signal with his sword for four cohorts of Batavians and two from Tongres to engage in hand-to-hand fighting. They were well trained for this, while the Britons with their small shields and disproportionately long spears were ill-equipped. The Britons' swords were not pointed and so unfitted for swordfighting of this sort. Thus, the Batavians began to strike out in the fray, using the bosses of their shields to hit the enemy while slashing their faces with their swords, and when they had routed the enemy lines on the plain they took up positions on the hills. At the same time the other cohorts, keen to emulate them, massacred all the enemy around them, though in their haste they left many half-dead or even unharmed. Meanwhile our cavalry squadrons put the British chariots to flight and then joined the infantry fray. Despite the immediate panic they caused, they remained trapped in the thick of the enemy's battalions and the uneven terrain. The battle no longer resembled a cavalry engagement, as the men already found it difficult to stand upright on the slopes without being also jostled by

the horses, and often driverless chariots careered through the ranks, taking them wherever their frightened horses pulled them. However, those Britons who had taken up positions on the top of the hills and had not yet joined in the fray, quite calmly and with complete disdain for our inferior numbers, started to come down and turn the victors from behind. Agricola had anticipated just such a possibility and he drew up against them four cavalry corps that he had held in reserve in case of emergencies. The attackers were put to flight and they were routed with even more confidence than they had shown themselves in their attack.

When the barbarians realized that they were beaten, some surrendered; they were held as prisoners until they could be sold as slaves, or executed on the spot.[179] Others fled, pursued by the Romans. At this point all the tacticians recommend the utmost prudence[180] so as not to fall into a trap or an ambush. The first thing to be done was for the legionaries to scour the surroundings.[181] Only then did the cavalry start to pursue the routed enemies.[182] A recently discovered inscription explains a scene on Trajan's Column which is also found on the Adamklissi monument:[183] Tiberius Claudius Maximus, born in Phillipi in Macedonia, caught up with King Decebalus of the Dacians, and killed him before he could commit suicide. He then cut off his victim's head and took it to Trajan. Finally, when they were sure that there was no risk the soldiers plundered the baggage of the losers.

After the battle the Romans had to display their *pietas*, that is give the gods and men their due. While doctors treated the wounded, the living buried their dead;[184] Marcus Caelius, a centurion killed during Varus' disaster, was buried in Xanten, in the province of Germany.[185] The victors erected a trophy. They dressed a dummy in the various arms taken from the enemy. To immortalize this monument of thanksgiving it could be reproduced in bronze or built in stone and faced with marble. The most imposing monument of the kind known today is at Adamklissi.[186] If the Roman general had been acclaimed by his soldiers on the battlefield, on his return to Rome he could receive from the emperor the honours of an ovation,[187] or if he did not warrant an actual triumph, the insignia of a triumph (in view of their religious implications these ceremonies will be studied in detail later).

CONCLUSION

The more our study advances the more we realize that the Roman army never gave the impression of being a rabble. When the units moved, each individual one found that it had been given a particular place; during sieges and open-country battles each corps had to occupy the spot allotted to it. No move was left to chance, and an important feature was that men

145

had given some thought to marching and battle orders. A Roman science of warfare did exist, therefore, even if it did draw inspiration from Greek models. But the implementation of these tactics implies a perfect collaboration between officers and ordinary soldiers, with the former having the knowledge and the latter obeying their orders. Such a harmonious arrangement could not exist without quality control at the recruitment stage and constant training afterwards.

$$\boxed{6}$$

STRATEGY

The study of tactics may well appear to have given a view of the army that was over-professional, over-technical. Yet this was necessary because a Roman general's strategy depended on his troops' armaments and ability to manoeuvre.

We assume that we have a fairly good knowledge of this military organization, and the mere mention of it immediately brings to mind some terms and images: the famous *limes*, the great fortresses and the provincial armies, the legions of Germany, Hadrian's Wall, the great camp at Lambaesis, another rampart built in Syria or in the countries around the Danube. In regard to the *limes* standard textbooks still contain inaccuracies, if not actual errors, about the word itself and the reality it describes.[1] Also, many permanent camps have been uncovered in excavations, and their layout presents much interesting material that ought to be better known than it is today.[2] As for the number of men deployed in each region, no attempt at a synthesis of our knowledge has been made;[3] a global geographical study of the Roman army still needs to be done. Before that, however, we shall consider two features that are always present: individual defences (forts) and linear defences (walls). But even before we can do that we need to recall the conditions that governed their construction.

ROME AND ITS ENEMIES: OFFENSIVE OR DEFENSIVE?

It seems logical to state that Roman strategy varied according to the actual or potential enemy. Even if the founder of the Empire was not inspired by such considerations, his successors were certainly forced to adapt their policy to take account of the attitudes of their different adversaries. It is obviously impossible to say in a few pages everything

147

that needs to be said about the barbarians, but all that interests us here is to define the military characteristics of each people in order to understand how Rome was forced to change its strategy accordingly.

The enemies

If we look at the problem geographically (probably the easiest way) we start with two particular cases, Spain and Britain. The Iberian peninsula required no less than two centuries of fighting to complete its conquest. The natives were renowned for their fighting qualities, and Rome was to recruit many of them for its auxiliary units. Nevertheless, after Augustus peace seems to have been achieved, and the *legio VII Gemina* probably watched over the mines in the north-west as much as it did over the men. In any case, with the sea behind them the men could not find safety anywhere else.

In Britain, by way of contrast, there were always some tribes who could not be kept under control: the Caledonians in the north were never part of the Empire. Their numbers and their fighting qualities always presented problems for the Roman command who must have been relieved that they were riven by political divisions. In the third century these problems became greater following the attacks of Saxon pirates.

On the continent, east of the Rhine and the Danube, the huge German peoples with their proven warrior qualities had three elements in their favour: their fighting spirit; their numbers; and the length of the border that Rome had to defend. The threat to Rome here became even more acute when the Sarmatian or Rhoxolan nomads joined forces with the Germans. Their political fragmentation, however, diminished their power. This is why the unification process, with the setting up of confederations, by Arminius, who defeated Varus, was particularly dangerous. Moreover, on the left bank of the Lower Danube, in present-day Romania, there were the Dacians. They possessed several assets, including their wealth (the so-called 'Dacian gold'), the lack of an inferiority complex vis-a-vis the Empire, and their organization. Indeed, they had come together to form a kingdom, although this was small in comparison with the extent of the Roman world. In the third century, however, a new situation affected these peoples on the northern frontier. Disturbances in the Far East drove nations westwards, and these in turn drove towards the Empire the nations on its borders.

To understand the importance of the third century it is also necessary to look at the Middle East. The only powerful, centralized state near the Roman Empire was in Iran. In the first two centuries AD, the monarchy in power there had relatively peaceful objectives, but between 212 and 227 there was a revolution, with the Parthian Arsacides being overthrown by the Sassanian Persians, who were more nationalistic in outlook, bellicose and fanatically religious. What historians of Rome call the 'great crisis of the third century' was the result of two attacks, the Iranian offensive in the east and the German in the north, albeit for different reasons.

The southern frontier presented other problems, the main threat being the nomadic and semi-nomadic Nobades and Blemmyes in Egypt, and Mauretanians and Numidians in present-day Maghreb. One particular factor in the situation here should be underlined, namely that these tribes lived both north and south of the frontier which they regularly crossed in their wanderings. Hence the principal task of the legions was to keep a watchful eye on these movements. Some historians give the impression that Africa experienced three centuries of continuous insurrection, but this can be misleading. A large part of the natives sided with Rome (this region has left countless remains dating to the Early Empire, and produced writers and even emperors). The few unorganized nomads cannot be compared with the Germans or the Persians, however courageous they may have been. However, it is a fact that in times of crisis on other fronts any turbulence on their part would put the Roman generals under even more pressure.

The strategic problem

What strategy did the Romans use when faced by all these peoples? What basic principles were held by those responsible for leading the Roman armies? Y. Garlan is in no doubt that they chose a defensive strategy:[4] 'As early as Augustus' reign the Empire's foreign policy aimed to conserve and stabilize what had already been acquired.' This assertion is based on the fact that at the time of Augustus' death in 14 the limits of Roman influence were already more or less definitively fixed. This view needs to be qualified somewhat as in theory the collective mentality recognized no limits to its power; it was Rome's right to rule the whole world, and this right was used to serve imperialism.[5] Addressing the citizens, Virgil speaks to them of the other nations: 'Impose on them the observance of peace; spare those who submit and tame the arrogant'.[6]

But in practice such an aim was utopian. Firstly, some neighbours could resist, sometimes successfully, and an episode like that of Varus undoubtedly tempered many ambitions. Secondly, the Romans did not have unlimited means; the Chiefs of Staff had never heard of Siberia or the Congo. Finally, some territories held no military or economic interest whatsoever. In this respect in time of peace Rome opted for a defensive strategy, but two exceptions to this rule must be pointed out. Firstly, from time to time Rome experienced episodes of aggression, since each conquest was preceded by the creation of one or more legions (see table p. 26 for their frequency). Moreover, we know that even after 14, several emperors conducted a bellicose policy. To mention only the most blatant examples, there was Caligula in Mauretania, Claudius in Britain, Trajan against the Dacians, the Arabs and the Parthians, Marcus Aurelius and Septimius Severus in the East.

Moreover, respect for others' rights did not stop the Roman military from practising preventative operations and reprisals. They watched their neighbours very closely and the destruction of a potential danger always seemed to them to be the best means of ensuring their own security. In view therefore of what imperialism proposed and what reality imposed we shall attempt to define imperial strategy by an oxymoron, offensive defence.

The evolution of ideas

In the course of three centuries changes are noticeable. These have been studied in two important works devoted to the strategy of Rome in general and in the Iberian peninsula in particular.[7] In the first, its author E.N. Luttwak defined the Roman Empire in its infancy as 'a hegemony', that is its territories were divided into three groups, those which were administered directly, those which were under diplomatic control and those that were merely influenced. The age of the Julio-Claudians was that of the 'experimental army' (P. Le Roux) when extremely mobile units were sometimes stationed on the borders, sometimes far from the borders. Camps in Gaul like Arlaines (near Soissons), Aulnay (Saintonge) and Mirebeau (near Dijon), the last-named dating from the Flavian era, perhaps demonstrate a desire to keep an eye on the interior of the Empire and not to expose the legions unnecessarily to enemy incursions and raids. The Danube also was defended from a long way away; in Africa the *legio III Augusta* was not stationed near all its potential enemies. A system of client states complemented the role of the soldiers.

Under the Flavians we find the 'permanent army' of P. Le Roux, when the Roman troops were stationed more or less permanently close to the frontier separating the Roman and barbarian worlds. There was a slow two-fold evolution. On the one hand there was a shift from the 'hegemonious Empire' to a 'territorial Empire' (E.N. Luttwak), in which the last regions to be placed under Roman influence or diplomatic control were gradually subjected to direct administration; on the other there was a 'forward defence', whereby not only did Roman soldiers camp on the borders but they even built roads in barbarian territory and set up outposts and watchtowers along them. So in the second century, after a period of trial and error, Roman command had at its disposal a 'scientific' protection, defined by Luttwak as 'preclusive'; in Spain there was an 'army of peace' as defined by P. Le Roux.

With the 'crisis of the third century' the situation changed once more. Those in power adopted a more defensive attitude, often abandoning outposts and stationing the garrisons well behind the frontiers (Luttwak's 'defence in depth'). Lack of imagination makes them appear a 'static army' (P. Le Roux), one in which the units hardly moved at all except perhaps to stop a gap; the initiative had been given to the enemy.

However, this pessimistic impression is not correct. The Roman State often acted as it pleased, since it had the means to do so. First came the psychological aspect: everyone knew what Rome wanted because its policy was clear. Secondly, diplomatic activity must be mentioned. While conferences and discussions admittedly played a large role, it was not so large as that played by the influence of money; Domitian had preferred to buy peace with the Dacians rather than fight them. Moreover treaties very often contained clauses that dealt with hostages (a subject that has received little attention[8]); rulers who wished to prove their loyalty sent some of their family to the imperial court. But of paramount importance for the security of the Empire were the military forces, the army and its fortifications.

DEFENSIVE ORGANIZATION: THE OVERALL STRUCTURE

To put its policy into practice the Roman state gradually built up what are generally called the *limes* (we shall explain later why this is not a totally appropriate term). This was a defensive zone that more or less encircled the Mediterranean basin. In the minds of its founders this military organization comprised three elements: gods, men, stones. Indeed, because they considered themselves the most religious people the Romans were firmly convinced that nothing could be done without the help of the gods (see pp. 236ff). Men were also needed of course, as legionaries, auxiliaries and sailors. But perhaps the most original aspect of this arrangement were the constructions, which can be divided into two groups, the 'linear defences' (long walls erected against the barbarians like a miniature Great Wall of China) and 'individual defences' like towers, forts and fortresses.

It was essential to ensure that these constructions were well looked after and that the soldiers stationed there were not left to their own devices. This was achieved by inspections. We know that in 128 Hadrian went to the north of the Aures to see if training was being properly carried out and the camp and parade ground properly maintained.[9] About the same time the general and strategist Arrian did an inspection tour of the Black Sea:[10] 'We were at Apsarus where five cohorts are stationed . . . I inspected the arms, the ramparts, the ditches, the sick and the food supplies.' He visited another garrison a short distance from there: 'On the same day we were able . . . to see the horses, the horsemen practising their riding, the hospital, the supplies before going around the walls and ditches.' These texts are important because they show that a Roman officer had permanently to watch over men and stones.

Theory of the defensive system

It is possible to present an ideal diagram of the defensive system of any province (pl.XXXI,29), since it was the same virtually everywhere. This sort of system has been uncovered gradually through excavations, or all at a stroke through aerial photography, as is the case in Syria and Numidia.[11] The extent of these discoveries leads to the conclusion that the Roman 'frontier' was never just a line, like frontiers today, but a strip of land of varying width containing a multiplicity of features. The main constituent of this strip was the road, the original meaning of the word *limes*. There was a road running on the enemy side of the fortifications, sometimes beside a natural obstacle, normally a river like the Rhine or Danube. Elsewhere it was associated with an artificial 'linear defence'; in Britain, Hadrian's Wall and the Antonine Wall both have a roadway running alongside them, as does the Seguia bent el-Krass in Numidia. When there was a continuous barrier like a river or a rampart we talk of a closed system, as opposed to an open system as found in the African and Syrian deserts.

At intervals all the way along the road were 'individual defences'. Large camps housed a whole legion and a supply depot. Less important forts also received supplies, with watch-towers acting as relays between them. When the road ran alongside a large river, ports were built to provide moorings for the ships of the fleet. In the case of the open systems of the deserts the army endeavoured to control the watering places, the oases. This practice is explained by Tacitus,[12] and aerial photography and excavation have shown how it was put into effect in Egypt, Syria and Numidia. Other forts were installed behind the road. Maps should be treated with caution as in military zones some archaeologists tended to name as camps many ruins, which, at the most, were no more than fortified farms.[13]

The role of *coloniae*, those cities founded near frontiers and populated by Roman citizens should also not be exaggerated. Admittedly if the need arose the farmers who lived there could take up arms, particularly if they were veterans; moreover, at the end of the Republic, in 63 BC, Cicero had said that they were the 'bulwarks of the Empire' (*propugnacula Imperii*).[14] It is also true that they constituted centres of Romanization, thus indirectly contributing to the pacification of the region in which they were situated. However, their real *raison d'etre* was economic – the exploitation of the soil.[15]

On the other side of the road both then and in the second century, during the period of 'forward defence', the Roman military were unceasingly active. The authorities thought it best to keep a watchful eye on the barbarians.[16] On a map, three successive zones can be distinguished: a sector of continuous military occupation; the territories brought under control; and the countries that remained defiantly independent. In the second zone the Romans carried out building operations, particularly roads that went deep into enemy territory. They also built towers, either as relay stations for couriers or for sending messages by a combination of torches.[17] Then there were outposts built by the engineers, at first of a temporary nature such as those Germanicus had built among the Ubii in the Cologne region,[18] and then permanent, like the series of forts in Tripolitania[19] and Numidia[20] under Septimius Severus.

This static organization served as a support for the mobile units. The roads were travelled regularly by messengers since the Romans attached much importance to information, whether oral or visual. Visual information could have many forms. A general used maps[20b] as well as the observations supplied by the watchmen in the towers; he also sent scouts, individually or in groups, far into enemy territory. He could also send out raiding parties; under Nero some Praetorians were sent up the Nile,[21] not the first time this had happened. In 174 a small expeditionary force went further than the Djebel Amour, a mountain situated well beyond civilian Africa.[22] Later on even major expeditions were launched, like the ones into the Sahara studied by J. Desanges.[23] But officers also used verbal information gleaned from their conversations with caravan drivers and their contacts among the native chiefs.

So there was a relatively wide defensive zone in which the frontier armies circulated. This strip included a central axis (a road) and other military constructions (secondary roads, fortresses, forts and towers), and backed on to a river or a 'linear defence'.

Terminology

We must now look at what the Romans themselves called this strip of land, particularly as contemporary historians have used several Latin words, often incorrectly, in their discussions.

The most important term, that of *limes*, has also been the most abused, and yet its precise meaning is clear today (see n. 1). In the beginning it designated a path, a road, or the line that separated one field from another. Very soon it took on a 'bidimensional' meaning (G. Forni) and can then be applied to a strip of land which contained a path and which had one or more uses. In legal language it was the space that divided two bits of land, or was necessary for an aqueduct; in a religious context it defined the space around a burial place; in military parlance it designated a space with a road or network of roads and some fortifications. But two points need making. Firstly, the military meaning appears only at a fairly late date, attested for the first time in 97. Secondly, the word does not define the actual defensive system as such in its entirety. It is normally used with an adjective or the genitive of a noun indicating its geographical limits.[24] In the first case (e.g. *limes tripolitanus*) we are dealing with a very limited part of a zone under the control of the army, a segment corresponding to a city, a tribe or a region. In the second case (e.g. *limes Rhaetiae*) this sector is extended to the dimensions of a province. We can thus talk of a Tripolitanian *limes* or the *limes* of Raetia, but should avoid speaking of *limes* alone, even though there are certain exceptions. In any case, it is important to remember that this military meaning is late in origin and not always attested by inscriptions or literary texts. It can be translated by the expression 'defensive system'.

In addition, within a given province it has been seen that security could be maintained by a series of interconnected organizations. In Africa for example the frontier protection was a complex affair with a central nucleus around the Aures, a few supplementary defences in the north of the military zone, particularly at Carthage, and 'linear defences' running from the mountain range, along the Numidian Sahara and covering Tripolitania.[25]

Other terms have been used.[26] One, *praetentura*, covers very diverse situations. Its strictest sense is found in the language of the *gromatici*, the land surveyors, when they were writing about camps. For them it was the part of the fortress between the *via principalis* and the *porta praetoria*, but it could also be used in the case of an outpost or a permanent fortress built in enemy territory.[27] Sometimes it means a road. Inscriptions mention that the emperors Septimius Severus and Caracalla 'gave orders for milestones to be set up along the new *praetentura*'.[28] Finally, its meaning could be very close to that of *limes*; another epigraphic document cites a man called Quintus Antistius Adventus Postumius Aquilinus who was 'imperial legate for the *praetentura* of Italy and the Alps during the campaign against the Germans' around 168.[29]

Since the frontier sometimes was a river it could be designated by the term *ripa*. This word was originally used for the river bank itself,[30] but later it came to mean the river bank defensive system of soldiers and fortifications.[31] In the third century the word became restricted like *limes* to a particular geographical usage. Thus a *dux ripae*, whose title is similar to that of the *dux limitis*, lived at Dura-Europos on the Euphrates.[32]

However, none of these terms (*limes*, *praetentura*, *ripa*) normally designated the whole defensive system of the Empire; their use was restricted to a geographical sector.

Linear defences

In the military zones the Romans sometimes built 'linear defences', long walls intended as much to hinder any barbarian infiltration as to indicate the legal limits of the Empire, the crossing of which would result in being called an enemy. They are also cultural and moral barriers that separate two civilizations.[33]

There is no need to repeat the discussion on *bracchia*, but special attention should be paid to some famous fortifications of this type found in Britain (Hadrian's Wall and the Antonine Wall), in Upper Germany, to the south of the Aures (Seguia bent El-Krass), and in Tingitanian Mauretania. The basic principle was very simple (pl.xxxi,30); an elementary fortification of the type discussed above, comprising a ditch, a bank and a rampart (pl.xxvi,19), was built over some distance.[34] The rampart could be made of soil or turf; it could be a wooden palisade or a brick or stone wall. Alongside it ran a track, a berm or one or more proper roads. This communication route was an essential part of linear defences and could be built behind or in front of the *vallum*. Towers and camps represent a no less important feature. As with an open *limes*, these could be built at a great distance from the road, either in Roman or enemy territory, but they could also be integrated more closely into the system, built against the rampart or straddling it.

Specialists have naturally questioned the effectiveness of these barriers, since they could probably be scaled by a large enemy band armed with rams and ladders, or the enemy could simply go around one of the ends. Perhaps this explains why the Romans did not surround their Empire with a gigantic 'Wall of China', which its engineers and soldiers would undoubtedly have been capable of building. In fact the Roman military authorities preferred a regular system of 'individual defences' to 'linear defences'.

'Individual defences': permanent camps

There is a fairly wide variety of Roman fortresses as the dictionary reveals. There are several words to designate enclosures of different sizes and different periods.

Latin fortification terms

Latin uses the term *munimenta* for several types of fortification,[36] but particularly for a simple rampart. The camp itself is *castra*, whatever its size, and there is no other term for a construction large enough to house a whole legion. Permanent fortresses are called 'winter camps' (*castra stativa*, *castra hiberna* or simply *hiberna*) to distinguish them from the 'summer camps' (*castra aestiva*) that were built at the end of every day during campaigns. These terms can be explained by the fact that Roman soldiers prepared for war in the cold seasons and embarked on campaigns when the weather got warmer.[37]

Various terms were used for smaller ramparts. A *castellum* was a small camp;[38] the word itself is a diminutive, but it is used in civil contexts to designate a small community that did not enjoy the status of *colonia* or *municipia*. It is therefore a legal definition in this case. The term *burgus* was also used in a non-military context to designate an association with some public rights, a small town on the way to becoming a municipality.

When used in conjunction with soldiers it could have several meanings, especially a tower (Latin *burgus* belongs to the same family as Greek *purgos*[39]), or a little *castellum*. What seems to be specific about this term is the implication of a function. In *burgus speculatorius* its function was to ensure the supervision and policing of roads,[41] and maintaining law and order in the villages.[42]

Statio is a term designating a small construction, similar to a *burgus*, without necessarily being fortified, but this term also has several meanings. We can omit one attested meaning, that of the police station in a large fortress, as it does not concern us here.[43] It seems to be used in the context of fighting banditry;[44] the soldiers sent to a *statio* were normally officers, especially *beneficiarii*. Furthermore, it contains some notion of permanence, the duration of the occupation of the site.[45] Sometimes it designates a garrison whose duty was ensuring security on the roads:[46] Aquileia, the home of some *beneficiarii*, was the starting point for numbering the milestones along the roads to Raetia, Noricum, Dalmatia and Pannonia. In Africa however, several of these posts were situated at long distances from the main roads,[47] and they were not the centres of administration in the imperial domains.

But this is not all. *Centenaria* are mentioned in inscriptions,[48] and the only thing we really know about these is that their name is based on *centum* (a hundred). It is hard to say what the hundred referred to, men or things, and of what sort. As far as is known, these camps were small and of late date; the oldest we know of was restored in 246, but was probably not built much earlier.[49] Perhaps Raetia provided the architectural model for this construction. The *praesidium* was another construction that was small in size. Strictly the word designated a garrison of men.[50] This meaning was maintained for a very long time, but then by metonymy the container was used for the thing contained, and so it came to designate the construction that housed the soldiers, a *castra* in the Early Empire and a *castellum* in the later period.

The smallest enclosure known to archaeologists has two names in Latin, *turris* and *burgus*.[51] Towers were isolated and fulfilled several functions, as observation posts, as information relays and as advance defences. They could also be a barrier when placed at the head of a valley or an additional fortification when situated between two camps. There was no set plan in their construction. The majority are rectangular or square, but some are trapezoidal or circular. The variety is not accidental; nothing military was left to the whims of architects. Square towers had the advantage of being the quickest to build, but the drawback of being less resistant to the impact of battering rams and stone balls than circular towers were. The latter were stronger, but more difficult to build.

Permanent camps: layout

To understand how the space inside a *castra* was organized it is necessary to study a fortress big enough to house a legion, as a maximum of constructions can be found there (pl.XXXII). The first rule to observe is not to oversimplify. There was no model that was repeated exactly every time a camp was built; it was not like a prefabricated house. Moreover, as J. Lander has shown (see n.53), changes did not occur at the same speed throughout the Empire. Nevertheless, certain broad outlines and permanent features can be picked out.

The first problem for the officers and the *metator* was to ensure the choice of a suitable site. They had to follow the same principles as when building a *castra aestiva*, choosing an easily defendable site with no danger spots above; it should have a slope to facilitate aeration and the drainage of dirty water and to give the right impetus to a sortie in case of siege. They should also make sure that there was an adequate water supply on the site, again in case of siege.

At the time of Hadrian, Arrian described one of these permanent camps when on his tour of inspection around the Black Sea:[52]

> The fort, situated at the mouth of the Phasis, houses four hundred elite soldiers. In view of the lie of the land it seemed to me to be very strong and well able to protect ships navigating on this side of the river. There are wide ditches on either side of the wall. In the past this wall was made of earth and had wooden towers on top of it, but now everything is made of brick. The foundations are solid. Machines have been placed on the wall, so now the position has everything necessary to prevent barbarians from approaching it or endangering the life of our soldiers by a siege. But since it was also essential to make the ships in the harbour safe, as well as the area outside the fort which is inhabited by men who have retired from active service and by merchants, I thought it preferable to dig another ditch, going from the double ditch to the river, to encompass the harbour and the houses outside the wall.

The rampart was the most important part of the fort.[53] It was built in a similar fashion to that of the temporary camps and linear defences, with its *fossa*, *agger* and *vallum* (pl.XXVI,19), and a wide empty space (*intervallum*) behind the wall. Nevertheless, there are some differences. As already noted, there were two or even three ditches, but the most interesting feature is the wall. In the first century it had an irregular quadrilateral profile (pl.XXXIV,32), but a rectangular one afterwards. This change reflects the change in the materials used. In the Julio-Claudian period it was built of earth, turves and wood; from 69 onwards, the Flavian era, generals realized that the defensive systems were to be permanent and consequently demolished the earlier walls and rebuilt them in brick and stone with earth buttresses. The width varied between 2 and 3m ($6\frac{1}{2}$ and 12ft). In the Late Empire, instead of obtaining materials from brickmakers and quarrymen, builders cannibalized other constructions, such as ruined monuments, old statues, altars and tombs, in order to incorporate these bits and pieces in their new ramparts. On top of the walls there were battlements (*propugnacula*) of various shapes and sizes: rectangular with a central loophole, or T-shaped.

Seen in a plan, the enclosure was usually a rectangle with rounded corners. When speaking of temporary camps in the Republican era Polybius remarked on the Roman preference for the square, but in the Early Empire the situation changed. At the beginning of the second century Pseudo-Hyginus recommended a length/width ratio of 3:2 for temporary camps. However, permanent camps built around the same time seem to obey different principles, with the result that at El-Kasbat (*Gemellae*) the ratio is 5:4 and at Lambaesis 6:5. In the fourth century Vegetius based his recommendations of a 4:3 ratio on earlier constructions. Nevertheless, in the first century camps were normally rectangular, very occasionally square. In the Late Empire virtually any shape, even circular, was possible. This period also saw the disappearance of the *intervallum* and the construction of buildings against the wall. These are categorized as 'having outlying barracks'.

The enclosure usually had four gates,[54] which were built with great care as they represented a weak spot during an assault (in urban walls of the Julio-Claudian era they were of the *clavicula* type). From Vespasian onwards they were set in the wall itself, with towers built on each side to strengthen the position. At first these towers were simply square or rectangular, but from Marcus Aurelius' reign onwards we find various shapes, some pentagonal, some rounded on one side.

In fact the towers,[55] together with their accompanying bastions, represent an important element of the rampart, not least for their role as supports for artillery pieces. According to J. Lander (see n.53) the first external corner towers made their appearance after the Marcomannic wars, but their use did not become widespread until well into the third century. It is useful to repeat what has already been said: the circular plan has the advantage of strength but the disadvantage of difficulty of construction, while the square plan was quicker to build but weaker. In the Early Empire the external façade of the wall was often flat; and constructions added to it were on the inside. In the second century the walls were flanked by bastions in the corners and in between. In the third century the rectangle was the most common form, with the semicircle appearing after 250. In the Late Empire, however, any additions made to the rampart were on the outside. Although the fortresses with square bastions are called 'tetrarchic' from the name of the political system set up by Diocletian, they probably made their appearance in an earlier period, during the great crisis of the third century. In the fourth century a surprising diversity of rectangles, circles and semicircles co-existed side by side, their presence governed by the circumstances that prevailed when the camp was built.

But architects did not start by building the rampart. Their first task was to organize the space within the fortress. They started with the *groma* (pl.xxvii,23), the instrument made up of four plumb-lines to enable them to position the roads at right angles. The spot on which it was placed was so important that at Lambaesis it was marked with a four-sided triumphal arch.[56] The camp was divided into three sections by two roads, with the *via principalis* separating the *praetentura* from the sides of the *principia* (see below); the *quintana* ran between the sides of the *principia* and the *retentura*. The *groma* marked the intersection of the *via principalis* and the *via praetoria*, which led to the nearest gate.

In the permanent camps built in the Early Empire the central part was occupied by the *principia*, often wrongly called the *praetorium*.[57] It consisted of a group of buildings that was the heart of the camp. When the camp covered more than 20 ha (50 acres) these buildings occupied two successive courts, of which the second, smaller one was converted into a basilica in the second half of the third century by building two rows of columns and covering it with a roof. At the far end was a chapel that housed the standards (*aedes signorum*), normally a single room which was occasionally made to look like a small temple built on a podium.[58] From the second century onwards a vault was built under this room to house the unit's funds and the deposits that soldiers had to pay on joining the army and which they would recover on retirement. Also at that end was a series of premises, fitted with apses from the time of Septimius Severus (with a wall that formed an arc), to which the name of *scholae* was given.[59] These were meeting places for colleges of officers that were recognized by Septimius Severus, and consequently are not earlier than the beginning of the third century. Other rooms were offices (*tabularium legionis, tabularium principis*, etc.). At Bu Njem in Libya, a two-sided sloping desk has been found.[60] The armories (*armentaria*) were situated on the sides of the first area.[61] Finally, a platform (*tribunal*) was built to enable the garrison's highest-ranking officer to address the troops; the ritual of the *adlocutio*, the speech to the soldiers, played a large role in Roman culture. It should be noted, however, that in some camps built in the fourth century the architects had sited the *principia* at the far end, against the wall.

The *principia* never took up the majority of the space inside a camp, which was always used for housing the men. Officers lived in proper houses, comprising several rooms around a central courtyard, on the opposite side of the *via principalis* to the *principia*. The largest residence was that of the commander-in-chief, an imperial propraetorian legate in the case of a camp housing a legion, and the term *praetorium* should be used for this building only in this situation. Centurions and officers had less privacy and lived in barracks, normally two series of rooms on either side of a courtyard, with the larger end rooms reserved for the centurions. According to H. von Petrikovits (see n. 53) some officers were perhaps slightly better housed; these would be the *immunes*, the *principales*, the artillery and cavalry officers. Other, less comfortable premises were reserved for the few auxiliaries allowed within the enclosure and for the domestic staff.[62]

With almost 5000 men, a legionary camp was the equivalent of a town. Consequently everything that was essential for the daily life of such a community – hospital, stores, workshops, baths, as well as public lavatories – was to be found.

We have a fair knowledge of military hospitals (*valetudinaria*). The one at *Vetera* (Xanten on the Rhine) gives a good idea of the architecture of these buildings.[63] It was square, 83.5m (270ft) long after rebuilding, with two rows of rooms on three sides, in a 'U' formation, separated by a central corridor. It could house two hundred sick or wounded at a time. In the middle was a courtyard 40.2m (130ft) square which could be reached from a hall. Even the doctor's room and the pharmacy have been identified. Other hospitals that have been studied, such as those at Haltern, Lotschitz, Altenberg (*Carnuntum*) and Neuss (*Novaesium*), sometimes have a rectangular form.

Those buildings that had an economic function occupied a larger space. Each legion had a workshop (*fabrica*)[64] to supply some of its weapons and the bricks (often stamped). Normally this building was divided in two, with one part set aside for the production rooms that formed a U-shape around a small courtyard, the other for stores to house the manufactured articles.

Warehouses were particularly necessary for keeping food, oil, wine and wheat, as not only everyday needs had to be met, but also supplies had to be abundant in case of siege. Granaries (*horrea*) posed two difficult construction problems.[65] The walls were subjected to very strong pressures from the grain, which behaved like a liquid, and the floors had to be kept dry to prevent it rotting. A drainage system was provided for each room, while the walls were built thick and then buttressed. They were built of wood at the end of the first century, but soon afterwards of stone. Generally they measured between 20–30m (65–100ft) long and 6–10m (20–33ft) wide. According to G. Rickman (see n. 65) there were four main types of *horrea*: single; double; paired; or end-to-end. Excavations have revealed the existence of regional differences. In Britain there were long, narrow rooms set around a central courtyard; in Germany millstones with their owners' names on ('century of C. Rufus', 'century of Vireius') indicate that each century had to grind its own corn supply.

Provision of water had also to be assured. Pipes, some of which ran underground, connected the camp to the nearest source of water, which was stored in tanks in case of any surprise attack. Its value was not restricted to drinking, as Roman concerns for hygiene meant that they needed huge quantites, and the problem was particularly pressing in desert regions. Legionaries bathed regularly, so in each camp there were *thermae*,[66] the only leisure facility in any camp, though even here the medicinal qualities were probably rated higher than the recreational. The baths that have been excavated in military constructions do not appear to have differed from civilian ones. There

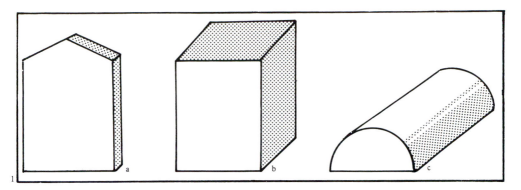

1. Funerary monuments. a) stela; b) altar; c) cupula: the three main types of funerary monument. Each tomb normally had an inscription and in addition there might be some form of decoration on the stone, reliefs or acroteria, etc. Chronological differences can be established: the stela was the earliest form, followed by the altar and then the cupula.

2a

2. Funerary reliefs. a) Bust of the deceased (unpublished drawing from the Bibliothèque de la Sorbonne); b) horseman charging (Tipasa Museum).

2b

2c

2. Funerary reliefs. c) Full-length portrait of the deceased (Cherchel Museum).

3. Haïdra and its military cemeteries. The cemeteries form a circle around the city, with the soldiers' tombs lining the roads leaving the camp. (Drawing based on F. Baratte and N. Duval, *Les ruines d'Ammaedara-Haïdra*, 1974.)

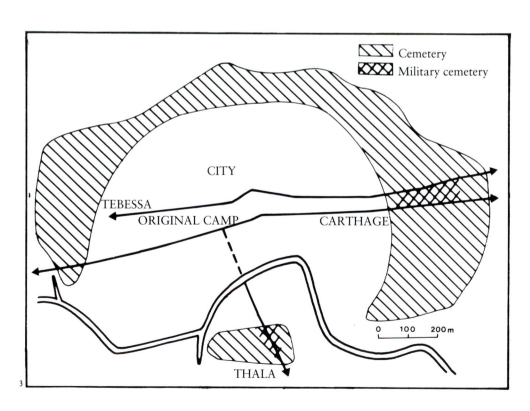

3

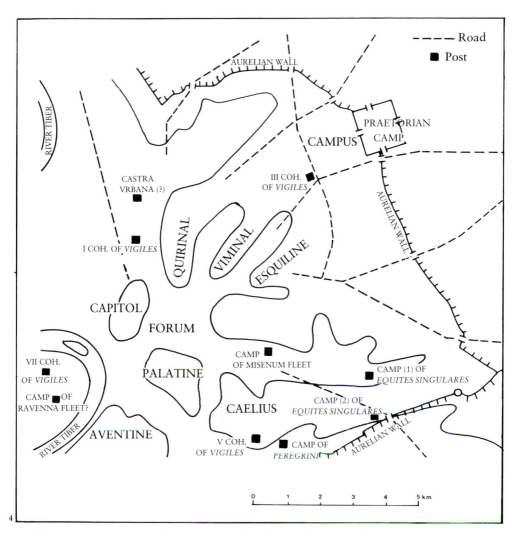

4. The garrison at Rome. The city was both policed and protected by the *castra praetoria*; smaller posts were eventually established throughout the city. (Drawing based on M. Durry, *Les cohortes prétoriennes*, 1968.)

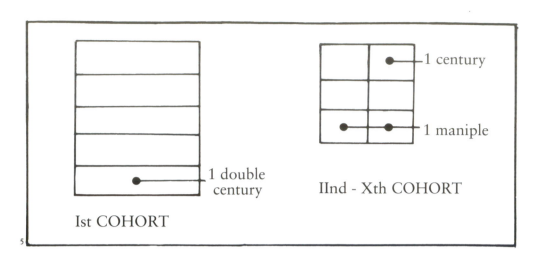

1 century

1 maniple

1 double
century

IInd - Xth COHORT

Ist COHORT

5

6

5. Organization of a legion. For administrative purposes a legion was divided into ten cohorts, each of which was subdivided into three maniples or six centuries. However, the first cohort contained only five centuries but with twice the number of men.

6. Auxiliary cavalryman charging. This cavalryman from an auxiliary cohort is killing an enemy on the ground with a lance almost 2m (6ft) long. He has a short sword on his right side and a coat of mail. (Algiers Museum.)

7

8

7. Eagle-bearer *(aquilifer)*. The sculptures on this panel from the Antonine Wall in Britain are in the form of an arch. In the centre a female figure who may personify Britain faces a soldier holding the eagle of his legion, the *XX Valeria Victrix*. He is wearing a tunic and short coat, with a dagger at his side. Each of the flanking panels contains a defeated barbarian. Underneath is the legion's emblem, a boar (Hutcheson Hill, Scotland). (Based on A.S. Robertson and M.E. Scott, *The Roman Collections in the Hunterian Museum*.)

8. Standard-bearer *(signifer)*. This funerary relief from Mainz, where the *Legio XIV Gemina* was stationed under the Flavians, shows a soldier wearing a corselet, sword and dagger. The *signum* is to his right, a spear shaft with six bossed disks. It has a lance point at its upper and a goat head at its lower extremity. (Mainz. Based on A. von Domaszewski, *Aufsätze sur römischen Heeresgeschichte*, 1972.)

9

9. Cavalry standards *(vexilla)*. Detail from the base of the column of Antoninus Pius at Rome (160-1), showing the mounted procession following the emperor's body (Vatican Museum). (Photo De Antonis, Rome.)

10. Music and religion. a) Music accompanied the purification of the camp as seen here on Trajan's Column. (Photo German Archaeological Institute.) b) Two *cornicines*: the one on the left is from Trajan's Column, the one on the right from a funerary relief from the *praetorium*. (Based on A. von Domaszewski, *Aufsatze*.)

10b

11

11. The *adlocutio* ceremony. This coin shows the emperor addressing his troops from a podium.

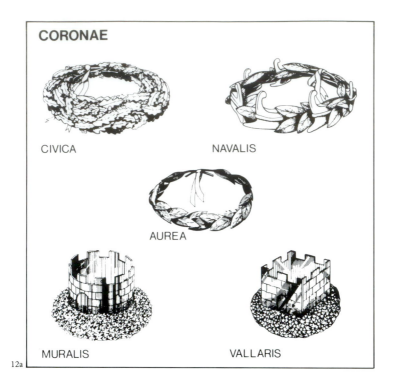

CORONAE

CIVICA

NAVALIS

AUREA

MURALIS

VALLARIS

12a

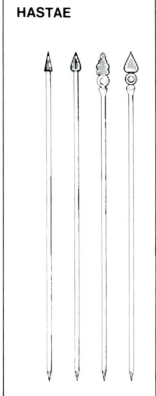

HASTAE

12b

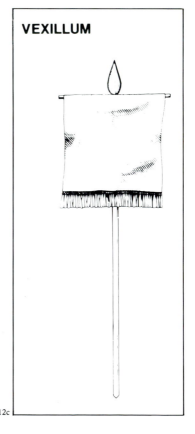

VEXILLUM

12c

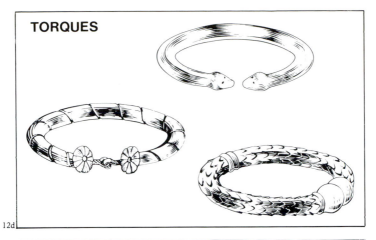

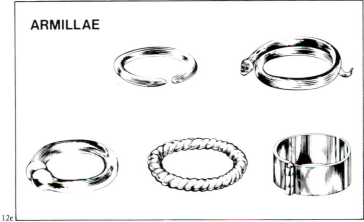

12. Decorations. a) Crowns; b) lances; c) standard; d) torques; e) armbands. Soldiers and officers were rewarded for bravery or for simply having taken part in a campaign. The decorations could be held at the same time since they were conferred in different circumstances.

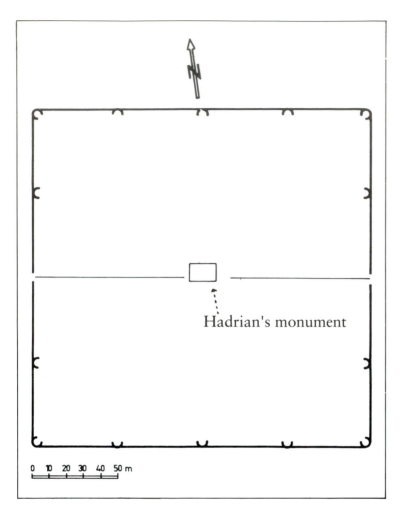

Hadrian's monument

0 10 20 30 40 50 m

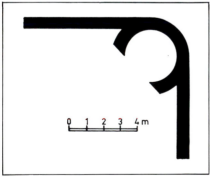

0 1 2 3 4 m

13. The training-ground at Lambaesis. This exercise-ground comprised a mud floor space surrounded by four thin walls with two openings. A podium was erected in the centre. (Based on *Cahiers du groupe de recherche sur l'armée romaine et les provinces*, I, 1977.)

14. Trajan's Column. (Drawings by S. Reinach, *Répertoire de reliefs grecs et romains.*
Text based on F. Coarelli, *Guida archeologica di Roma*, 1974.)
1-58: Trajan's first war against the Dacians:
       1-23: first campaign;
       24-33: second campaign;
       34-58: third campaign.
59-114: Trajan's second war against the Dacians:
       59-75: fourth campaign;
       76-114: fifth campaign.

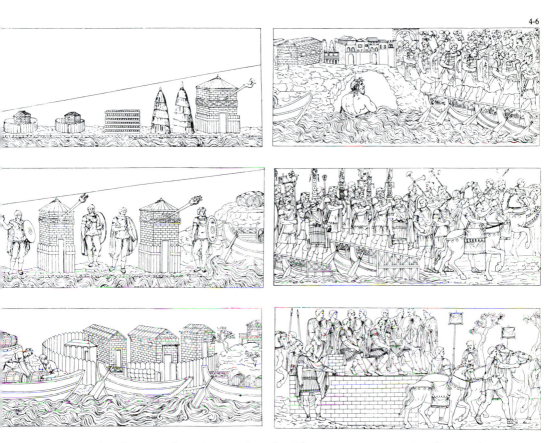

4-6

1, 2, 3 Roman fortifications along the Danube. *4, 5* The Roman army crossing the Danube on a bridge of boats. *6* Trajan's first council of war.

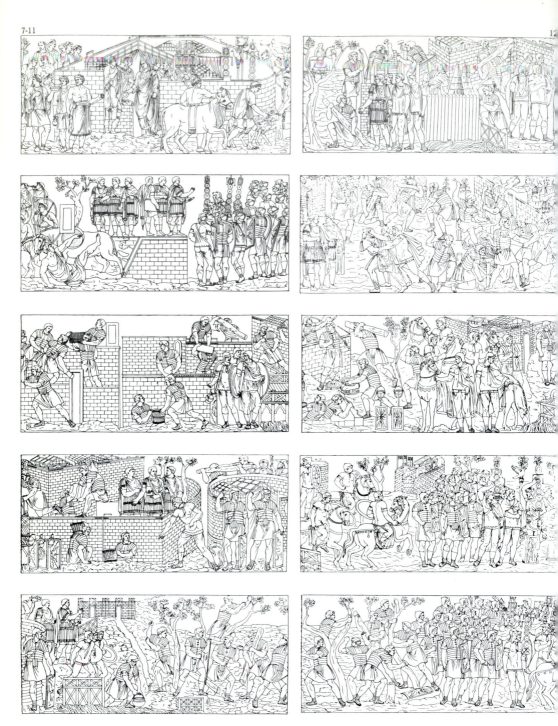

7 Sacrifice and purification before occupation of a new camp. 8 Trajan addresses the troops.
9 Construction of a camp. 10 Trajan inspects the construction work. 11-12 Soldiers cutting
down trees for another camp. 13 An enemy spy is brought before the emperor while soldiers
build a bridge and a small fort. 14 The cavalry about to ride out. 15 The cavalry and infantry
about to leave. 16 The army marching through a wood.

17-18 First military engagement with the Dacians. *19* The Romans burning Dacian homes as the inhabitants flee. *20* The Dacian ambassadors received by the emperor. *21* Trajan with prisoners. *22* Dacian cavalrymen drowning as they try to cross a river; Dacian attack on Roman camp. *23* Another detail of the same scene. *24* Transport of provisions by boat. *25* Trajan embarks. *26* The emperor at the head of the cavalry charging the enemy cataphracts.

27 The emperor at the head of the cavalry charging the enemy cataphracts. 28 Continuation of the battle; submission of the old men, women and children. 29 Construction of a camp in the presence of the emperor; torture of enemy prisoners; treatment of Roman wounded. 30 Departure of army and new battle. 31 Dacians flee. 32 The emperor addresses soldiers; Dacian prisoners in a fortress. 33 The army pays homage to the emperor; Roman prisoners tortured by women; barbarian chiefs submit to Trajan. 34 The Roman army crossing the Danube. 35 Trajan with a group of soldiers in front of a camp. 36 Another scene of the emperor with soldiers; cutting down trees to build a camp.

37 Purification of a camp. 38 Trajan addresses his troops. 39 The Roman army advancing through a forest between enemy fortifications. 40 The emperor crosses a river by a bridge; burning of enemy fortifications. 41 Construction of a camp; surrender of a barbarian chief. 42 Convoys making for a camp. 43 The emperor present at charge of Numidian cavalry. 44 Dacians routed in a forest. 45 Construction of a camp; surrender of Dacian chiefs to Trajan. 46 Battle in front of the Roman fortifications.

47 Dacians cutting down trees to build fortifications. 48 The Romans building a camp.
49-50 The Dacians driven back inside their fortifications; Romans using 'tortoise' technique
for protection. 51 Trajan receiving the heads of two Dacian chiefs. 52 New battle. 53 Trajan
inspects building of a camp. 54-55 Surrender of King Decebalus and other Dacian chiefs to
Trajan. 56 The Dacians destroying their fortifications.

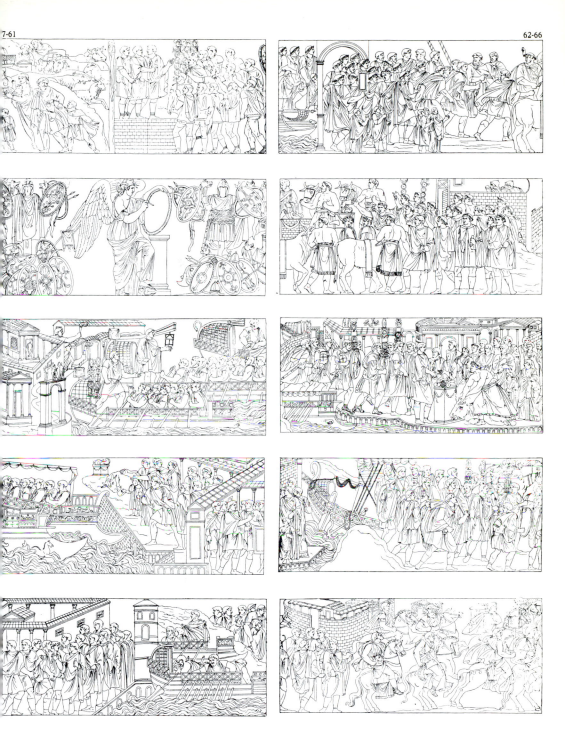

57 Departure of old men, women and children with the animals; last speech of Trajan to
his troops. 58 Victory writing on a shield between two trophies. 59 Ships leaving Ancona;
beginning of the second Dacian war (spring 105). 60 Arrival in an Italian harbour?
61, 62, 63 Triumphal entry of the emperor and ritual sacrifice. 64 Entry into another city;
another sacrifice. 65-66 Disembarkation (on the Dalmatian coast?) and start of Roman
army's march.

67-68 Surrender of a city and ritual sacrifice on altars. 69 Cutting down of trees to build a camp. 70 Dacians take refuge in a fortress. 71 The Dacians' unsuccessful attack on a Roman fortress. 72 Another Dacian attack. 73 Trajan arrives at the head of his cavalry. 74 The emperor sacrificing against a backdrop of a great bridge over the Danube built by Apollodorus of Damascus. 75 Trajan accepts the surrender of barbarian chiefs in a Roman city with amphitheatre. 76 The Roman army crossing a river.

77 Sacrifice. 78-79 Sacrifice and purification of a camp; speech to troops. 80-81 Departure of the Roman army and arrival in a camp. 82-83 Soldiers foraging. 84 Dacians talking in a fortress. 85 Battle. 86 Assault on Sarmizegethusa; the emperor's council of war.

87 Assault on Sarmizegethusa; the emperor's council of war. 88-89 Continuation of assault with siege machines. 90 The Romans build wooden palisades. 91 Dacian chief comes to Trajan as an ambassador. 92 The Dacians set fire to Sarmizegethusa to prevent it falling into Roman hands. 93 Dacian chiefs take poison. 94 Flight of the Dacians. 95 Surrender of the Dacians to Trajan. 96 The Romans occupy Sarmizegethusa.

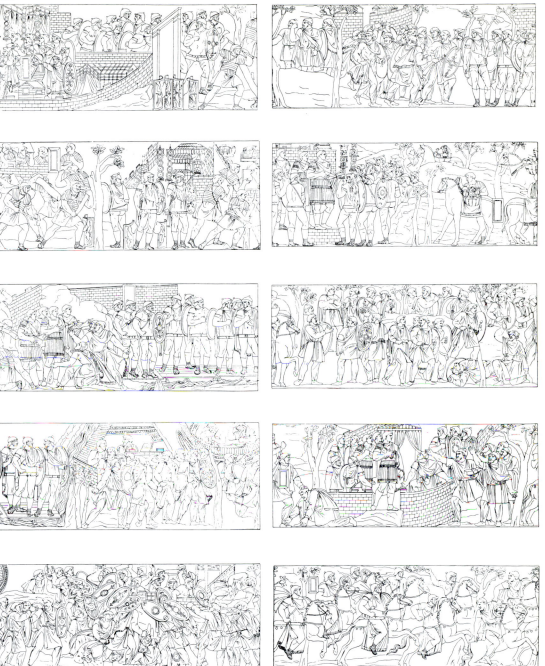

97 The Romans occupy Sarmizegethusa. 98 Construction of a camp. 99 Surrender of Dacian chiefs to Trajan. 100 Crossing a river; the Dacians abandon a fortress. 101 The Dacians under the leadership of Decebalus attack a Roman camp. 102 Defeated Dacians flee. 103 Trajan's speech to the troops; the Dacian treasure is carried off on mules. 104 Flight of the Dacians; suicide of some of their chiefs. 105 Surrender of the Dacians to Trajan. 106 Roman cavalry in pursuit of Decebalus and the last of the Dacians to remain faithful to him.

107 Roman cavalry in pursuit of Decebalus and the last of the Dacians to remain faithful to him. 108 Death of Decebalus when caught by the Romans. 109 Capture of Decebalus' sons; the king's head is brought into the Roman camp. 110 Capture of more Dacians. 111 Fall of the last Dacian stronghold and assault on a city. 112 The city is set on fire. 113-114 Deportation of old men, women and children.

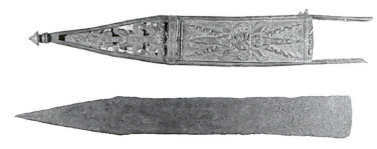

15a

15. Weaponry.
a) Sword and scabbard (early first century AD) (Strasbourg Museum).
b) Legionary saluting (early first century AD). Note the corselet, helmet and shield (terracotta figure, Strasbourg Museum).
c) Deceased legionary (beginning of Early Empire) with sword at his right side (Strasbourg Museum). (Photos Musée Archéologique de Strasbourg.)

15c

15b

16a

16. Auxiliaries and legionaries. a) Auxiliaries (early second century AD). Depicted on this bas-relief are the famous Mauretanian cavalrymen under Lusius Quietus. (Photo P.M. Monti. Cf. also figs 2b and 2c and fig. 6.)

16b

16. Auxiliaries and legionaries.
b) Legionary (early second century AD).
(Trajan's column; Photo P.M. Monti.)

17. A legionary (late second
century AD). This legionary probably
died in action in Pannonia. Here he is
represented in a victory scene
(Archaeological Museum, Budapest;
from cast in Rome; Photo Alinari.)

C·SEPTIMO OPT·LEG·I·
DESIDERATVS·EST

17

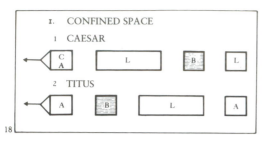

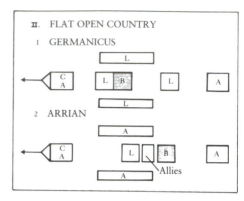

18. **The Roman army on the march.**
A: auxiliaries; B: baggage; C: cavalry;
L: legionaries.
I. Confined space
1. Caesar (*Gallic War* II, 19, 2-3).
2. Titus' army in Samaria. (Josephus, *Jewish War* V, 2, 1 (47-49).

18. II. Flat, open country.
1. Roman army in Germany at the beginning of Tiberius' reign. (Tacitus, *Annals* I, 51, 5-6.)
2. Arrian (*Alans*).

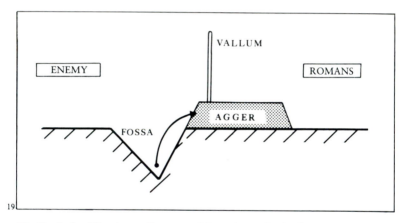

19. **Basic fortifications.** Roman soldiers dug a ditch (*fossa*) and used the earth from it to make a mound (*agger*), with possibly a palisade on top, the whole forming a *vallum*.

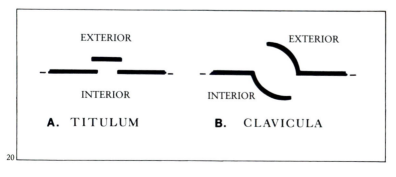

20. **Gates of Roman marching camps.**
a) *Titulum*
b) *Clavicula*
For these temporary camps only a simple obstacle was necessary in case of enemy attack, a small wall (*titulum*) in front of the opening or an arc-shaped extension of the two ends of the wall (*clavicula*).

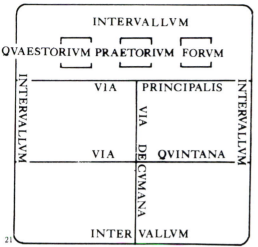

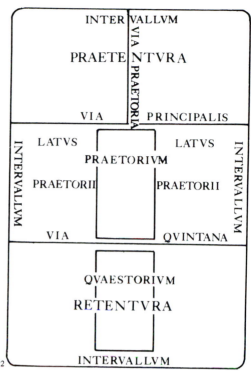

21. A temporary camp (Polybius). In the middle of the second century BC (i.e. Republic) the Greek writer Polybius enthused over a temporary camp (VI, 27-42) consisting of ramparts with an open space (*intervallum*) alongside forming an almost perfect square; in the centre along with the living quarters was a *forum*, the general's quarters (*praetorium*). Roads intersected at right angles.

22. A temporary camp (Pseudo-Hyginus). An anonymous treatise, wrongly attributed to Hyginus, in describing a temporary Roman camp at the beginning of the second century AD shows how it had evolved in the intervening period. The ground plan is now rectangular and is divided into four sectors: *praetentura* in front of the *praetorium*, *latus praetorii* on each side and the *retentura* behind. The *intervallum* still runs alongside the rampart, and the roads still intersect at right angles.

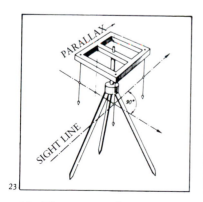

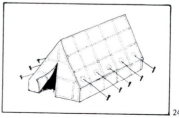

23. The groma. This was an instrument used for marking out the camp in right angles. (Drawing by F. Kretzschmer, *La technique romaine*, 1966 from a *groma* in the Saalburg.)

24. A tent. Bar Hill camp in Scotland yielded a remarkable quantity of leather, including fragments of tents. (Based on A.S. Robertson and M.E. Scott, *The Roman Collections in the Hunterian Museum*.)

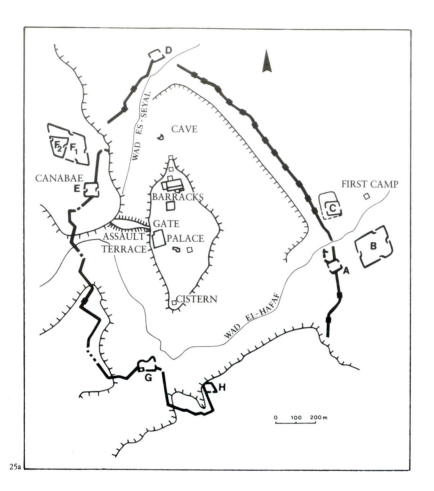

25a

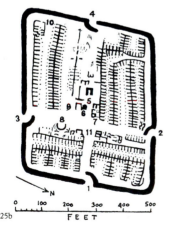

25b

25. The siege of Masada. a) General view. In order to isolate the Jews who had fled to the citadel of Masada in AD 72 Flavius Silva built eight small forts and a linear defence. In addition the Romans had to construct an assault platform to reach the citadel. b) Detail of camp B. *1* Praetorian gate. *2* Principal gate (right). *3* Principal gate (left). *4 Porta decumana. 5 Principia* (to be preferred to *praetorium*). *6* Podium. *7 Auguratorium. 8 Schola* (?). *9* Standards. *10* Hospital (?). *11* Officers' quarters. (Based on C. Hawkes, *Antiquity* III, 1929.)

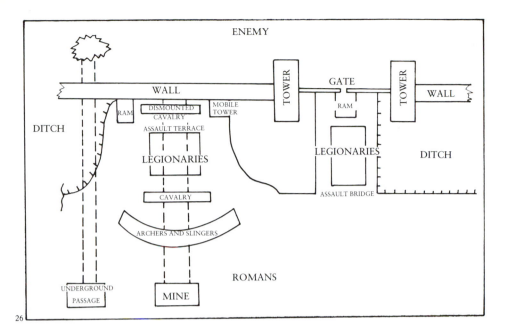

ENEMY

WALL | TOWER | GATE | TOWER | WALL

RAM | DISMOUNTED CAVALRY | MOBILE TOWER

RAM

DITCH | ASSAULT TERRACE | LEGIONARIES | DITCH

LEGIONARIES

CAVALRY

ASSAULT BRIDGE

ARCHERS AND SLINGERS

ROMANS

UNDERGROUND PASSAGE | MINE

26

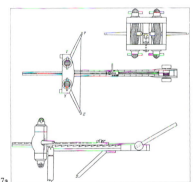

27a

26. An assault on a besieged city. To storm a besieged city the Roman general had several options open to him. He could use a ram on the gate, the weakest spot in the defences, after building an assault bridge if there was a ditch. Confronted by a huge wall he could build an assault platform, dig a mine into which the wall would collapse or else dig a tunnel underneath the wall.

27. Artillery pieces. a) This machine was used for firing arrows. Viewed frontally, from above and from the side. b) This machine fired stones. (E.W. Marsden, *Greek and Roman Artillery*, 1971.)

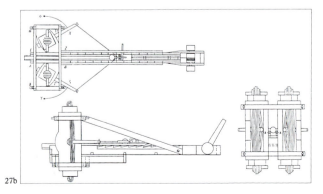

27b

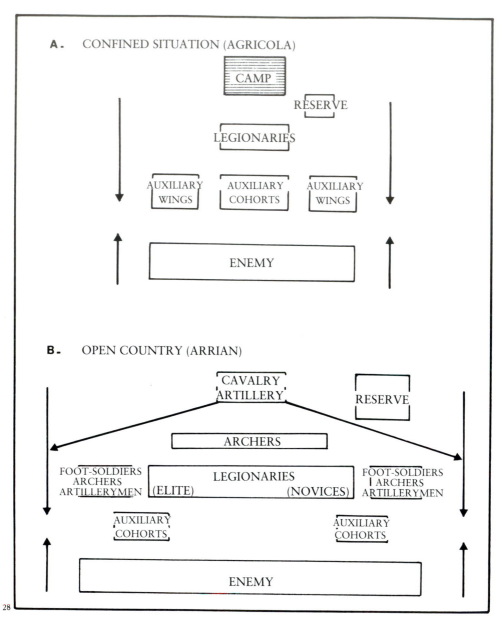

A. CONFINED SITUATION (AGRICOLA)

CAMP

RESERVE

LEGIONARIES

AUXILIARY WINGS   AUXILIARY COHORTS   AUXILIARY WINGS

ENEMY

B. OPEN COUNTRY (ARRIAN)

CAVALRY ARTILLERY   RESERVE

ARCHERS

FOOT-SOLDIERS ARCHERS ARTILLERYMEN   LEGIONARIES (ELITE)   (NOVICES)   FOOT-SOLDIERS ARCHERS ARTILLERYMEN

AUXILIARY COHORTS   AUXILIARY COHORTS

ENEMY

28. Battle formation. a) Initial battle formation of Agricola in a confined situation: the auxiliaries in front of the legionaries, who were themselves in front of the camp. Reserve force stationed near the camp. b) Arrian's initial battle formation in open country. With more space at his disposal than Agricola had, Arrian could spread his legionaries wider and put the auxiliaries on the flanks. Artillery and archers were placed behind and on the sides.

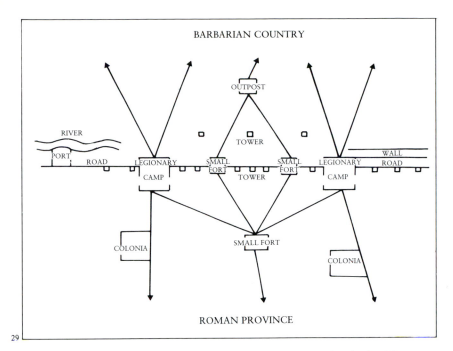

29. Defensive organization: theoretical structure. The road is the backbone of what is customarily called 'limes'. It runs alongside fortresses, small forts and towers, flanked either by a river or a linear defence. It is joined by other roads coming from Roman territory or going out into barbarian country, where outposts and watchtowers were set up.

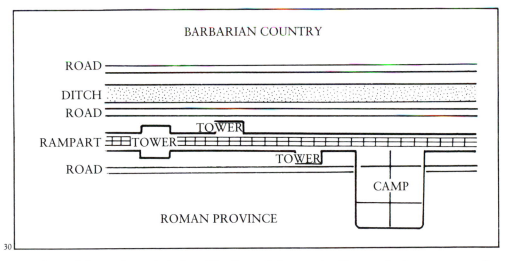

30. Linear defence: theoretical plan. The linear defence or 'wall' comprised a stone or earth rampart with towers and small forts set in it. Alongside it ran up to three roads and a ditch (see figs 19 and 34).

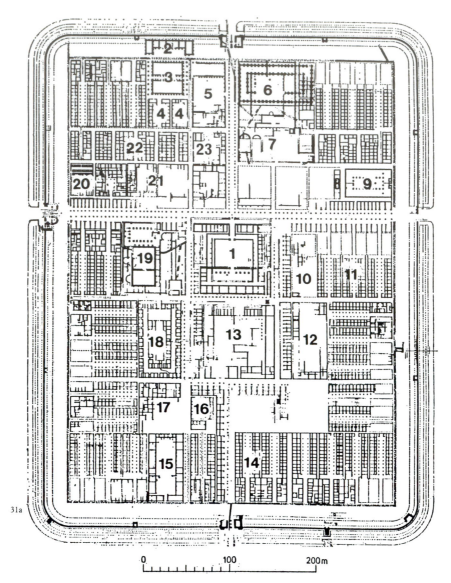

31. Camps. a) *Novaesium* (Neuss): legionary camp. *1 Principia.*
2 Workshop. *3* Granaries. *4* Quarters of *immunes. 5* Shop. *6* Shop.
7 Baths. *8* Quarters of *immunes. 9 Scholae* (?) of the 1st cohort. *10* Quarters
of *immunes. 11* 1st cohort's barracks. *12* Shop. *13 Praetorium. 14* Barracks
of a century. *15* Shop. *16* Quarters of *immunes. 17* Shop. *18* Hospital.
19 Baths. *20* Barracks. *21* Officers' quarters. *22* Auxiliary unit's quarters.
23 Auxiliary unit's quarters. *23* Auxiliary unit commander's headquarters.
(Based on H. von Petrikovits, *Die Innenbauten römischer Legionslager*, 1975.)

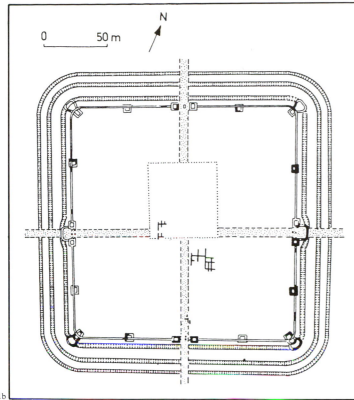

31. Camps.
b) *Campona*
(Nagytetény). This
ala camp, measuring
178 x 200m (580 x
660ft) was probably
built in the time of
Domitian for the
ala I Tungrorum. It
was occupied by the
ala I Thracum at the
beginning of the
second century and
was still being used at
the end of the fourth
century. (After J. Fitz,
*Der römische limes in
Ungarn,* 1976.)

31b

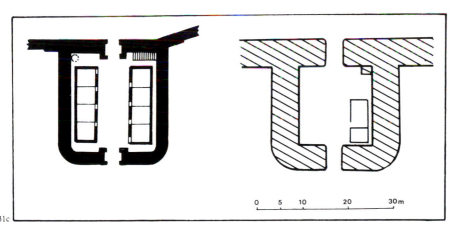

31c

31. Camps. c) (left) Poltross Burn: milecastle. Along the length of Hadrian's Wall
are small forts approximately one mile apart (hence their name). This one measures
less than 24 x 27m (80 x 90ft). That on the right is milecastle 50 (High House).
(D.J. Breeze and B. Dobson, *Hadrian's Wall,* 1976.)

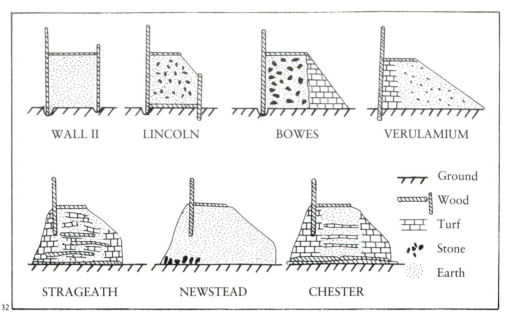

WALL II   LINCOLN   BOWES   VERULAMIUM

Ground

Wood

Turf

Stone

Earth

STRAGEATH   NEWSTEAD   CHESTER

32. Rampart sections. All these ramparts were built before the reign of Hadrian. (M.J. Jones, *Roman Fort-Defences*, 1975.)

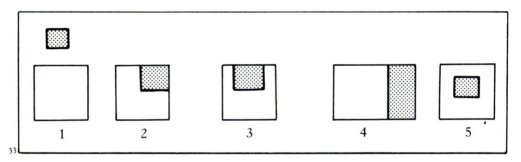

1   2   3   4   5

33. Camps: surface-area changes. There were several ways to increase or decrease the size of a camp to accommodate a different type of unit: building a new enclosure outside the original camp or inside it (2-5).

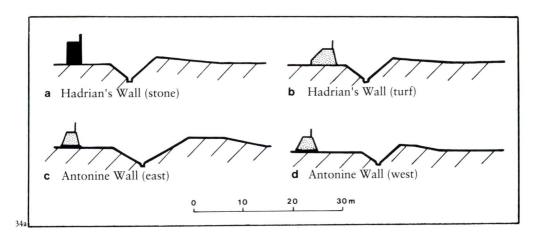

a Hadrian's Wall (stone) b Hadrian's Wall (turf)

c Antonine Wall (east) d Antonine Wall (west)

0   10   20   30 m

34a

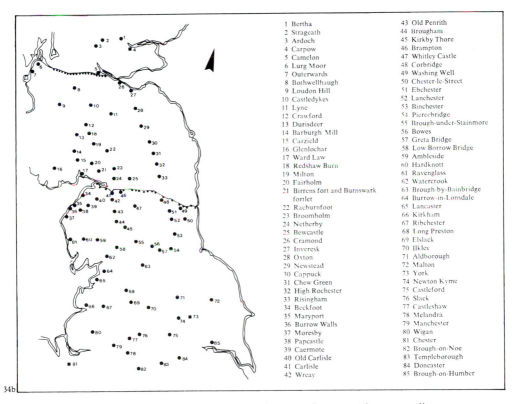

1 Bertha	43 Old Penrith
2 Strageath	44 Brougham
3 Ardoch	45 Kirkby Thore
4 Carpow	46 Brampton
5 Camelon	47 Whitley Castle
6 Lurg Moor	48 Corbridge
7 Outerwards	49 Washing Well
8 Bothwellhaugh	50 Chester-le-Street
9 Loudon Hill	51 Ebchester
10 Castledykes	52 Lanchester
11 Lyne	53 Binchester
12 Crawford	54 Piercebridge
13 Durisdeer	55 Brough-under-Stainmore
14 Barburgh Mill	56 Bowes
15 Carzield	57 Greta Bridge
16 Glenlochar	58 Low Borrow Bridge
17 Ward Law	59 Ambleside
18 Redshaw Burn	60 Hardknott
19 Milton	61 Ravenglass
20 Fairholm	62 Watercrook
21 Birrens fort and Burnswark fortlet	63 Brough-by-Bainbridge
	64 Burrow-in-Lonsdale
22 Raeburnfoot	65 Lancaster
23 Broomholm	66 Kirkham
24 Netherby	67 Ribchester
25 Bewcastle	68 Long Preston
26 Cramond	69 Elslack
27 Inveresk	70 Ilkley
28 Oxton	71 Aldborough
29 Newstead	72 Malton
30 Cappuck	73 York
31 Chew Green	74 Newton Kyme
32 High Rochester	75 Castleford
33 Risingham	76 Slack
34 Beckfoot	77 Castleshaw
35 Maryport	78 Melandra
36 Burrow Walls	79 Manchester
37 Moresby	80 Wigan
38 Papcastle	81 Chester
39 Caermote	82 Brough-on-Noe
40 Old Carlisle	83 Templeborough
41 Carlisle	84 Doncaster
42 Wreay	85 Brough-on-Humber

34b

34. Roman walls in Britain. a) Sections on scale 1:432. b) Map. The two walls were protected by towers and forts of differing sizes. Many other individual defence posts can be seen south of the walls and even to the north. (D.J. Breeze and B. Dobson, *Hadrian's Wall*, 1976.)

35. **Coin of Clodius Macer.** This coin was intended to encourage the allegiance of the African legion to the usurper Clodius Macer. Soldiers received well-minted silver coins while the unit was given the honorific title of *liberatrix* to mark its role in the ending of tyranny. (H. Cohen, *Description historique des monnaies frappées dans l'Empire romain*, I, 1859. Photo British Museum.)

36. **Coin of Septimius Severus.** On the reverse of the coin can be seen an eagle between two *signa*. It was struck to honour the *Legio XIV Gemina*, stationed at *Carnuntum* (Petronell) in Pannonia under Septimius Severus (193-211). (H. Cohen, *Description historique...*, III, 1860. Photo British Museum.)

37. **Coins.** a) Money of Gallienus. These *antoniniani* (double sesterces) of Gallienus were struck *c*. 261 to honour the *Legio III Italica* and the *Legio XI Claudia*. (H. Mattingly, *Roman Coins*, 1962.)

37. **Coins.** b) Money of Victorinus. During the 'crisis of the Empire' coins became lighter and debased. The last of the 'Gallic Emperors', Victorinus (268-70), nevertheless had to buy the allegiance of his troops. (Photo Bibliothèque Nationale.)

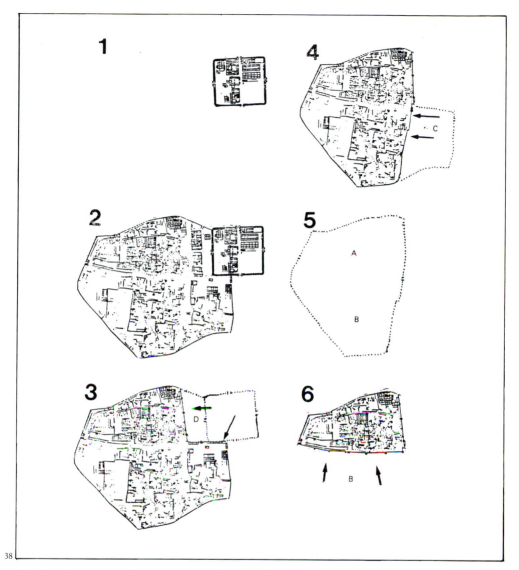

38. Rapidum (Sour Djouab): town and camp. These six drawings show the rise and fall of a little town that grew up from a camp in Mauretania. *1* Construction of a cohort camp 135 x 127m (440 x 415ft) in 122. *2* In 167 a wall was built to protect the civilian settlement that had grown up around it. *3* At the height of the 'crisis of the Empire' in the middle of the third century the camp and sector D were abandoned. *4* Abandonment of sector C about 270. *5* Shortly after 270 the city was captured and destroyed, resulting in its total abandonment for several decades. *6* At the very end of the third century sector A was reoccupied. (J.-P. Laporte, *Bull. Soc. Antiq. France*, 1983, p.264.)

39. Coin to honour *Disciplina*. A soldier's job had to be learned: it was a 'discipline' just like grammar or rhetoric and required obedience, the second meaning of 'discipline'. This dual concept resulted in the creation of a deity, *Disciplina*. (Photo Bibliothèque Nationale.)

40a

40. Triumphs. a) Triumph of the Augustan era showing two barbarians in fetters and a trophy in the midst of victors; also a sacrificial bull. This frieze, dating from about 20 BC, was inside the temple of Apollo at Rome. (Photo U. D. F.) b) Triumph of Titus. These reliefs were placed inside the Arch of Titus that dominated the Forum. They show the victor in his chariot and the booty from the Temple of Jerusalem, in particular the famous seven-branched candelabra. (Photo Alinari.)

40b

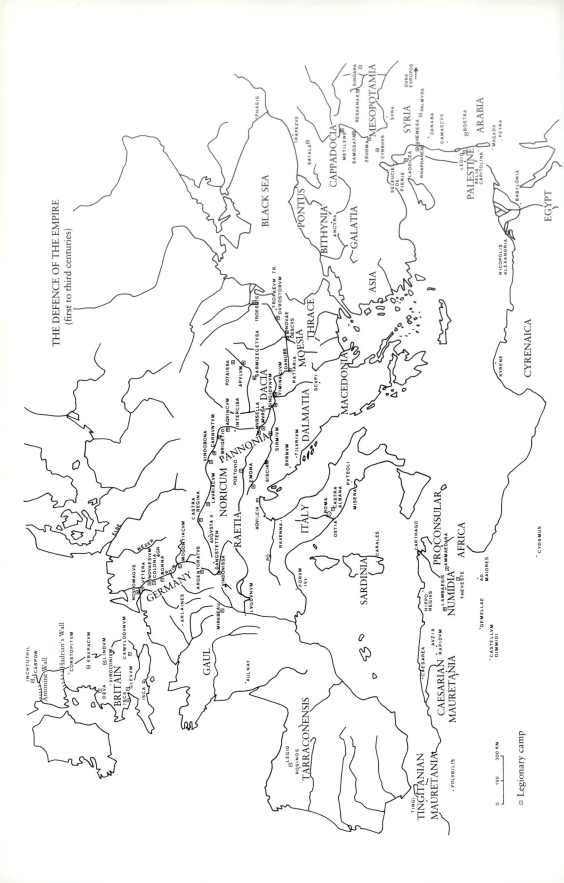

THE DEFENCE OF THE EMPIRE
(first to third centuries)

□ Legionary camp

BRITAIN
Hadrian's Wall
Antonine Wall
INCHTUTHIL
CARPOW
CORSTOPITVM
EBVRACVM
LINDVM
VIROCONIVM
CAMVLODVNVM
DEVA
ISCA
GLEVVM
ISCA D.

GAUL
AVLNAY
LVGVNVM

GERMANY
NOVIOMAGVS
VETERA
NOVAESIVM
COLONIA AGR.
BONNA
MOGONTIACVM
ARGENTORATVS
ARLANES
MIREBEAU
WESER
ELBE
RHIN

RAETIA
CASTRA REGINA
AVGVSTA V.
LAVRIACVM
DANGSTETTEN
VINDONISSA

NORICUM
BRIGETIO
VINDOBONA
CARNVNTVM
POETOVIO
EMONA

PANNONIA
AQVINCVM
INTERCISA
MVRSELLA
MVRSA
SINGIDVNVM
SIRMIVM
BVRNVM
SISCIA

DACIA
SARMIZEGETVSA
POTAISSA
APVLVM
TIBISCVM

DALMATIA
TILVRVM
DANUBE
RATIARIA
VIMINACIVM

MOESIA
TROPAEVM TR.
NOVAE
DVROSTORVM
OESCVS
SCVPI

THRACE
TROESMIS

MACEDONIA

ITALY
ROMA
CASTRA ALBANA
MISENA
OSTIA
RAVENNA
FORVM IVL.
PO
PYTEOLI
AQVILEIA

SARDINIA
CARALES

BLACK SEA

PONTUS
SATALA
TRAPEZVS
PHASIS

BITHYNIA
ANCYRA

GALATIA

ASIA

CAPPADOCIA
METILENE
SAMOSATA
ZEVGMA
CYRRHVS

MESOPOTAMIA
SINGARA
RESAENAE
DVRA EVROPOS

SYRIA
HEMESA
PALMYRA
DANABA
DAMASCVS
SELEVCIE DE PIERIE
LAODICEA
RHAPHANEAE

PALESTINE
AELIA CAPITOLINA
LEGIO
MASADA

ARABIA
BOSTRA
PETRA
BABYLONIA

EGYPT
NICOPOLIS
ALEXANDRIA

CYRENAICA
KYRENE

PROCONSULAR
CARTHAGO

AFRICA
AMMAEDARA
THEVESTE
AD MAIORES
GEMELLAE
CASTELLVM DIMMIDI
CYDAMUS

NUMIDIA
HIPPO REGIVS
L'AMBAESIS

CAESARIAN MAURETANIA
CAESAREA
AVZIA
RAPIDVM

TINGITANIAN MAURETANIA
TINGI
VOLVBILIS

TARRACONENSIS
LEGIO
ROSINOS

0 150 300 KM

was a changing room, a cold bath, a warm bath, a sauna room and a hot bath.

Roads, squares and an administrative centre, a hospital, grain stores, a workshop, baths and barrack-rooms are the main constructions identified by archaeologists and epigraphists in Roman camps. But the ramps varied in size.

Permanent camps: size

Permanent camps were much bigger than temporary camps – their size was a function of the unit housed and those built for one or two legions are the ones best known. We know that at the beginning of the Empire, Roman generals favoured large concentrations of soldiers, and regularly put two such units together. Gradually the practice was changed until Domitian actually banned two legions in the same camp because he feared a coup d'état.[67]

The following table shows that a legion was allotted an area of between 17ha (42 acres) and 28ha (70 acres). There is only one problem case, that

PERIOD	PLACE	SIZE IN HECTARES	NUMBER OF UNITS
Augustus	Haltern	36	2
	Oberaden	35	2
	Mayence (*Mogontiacum*)	35–36	2
Julio-Claudians	Xanten (*Vetera*)	50	2
	Neuss (*Nouaesium*)	23–25	1
Tiberius	Altenburg (*Carnuntium*)	20	1
	Windisch (*Vindonissa*)	*c.* 18	1
Claudius	Bonn (*Bonna*)	27	1
	Lincoln	17	1
Vespasian	Chester (*Deua*)	*c.* 24	1
	Caerleon (*Isca*)	*c.* 19	1
	Nijmegen (*Nouiomagus*)	*c.* 28	1
	León	*c.* 20	1
Domitian	Inchtuthil	22	1
Trajan	Strasbourg (*Argentorate*)	19	1
	Budapest (*Aquincum*)	24	1
Trajan-Hadrian	Lambèse (*Lambaesis*)	20	1
179	Regensburg (*Castra Regina*)	25	1
c. 190	Lorch (*Lauriacum*)	22	1
Septimius Severus	Albano	10	1

Table 31: Legionary camps in the Early Empire

of Albano, where the *legio III Parthica* had only 10ha (25 acres). Two hypotheses are possible: as it was founded by Septimius Severus, who allowed soldiers 'to live with their wives',[68] only bachelors were housed in the camp and consequently the amount of space needed to house them was reduced. Alternatively, the legion could have had far fewer than 5000 men. But it must be remembered that these are only hypotheses.

	G.-ch. PICARD	G.C. BOON	G. WEBSTER	R. REBUFFAT	Y. LE BOHEC	M. REDDÉ
1000-STRONG WING	5.2–6				5.2–6	4–5
500-STRONG WING	3.8–4.3	1.8	2	2	2.3–3.8	2–3
1000-STRONG COHORT	3.1	1.8			2.2–3.1	
500-STRONG COHORT						
EQUITATA	2.1–3.3		1.5			
500-STRONG COHORT	1.7–2.7	1.2		1		

Table 32: The auxiliary camps in the Early Empire (in hectares)[69]

Turning to auxiliaries, the situation becomes even more complicated. There are three reasons for this. Firstly, the very wide diversity of units – all the soldiers in an *ala* had horses, against only a few in a *cohors equitata*, while among the *numeri* the diversity was great; in addition some units contained 500 men, others 1000. Secondly, when we find an inscription in an auxiliary camp its text does not always mention the total nature of the troops that occupied it. Thirdly, there are plenty of examples of a camp being built for 1000 men, and then being occupied by only 500 men after the other 500 had been sent elsewhere. These complications explain the disagreement on this question among historians. It seems preferable in the present context to give the different conclusions reached (**Table 32**); perhaps the future will resolve the problem.

It seems difficult, therefore, to come to any firm conclusions. At best we can say that a 1000-strong *ala* has 5/6ha (12/15 acres), a 500-strong *ala* a maximum of 4ha (10 acres), a 1000-strong cohort 3ha (7½ acres).

The significance of another difficulty that has already been mentioned is shown by the following inscription from Kopaceni, in the ancient province of Dacia:[70]

> Under the Emperor Caesar Titus Aelius Hadrian Antoninus Pius, Augustus, tribune for the third time, consul for the third time [140], the emperor has ordered the enlargement of the camp of the *numerus* of the police [*burgarii*] and the couriers [*veredarii*] because this unit lived in cramped conditions, by doubling the length of the rampart and installing towers. This task was undertaken by the imperial procurator Aquila Fidus.

This document clearly shows that the principal wall was lengthened but not how. It is not difficult to envisage the opposite situation either; if a

1000-strong unit was replaced by a 500-strong cohort the officers would have been tempted to shorten the rampart to defend it more easily. Archaeologists have revealed the existence of multiple enclosures, even superimposed on each other, on the same spot, without being able to determine precisely whether the original camp was enlarged or reduced in size. The absence of inscriptions or the inadequacy of excavations often prevent us from recognizing the elements necessary for establishing even an approximate chronology.

Be that as it may, the plans which we have can be divided into five categories (pl.XXXIV,33):

1 Two camps separate from each other: this situation is found at Lambaesis in Africa, to the north of the Aures, where a cohort was settled in 81 and an entire legion around 115–120.
2 A small enclosure occupied the corner of a larger one; this set-up can be seen at Masada in Judea (see F1 and F2 pl.XXVIII,25a) and at Eining in the ancient province of Raetia.
3 At Hirbet Hassan Aga in the Syrian desert a small post inside a larger one used only a small part of its wall.
4 At Halton Chesters in Britain a small rectangle is placed against a larger one.
5 Ramparts are built inside and parallel to other ramparts, as archaeologist have shown to be the case at Saalburg in Upper Germany.

Different situations can therefore arise, 'linear defences' or 'individual defences', fortresses or forts. What is always surprising is the mix of simplicity and technical expertise that is found in these monuments, monuments that are all alike from Scotland to the Sahara and from the Atlantic to the Euphrates.

THE STRATEGIC SECTORS: REGIONAL DIVERSITY

The range of the geographical conditions and the diversity of potential and actual enemies that lived outside the frontiers of this immense territory caused Roman strategists to develop new practices in the various sectors they had to defend (see map).

General characteristics

Each frontier province had an army (*exercitus*) composed of either legionaries and auxiliaries[71] or else *ala* cavalry and cohort infantry. Certain regions of the Empire, particularly those in the middle, are said to have been 'without armies' (*inermes*), but this term does not signify 'without soldiers'. Each sector had a minimum number of troops in order to police it, guard the mines and the mints, and act as escort to the governor. In a passage quoted above (pp. 19–20) Tacitus shows the positions of the troops, but he only deals with the major concentrations of soldiers, and we shall see later that the situation was infinitely more complex than he suggests.

In any case, it should not be imagined that frontier armies had only one function, that of awaiting an attack from the outside. Tacitus clearly states that the units based by the Rhine had to keep a watch on Germans and Gauls.[72] On the other hand, a century later Herodian insists on the danger the barbarians represented for the provinces along the Danube; the peoples living inside the Empire were no longer to be feared.[73] At certain periods men were stationed a long way behind the frontier, as was the case of the garrisons of Illyria–Dalmatia, who in the first century ensured the protection of Italy and provided reserves for the legions of Pannonia and Moesia.[74]

The role of the navy and the ports

In one way the navy can be seen to represent the Empire's ultimate reserve of soldiers; in effect the Mediterranean was a Roman lake from the time of Augustus. But the hypothesis of its acting as a police force must be rejected.[75] M. Reddé notes that sailors were considered as proper soldiers from Augustus' reign, and consequently fulfil a military function. The advent of the Empire saw the setting up of permanent fleets, a legacy of the naval concentrations of the Triumvirate, based mainly in the West. Misenum guarded the western Mediterranean basin; Ravenna took part in the operations against the Parthians, while ships were scattered all along the northern border, on the Rhine, the Danube and the Black Sea.

As a result, the soldiers of the Italian fleets were sent as reserves during the wars against the Germans and the Parthians. Above all, and this is their essential role, they provided the logistic support for campaigns. One of the first scenes on Trajan's Column shows ships on which soldiers have loaded provisions.[76] Indeed, the ships transported both supplies and men. This function explains the systematic reactivation of the port of Seleucia Pieria in Syria; during each of the emperor's expeditions against the Parthians there were soldiers of the 'praetorian' fleets.

This ship-based activity leads us to dub the naval strategy of the first two centuries AD as 'active defence' as opposed to the 'passive defence', which characterized the Republic when a navy was raised only in time of war, and the great 'crisis of the third century' when fortifications played the dominant role. But this role also explains the fact that no model for a military port existed; nothing really distinguishes Misenum from Ostia or Puteoli since in the three places the essential feature was the loading and unloading of men and supplies. Ravenna is well situated because of the lagoon with its canal link to the river Po, and its lighthouse to aid navigation.[77] But no record exists there to testify to the presence of an important war fleet. A future task for archaeologists will be to find the sailors' barracks and training grounds.

The interior

Thus the fleets provided soldiers in the heart of the Empire, but other soldiers were to be found in other regions far from the frontiers, in zones called 'without armies', but as already noted, not without soldiers.[78]

Italy

The most numerous garrisons of soldiers in this type of zone were most certainly to be found in Italy. There was the garrison at Rome with its Praetorian cohorts, *urbaniciani* and *Vigiles*, plus various other smaller units. There were also the fleets at Misenum and Ravenna, just mentioned; detachments from these were sent in the first century to Ostia and Puteoli.[79] Also at each of these two sites there was a cohort of vigils.[80] Finally it should be remembered that in 202 Septimius Severus set up the *castra Albana* 20km (12 miles) south-east of Rome to house the *legio II Parthica*.

The West

The province of Sardinia, very close to Italy, was the home of no fewer than four cohorts in Tiberius' and Claudius' reigns; afterwards a group of soldiers from Misenum were based at Cagliari. Soldiers were also to be found almost everywhere in the West, especially in proconsular Africa, whose governor commanded the legionaries until the reign of Caracalla, and even after that had around 1000 men under his orders. Carthage served as a retreat camp, a citadel;[81] the camp was situated in all probability on the Bordj Djedid plateau in what is now the presidential palace gardens.[82] An urban cohort (the XIIIth under the Flavians, the Ist afterwards) lived there, as did a cohort taken from the *legio III Augusta* and some *beneficiarii*.[83] Other units are known in the Maghreb: the *ala Siliana* under the Julio-Claudians and perhaps foot-soldiers subsequently, various detachments and even a short-lived legion, the *legio I Macriana* of the 68–9 crisis. On the other hand only 500 auxiliary infantrymen were to be found in the senatorial province of Baetica.

The Gauls seem to have received more soldiers, but only in the first years of the Empire. After the battle of Actium, Octavian as he was still called, berthed his fleet at Fréjus in Gallia Narbonensis.[84] Lyon was always home of at least one cohort, notably to protect the mint (*cohors XVII ad Monetam*, or *cohors I* then *XIII Urbana*). But recent discoveries have attested the existence of camps situated far from the Rhine frontier and built during the early Empire; recent work on the enclosure at

Arlaines near Soissons, which has been known about for some time,[86] has revealed that it dates to the Julio-Claudian period, like the other one discovered at Aulnay de Saintonge.[87] Finally several camps that have been discovered at Mirebeau near Dijon can be dated by stamped bricks to the Flavians.[88] These constructions are perhaps connected with the conquest and the insurrections of Florus and Sacrovir under Tiberius, and those of Civilis, Classicus, Tutor and Sabinus in 68–70. But we must not forget that Gaul was also the theatre for violence in the third century. The provinces of the Alps received *auxilia* right from their constitutional beginnings.

But the most important concentration of troops in the West was to be found in the first century in Illyria–Dalmatia (by 'the West' is meant that part of the Roman world in which Latin was the standard language, as opposed to 'the East' where Greek was spoken; see map). This position formed a barrier to people getting into Italy and also could supply aid to the armies stationed on the right bank of the Danube if necessary, whether in Moesia in the east or Pannonia in the north. However, throughout the first century their numbers shrank. They were reduced from five legions under Augustus (*VIII Augusta, IX Hispana, XI* (future) *Claudia, XV Apollinaris* and *XX Valeria*) to one under Claudius (*XI Claudia* then *IV Flavia*). Under Domitian the *IV Flavia* left the region, which was then defended only by auxiliaries.[89] At the end of the second century the sector was still important, when the Danube border was again under threat.[90]

The East

In the interior regions of the East there were never any similar permanent concentrations of troops, but there were small units sprinkled here and there. Macedonia was protected by the two Moesian legions (*IV Scythica* and *V Macedonica*) in the early years of the Empire;[91] auxiliary cohorts were also present in Achaia (see n. 91) and in Thrace, Asia Minor,[92] notably in Bithynia and Pontus.

This rapid tour leads to an important conclusion. Contrary to what has often been written, Augustus did not station all his troops near the frontiers where there were potential enemies. He kept important reserves in the rear, who only moved up to the front line very gradually. The *legio III Augusta* in Africa was nearer to Carthage than to the Garamantes; the camps at Aulnay and Arlaines, the garrisons of Macedonia and Illyria–Dalmatia were far from the Rhine and the Danube. Nevertheless, especially from the end of the first century, the main part of Rome's forces camped close to the barbarian world. It is possible to distinguish three major fronts, based on geographical criteria and potential enemies.

The northern front

The northern front, from the Atlantic to the Black Sea, was itself made up of three sectors, each threatened by large bellicose populations.

Britain

The island of Britain, occupied only in its southern part, was no more than a narrow strip of land at the limit of Roman domination.[93] Blocking this passage presented no difficulties, but on the other hand it was not so easy to prevent ships from going round one or other side of the island. It was in order to ensure the defence of the Roman province that immediately after the conquest, a British fleet (*classis Britannica*) was formed. In addition there was a garrison of four legions at the time of the conquest in 43/4 (*II Augusta*, *IX Hispana*, *XIV Gemina*, *XX Valeria*). Under Vespasian there were still four, with the replacing of the *XIV Gemina* by the *II Adiutrix*. The first camps were built at Gloucester, Lincoln and possibly Wroxeter. In the second and third centuries the numbers were reduced to three units each occupying a large camp: the *II Augusta* at Caerleon (*Isca*); the *VI Victrix* at York (*Eburacum*); and the *XX Valeria* at Chester (*Deva*).

The major characteristic of the defensive system of this province, however, lies in the two linear defences the Romans built there (pl.xxxv,34). Hadrian's Wall, the older of the two, measuring 128km (80 miles) long, linked the Tyne estuary to the Solway Firth. A north–south cross-section of this defence indicates four elements: a ditch, a berm, the stone wall (where it was made of earth it was topped by a palisade) and a road. A plan shows the presence, every 500m (1640ft) of towers built against the wall, gates and small forts now called 'mile-castles' every 1600m (5250ft), and forts built against the wall every 10km (6 miles). The Antonine Wall presents the same north–south cross-section of ditch, berm, wall, road, but it is made of earth and wood only. There are also small and large forts, and towers. It covers only 60km (37 miles) between the Firth of Clyde and the Firth of Forth, and is thus situated farther north.

There is a chronological question. Hadrian's Wall, built *c.*122, was abandoned in favour of the Antonine Wall between 138 and *c.*160, reoccupied between 160 and 184, abandoned again between 184 and 197, only to be reoccupied yet again from 197 until it was definitively abandoned in 367. British historians do not fully understand the reasons behind these moves.

Thus in the second century just over 30,000 men were using a fleet, three camps and a wall.

The 'Army of the Rhine'

On the northern extremity of the Empire lived the huge Germanic people who threatened the Rhine frontier to the west and the Danube frontier to the south. The military occupation of the left bank of the Rhine was organized by Drusus between 12 and 9 BC,[94] then Tiberius made it his personal concern before becoming Emperor. We know that Augustus had planned to extend the Roman world further eastwards as far as the Weser and the Elbe, but the disaster suffered by Varus in the Teutoburgwald in

9 and the troubles experienced by Germanicus between 14 and 16 put an end to ideas of this sort. However, the territory remained a constant worry to the Roman strategists as their maintenance of important numbers of troops there testifies. Under Augustus there were at least five legions stationed there, while for most of the first century this number rose to seven. From Trajan onwards it was reduced to four which seems to suggest that it was felt that the threat from this direction had receded somewhat. If we include the fleet (*classis Germanica*) and the auxiliaries, there was a reduction from 90,000 men in the first century to 45,000 in the second and third centuries.

Augustus	5 min.	*V Alaudae* or *XVI, XIV Gemina, XVII, XVIII, XIX*
Tiberius	8	*I Germanica, II Augusta, V Alaudae, XIII Gemina, XIV Gemina, XVI, XX Victrix, XXI Rapax*
Claudius	7	*I Germanica, IV Macedonica, V Alaudae, XV Primigenia, XVI, XXI Rapax, XXII Primigenia*
Vespasian	7	*I Adiutrix, VI Victrix, X Gemina, XI Claudia, XIV Gemina, XXI Rapax, XXII Primigenia*
Trajan-Aurelian	4	*I Minervia, VI Victrix* (replaced by *XXX Ulpia*), *VIII Augusta, XXII Primigenia*

Table 33: Legions in Germany

The left bank of the Rhine constituted a *de facto* province until its actual creation and division into Upper and Lower Germany in 89–90. Lower Germany had several large fortresses, at Haltern and Oberaden from the Augustan age, also Neuss (*Novaesium*) and Nijmegen (*Noviomagus*). In the second century *legio I Minervia* was stationed at Bonn (*Bonna*) and *XXX Ulpia* at Xanten (*Vetera*), while the legate governor had his residence at Cologne. As these fortresses backed on to the Rhine there was no need to build a linear defence system.

This was not the case in Upper Germany, however, because the region situated between the upper reaches of the Rhine and the Danube had been annexed in the Flavian era. It was called the *Agri Decumates*.To protect these lands and establish the frontier between Roman and barbarian territories, legionaries had built a barrier 382km (240 miles) long, running east from just north of Koblenz, to the north of Wiesbaden, via the south of Giessen and east of Frankfurt. From there it headed due south and towards the end divided into two. The older part (first century) went towards Stuttgart and the more recent (third century) towards Lorsch. The main element consisted of a palisade built on an earth bank (from Commodus' time the palisade was replaced by stone), with ditches on either side. Towers were built every 500 or 1000m (1640 and 3280ft) and small forts at irregular intervals of anything between 5 and 17km (3 and 10½ miles). Needless to say, a road network completed the system. The large fortresses were to be found at Windisch (*Vindonissa*), Strasbourg (*Argentorate*) and Mainz (*Magontiacum*), the home of the legate-governor. In the second century they housed respectively the following legions: *XI Claudia, VIII Augusta, XXI Primigenia*. Under the Flavians the *VIII Augusta* had been stationed at Mirebeau near Dijon, which was also in Upper Germany.

Thus the security of the Rhine was entrusted to eight legions in the first century and to four in the succeeding ones. Upper Germany was protected by a linear defence 382km (240 miles) long.

The Danube sector

The Danube sector of the northern front[95] was far more important to the minds of Roman imperial strategists.[96] In fact, throughout the whole of the Early Empire the greatest concentrations of troops were to be found there. The Germans were not the only danger; peoples from the kingdoms of Bohemia and Dacia, sometimes celticized, as well as nomads from the steppes of southern Russia, were permanent threats of a different nature, often difficult to detect. Also, this frontier was relatively long. Its conquest was organized largely by Tiberius between 12 and 10 BC. At the beginning of the imperial era the right bank of the Danube was defended by the legions stationed in Illyria and Macedonia. Not only were they far away, there were only nine of them. This number rose to 15 in Tiberius' reign and then to 18 and to 20 in the reign of Claudius. It stayed at this high level until the end of the third century. With the auxiliaries and the Danube fleets the total number of men stationed there was about 200,000, more than half of the entire Roman army!

Because of the length of this frontier we must proceed by province to province. Raetia was occupied by Drusus in 15 BC and defended by two legions (*XIII Gemina, XXI Rapax*) in the Augustan age. In Tiberius' time there were only auxiliaries to be found there, a state of affairs that was to continue until the time of Marcus Aurelius who established the *legio III Italica* at Regensburg (*Castra Regina*) c.165. Archaeologists have studied a linear defence, 166km, (103 miles) long that was a continuation of the one in Upper Germany, but known for years as the 'Devil's Wall'. It went east–west in the shape of an arc from Lorsch to the west of Regensburg. A palisade, followed by a stone wall 1m (3¼ft) thick and 2.5m to 3m (8 to 10ft) high, formed the main part, and a road network, towers and forts completed the system.

There were no continuous barriers in the neighbouring province of Noricum, whose garrison consisted solely of auxiliaries until Marcus Aurelius established the *legio II Italica* at Enns (*Lauriacum*). Moreover, elements of the Pannonian fleet covered the part of the Danube attributed to Noricum.

Like Noricum, Pannonia backed on to this major river that made the construction of a linear defence unnecessary.[97] However, the river made the creation of a fleet (*classis Pannonica*) essential, and it was probably Vespasian who was responsible for this. Strategies were preoccupied with the problem presented by the bend in the Danube in this province, and at different times came to different conclusions about how to solve it. Shortly after the conquest of 12–9 BC Augustus positioned his troops a long way back from the frontier. The three legions were at Ptuj (*Poetovio*: *VIII Augusta*), Ljubljana (*Emona*: XV Apollinaris), and Sisak (*Siscia*: IX *Hispana*). Tiberius reduced the number of units to two, which from Claudius' time were to be *XIII Gemina* and *XV Apollinaris*. But gradually, and as early as 15, the troops moved northwards and set up camp on the right bank of the Danube. During the Dacian wars Trajan had a better understanding of the situation, and between 103 and 106 he divided the province in two. From then on the distribution of the troops was decided upon with the potential enemies in mind and it remained stable until the end of the century. Upper Pannonia had two fortresses, Vienna (*Vindobona*: *X Gemina*) and Altenburg (*Carnuntum*: *XIV Gemina*), whose job it was to keep an eye on the Marcomanni, and another to deal with the Quadi at Szony-Komaron (*Brigetio*: *I Adiutrix*). There was only one major camp in Lower Pannonia, at Budapest (*Aquincum*: *II Adiutrix*), which had to counter the Sarmatians. Under Caracalla the number of men was increased by the arrival of the *legio I Adiutrix*.

An analogous situation can be observed in the military history of the provinces located on the right bank of the lower Danube. Indeed, the three legions that Augustus had established in Moesia[98] (*IV Scythica*, *V Macedonica* and *VII* future *Claudia*) were stationed very far from the frontier. Claudius increased their number to four by sending the *VIII Augusta*, and Trajan to five. From that time on the military geography of the region remained very stable. A linear defence was built in Dobroudja, by Trajan according to some archaeologists. Upper Moesia was defended by two fortresses, one at Kostolac (*Viminacium*: *VII Claudia*), the other at Belgrade (*Singidunum*: *V Alaudae*, then *II Adiutrix*, and finally *IV Flavia*). Lower Moesia had three large camps, the first at Swislow (*Novae*: *I Italica*), the second at Iglita (*Troesmis*: *V Macedonia*) the third at Silistra (*Durostorum*:*XI Claudia*). There was also the fleet (*classis Moesica*) that was probably created by Vespasian. What is surprising in the defensive organization of Moesia is the relatively uncommon stability of the units stationed there, perhaps due to the fact that once a certain equilibrium had been achieved it was not interfered with.

The same impression emerges from an examination of the situation in Dacia,[99] yet this province was in a very exposed position and was annexed only at a fairly late stage. Shortly after its conquest Trajan left three legions there (*I Adiutrix, IV Flavia, XIII Gemina*). The first two were very soon called elsewhere and only the *XIII Gemina* remained, in its camp at Alba Julia (*Apulum*). In the third century the *legio V Macedonica* arrived as a reinforcement. On this territory on the left (north) bank of the Danube was a linear defence; in the early second century, perhaps, an earth rampart, 235km (146 miles) long, supported by small forts, was built in Oltenia.

The Black Sea

As soon as the banks of the Danube were left behind, Rome's military presence was less noticeable. The Black Sea was surrounded by small posts only,[100] with a fleet, created by Nero, to back them up logistically. To the north the Cimmerian Bosphorus (modern Crimea) remained an independent kingdom, at least theoretically; a garrison did actually keep an eye on it at all times.

The eastern front

This survey has eventually brought us around to the frontier between the Roman world and Iran.[101] Here more than anywhere else imperial strategy was dependent upon the physical and human geography. To the north, mountains corresponded with Armenia, a small state tossed between two superpowers. To the south Palestine, Syria and Phoenicia, were cut off by desert. By its position the caravan city of Palmyra controlled all the civilian and military movements of the region. In the centre, the valleys of the Euphrates and the Tigris acted as two thoroughfares, but an invader from the West would have to head south and would therefore always have exposed his left flank to an enemy.

Trajan had tried to annexe Mesopotamia; he had actually managed to take control of it after reducing Arabia (in fact the western part of modern Jordan) to provincial status. But his pacifism, as much as circumstances, made Hadrian reinstate the upper Euphrates as the frontier of the Empire. Expansionist policies returned with Lucius Verus who reached the Khabour in his campaigns between 161 and 166. Septimius Severus completed the annexation; henceforth Nisibe and Singara belonged to Rome, and the frontier with Iran became the Upper Tigris. But the revolution of 212–27 that had witnessed the replacement of the Arsacid Parthians by the Sassanian Persians caused incessant problems for the rest of the century. The middle of this crisis saw the emergence of an exceptional figure, Zenobia, Queen of Palmyra.

The study of this eastern front reveals a constant increase in the number of Roman troops involved. The three legions of Augustus became four under Tiberius, six under Vespasian, seven under Trajan, eight under Antoninus Pius, ten under Caracalla and twelve under Aurelian, showing an increase from approximately 30,000 men to 150,000. This is the opposite of what we have seen on most of the other fronts. Nevertheless, even at the end of the third century the number of men in this sector never equalled those deployed to face the Germans on the Rhine and particularly the Upper Danube. Furthermore, it seems that no linear defence was ever built in this region. Four principal sectors can be distinguished.

Cappadocia

Reduced to the status of a province in 17, Cappadocia, opposite Armenia, always had two legions, *XII Fulminata* at Melite in the south, and the *XVI Flavia* (afterwards *XV Apollinaris*) at Sadag (*Satala*) in the north.

Syria

To simplify this survey Judaea or Palestine will not be included under the name of Syria, but Commagene in the north will. This was annexed by Tiberius, abandoned by Caligula in 38 and recaptured definitively by Vespasian in 72. The caravan city of Palmyra, which was so important from a military point of view, was also part of the same strategic system, even though it enjoyed a certain autonomy as a sort of protectorate. Dura-Europos with its cohort garrison served as an outpost.

In the absence of a linear defence the main axis of the military organization was made up of large camps of legionaries, of which only three were operational at any given time. Emesa housed the *III Gallica* in the first two centuries AD, before this legion left for the southern part of Phoenicia; Laodiceia had the *VI Ferrata* (first century), the *II Trajana* (early second century); at Cyrrhus was the *X Fretensis* (Julio-Claudian era) then the *IV Scythica*. From the beginning of the second century the *XVI Flavia* was at Samosata. From the time of Septimius Severus onwards must be added the *I* and *III Parthica*. There were also many auxiliary cavalrymen, particularly during the third century crisis, and the Syrian fleet (*classis Syriaca*) from either the Flavian or Trajan period. Aurelian established the *I Illyriciana* in the south of Phoenicia. All these troops were used to protect the fords, watering places and the bridges; these militarily sensitive spots were guarded by many posts, often no more than simple towers. A road network linked up the different elements, but it did not become a really efficient system until the time of the Tetrarchy when the *strata Diocletiana*,[102] the road that went from Damascus to Soura via Palmyra, was adequately provided with forts.

Judaea or Palestine

Further south, Judaea presented a special case. Reduced to provincial status in AD6, its extent was increased by the addition of the Hauran in 34 and Galilee in 39. There were violent uprisings in 66–70 and 132–5, while some Jews of the Diaspora caused trouble towards the end of Trajan's reign. This is a clear indication that the troops stationed there had to watch the native inhabitants rather than the desert for a potential enemy. For the most part there were two legions, the X *Fretensis* in Jerusalem from the time of Vespasian and the *VI Ferrata* at Caparcotna in the north from Hadrian's time.

Arabia

Palestine's flank (modern Jordan) was protected by the province of Arabia,[103] where there was only one legion, probably the *VI Ferrata* immediately after the annexation at the beginning of the second century, and the *III Cyrenaica* from Hadrian onwards. The general head-quarters had been set up at Bostra, and the defensive system's backbone in the sector was Trajan's 'new road' that went from there to Aqaba, via Jerash, Amman and Petra. Many forts and towers were built along this route, especially in the southern part, and to keep a watch over the desert patrols were sent as far as the Hedjaz and to the edge of the Nefoud.[104]

The southern front

If the need arose, help could be brought to Palestine and Arabia by the army in Egypt, which brings us to the southern front of the Empire, a sector judged secondary by Roman stategists. The result was similar to that seen in Germany: a rapid decrease in the number of troops stationed there. There were never very many, and three provinces, Cyrenaica and the two Mauretanias, were defended only by auxiliaries. On the northern front this situation held good only for Raetia and Noricum before the reign of Marcus Aurelius.

Egypt

By 29BC at the latest, the Roman army of Egypt was fully operational.[105] This province was special in many respects. The alluvium of the Nile provided an important wheat crop that was Rome's major supply under the Julio-Claudians. From a juridical point of view it was the province of the ruler, appearing to have been conquered by Octavian personally after the battle of Actium. It was like some immense imperial property, a fact that excluded senatorial interference in its affairs. Alexandria, its main city, was not considered by some ancients to be 'in Egypt', but 'near Egypt'.

Alexandria was so important strategically that the Romans treated it in a unique way. They did not deploy a defence system on an east–west axis, to protect the north from the south, as might be expected from our knowledge of the northern and eastern fronts. On the contrary, a totally different organization is discernible, that reflected the juridical and economic realities of the country.

Indeed, it would be wrong to speak of a defensive system in Egypt.

Troops were concentrated in the camp of Nicopolis at Alexandria. Under Augustus the army consisted of three legions (*III Cyrenaica, XII Fulminata, XXII Deiotariana*), with auxiliaries and the fleet (*classis Alexandrina*), created by Augustus himself in all probability. Under Tiberius the *XII Fulminata* left, and under Trajan, possibly, the *III Cyrenaica*. Moreover, the *XXII Deiotariana* was destroyed in the second century. At Nicopolis only one unit remained, the *II Trajana*, created by Trajan, but from then on its destiny is identical with Egypt's. But this is not the complete picture. In addition to the large camp near Alexandria there were two series of smaller forts, one along the road that borders the Nile and constitutes the main military axis, the other on the margins of the desert and in oases, as outposts. So the defence of this province was orchestrated along a north–south, and not east–west, axis; troop numbers decreased regularly in the first century.

Cyrenaica

Cyrenaica presents a different desert defensive system,[106] as far as can be seen from the paucity of our sources. The objectives of the strategists were to ensure the security of the cities and of the fertile plateau near the Mediterranean. R.G. Goodchild considered that it was not impossible for this province to have had a military organization as early as the first century, strengthened after the Jewish uprising of 115 and yet again during the third-century crisis. Stone was used to protect men and goods; fortified farms and little camps, towns with ramparts. The garrison in Cyrenaica consisted of one or two auxiliary cohorts. In times of crisis legionaries arrived from neighbouring provinces. Many of the walls described by Goodchild seem to have been built at a fairly late date, probably during the third-century crisis.

Africa–Numidia

The situation in Africa, from which Numidia was removed by Septimius Severus, was totally different. This region was more populous and much more wealthy. The fact that from the mid-first century it tended to replace Egypt as the main supplier of Rome's wheat gives a clear indication of its importance.

The evolution in the defensive organization is fairly well documented. Under Augustus the proconsul commanded two, or perhaps three, legions, though we do not know where they were stationed. This aspect must be emphasized, since a magistrate of such a rank normally had no authority over an army. One of these legions, the *III Augusta*, set up camp at Haïdra before 14. By the end of Tiberius's reign, it was the only legion in Africa, and its destiny was linked with that of the province thereafter. Under Caligula the situation returned to normal; the command of the army was withdrawn from the proconsul and entrusted to a propraetorial legate who was directly answerable to the emperor. Under Vespasian the general headquarters were transferred, for reasons unknown, to Tebessa, 35km (22 miles) west of Haïdra. Finally, around 115 or 120 the *legio III Augusta* established their camp at Lambaesis, to the north of the Aures, where it remained for two centuries apart from the period 238–53.

The military system of the second and third centuries is fairly well known thanks to excavations,[108] aerial photography,[109] and studies on the ground in southern Tunisia[110] and Libya.[111] The region of the Aures was encircled by a road with fortifications. Productive Africa was separated from the desert by another road, also equipped with camps, and divided into three sections – Numidia, Western Tripolitania and Eastern Tripolitania. Outposts were built in the desert, at Messad and Ghadames, for example, while some other garrisons were set up to the north of the military zone. The presence of linear defences has been turned up in Tunisia and Algeria, especially to the south of the Aures; the Seguia bent El-Krass, probably dating from the early second century, forms an arc more than 60km (37 miles) long to the south of the wadi Djedi. A cross-section of it shows that from the desert to the north it consists of a glacis, berm, ditch, berm, wall (mainly of stone). On a map a road network and camps can be picked out. Towers were built on or behind the wall, or else at a distance from it.

Mauretania Caesariensis

Moving west from Numidia the Roman world narrows to no more than a coastal strip. The defence of Mauretania Caesariensis was left to auxiliaries,[112] detachments from the Alexandrian or Syrian fleets that occasionally anchored in the harbours of the province. This strategy was unusual as it was based on two elements. The procurator governor's residence at Cherchel nearly always contained some soldiers and sailors, a situation not dissimilar to that of Alexandria in Egypt. In addition a series of camps placed alongside a road running east–west separated the Roman world from independent Mauretania. Under Trajan this frontier followed the wadi Chelif as far west as Aïn Temouchent and as far east as Sour el-Ghozlan (Aumale). A new *praetentura* was established under Septimius Severus; this route, equipped with forts, went further south, from Tarmount, north of Chott el-Hodna, to Tlemcen and Marnia. The original Caesarean Mauretania was seldom more than 50km (30 miles) wide; the new one was virtually double the size.

Mauretania Tingitana

From many points of view, including military and economic, the two Mauretanias had only their name in common. Some historians even believe that there was never any land communication between them. Indeed, Tingitanian Mauretania was a very compact area,[113] and in its administration and material life it had more in common with Spain than with the rest of the Maghreb.

Its defensive system also shows some originality.[114] Again it relied on the use of auxiliaries only, but a series of camps, particularly dense around Volubilis, covered the province. There was no east–west strip like the one in Caesarean Mauretania. Archaeologists have discovered a linear defence that starts on the coast, approximately 6km (4 miles) to the south of Rabat and goes east for some 12km ($7\frac{1}{2}$ miles). South–north it comprised a ditch, a berm and a stone wall, plus a few towers. It is obvious from its position and layout that its function was to protect the colony of Sala, which was near the modern Rabat.

Southern front: conclusions

There were probably very few soldiers in Mauretania Tingitania, a feature that characterized the southern front as a whole. If we add the Maghreban troops to those in Egypt and Cyrenaica we arrive at a total of approximately 60,000 men under Augustus, but only 50,000 under Tiberius, 40,000 under Claudius, and about 30,000 from Trajan right through to Diocletian. The numbers are not high if we remember their mission, to guard a territory stretching from the Atlantic to the Red Sea. These reductions are witness to the fact that Roman strategists were not overly worried by the security aspects of the region. When we also remember the economic importance of Africa this seeming lack of interest can only be explained by the success of the process of pacification and Romanization in the provinces concerned.

Hispania Tarraconensis

Another exceptional case is presented by Hispania Tarraconensis which had no frontier with barbarians, and yet had soldiers stationed in it.[115] The end of its conquest was marked by a series of operations in the north-west between 29 and 19 BC, in which Agrippa distinguished himself. At that period there were some eight legions, the *I* (probably *I Augusta*), *II Augusta*, *IV Macedonica*, *V Alaudae* (or the *XVI*), *VI Victrix*, *IX Hispana*, *X Gemina*, and *XX*. Under Tiberius only three remained (*VI Victrix*, *X Gemina*, *IV Macedonica*). Then the *IV Macedonica* left under Claudius, and *X Gemina* under Nero. Galba created the *VII Gemina* in the province, but took it with him when he left. After a brief episode that saw *X Gemina* return to Spain with *I Adiutrix*, Vespasian decided that the province needed only one legion, the *VII Gemina*, which stayed there until the end of the Early Empire. It is generally considered that only a few auxiliaries accompanied it.

The defensive organization of this province took into account the local situation. There was no question of defending a border against an enemy, but rather of keeping watch over the most turbulent inhabitants and ensuring the security of the mines. According to P. Le Roux and A. Tranoy there was no military zone as such in the form of a strip of a land, no *limes* as in Britain, on the Rhine or the Danube, but a main centre with secondary positions. The general headquarters were installed at León (the name itself derived from *legio*) in a large camp 570 × 350m (1870 × 1150ft), nearly 20ha (50 acres). Another enclosure, covering nearly 5ha (12 acres), that housed a cavalry *ala*, has been discovered at Rosinos de Vidriales. Also one or several auxiliary cohorts were deputed to guard the *ora maritima* on the Mediterranean. In all, Spain was defended by less than 10,000 men.

Strategy: an assessment

A good guide to the evolution of imperial strategy is the distribution of the legions. A table enables us to see the ways numbers fluctuated on each front and to compare the different fronts at different periods.

	AUGUSTUS	TIBERIUS	CLAUDIUS	VESPASIAN	TRAJAN	ANTONINUS	CARACALLA	AURELIAN
INTERIOR								
ITALY							1	1
ILLYRIA-								
DALMATIA	3	2	1	1				
MACEDONIA	2(?)	2						
TOTAL	5	4	1	1			1	1
NORTH								
BRITAIN			4	4	3	3	3	3
RHINE	5*	8	7	7	4	4	4	4
DANUBE	4	3	8	6	12	10	13	12
TOTAL	9	11	19	17	19	17	20	19
EAST	3	4	4	6	7	8	10	12
SOUTH								
EGYPT	3	2	2	2	2	1	1	1
AFRICA	2*	2	1	1	1	1	1	1
TOTAL	5	4	3	3	3	2	2	2
SPAIN	5	3	2	1	1	1	1	1

* = minimum

Table 34: The distribution of legions

The above table shows that at the beginning of the Empire, the Rhine and Africa were the sectors considered to be the most at risk. In addition, an important concentration of troops that had escaped the notice of historians was centred on Illyria and Macedonia. After a fairly lengthy period of experimentation the armies of the Rhine, Britain, Spain and Africa were reduced numerically, whereas the defence of the Danube was reinforced even more strongly than in the East. Nevertheless, it seems that the Roman strategists always felt that the main threat came from Germany and not from Iran. Their calculations were not far out, as it was the Vandals, the Alans and the Suevi (after the Franks, the Alemanni and the Goths) who finally succeeded in breaking through the defences of the Empire. But the generals made one mistake: the barbarians crossed the Rhine, not the Danube.

CONCLUSION

The strategy put in place by the Romans, therefore, was based on several elements. While not forgetting the gods, they put most of their trust in roads, walls and soldiers. In order to build fortresses and linear defences the soldiers had to acquire certain techniques. The same demands were highlighted in the previous chapter on tactics: to build a temporary camp, keep in step in a moving column or on the field of battle, cross swords with the best chance of staying alive, required a legionary to have learned his métier. The officers too had to be prepared for the tasks of choosing a site to spend the night, of drawing up the troops for battle, or organizing a defensive system. Strategy and tactics, the things that made Rome what it was, could not be used without intensive training and exercise.

III

THE ROLE OF
THE ARMY IN
THE EMPIRE

HISTORY OF THE ROMAN ARMY

So far it has seemed preferable to study the Roman army by successively examining each of its aspects, and this has entailed highlighting the fact that sometimes these aspects changed over the centuries. However, it would be a pity to ignore evolution in a history book. Obviously it would be impossible to summarize the events that took place in the Mediterranean basin in the course of the first three centuries AD. Nevertheless, scholars will note, perhaps with regret, that no military history of the Empire actually exists. Without going into great detail, therefore, it is necessary to sketch in the broad outlines of these questions.[1]

Changes occurred in two areas, essentially, but most importantly in the purely military. Virtually every emperor did his best to follow some policy, whether offensive or defensive. Some conducted vast operations which occasionally brought them triumphal processions on the Capitol, while others had to conceal disasters. Others still had to wage inglorious wars that were more like police operations keeping law and order. Yet others reacted to the future they foresaw or the failures of the past and attempted to modify structures that they felt to be outdated. Secondly, the army interfered in politics. With the ruler as its head, it was a force that had to be reckoned with. In the context of a civil war it was even more powerful as it could join with the inhabitants of a province to make or break emperors. This was the 'secret of the Empire'[2] that has been the subject of recent study.[3]

When examining the period as a whole[4] it is noticeable that convenient reference points like reigns and dynasties very often correspond to the major historical changes. This phenomenon can be explained in several ways, of course. Some emperors had a big enough personality to make their mark on an era, or they had enough intelligence to choose the right sort of advisers. It is often the inadequacy of a ruler and his advisers in the face of pressing circumstances that brought about a palace revolution; in this situation the army always intervened.

ORGANIZATION AND NATIONAL REBELLIONS

Assuredly, Augustus did not create his army from scratch. He benefited from the Republican inheritance, in particular the modifications linked with Caesar's Wars and again those of the Triumvirate. But that is not within the scope of this book.[5a]

With regards to the first century as a whole, the prodigious amount of work accomplished under Augustus must be emphasized, which was no more than tinkered with by his successors for a long time. They transformed the 'experimental' army into a 'permanent' army.[5b]

Augustus and the creation of the imperial army

Contemporary historians have often concurred in denying Augustus any military talents,[6] by insisting on the fact that he seldom set foot personally on the battlefield. However, echoing an ancient tradition, Aurelius Victor painted a more flattering portrait of this ruler,[7] and following him, we should rehabilitate Augustus as a general.

Firstly, his reign was responsible for organizing the army in the way it was to remain for the whole of the period of the Early Empire.[8] Admittedly he did not do this from scratch, since the Republic had already had at its disposal forces that were sufficiently well organized to conquer a large part of the Mediterranean world. But the distinction between the garrison at Rome and the provincial army, between auxiliary units and legions, their command structures, their recruiting standards and frontier strategy, all of these date from the very beginning of the new regime. No doubt we should not attribute all these innovations to one person, but nevertheless in a monarchy the role of the ruler is of the greatest importance. The ruler is the one who makes the final decisions and is the one responsible for the choice of advisers. In this respect Augustus made good choices. It is true that the Civil War had revealed the talents of a large number of efficient generals, who in turn trained their successors. Many names should be cited with those of Caius Sentius Saturninus, Lucius Domitius Ahenobarbus and the unfortunate Publius Quinctilius Varus, but it was a lucky coincidence for Augustus that he found his best officers in his family circle. We know that he was married twice; his son-in-law Agrippa, his step-sons Tiberius, Drusus and Germanicus, as well as his grandson Gaius Caesar, were among his most competent generals.

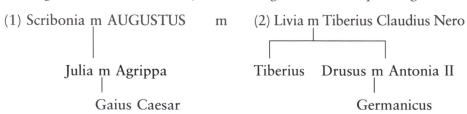

In addition a large number of high-quality officers were required as the Romans were fighting in many different places. Four major sectors of military activity can be distinguished. Firstly, Augustus himself, with the aid of Agrippa, made a huge effort to bring about Spain's definitive submission. This conquest had been started as long ago as the third century BC but had never been completed, leaving the north-west region of the Iberian peninsula still independent of Roman control. Seven legions and their auxiliaries fought for ten years (29–19), but even then troubles started up again three years later. In 29 also Marcus Valerius Messala Corvinus' troops marched through Aquitaine, quelling the unrest of the inhabitants.

Secondly, Augustus was most preoccupied by the northern front. In order to ensure safe communications between Gaul and Italy, between Rome and the northern frontier, the Alps had to be brought completely under Roman rule. In 25 the Salassi were made to surrender and in 7 it was the turn of the rest of the major valleys. This success was commemorated by the erection of the famous trophy at La Turbie. But the northern front comprised two sectors, the Rhine and the Danube. It looks as thought it was Augustus's intention to push back this frontier as far as the Elbe, but the Sicambri had already inflicted a setback on Lollius in 16, so Drusus immediately set about strengthening this frontier. Between 12 and 9 he succeeded in reaching the Elbe after a series of brilliant campaigns, but he died on the way back. Tiberius consolidated his defensive work in 8–7 BC and in AD 4. But the Roman strategists were brought back to reality by the defeat of Varus at the hands of Arminius in 9, and had to abandon all ideas of extending their domination over Germany. At the most, a few operations by Tiberius and Germanicus enabled this front to be stabilized.

The northern sector also consisted of the Danube regions. In 15 BC Drusus and Tiberius captured Raetia and Vindelicia, to which was added Noricum. It was particularly between 12 and 10 that the most important events took place. Tiberius completed the pacification of the territories situated on the right bank of the Danube which others had prepared. As early as 19 Pannonia had been reached, and in 13 Lucius Calpurnius Piso had made an armed incursion into Moesia. Combined operations had meant that the Elbe was reached from the Danube as well. The security of this region was also ensured by making the kingdoms of Thrace, Crimea and Pontus protectorates. But Bohemia, which was very celticized, was invaded by the Marcomanni, whose king, Marbod, fought against Tiberius from 6 to 9. This war came at a particularly bad moment, since Pannonia and Dalmatia rebelled in 6.

The third factor to which Augustus addressed himself was the East. Firstly, the emperor reinforced the Roman presence there. In 25 BC he reduced Galatia to the status of a province; between 1 BC and AD 4 he sent his grandson Gaius to Armenia, where he was to die at the end of his mission. Finally, Judaea, which was left to its kings (Herod being the most famous), was divided, and entrusted to prefects from 6 to 42. Relations with the Parthians were fairly peaceful and were on a diplomatic rather than a military footing. In 20 Tiberius received the standards that had been taken from Crassus and Mark Antony (this scene was represented on the breastplate of the famous statue of Augustus found at Prima Porta). Finally, though this has no bearing on military history, ambassadors came to the imperial court from the Indian kingdoms.

The southern front posed different problems in its eastern and western sectors. Egypt, which had been captured following the battle of Actium in 31 BC, soon became a launching pad for expeditions to remote places. Its first governor, Cornelius Gallus, had to quell a rebellion in the south. Then Aelius Gallus explored Arabia, but if this was an attempt at an expansion eastwards it failed, as did that of C. Petronius in the direction of Ethiopia (24–21 BC). The province of Arabia was the scene of two major periods of war. Between 35 and 20 BC Rome fought the Garamantes (inhabitants of modern Fezzan); the dates for the second wave of troubles are uncertain – either from AD 1 to 6 or from 6 BC to AD 9. This time the rebels were Nasamones of Tripolitania, the Musulamii from the region of Tebessa and the nomadic Gaetuli on the borders of the desert and 'useful' Africa.

At the end of this brief analysis it is apparent that difficulties accumulated towards the end of Augustus' reign, with the revolt of Pannonia and Dalmatia in AD 6, the war against Marbod from 6 to 9 and the disaster of Varus in 9. Nevertheless, the overall achievement remained considerable and historians too often forget this. Firstly, the conquests covered immense territories (north-west Spain, the Alps, the right bank of the Danube, Egypt, the provincialization of Galatia and Judea); secondly, the institutional and strategic achievements mentioned above cannot be dismissed as worthless either. For both these reasons it is time that at least the importance of the military achievements of Augustus' reign was recognized, even if he himself is not rehabilitated as a general.

Augustus' successors in the first century

The Julio-Claudians

Several of Augustus' successors are generally thought of as lunatics or even monsters. This is the case with Tiberius, Caligula and Nero; as for Claudius, he is seen as a drunkard, the plaything of his freedmen and successive wives who had no qualms about being unfaithful to him all the time, even in public. Nevertheless, whether merit·is due to the rulers or to their advisers, their reigns were marked by many successes.

The first of the rulers, Tiberius, had proved a good general before becoming Emperor,[9] but his reign got off to a bad start with the mutiny of the legions in Pannonia and Germany;[10] Germanicus restored discipline, and then set off with them across the Rhine (14–17) to consolidate his power over them. Moravia, on this front, also became a protectorate. Immediately after these events (18–19) Germanicus was sent to the East. There Rome's empire increased; in 17 Cappadocia was reduced to a province, Armenia became a protected kingdom, and Judaea was annexed in 34. This progress did not prevent the situation from becoming strained again towards the end of his reign. However, most characteristic of Tiberius' reign were the national revolts. Drusus was sent to Illyria, and Thrace became unsettled in 20–2.[11] It is above all Africa and Gaul that were the scenes for the biggest crises. In Africa, whose army was responsible to the Senate, a deserter by the name of Tacfarinas encouraged his Musulamii people to revolt. This spread,[12] and it appears that Tiberius was not too unhappy at exposing the inadequacies of that illustrious assembly who allowed the situation to drag on from 17 to 24. In Gaul in 21 there was the revolt of the Treveri and Aedui, named after their leaders as that of Florus and Sacrovir.[13]

Caligula was no keener than Tiberius to undertake any important reforms, as Augustus' structures still held good. But problems continued to arise on the frontiers. On the negative side of the balance for this mad ruler there was the abortive campaign against the Chatti in 39 and a temporary abandonment of Armenia and Judaea. On the positive side there was the setting up of a vast Thracian state and the inauguration of a new policy for Africa. The assassination of Ptolemy, King of Mauretania, in 40 was part of a coherent policy geared to a new annexation, even if one of Caligula's motives was probably psychopathic.

When Claudius came to power he was confronted immediately by the new situation in the west of the Maghreb caused by the death of the ruler; Aedemon, one of his freedmen, had incited an insurrection. In 42 an excellent general named Suetonius Paulinus was sent to this new theatre of operations with a large number of troops. The Caesarean Mauretanians of Cherchel and the Tingitanian Mauretanians of Tangiers were added to the list of provinces. But the major achievement of Claudius' reign was the conquest of Britain,[14] something Julius Caesar had failed to do. In 44 Judaea was annexed once more and entrusted to procurators. It kept this status until 66. In 45 or 46 it was the turn of Thrace to be integrated into the Empire. These successes make Claudius' reign an important milestone in Rome's military history. Moreover, this ruler, who was the first reformer of Augustus' work, was also respected by the soldiers.[15] He passed a number of laws and reorganized the career structure of equestrian officers: according to Suetonius 'the military career of equestrians was regulated in this fashion; after command of a cohort he prescribed the command of a cavalry *ala* then the tribunate of a legion.'[16] But Claudius experienced problems. He had to send Vespasian[17] to Strasbourg in 41–2 to control the Chatti in Germany, then Corbulo[18] to subdue the Chauci and the Frisians in 48–9. At the end of Claudius' reign came the most unpleasant surprise: Vologeses invaded Armenia.

Nero was therefore confronted with a difficult situation straight after his accession. Unfortunately he was both unable and incapable of embarking upon reform or conquest; the fact that all his wars were defensive differentiated him from the other emperors. The first task then was to fight the Parthians (58–63);[19] Corbulo conquered Armenia then ran into difficulties; but then even Adiabene was occupied in 61. At the same time, at the other end of the Empire, Britain still refused to be dominated by the Romans[21] and a woman, Queen Boudica, symbolized the resistance of her people. Suetonius Paulinus, who was still available, was unable to get the better of the Britons. Here again, it must be said that the wars waged under Nero had their origins in the policies of Claudius. In 66 an insurrection broke out in Judaea;[21] Vespasian and his son Titus were sent to restore order in this sector, but in 68 Nero died before they carried out their task.

The crisis of 68–9

Nero's failure gave rise to a crisis, which had three effects of a military nature. First, the war in Judaea dragged on; second, the different provincial armies, supported by their civilians, sought to promote their own generals to the imperial purple; and third revolts broke out in various nations of the Empire.

The legate of Gallia Lugdunensis, Vindex, and the commander of the *legio III Augusta*, Macer, became political dissidents but were unable to achieve their ambitions, as Galba, with the help of Spain, was the first to have himself acknowledged as emperor. Coins were minted celebrating the legions (pl.xxxvi,35). But Galba was abandoned by his troops because he was too authoritarian,[22] and with the support of the Praetorians Otho tried to replace him. Then it was the turn of the legions in Germany to impose their candidate, Vitellius.[23] Taking advantage of the fact that the Romans were fighting among themselves some peoples tried to assert their independence. In 69 Civilis persuaded the Batavians to rebel; in 70 Classicus, Tutor and Sabinus proclaimed a Gallic empire. According to Tacitus the rebels were fighting for a variety of reasons, 'the Gauls for their freedom, the Batavians for glory and the Germans in order to pillage.'[24] Order was restored when Vespasian decided to march on Rome, backed by the legions of the East and of the Danube;[25] when it is recalled that it was there that the greatest concentrations of troops were to be found, the reasons for his success are understandable.

The Flavians

In any case Vespasian was rightly considered to be an officer of outstanding quality.[26] He had left his son Titus to solve the Jewish problem, and in 71 he was successful, as shown by an arch in the forum bearing the portrayal of the seven-branched candelabrum taken from the

Temple of Jerusalem. But the last pocket of resistance, the citadel of Masada, held out until 73. In Britain, too, several great generals came and went, Cerialis (71–4), Frontinus (74–7) and Agricola (77–84). At the same time a policy of expansion was adopted; in Germany the valley of the Neckar was occupied and the resistance orchestrated by the prophetess Velleda was met. In 72 Commagene was definitively annexed to the province of Syria.

Vespasian's eldest son, Titus, was not emperor long enough to be able to embark on any sort of project. The same cannot be said for his brother Domitian,[27] who inherited the problem of the Britons and left Agricola to bring the situation to a successful conclusion. The Germans were the first to cause problems. In 83 (or 81?) the Emperor sent Frontinus to fight the Chatti. Then a legate, Lucius Antonius Saturninus, attempted an insurrection (88–9), which probably brought about the disappearance of the *legio XXI Rapax*. In 89–90 Domitian decided on the annexation of the Agri Decumates (the angle formed by the Upper Rhine and Upper Danube), and he divided the province of Germany into Upper and Lower Germany. On the Danube in 85 the Quadi and the Marcomanni were becoming restive, as were the Jazyges and the Sarmatians, who were to be much talked about from then on. But it was the Dacians who caused Domitian the most problems; an altar and a mausoleum erected at Adamklissi at the time (the trophy itself dates from Trajan) could not allow Roman generals to forget that it had been necessary to buy off these barbarians because they could not be defeated. In Africa Domitian ordered the annihilation of the Nasamones of Tripolitania. Finally he received a request of an alliance from Vologeses to repel the Alans.[28] His failure to defeat the Dacians was instrumental in the fall of this emperor, and yet he had been well received in military circles, enjoying their support in the first three years at least of his reign (see n.27).

THE GREAT WARS

If the troops in Spain in the second century can rightly be called an 'army of peace',[29] the same cannot be said of the other legions which enjoyed a precarious calm.

Trajan and offensive wars

It seems unnecessary to waste much time on Nerva; in the eyes of many historians the principal merit of his short reign was to have chosen a worthy successor. At the end of 97 troubles broke out in Germany and the heir designate therefore found his place in history.[30]

This famous man has not received universal acclaim. For J. Carcopino

Trajan was the ruler who brought the Empire to its highest point.[31] P. Petit on the other hand sees in him only 'a roughneck soldier of low intelligence' with a weakness for 'wine and young boys'.[32] In military affairs his only attempt at reform seems to have been his effort to increase Italy's population in order to facilitate the recruitment of legions (p. 88). His reign was marked by the strong military character he exhibited, which did not displease the army.[33] In fact he was essentially an active ruler whose policy was war. With him the age of conquests had returned.

Historians have often ignored his policies, and yet it was in his reign that the Aures was reached and began to be enveloped. This expansionist phase has sometimes been forgotten because the emperor did not feel it necessary to add to his title a name celebrating the event. This is why epigraphists have not paid enough attention to the fact.[34] Another reason is that at the same time the much more complicated conquest of Dacia was underway. The ruler himself crossed the Danube and had to lead several campaigns between 101 and 105, though pacification was achieved only in 107. This victory allowed him to call himself 'Dacicus'; it was the source of two important monuments: a trophy dedicated to Mars Ultor on the site of Adamklissi,[35] and the famous Trajan's Column at Rome. It is this campaign that explains why Romanian is a Romance language.

The campaign in Dacia was hardly over, yet soldiers were sent to the East;[36] in 105–6 the province of Arabia (modern Jordan) was created, not for any intrinsic value of its own, but as part of a strategic system that would enable the Romans to conquer Mesopotamia. This conquest in turn would be the prelude to the destruction of the Parthian state. Chronologically it was the second major military project of his reign, but in view of what was at stake it was the first in strategic importance.

Various reasons could be advanced to explain this enterprise.[37] Economically it was hoped to be able to have greater control over trade with India; politically the emperor was keen to add even more glory to his name; strategically the concept of a new defensive line covering Armenia and the whole of northern Mesopotamia made sense since Rome could not destroy the enemy. At least ten legions with their auxiliaries were brought in between 113–14 and Trajan's death. In 115 the Upper Tigris and the Upper Euphrates came under the control of Romans who pushed further on in the following year to reach Nisibis, Edessa and Ctesiphon. Adiabene (ancient Assyria) was also conquered. But in 117 the Parthians reacted and there was a rebellion of the Jews who were dispersed among the provinces at the death of Trajan.

'Pax Romana'

Trajan's successor, Hadrian, poses the difficult historical question of whether or not he was a pacifist. Indeed, was such an attitude even conceivable in the ancient world? Whatever the answer, this ruler's moderation earned him the reputation of a mediocre strategist.[38] As soon as he became emperor he gave orders for Trajan's conquests in Mesopotamia to be abandoned on the grounds that even if their defence was possible, the financial cost would be too high. He even went so far as to meet the King of the Parthians in 123 and concluded a peace treaty with him. Some historians have perhaps wrongly interpreted his decisions as a profound change in imperial strategy. In any case, the Jewish problem had to be settled. It had been taken on by Lusius Quietus, one of Trajan's generals, in 117, and renewed fighting between 132 and 135, this time in Judaea, enabled the question to be settled for some time, even if a few massacres were necessary to achieve a result. Sesterces were minted celebrating the armies of several provinces (Spain, Britain, Germany, Raetia, Noricum, Moesia, Dacia, Cappadocia, Syria and Mauretania).

Hadrian may not have been a conqueror, but he did ensure that traditions were upheld. Some new regulations that he instituted were still in force a century later.[39] Above all he saw to it that the Empire was ready to defend itself. Fortifications were built in Germany, Raetia and Britain (the famous Hadrian's Wall),[40] as well as perhaps in Africa if the Seguia bent el-Krass does in fact date to this period. The Emperor inspected camps and ramparts (see n.39) and often made a personal visit to see whether the troops were training regularly (p. 115f.). He is often credited with the creation of ethnic *numeri*, but the view today is that Trajan, or even Domitian, was actually responsible for this innovation. Finally, it was in this period that two legions possibly disappeared, the *XXII Deiotariana* and the *IX Hispana*, the latter being cashiered because of lack of discipline or possibly annihilated by the Brigantes in Britain.

Were it not for the Jews and perhaps the Britons, Hadrian's reign could pass for a period of great calm from the military point of view. Antoninus Pius, whose reputation as a general was considerable,[41] did not have to face any major conflict either, but his reign was marked by a series of small tremors. A new wall in Britain extended the imperial frontier northwards, but is often said to have been built to counter an attack. On the northern frontiers a few conflicts with the Germans and the Dacians needed to be settled. To the east a treaty was made in 155 with Vologeses, but this did not prevent war breaking out again in Armenia in 161–3, while the Jews were restive once more. On the southern front an insurrection in Egypt and a bigger one in Mauretania have been identified.[42] On the whole there was nothing very serious, just a series of small uprisings all around the edges of the Empire.

The alarm sounds

The situation worsened under Marcus Aurelius, the philosopher-emperor. He was to prove a fine war leader[43] with a good eye for the competent adviser.[44] Some relatively minor disturbances were marking certain provinces, such as the two Mauretanias again; Egypt was the scene of the *boucoloi* movement in 172–3; Greece was invaded by Costoboci barbarians.[45] But the Empire's military history was shaken by two major wars.[46]

In the east the Parthians invaded Syria, but there is no indication that the Romans were particularly worried about this at the time. The war lasted four years, from 162 to 166, with Lucius Verus backing up Marcus Aurelius.[47] If it had not already happened, it is possible that it was during these hostilities that the *XXII Deiotariana* disappeared and the *II* and *III Italica* were created. The conflict had a successful outcome with the establishment of a new province, Mesopotamia, that was put in the hands of Avidius Cassius.

But worse was to come. Marcus Aurelius' Column tells of a series of struggles that took place on either side of the Danube.[48] As early as 166–7 a first German assault crossed Pannonia and stopped at the Adriatic. The Goths were pushing at the backs of the Quadi, the Marcomanni, the Jazyges and the Roxolani. Marcus Aurelius fought them until 169. Then, in 171, a second offensive began. Every year a new wave of barbarians reached the frontier, the Quadi in 172, the Sarmatians in 173, the two tribes together in 174, the Sarmatians on their own in 175. Marcus Aurelius had to be on the Danube from 172 to 175 fighting an increasingly difficult war. Again the Emperor had to join his soldiers for the third wave of fighting from 177 to 179, and he died among them the following year.

The end of the Antonine period was marked by a certain return of peace. Despite the faults attributed to him, Commodus was capable of conducting a relatively effective military policy, probably partly thanks to those around him.[49] To check the spread of banditry,[50] observation posts (*burgi*) were built, garrisons (*praesidia*) installed from the Danube to the Aures, and favourable conditions given to soldiers.[51] Britain experienced another period of unrest, but the main problem area was the Danube, where the legions had to fight the Sarmatians and the Jazyges (or Roxolani) yet again in 184–6, and then the Quadi and the Marcomanni in 188–9.

The Antonine dynasty ended with the assassination of Commodus. The second century, often considered to be Rome's golden age, did not bring many modifications to the military domain; apart from the construction of several fortifications and the setting up of ethnic *numeri* (if these were not in fact earlier) there is little that can be credited to its balance sheet. As for campaigns, the era was characterized by the offensive wars of Trajan and of Marcus Aurelius, though even the latter's final ones were more defensive in nature.

THE THIRD CENTURY: THE SEVERI AND THE MILITARY CRISIS

The Severan era: reforms and wars

With the death of Commodus and with it the end of the Antonine dynasty, power passed into the hands of a certain Pertinax, but not for long. He was considered to be an officer of high quality, but perhaps too authoritarian.[52] The *Historia Augusta* gives an interesting piece of information for this point in time, saying that already nobles were seeking to avoid their military obligations, but its evidence is not entirely trustworthy. Certainly some were influenced by the harshness of the wars fought under Marcus Aurelius, but they must have been the exception.

At this point one of the Early Empire's most militarily important reigns began. Septimius Severus proved himself not only a great strategist but also an active reformer.[54] He was familiar with civil and foreign wars. Indeed, as soon as Pertinax was assassinated, a situation analogous to that at Nero's death arose. Four people said they had legitimate claims to rule the Empire. At Rome the Praetorians auctioned the Empire to Didius Julianus, the highest bidder,[55] while the legions of Pannonia, backed by those of the Danube, proclaimed their leader, Septimius Severus as Emperor. Coins from 193–4 (pl.XXXVI,36) list the legions already bought or still to be bought: *I Italica, I Adiutrix, I Minervia, II Adiutrix, II Italica, III Italica, IV Flavia, V Macedonica, VII Claudia, VIII Augusta, XI Claudia, XIII Gemima, XIV Gemina, XXII Primigenia, XXX Ulpia.* At the same time the soldiers of Syria supported their legate, Pescennius Niger,[56] a good but too authoritarian general. The actions of the soldiers of Britain were cleverly anticipated by Septimius Severus who offered the title of Caesar to their general, Clodius Albinus.[57] He too was a talented officer and just as demanding as the others. Such a stalemate could obviously not persist for ever; one had to eliminate the other three. Septimius Severus was able to display the full extent of his military qualities as he fought on several fronts, both against his rivals and against the Parthians. The first campaign took place in the east in Osrhoene and Adiabene, the second saw him lead his troops as far as Ctesiphon. Upper Mesopotamia was annexed and the rival generals were eliminated.

But Septimius Severus should not be regarded as a mere swashbuckler. He proved a great reformer of the army, probably second only to Augustus, a fact often overlooked by historians. His role in this domain was considerable. The measures he took were based on a conscious decision to use the army against the Senate.[60] On his deathbed he is reported to have advised his sons to 'make the army rich and never mind about the others'. The words are too good to be true, but nevertheless they do give an accurate indication of the feelings at that time.

191

Dates	Official name of the conflict	Adversaries
194	*expeditio urbica*	Didius Julianus
194/5	*expeditio parthica*	Parthians; Osrhoene; Adiabene
195/6[59]	*expeditio asiana*	Pescennius Niger
196/7	*expeditio gallica*	Clodius Albinus
197/8	*expeditio parthica mesopotamica*	Parthians; Mesopotamia

Table 35: The wars of Septimius Severus 194–8

Indeed, some of the measures taken by him were solely meant to improve the living conditions of the soldiers. First there was a pay rise,[61] only the second since the amount had been fixed by Augustus, that established a new relationship between prices and salaries. Secondly, the everyday fare was improved by the organization of a military *annona*;[62] the word designates the amount of payment in kind that was sent directly to the army for its food (it does not seem therefore that a new tax was created, contrary to certain beliefs). Furthermore, the soldiers were allowed to live with women outside the camp (see n.61); it is therefore inaccurate to say that Septimius Severus allowed them 'to marry'.

The Emperor also favoured the creation of military colleges.[63] The first of the associations had been created at the time of Augustus, but were authorized only for veterans and for burial reasons; on leaving the army each soldier paid a sum of money to the treasurer of the community in return for a guaranteed decent burial. Colleges also existed in civilian society with a similar burial, or more generally religious, function. They existed well before Augustus' time. Their organization into trade guilds occasionally gave them a protest quality (some historians believed that these institutions were the embryo of a trade union movement). The Roman state was therefore very suspicious of them and insisted on their being authorized in order to keep them under control.

Septimius Severus extended the right to form colleges to soldiers who were still on active duty. However, this authorization was granted to officers only. We know of associations of *duplicarii*, *beneficiarii*, *tesserarii*, *cornicularii*, *optiones*, musicians, horsemen, hospital staff, 'accountants' (*librarii*) and armoury wardens (*custodes armorum*), and the list is by no means exhaustive. We know also that the soldiers concerned paid money into a fund (*arca*) managed by a treasurer (*quaestor*); they held meetings in a small room of the *principia* called a *schola*, containing stone benches and an apse. Many inscriptions giving the regulations (*leges*) of these colleges have been found. They were always divided into three sections, beginning with a preamble honouring the Emperor. Then came the list of 'founding fathers'. Finally there were the articles fixing the enrolment fee, the amount to be paid to the soldier in the event of promotion, retirement, a voyage and even demotion, and that to be paid to his heir in the event of death.

Historians are divided as to the function these associations performed. Some feel that they were religious, particularly funerary, like the colleges of veterans. Others feel that their meeting in a *schola* proves that they were there to celebrate the cult of the Emperor. Neither of these suggestions is particularly convincing since their *leges* make no mention of either function. Other specialists argue that these associations ensured the defence of the professional interests of their members, but again there is no mention of this in the texts. On the other hand, they do show clearly that the officers in question were concerned about having both a deposit bank and an insurance company, playing a similar role to a pension fund. These military colleges, which were set up in 197–8, were still functioning in the reign of Alexander Severus.

Besides these concrete material advantages, Septimius Severus also endeavoured to flatter the soldiers' self-esteem. He granted centurions the right to parade in white uniform (*albata decursio*) and the men (probably only the *principales*) to wear the golden ring (see n.61). Finally he had coins struck to commemorate certain legions. All this was not the result of chance. It has been said that the Emperor wanted to use the army against the Senate, but it should be noted that he gave greater privileges to the officers than to the ordinary soldiers, and this fact may prompt the question as to whether he had something else in mind. Perhaps he was attempting to improve recruitment, to attract to the camps the elite of the younger generation and to encourage officers to strive for promotion.

He did not limit his activities to trying to please the troops however, but played an active part in the reorganization of strategy. Firstly he increased numbers,[64] notably by creating three legions (*I, II, III Parthica*); two of these were based in Mesopotamia, the third near Rome. They were commanded by equestrian prefects, not senatorial legates, and this choice was politically motivated, since equestrians were directly responsible to the emperor. In any case, it was probably becoming increasingly difficult to find volunteers among the aristocracy. If we also take into account the increasing use of detachments (*vexillationes*),[65] led by *duces* or *praepositi* who were chosen by the central authority when large numbers of troops were involved, it is understandable that the spread of these practices would lead to a separation of civilian and military powers in the provinces.

A. von Domaszewski has criticized Septimius Severus for having 'barbarianized' the army. G.R. Watson and R.E. Smith on the other hand have come to the Emperor's defence.[66] In their eyes he did not drive Roman citizens away from the army any more than Vespasian had excluded Italians from it. In point of fact, the intentions of the Emperor are irrelevant. What we observe is that there was no profound change in the quality of recruitment at the beginning of the third century, just a steady decline, though the momentum of the decline is probably slightly greater than that which was already taking place at the end of the previous century. Soldiers were speaking a more vulgarized Latin and the *origo castris* soldiers increased in relation to the Romanized citizens. In addition, the legionaries were more often employed to carry out more menial tasks such as policing the roads. We do not know if this downgrading was intentional or not, but we can say that the measures Septimius Severus took did at least slow down this lessening of status. It also remains a fact that his military policies were more reforming than all those found during the first two centuries of the Early Empire with the exception of Augustus' organization of the army.

In 206 the Emperor left to fight in Britain, where he was to die five years later. His son and heir, Caracalla, was left to fight on three fronts. Firstly, he had to complete the task of pacification of the island begun by his father. Secondly, he had to repel the Alamanni who were threatening the Agri Decumates, and the Goths who were threatening the Danube defences (212–14). Thirdly, he went to the East to wage war against the Parthians of Artabanus IV (215–17). It was during this conflict that he died, apparently lamented by all the soldiers.[67]

After an interruption, caused by Macrinus' usurpation of power, the Severan dynasty resumed, but in order to achieve this Elagabalus had to 'bribe' the *legio III Cyrenaica*, stationed near his home. During his reign there was another campaign against the Marcomanni,[68] and there were still noblemen seeking posts of command in the army.[69]

The history of the dynasty finished with another important reign, that of Severus Alexander. The first offensive was on the eastern border in 223 when the army had to fight the Sassanian Persians under Ardaschir. In 232 the Emperor himself went to the warfront.[70] Elsewhere the legions had to repel the Alamanni who were attacking Gaul.[71] At the same time a series of insurrections broke out in the two Mauretanias,[72] in Illyria, in Armenia and perhaps in Isauria.[73] In all probability it was these attacks as much as his own personal nature that led him to change the structures of the army, and the time was propitious. The success of Severus Alexander's military exploits is attributable partly to his own personal qualities,[74] partly to those of his generals.[75] The soldiers too were not slow to approve his plan of action, although not all the officers were over-enthusiastic about following him every time. An important change in tactics can be traced to his reign, namely the very frequent use of archers and cavalrymen, particularly the armoured variety, the cataphracts (see n.29). To meet new demands many auxiliaries were recruited in the East and in Mauretania. Thus gradually the Roman army was changing.

The third-century crisis: characteristics

The mid-third century was marked by a profoundly serious crisis whose origin was essentially military. It stemmed from a combination of

German and Iranian offensives. The barbarians living near the northern frontier were pushed forward like billiard balls by others coming up behind. The origin of this pressure is to be found in the Far East. To the east the Arsacide Parthians were overthrown by a revolution that brought to power the Sassanian Persians, who were characterized by an unusually intolerant religion and a particularly aggressive nationalism. Rome found it difficult to cope with both these fronts at the same time.

As if that were not enough, the invasions caused widespread disruption in other areas. In politics the demands of the war caused the nature of power to change. Rulers were often generals, whom soldiers could make or break.[78] Assassinations meant that reigns were short-lived. In terms of the economy there was a downturn as traders, towns and rural areas were ruined. Society also suffered from another aspect of the disruption as bands of brigands ran wild in the provinces and noblemen could no longer manifest their generosity towards the community. Finally, consciences were troubled; if the gods allowed these disasters it was because they wanted to manifest their irritation, but about what? They invoked the famous 'impiety' of the Christians who did not honour Jupiter or Mars or any of the heavenly powers, and this explains the persecutions.

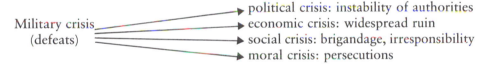

Military crisis
(defeats)
political crisis: instability of authorities
economic crisis: widespread ruin
social crisis: brigandage, irresponsibility
moral crisis: persecutions

Table 36: The third-century crisis

Nevertheless, the scale of the disaster should not be exaggerated, and modern historiography tends to emphasize the things that were untouched by the crisis; every region was not affected equally, every social class did not suffer to the same extent, every reign did not see the same troubles. Moreover, some rulers were able to react, even if this did mean a certain militarization of their regime. On the whole, strategy becomes more defensive[79] and tactics were more often based on armoured cavalry and archers. To demonstrate this evolution we need to return to our chronological line of enquiry.

The limits of the crisis

The third-century crisis is considered to have become serious under Maximinus I, the Thracian. This emperor was a good general;[80] he changed the structure of the senior staff[81] and in his reign it was still possible to find senators capable of holding a command.[82] What is more, the eastern front experienced a period of calm. It was essentially the

Germans, then the Sarmatians and the Dacians that threatened the security of the Empire. Two facts can be highlighted as they mark the beginning of a new era. Firstly, no previous emperor had come up through the ranks from a humble background. Secondly, the military alert seemed serious enough for important steps to be taken. Crushing taxes were levied to find the money that needed to be raised. This led to revolts breaking out in 238 in the proconsular province of Africa as the inhabitants rebelled against the tax burden and proclaimed their governor and his son emperors. We know them as Gordian I and Gordian II. The legion of Numidia hesitated before savagely crushing this movement. But the Italians had also revolted and despite the death of the two Gordians, Maximinus disappeared.

He was succeeded by Gordian III, grandson of Gordian I, whose reign seemed to his contemporaries to symbolize a return to tradition. The situation appeared to have some positive elements in that Timesitheus, his first Praetorian prefect, was a competent stategist,[83] noblemen were still supplying at least a good number of the army's officers[84] and the soldiers were not averse to their new commander-in-chief. However, his reign was marked by the horrendous military situation that was the third-century crisis – the conjunction of the attacks on the eastern and northern fronts. In 238 the Carpi and the Goths crossed the Danube, only to be repulsed, but the Persians also launched an assault.[86] The strain of these continual wars eventually wore down the soldiers' resolve, and they switched allegiance from Gordian III to his latest Praetorian prefect, Philip.

He bought peace in the East in order to hurry back to the West.[87] In 244 the Alamanni invaded Alsace and in 245–7 other Germans attacked the provinces in the Danube regions; in 248 the Carpi and the Goths launched another attack. The crisis deepened as rulers came and went in quick succession. The first Illyrian emperor, Trajanus Decius, (coins celebrated the *exercitus illuricianus*) may well have possessed good military qualities,[88] but they were of little avail when he faced King Kniva and his Goths. These pushed forward as far as Beroia and Philippopolis in 250, and were not appeased by the first major persecution of the Christians.

The darkest moments of this third-century crisis no doubt occurred during the joint reign of Valerian and his son Gallienus. In 252–3 the Alamanni and the Franks breached the Roman defences, ravaged Gaul and even reached Spain without meeting any resistance, but they were not so dangerous as the Goths. They sacked Asia Minor and the right bank of the Danube in 252–3, Greece and Asia Minor again in 256. In 258 they were once more in Anatolia. At the same time insurrections broke out in Numidia in 253–60, and Dacia was overrun in 256. It is uncertain whether Valerian's bad luck[89] or lack of energy[90] was the main reason for all this. He did indeed send his son Gallienus to Gaul from 254 to 258; the Franks and the Alamanni joined battle between 256 and 258, and were forced to sign a formal surrender. In 258 he sent an expeditionary force to endeavour to liberate the Danubian provinces. But the Romans were faced with a difficult, even frightening, situation, for as they struggled to contain the Germans in the north the Persians launched their offensive in the east.

In 256 Sapor conquered Antioch. Valerian set off to fight him, and was captured and executed in 259 or 260. This was a supreme humiliation for the Empire.[91] Simultaneously the Quadi and the Sarmatians were threatening Lower Pannonia. Its governor, Ingenuus, proclaimed himself Emperor and had coins struck to honour those legions whose support he was counting on.[92] The Roxolani arrived at the borders of Lower Moesia, where Regalianus, also appointed by the state, proclaimed himself Emperor too. He had the support of the armies of Upper Pannonia and Dacia. The invasions and usurpations that are so characteristic of the third-century crisis were happening simultaneously.

Reactions to the crisis

On Valerian's death the situation of Gallienus was particularly precarious.[93] According to the senatorial tradition he was a debauchee; while the barbarians were attacking the Empire 'the Emperor was spending his time in bars and taverns making friends with pimps and drunkards, when he wasn't with his wife Salonina or indulging his shameful lust for Pipa, one of the daughters of Attalus, King of the Germans.'[94] He proved, however, to be a great reformer and historians today therefore tend to rehabilitate him, but the situation that he inherited was difficult.

Abroad, the conjunction of enemy attacks remained unchanged. While Gallienus was making preparations for war against the Persians, in 259–60 the Franks launched their second major successful invasion of Gaul; Postumus was sent to counter them. In 261 the Alamanni reached Italy; a large army was raised in Milan, and according to M. Christol some of Gallienus' coins honour the military units that made up this force.[95] On those coins struck by this Emperor, probably in 258–9, we find the following units mentioned: Praetorian cohorts and legions *I Adiutrix, I Italica, I Minervia, II Adiutrix, II Italica, II Parthica, III Italica, IV Flavia, V Macedonica, VII Claudia, VIII Augusta, X Gemina, XI Claudia, XIII Gemina, XIV Gemina, XXX Ulpia* (see pl.xxxvi,37a). But that did not prevent the Goths ravaging Thrace, Greece and Cappadocia in 267, while the Alamanni were once more on the offensive, this time in Raetia. The Emperor himself intervened against the Germans.[96] Pirates were pillaging the coasts of Britain and northern Gaul. The valley of the Nile was under attack from the Blemmyes.

These disorders facilitated usurpations of power, which in turn added to the military difficulties. In the West, Postumus created a Roman Empire of the Gauls, while in 268 a plot enabled Aureolus to be named Emperor.

Victorinus succeeded Postumus (pl.xxxvi,37b). In the East several usurpers of the imperial power came and went, Macrianus and Quietus in 260, then Aemilianus. But the major role was played by the city of Palmyra. Urged on by his wife, the famous Zenobia, King Odeynath created his own Empire which he dreamed of extending towards Anatolia and Egypt. He did actually reach the latter.

Gallienus' main merit was perhaps to have understood that he did not have sufficient means to resist these separatist forces. Furthermore, he realized that even if these usurpers were not fighting for him they were at least fighting for Rome in as much as they were countering the Persians and the Germans. But he did better in reforming the army that he had under his orders. He established a new bodyguard corps (*protectores*, who may have been created earlier, it is true), but more importantly he modified the legions, probably in 262. According to Aurelius Victor 'he banned Senators from taking up a military career or even access to the army'.[97] In point of fact, all he did was to give legal confirmation to what was by now the practical reality, as senators proved unwilling to serve because of the harshness of the wars. Gallienus then abolished the posts of legate and laticlavian tribune, which meant that the camp prefects found themselves at the head of the legions since the two superior ranks had disappeared. All the legions now had a uniform command structure based on those that were stationed in Egypt or those that were called Parthica. At the same time the governors of the senatorial provinces were progressively replaced by the *praesides* of equestrian rank, to whom the prefects of the legions remained subordinate. It is possible that for a little while some exceptions continued to exist as provinces were still ruled by Senators, but in general this change reinforced the professionalism of the officer corps.

Another factor was the greater importance Gallienus gave to the tactical and strategic role of the cavalry. In doing this he was drawing his own conclusions from the events of 252–3 and 259–60 (having breached the defences, the barbarians met no further obstacles). The number of *equites* in a legion was increased from 120 to 726 men; detachments were entrusted to equestrian *praepositi* and larger units to *duces*; new mounted units were created; those that already existed, the Dalmatians, the Mauri, the *promoti*, the *scutarii*, the *stablesiani*, were increased in number by the Emperor. When these changes had been completed, they gave rise to a mobile reserve stationed behind the frontier, a strategic innovation that represented a small revolution. Nevertheless, the infantry still remained 'the queen of the battlefield'.

All these reforms pleased the soldiers,[98] as did the added one of the right to parade in white (*albata decursio*), which had been the privilege of centurions since the time of Septimius Severus. Taken as a whole, this Emperor's reign was more positive then senatorial tradition would have us believe. Admittedly enemies were attacking the Empire on all sides at

198

once, usurpations were an increasing problem, but the Empire did not collapse, and the army was better adapted to its mission. There was even some sign of a cultural renaissance in the arts and philosophy, with Hellenism at its centre. Persecution of the Christians halted; Salonius and Plotinus attempted to put Neoplatonism at the centre of a rebuilding programme of Roman morality.

The situation gradually improved from that time. But when Gallienus died *en route* to fight with Aureolus, the task of putting an end to this attempt at usurpation fell to his successor, Claudius II Gothicus. The Alamanni were once more defeated, this time near lake Garda, but the major success of his reign, that earned him his nickname, was his defeat of the Goths at Nish in 270. In the same year Zenobia finally extended her power to include Egypt and Asia Minor; Claudius II died without being able to do anything on this front. Scholars agree that he is to be credited with the increasing use of barbarian *auxilia*.

The subsequent reign is no less interesting. Aurelian tried to achieve unanimity once more in the Empire, this time through the worship of the sun god. Most of his time was spent fighting, either personally or through his generals. In 270 the Franks and the Alamanni were pushed back from the frontier of the Rhine. The same year saw the Marcomanni, the Vandals and the Sarmatians pushing against the Danube frontier, and the following year it was the turn of the Goths. But the Emperor led two campaigns in the east, in 271–2 and 272–3, to subdue Zenobia and her son Waballath.[99] As soon as he returned from there in 273, Aurelian waged war against the Alamanni, the Franks and probably the Carpi.[100] In 274 the Alamanni, abetted by the Juthungi, attacked Raetia, and later in the year joined with the Franks to cross the Rhine. In the same year Dacia was abandoned, troubles broke out in Britain.

None of these conflicts was of major importance, involving some brilliant victory or disaster. This state of affairs continued through the next reign, that of Tacitus. In 275 the Goths launched another assault on Asia Minor while the Alamanni, with the Franks, crossed over into Gaul in 275–6. It is sometimes claimed that the Senate found favour again in this reign, but if this actually was the case it was of short duration and had no effect on the army.

The following reigns tended to be short but reasonable, as the Emperors of the late third century, often Illyrians, were regarded as being good generals. Probus was no exception;[101] he managed to keep the soldiers' sympathies[102] while leading them on many campaigns.[103] In 276–8 the Franks and the Alamanni were expelled from Gaul, the Burgundians and the Vandals from Raetia. In 278–9 a campaign saw the expulsion of the Goths and perhaps the Getae from Thrace and Illyria. In 280–1 the Emperor advanced into Asia where he apparently clashed with the Persians, then into Egypt where he crushed the Blemmyes. During his reign a curious but significant event occurred when some Franks who had been driven towards the shores of the Black Sea stole ships, crossed the straits and sailed the Mediterranean. They paused en route only to pillage, travelled on through the straits of Gibraltar, turned north and returned to their homeland.[104] Their journey is an eloquent testimony to the fact that the Roman navy was no longer equal to its mission.

In fact, piracy was still rampant, particularly in the English Channel and off the coasts of Britain. The last rulers of the Early Empire, Carus, his sons Carinus and Numerianus, could do little of any consequence in this respect. The *Historia Augusta* accuses Carus of having militarized the State in order to pander to the soldiers, but this situation had already begun long before.[105] His main tasks were to push back the Sarmatians and the Persians on two fronts.[106] He died after a successful invasion of Mesopotamia. His sons, who were less energetic than their father, abandoned the conquered territories.[107] When they died, the elder probably assassinated, the younger certainly, power passed into the hands of Diocletian, but that is another story, another era.

THE ARMY, WAR AND POLITICAL PROPAGANDA

In the previous pages we have had many occasions to highlight the links established between the rulers and the armies. The Empire lived under a military monarchy as the Emperors themselves clearly recognized. With no compunction they utilized striking political propaganda which we can chart through inscriptions and coins.

The theme of victory

To start with they tried to persuade their subjects that their mere presence was enough to guarantee victory by skilfully playing on the word *imperator*. In the Republic the title was used to designate a victorious general whose success had been acknowledged by his own soldiers. It was they who conferred the title on him as a recognition of his worth. This tradition was maintained during the Empire. Two writers explain how Titus was honoured in this way. Suetonius wrote: 'During the final assault on Jerusalem Titus personally shot twelve defenders with twelve arrows, and captured the city on his daughter's birthday. His soldiers' joy and affection for him were so intense that they saluted him as *imperator*.'[108] Josephus recounts the same episode, but uses a different tradition: 'Now that the rebels had taken refuge in the city, and the Sanctuary itself with all the buildings around it was on fire the Romans brought the insignia to the Temple courtyard. They set them up facing the east gate, offered sacrifices to them on the very same spot, and loudly proclaimed Titus *imperator*.'[109]

At first this honour went to the general who had actually been in command during the battle and it could be followed by a triumph in Rome. From 9 BC however, Augustus reserved for himself the exclusive rights to such a prestigious ceremony; he then acted as though every victory of the Roman army was not due to some officer but to his own divine power (*numen*) that had inspired the general on the field of battle at the time in question. After this date only the ruler had the right to a triumph and he accumulated the acclamations. Augustus collected 21, Tiberius 8, Claudius 27, etc. This use of victory as a means of political propaganda became so important that some Emperors attributed to themselves titles of success even when their troops had been defeated. To get rid of the Dacians Domitian bought peace, yet he still claimed for himself the title of *imperator* on this occasion.[110] However, this title then takes on a meaning other than the two just discussed, and comes simply to designate the Emperor.

Very soon afterwards other victory titles appeared. As early as the reign of Augustus a ruler was called Germanicus to celebrate Rome's domination over Germany, while later another was to receive the name of Britannicus for a similar reason. Caligula was the first to give himself a triumphal title; he called himself Germanicus. Claudius called himself Germanicus and then added Britannicus. Henceforth inscriptions mentioning rulers use both of these titles as well as any *imperator* acclamations. The famous arch at Beneventum has an inscription in which Trajan not only has the title *imperator* in both its connotations but also is honoured by the mention of his military successes:

> To the Emperor [*imperator*] Caesar Nerva Trajan, son of deified Nerva, the best (of the rulers), Augustus, Germanicus, Dacicus [= conqueror of the Germans and the Dacians], Supreme Pontiff, tribune for the eighteenth time, acclaimed victor [*imperator*] seven times, six times consul, father of the homeland, very courageous ruler, the Senate and the people of Rome (had this arch erected in his honour).[111]

The custom of having titles evoking conquered peoples lasted until the Late Empire. From Marcus Aurelius' time a superlative was added when he styled himself 'greatest conqueror of the Parthians'. By contrast, from Gordian III onwards Emperors stopped adding on their real or fictitious triumphs.

Links between the Emperors and particular units

In addition, especially in the third century, emperors strove to establish personal and political links between themselves and the different corps by bestowing honorary titles on them. Roman troops could receive three sorts of adjectives to describe them. First was that based on the name of

EMPERORS	TITLES	IMPERIAL SALUTATIONS
Augustus[113]		21
Tiberius		8
Caligula	Germanicus	
Claudius[114]	Germanicus Britannicus	27
Nero	(Germanicus)	
Vitellius	Germanicus	
Vespasian		20
Titus		17
Domitian	Germanicus	22
Nerva	Germanicus	2
Trajan	Germanicus (with Nerva)	
	Dacicus	13
	Parthicus	
Hadrian		2
Antoninus Pius	Germanicus?	2
Marcus Aurelius	Armeniacus	
	Parthicus maximus	
	Medicus	10
	Germanicus	
	Sarmaticus	
Lucius Verus	Armeniacus	
	Parthicus maximus ⎫ with Marcus	5
	Medicus ⎭ Aurelius	
Commodus	Germanicus ⎫ with Marcus	
	Sarmaticus ⎭ Aurelius	8
	Britannicus	
Septimus Severus	Arabicus	
	Adiabenicus	
	Parthicus maximus	15
	Britannicus maximus	
Caracalla	Parthicus maximus ⎫ with Septimius	
	Britannicus maximus ⎭ Severus	
	Germanicus	3
	Arabicus	
	Adiabenicus	
Geta	Britannicus with Septimius Severus	

EMPERORS	TITLES	IMPERIAL SALUTATIONS
Maximinus	Germanicus maximus	
	Sarmaticus maximus	7
	Dacicus maximus	
Gordian III		6
Philip	Parthicus maximus	
	Persicus maximus	
	Carpicus maximus	
	Germanicus	
Philip (son)	Carpicus ⎫ with Philip	
	Germanicus ⎭	
Decius	Dacicus maximus	
Valerian	Germanicus maximus	
Gallienus	Germanicus maximus	
	Dacicus maximus	
	Parthicus maximus	
	Persicus maximus	
Postumus	Germanicus maximus	
Claudius II	Germanicus maximus	
	Gothicus maximus	
	Parthicus maximus	
Aurelian	Germanicus maximus	
	Gothicus maximus	
	Parthicus maximus	
	Carpicus maximus	
	Dacicus maximus	
	Britannicus maximus	
	Sarmaticus maximus	
Waballath	Persicus maximus	
	Arabicus maximus	
	Adiabenicus maximus	
Tacitus	Gothicus maximus	
Probus	Germanicus maximus	
	Gothicus maximus	
Carus	Persicus maximus	
	Germanicus maximus	
Carinus	Persicus maximus ⎫ with	
	Germanicus maximus ⎬ Carus	
	Britannicus maximus	

Table 37: The victory theme in imperial titles[112]

the Emperor under whom the unit had been formed, e.g. *ala I Flavia*, *legio I Claudia*. Only in the first and second centuries did rulers use this method; we can count Augustus, Claudius, Galba (Sulpicius), the Flavians, Vespasian, Nerva, Trajan (Ulpius or Traianus), Hadrian and Antoninus Pius (Aelius), Marcus Aurelius and Commodus (Aurelius), and finally Septimius Severus (Septimius) among them. A particular case is that of a *legio Gemina*, so-called from the merger of two already-existing units.[115] Secondly came the adjectives denoting virtues; the *legio VII Gemina* was proclaimed *Felix* ('lucky') in 73–4 and 'pious' at the beginning of the third century; the *legio III Augusta* was called 'pious and vengeful' from Septimius Severus to 238, 'pious and loyal', under the Tetrarchy.

The third sort of adjective is that called 'variable'[116] since it changed with every ruler, being added to that of its founder; thus the *legio III Augusta* also became *Antoniniana*, then *Alexandriana*, then *Maximiniana* and so on. This practice originated with Domitian who wanted to honour the troops in Germany, was then copied by Commodus, but did not become common until the beginning of the third century. It spread fairly widely and affected the garrison at Rome just as much as the border armies or the fleet. The attested adjectives are as follows:

Domitianus -a	Gordianus -a
Commodianus -a	Philippianus -a
Septimianus -a	Decianus -a
Severianus -a (from Septimius Severus on)	Gallianus -a, Volusianus -a
Antoninianus -a	Valerianus -a, Gallienus -a
Alexandrianus -a	Postumianus -a
Severianus -a, Alexandrianus -a	Claudianus -a
Maximinianus -a	Tetricianus -a
Pupienus -a, Balbinus -a	Aurelianus -a

The significance of this third type of epithet has been analysed by J. Fitz,[118] who believes that they are purely chronological mentions; thus in a career structure (*cursus*) when a person states that he has been a tribune of the VIII Praetorian Cohort *Philippiana*, this simply means that the inscription was written in the time of Philip. A certain number of inscriptions seem to confirm this interpretation. However, in other cases, particularly for the beginning of the third century, these epithets do seem to have been bestowed as an honour. From then on it became almost automatic, but it is hard to believe that Emperors never had any ulterior motives in following this practice.

CONCLUSION

When considering the first three centuries as a whole from the Roman soldiers' point of view, the historian notes that change played only a secondary role. It was the permanent features that were important. Only four rulers were capable of introducing changes of any consequence, of whom the most active was Augustus. He not only set up the new structure, he was also a great conqueror, whereas Trajan was no more than an active leader, carrying out major expeditions while making few changes to the structure he had inherited. On the other hand, Septimius Severus, in particular, and Gallienus promoted reforms that were much more significant than has been recognized. During the third century, moreover, changes whose details our meagre documentation only allows us to guess at were introduced. The crisis involved a huge shake up in tactics, strategy and recruitment. It is here that we can see an essential element to help us understand the efficiency of the Roman army, that is its capacity to adapt to changing circumstances.

The best-known legions and their major changes of location are listed below.

I *Adiutrix*	Germany (Vespasian to Domitian), Pannonia (Domitian), Dacia (early second century), then Pannonia.
I *Germanica*	Germany (Julio-Claudians).
I *Italica*	Moesia (from Vespasian).
I *Minervia*	Germany (from Domitian).
I *Parthica*	Mesopotamia (from Septimius Severus).
II *Adiutrix*	Britain (Flavians), Pannonia (from Domitian).
II *Augusta*	Spain (Augustus), Germany (Tiberius), Britain (from Claudius).
II *Italica*	Noricum (from Marcus Aurelius).
II *Parthica*	Italy (from Septimius Severus).
II *Trajana*	Syria (Trajan), Egypt (from Hadrian).
III *Augusta*	Africa-Numidia (Augustus to Diocletian).
III *Cyrenaica*	Egypt (Augustus to Trajan or Hadrian), then Arabia.
III *Gallica*	Syria.
III *Italica*	Raetia (from Marcus Aurelius).
III *Parthica*	Mesopotamia (from Septimius Severus).
IV *Flavia*	Dalmatia (Claudius to Domitian), Moesia (Domitian and Trajan), Dacia (early second century), then Moesia.
IV *Macedonica*	Spain (Augustus to Claudius), Germany (Claudius).
IV *Scythica*	Moesia (Julio-Claudians), Syria (from Nero).
V *Alaudae*	Germany (Julio-Claudians), Moesia (Flavians).
V *Macedonica*	Moesia (except when in Syria under Nero).
VI *Ferrata*	Syria (first century), Arabia (Trajan), Judaea (from Hadrian).
VI *Victrix*	Spain (Julio-Claudians), Germany (Flavians and Trajan), Britain (from Hadrian).

VII Claudia	Dalmatia (Claudius), then Moesia.
VII Gemina	Spain (from Vespasian).
VIII Augusta	Dalmatia, Pannonia, Moesia (Julio-Claudians), Germany (from Vespasian).
IX Hispana	Dalmatia, Pannonia (up to Claudius), Britain (Claudius to Domitian).
X Fretensis	Syria (Julio-Claudians), then Judaea.
X Gemina	Spain (up to Claudius), Pannonia (Nero), Germany (Flavians).
XI Claudia	Dalmatia (Claudius and Nero), Germany (Flavians), Moesia (from Trajan).
XII Fulminata	Egypt (Augustus and Tiberius), Syria (Tiberius to Nero), Cappadocia (from Vespasian).
XIII Gemina	Raetia, Germany (Augustus to Claudius), Pannonia (Claudius to Trajan).
XIV Gemina	Germany (Augustus to Claudius), Britain (Claudius and Nero), Germany (Vespasian to Domitian), then Pannonia.
XV Apollinaris	Dalmatia, Pannonia (up to Trajan) except Syria (Nero), then Cappadocia.
XVI Flavia	Cappadocia (Vespasian to Trajan), Syria (from Hadrian).
XX Valeria Victrix	Dalmatia, Germany (Augustus and Tiberius), Britain (from Claudius).
XXI Rapax	Raetia, Germany (up to Domitian).
XXII Deiotariana	Egypt (up to Hadrian).
XXII Primigenia	Germany.
XXX Ulpia	Pannonia (Trajan), Germany (from Hadrian).

Table 38: Legion movements in the first two centuries

206

8

THE PRACTICAL ROLE

It is quite obvious that a soldier's main *raison d'etre* was to wage war, to kill without being killed. We have seen above how Rome was able to prepare for this eventuality and to face up to it when it happened. But the soldiers also had an economic function that arose from their military function. As the demands of defence occupied a dominant place in the lives and thoughts of the Romans under the Early Empire, the army became an important group in society.[1] Juvenal asks 'Who could enumerate, Gallius, the privileges of a military career?'[2] On the other hand in the provinces, as P. Salway has shown, admittedly for a small region,[3] both the countryside and the material existence of populations were changed by the dynamic presence of soldiers.

To give a simplified picture of the situation we can say that these changes had a direct influence in two areas, those of the economy and demography.

ECONOMY

The economic life of the Mediterranean was transformed in several different ways by the presence of soldiers, and we can see first what was affected by their professional military activities.

Economic consequences of the military role

Pax Romana[4]

The legions' first duty was to prevent a potential army from entering the provinces. However, every historian knows that war ruins the territories on which it is fought; fields were burned, roads blocked, towns pillaged. The expression *pax Romana* is therefore doubly significant, implying both the absence of conflict and the consequent presence of material

207

wealth. Imperial ideology was built mainly on a string of advantages, victory – peace – prosperity.

But if the barbarian on the outside was a danger, the brigand on the inside was too.[5] Repression of these two forms of danger was the responsibility of the army. The State's objective of maintaining order formed an indissoluble whole in the mentality of the time; it could not conceive of an independent police force, apart from the *vigiles* of Rome and the few men attached to each municipal magistrate to catch chicken-thieves. But several corps in fact played a largely non-military role (see Chapters 1 and 2). Besides the *vigiles*, Rome had the *peregrini* and *frumentarii*, the first to carry out discreetly the authorities' dirty work, the second to act as spies, just like the Security Services today. In Italy and the provinces posts (*stationes*) were set up mainly along the roads; the soldiers stationed in them (see Chapter 2) went under various names, *burgarii* or *stationarii* or occasionally *beneficiarii*. On completion of their period of secondment (*expleta statione*)[6] they gave thanks to the gods before returning to their unit of origin. Use was also made of soldiers whose tactical role was that of mobility, notably *frumentarii* and *speculatores*. Finally, there is no doubt that the units placed under the orders of a provincial governor also acted as a police force, particularly where there was no threat of an external attack. The garrisons at Lyon and Carthage are good examples, but it should be remembered that there was no part of the Empire without troops.

The army therefore carried out the function of a police force in every place that lacked one, thus supplementing the role of the municipal authorities.

'Explorations'

Obviously the maintenance of law and order was a help towards prosperity, but it is not the only aspect to be considered. For a long time now historians have drawn attention to what they mistakenly have called explorations.[7] In fact they are more often than not expeditions organized, according to some, by the army with the sole aim of bringing back riches.

Thus in 30–29 BC the prefect of Egypt, Cornelius Gallus, sailed up the Nile as far as Philae. In 25–24 Augustus put Aelius Gallus, also prefect of Egypt, in charge of a reconnaissance mission to Arabia. He probably reached the edge of the Hadramaout and the Yemen before disaster struck. His successor Petronius took up Cornelius Gallus' project again and made the area further to the south a sort of marcher country.[8] Under Nero some Praetorians sailed up the Nile as far as the kingdom of Meroe.[9] Farther west, in the Mahgreb, the relationship between war and commerce can be demonstrated in the case of Phazania. Ch.-M. Daniels has established that the abundance of so-called Roman ceramics follows the soldiers' reconnoitres in this area. Thus in 19 BC L. Cornelius Balbus received triumphal honours for having fought his way as far as this region, but we find very little pottery dating from the Julio-Claudians. It was not until the Flavians that trading really developed, at precisely the date of the expeditions of Valerius Festus and Septimus Flaccus, as well as that of Julius Maternus to the mysterious country of Agisymba. Archaeologists have no difficulty in recognizing the second-century vases and amphorae as the consequences of this policy. Other parts of the ancient world could give us other examples.

Nevertheless, it would perhaps seem excessive to see only economic motives in these ventures. Security must have been a factor; in order to protect a territory it would not be a bad idea to be familiar with the peoples surrounding it. Furthermore, must one consider that these officers were totally devoid of any curiosity? They too had a natural thirst for knowledge; it may well be supposed that intellectual factors, culture even, played a role at the same time as security and the economy in defining the motives that justified these expeditions.

Civil engineering works

Soldiers also trained, and it should be remembered that officers made them undertake civil engineering tasks in order to increase their physical strength (p. 110). They built towns and monuments, they marked out roads. One example that rewards study is the aqueduct of Bejaia (Bougie) in Caesarean Mauretania.[11] Since the inhabitants of the city could not build it they asked their governor, who in turn asked his colleague, the legate of the *legio III Augusta*, to send him an architect. In 137 the *librator* Nonius Datus submitted a plan, but because the civilian population was unable successfully to put it into practice he went there himself, in 149 and 151–2. The workforce was drawn from the citizens at first but later supplemented by the Mauretanian army. On completion of the work, water could travel 21km (13 miles), descending from a height of 428m (1400ft) to 86m (280ft), via a tunnel.[12]

Maintaining the peace, keeping watch over the Empire's neighbours and keeping fit were all activities whose aim was military; the economic spin-off was only an indirect consequence of this but there is better information on this subject.

Soldiers as agents of the economy

Soldiers were an important link in the chain from production to consumption. The wealth of soldiers was a commonplace in literature particularly of the Early Empire,[13] but also of the Late Empire.[14]

Salaries

The fundamental factor of this affluence was their pay, to which historians have given too little prominence, because it was considerable and regular. Soldiers formed part of the rare salaried class in antiquity, and they were relatively affluent. One point needs to be made, however: in antiquity the 'salary scale', that is the difference between the highest and the lowest incomes, was far greater than is the case today. Hence an ordinary soldier seems to have been poorly paid in comparison with a procurator, but well paid in comparison with a peasant, a farmworker or a slave.

The importance of these sums is demonstrated by the ceremonies that accompanied their payment. In the Black Sea area under Hadrian it was left to an officer who was on a tour of inspection.[15] At Dura-Europos in the third century men went to fetch the pay (ad opinionem stipendii). They returned with it, following a set pattern of duties; foot-soldiers ensured the protection of the dromedaries carrying the money, while they in turn were escorted by mounted troops. The distribution in the camp was followed by a parade and then the accounts (ratio) were sent back to the procurator.[16]

While we know the methods of distribution, it is not easy to ascertain the amounts involved; the few facts have been so manipulated by scholars that the resulting statistics are unreliable by their very divergences. It is true that some elements are unproblematic. The Roman army stuck to one basic principle, namely that salaries were linked to status.[17] An officer was paid more than a centurion who was paid more than a soldier. Ordinary soldiers were paid less than a sesquiplicarius who received 1.5 times their salary, or a duplicarius (double their salary) or even a triplicarius (three times their salary). Moreover even the same rank could receive different amounts according to the prestige of the unit; a Praetorian centurion received more than a cohort centurion, a legionary more than an auxiliary. It is known that salary increases were certainly granted on several occasions in the Early Empire.

The problems begin when we try to put forward some figures, as the few we have are not clear-cut. All calculations have been made from the best documented case, that of the legionary on single pay. We now know that payment was instituted from the end of the Republican era. The actual amount is not important here, but what is, is the fact that at the end of Augustus' reign it was fixed at 225 denarii per year (i.e. silver coins).[18] The first pay rise was decreed only about 83 under Domitian, who increased the amount to 300,[19] by adding a fourth payment equal to the three others. It was not until Septimius Severus, around 193, that the next pay rise was decided.[20] Although we do not know the actual size of the increase we do know that it was substantial. In their uncertainty historians have put forward three hypotheses: low (400 denarii a year), middling (450) and high (500). The middling solution may be preferable,[21] but the other two are worth considering. After that Caracalla increased his father's payment to ordinary legionaries by 50 per cent,[22] but as we do not know what this increase meant in numerical terms we have once again three suggestions: 600, 675 and 750 denarii per year. Be that as it may, these increases must be viewed in the context of a corresponding rise in prices from the time of Marcus Aurelius.

For the third century the situation is even more complex. The theory of a universal doubling of salaries under Maximinus seems to be destroyed by the papyrological evidence from Panopolis which prompts us to believe that wages were very stable during the period from Caracalla to Diocletian.[23] Nevertheless, the depreciation of money, which is well attested for this century of crisis, had to be compensated for. The military *annona* went some way to solving the problem of supplies, and emperors multiplied the exceptional distribution occasions such as the *donativa* and the *liberalitates*. Finally, some of the payments were made in kind.[24] As M. Christol has pointed out, the crisis between 250 and 274 caused a decentralization of the mints; they were set up near the *limes* and their production standardized.[25]

The pay of soldiers serving in other units is often calculated from the legionary data, as information is scarce. The garrison at Rome is best documented for the end of Augustus' reign.[26] A Praetorian's salary may well have been 375 denarii per year in AD 6, rising to 450, then to 750 in 14. When Augustus died the salary of the *urbaniciani* was probably 360 or 375 denarii, while that of the *vigiles* was only 150. Under Tiberius their pay caught up with, and then passed, that of the legionaries. Among the auxiliaries the mounted soldiers earned more than the foot-soldiers, but the amount the latter actually earned can only be guessed. One school of thought puts it at $\frac{5}{6}$ of a legionary's wage,[27] another at $\frac{2}{3}$,[28] while a third, more plausibly, puts it at $\frac{1}{3}$.[29] The salary of mounted soldiers in cohorts is not known; all we can say is that A. von Domaszewski was wrong to suppose that they earned less than a legionary.[30] The salary of sailors, too, is an unknown quantity, and has given rise to hypotheses;[31] sailors of the provincial fleets were probably on the same level as auxiliaries, while sailors of praetorian fleets were on a parity with the *urbaniciani*, or rather with the *vigiles*.

When we try to evaluate the salaries of high-ranking officers, more questions remain unanswered, as we rarely have any precise figures. In the third century the salary of a tribune, though we do not know for sure what sort of tribune he was, an angusticlavian, or more likely, a *sexmenstris*, was 6250 denarii according to the Thorigny marble.[32] Furthermore, it can be stated with confidence that the other equestrian officers must have been paid less than the lowest-paid procurator, who received 60,000 sesterces or 15,000 denarii per year. Historians have filled in the gaps in our knowledge with plausible figures. But it must be remembered that, despite the common belief, there is no certainty that the pay of centurions and officers rose in ratio to that of the ordinary soldiers. To give an indication of a possible income scale, we can use B. Dobson's findings to create **Table 39**.[33]

If we accept the figures in these two tables, based, it must be remembered, on several hypotheses, we can get some idea of the annual salary bill for the Roman army. Supposing that ordinary soldiers each received only the minimum salary, on a basis of 15,000 men for the garrison at Rome, 125,000 legionaries, 125,000 auxiliaries, and 40,000 sailors, we arrive at a very substantial military budget.

SOLDIERS		Augustus – Domitian	Domitian – Septimius Severus	Septimius Severus – Caracalla	Caracalla – Diocletian
Garrison at Rome	Praetorian	750	1000	1500	2250
	Urbanicianus	375	500	750	1125
	Vigiles	150	200	300	450
Legion	Foot-soldier	225	300	450	675
	Cavalryman	300	400	600	900
Auxiliary	Foot-soldier	75	100	150 (133⅓ ?)	225
	Cohort Cavalryman	150–200	200–266⅔	300–400	450–600
	Wing Cavalryman	250	333⅓	500	740
Fleet	Praetorian Fleet	150	200	300	450
	Provincial Fleet	75	100	150	225

OFFICERS AND NCOs	Augustus – Domitian	Domitian – Septimius Severus	Septimius Severus – Caracalla	Caracalla – Diocletian
Sexmenstris Tribune	1875	2500	3750	6250
Centurion = Cohort Prefect	3750	5000	7500	12,500
Primus Ordo = Angusticlavian Tribune	7500	10,000	15,000	25,000
Wing Prefect	11,250	15,000	22,500	37,500
Primipilus = Camp Prefect = 1000-Strong Wing Prefect	15,000	25,000	37,500	56,250

Table 39: Annual salaries in the Roman army (in denarii)

A comparison can be made with the sums spent on imperial procurators in the reign of Trajan,[34] when twenty-one of these state servants received 60,000 sesterces per year, twenty-nine 100,000, thirty-four 200,000, representing an outlay of 2.74 million denarii. It is not difficult to see therefore that the army was one of the largest factors of state expenditure.

Soldiers				
Garrison at Rome	4.50	6	9	13.50
Legions	28	37.30	56	84
Auxiliaries	9	12	18	27
Fleets	4	5.30	8	12
Centurions	13	17.30	26	39
Officers	6.25	8.30	12.50	19
Estimated Total	64.75	86.20	130	195

Table 40: The Roman State's annual salary bill (in millions of denarii)

As a result, imperial finances were in a constant state of precarious balance, and in an emergency recourse had to be made to expedients. The *Historia Augusta* reveals that Marcus Aurelius had to sell his tableware;[35] in 217 Macrinus wrote informing the Senate of his financial difficulties:[36] 'Leaving aside the other advantages that they (the soldiers) obtained from Severus and his son . . . it was impossible to pay them their salaries in full because they were so high, and impossible not to pay them.' In ordinary times it was not possible to have more men in the army than the Empire actually had without lowering their pay, but as this was a considerable encouragement to young men to join the army, a decrease in salary would entail sacrificing quality for quantity. This was the choice Diocletian made.

Supplementary incomes

While his salary represented the main part of a soldier's income, it was not all he received. Just like twentieth-century workers Roman soldiers had negotiated bonuses; cavalrymen got a fodder allowance for their horses,[37] infantrymen a bootnail and shoe allowance (*clavarium*[38] and *calciarium*[39]). Moreover, on discharge a soldier received the savings he had been forced to make, and he also received the *praemia militiae*, amounting to 3000 denarii under Augustus and 8250 in 212.[40] In addition, like every citizen, the soldier could inherit and he had his 'wife's' possessions, not to mention the fact that his parents could give him a *viaticum* of 75 denarii when he joined up.[41]

But these were not the only extras. The most profitable were the exceptional and extraordinary income derived from two other sources. In time of war troops carried out on Roman territory requisitions that were often deemed excessive by the civilians who made complaint to their emperor.[42] The 'rescript of Scaptopare' is mentioned on an inscription found on the boundary between Macedonia and Thrace;[43] this text makes known a complaint addressed in 238 to the Emperor Gordian III by the inhabitants of Scaptopare who were unhappy with the depredations of the troops passing through.

Afterwards, in enemy territory, pillaging was allowed under the laws of war, and many texts testify to the importance of the loot acquired. According to the jurist Gaius,[44] 'What we take from the enemy becomes ours also by natural consideration'. Custom has it that 'the spoils of a city taken by storm belong to the soldiers and those of a city that has capitulated to the officers'.[45] In the first case the soldiers kept what they had gained; in the second the officers became the owners of the possessions that had belonged to those who had surrendered. In many circumstances we glimpse the size of the booty.[46] After the capture of Jerusalem 'while the sanctuary was on fire, the soldiers pillaged everything that fell into their hands'. The consequence of the victory was that 'all the soldiers were overflowing with spoils to the point that in Syria gold was being sold by weight, at half its previous value.'[47] Trajan's Column shows soldiers carrying a chest and heavy bundles after their successful siege of Sarmizegethusa;[48] it also evokes the fabulous 'Dacian gold'. On

Benefactor	Circumstances	Beneficiaries	Total	References
Augustus	entry into Rome	soldiers	2500 d	HA: S.S.VII, 6
	Gaius in army	soldiers	?	Dio LV, 6,4
	will	Praetorians	250 d	Tac. Ann. CI, 3;
		urbaniciani	125 d	Dio LVI, 5,3, and
		legionaries and auxiliaries of cohorts of citizen soldiers	75 d	6,4
Tiberius	revolts in Germany and Pannonia	soldiers	2 × Aug's will	dio LVII 5,3 and 6,4; Suet. Tib. XLVIII, 4
	Sejanus affair	Praetorians	1000 d	Suet, Tib. XLVIII, 4
	will	Praetorians	250 d	Suet. Tib. LXXVI, 2; Dio LVIII, 18 and LIX, 2,2
Caligula	accession	Praetorians	2500 dr	Dio LIX, 2,4
		urbaniciani	125 dr	
		others	85 dr	
			double Tiberius' will	
	death of Lepidus	soldiers	?	Dio LIX, 22
	affair in Britain	soldiers	?	Dio LIX, 25
Claudius	accession	Praetorians	3750 d or 5000 d	Suet. Claud. X, 8; Josephus J.A. XIX, 4,2 (247)
	anniversary of accession	Praetorians	25 d	Dio LX, 12,4
	Nero's taking of man's toga	soldiers	?	Tac. Ann. XII, 41, 3; Suet. Nero VII, 6

Benefactor	Circumstances	Beneficiaries	Total	References
Nero	accession	Praetorians	?	Tac. *Ann.* XII, 69,4; Dio LXI, 3,1 Suet. *Nero* X, 2
			monthly corn	
	death of Agrippina	Praetorians	?	Dio LXI 14,3; Tac. *Ann.* XIV, 11
	Piso conspiracy	Praetorians	500 d	Tac. *Ann.* XV, 72,1; Dio LXII, 27,4
Galba	refuses *donativum*	Praetorians	0	Suet. *Galba* XVI, 2 and XVII, 1; Dio LXIV, 3,3
	promises *donativum*	Praetorians legionaries	7500 dr 1250 dr	Dio LXIV, 3,3; Plutarch, *Galba* II, 2 Suet. *Galba* XX, 1 Tac.*Hist.* I,5,1
	promise broken		0	Plut. *Galba* XVIII, 3 XXIII, 4
Otho	promise	Praetorians legionaries soldiers	1250 d ? ?	Tac. *Hist.* I, 82,5 and III, 10,4 Tac. *Hist.* IV, 36,2
Vitellius	gift not possible	soldiers	0	Tac. *Hist.* II, 94,5
Vitellius or Vespasian	gift made	legionaries	?	Tac. *Hist.* IV, 58,6
Vespasian	69	soldiers Praetorians	pittance 25 dr	Tac. *Hist.* II, 82,4 Dio LXV, 22,2
Titus		Praetorians	?	Dio LXVI, 26,3
Domitian	accession Dacian War	Praetorians soldiers	as Titus ?	Dio LXVI, 26,3 Dio LXVII, 7,3
Nerva				Mattingly, *Coins* B.M. III, 46
Trajan		soldiers	?	Pliny, *Pan.* XXV, 2 and XLI, 1
Hadrian	accession	soldiers	double *largitio*	*HA*: Hads. V, 7
	adoption of Aelius Caesar	soldiers	75,000,000 in all!	*HA*: Hads XXIII, 12 and 14; Ael. III, 3 and VI, 1
Antoninus Pius	daughter's wedding	soldiers	?	*HA*: AP VIII, 1 and X, 2

. . . cont.

Benefactor	Circumstances	Beneficiaries	Total	References
Marcus Aurelius	accession Marcomannic war	Praetorians soldiers	5000 d or 3000 d refusal	*HA*: MA VII, 9; Dio LXIII, 8,4 Dio LXXI, 3,3 and LXXIII, 8,4
Commodus	accession	Praetorians	?	Herodian I, 5,1 and 8
Pertinax	accession promise gift	Praetorians Praetorians	honours Commodus' promises 3000 d 1500 d	*HA*: P. VII, 5 *HA*: P. XV, 7 and VII, 5 and 11; Dio LXXIII, 8,4
Didius Julianus	promise gift	Praetorians	6250 d 7500 d	Herodian II, 6,8 and 11,7; Dio LXXIII, II, 4,5; *HA*: DJ. III, 2; Zonaras XII, 7
Clodius Albinus	promise	soldiers	3 *aurei*	*HA*: CA. II, 4
Septimius Severus	193 197 198 203 (10th anniversary)	soldiers soldies soldiers Praetorians	2500 d ? looting Parthian capital 10 *aurei*	Herodian II, 14,5; *HA*: 55 VII, 6 Herodian III, 6,8 and 8,4 *HA*: SS. XVI, 5 Dio LXXVI, 1,1
Caracalla	various 211 murder of Geta	soldiers Praetorians[54] Praetorians	various amounts ? 2500 dr	Herodian IV, 7,4 Tertullian, *DC* I Herodian IV, 4,7 and 5,1
Macrinus	crisis promise gift	soldiers	750 dr 5000 dr 1000 dr 8 *aurei*	Dio LXXVIII, 19,2 Dio LXXVIII, 34,2 *HA*: Diad. II, 1
Elagabal	crisis	soldiers	500 dr	Dio LXXIX, 1,1
Alexander Severus	 war in east 231	soldiers soldiers	3 *donativa* generous	*HA*: AS. XXVI, 1 Herodian VI, 4,1

. . . cont.

Benefactor	Circumstances	Beneficiaries	Total	References
Maximinus	civil war 238 (two occasions)	soldiers	enormous sums	Herodian VII, 8,9
Gordian	civil war 238	soldiers	biggest *donativum* known	Herodian VII, 6,4
Philip	assassination of Gordian	soldiers	large amount	Zosimus I, 19,1
Tacitus	accession	Praetorians	usual sum	*HA*: Tac. IX, 1

Table 41: *Donativa* and *Liberalitates*

the Aurelian Column there are several scenes of soldiers carrying off livestock and women.[49] Septimius Severus is said to have promised his soldiers the pillage of the Parthian capital as an extraordinary gift to mark his accession to the purple.[50]

In times of peace the emperors kept the soldiers happy with occasional acts of exceptional generosity. Augustus did not forget them when he made out his will;[51] Septimius Severus organized a distribution of clothes for them.[52] The habit of making these exceptional gifts (*liberalitates* or *donativa*) was soon adopted and thus become standard practice, particularly at the beginning of a reign. The only question remaining is to determine whether entitlement to these gifts was general or restricted to the Praetorians; in point of fact, the list of beneficiaries varied according to circumstances, but rare were the emperors like Galba who refused because 'he was in the habit of enlisting soldiers and not buying them'.[53]

All these incomes, which made the soldiers relatively well-off, created a zone of personal wealth. The soldiers were a sort of engine, driving a machine: on the one hand the State took from ordinary people to pay the soldiers' salaries, while on the other the same ordinary people recovered the money when the consumers in the army spent it.

But from a strictly economic viewpoint all triumphalism should be avoided. The men who lived in the first three centuries AD were ignorant of financial mechanisms, and consequently made many mistakes, of which three need to be highlighted. Firstly, as we have already seen, the State was a 'bad employer' because it awarded pay rises that failed to match price rises, thus causing a deflationist tendency (the situation in the Early Empire should not be reduced to a simple inflationary tendency, which was real and pervasive, because this would not explain everything). Secondly, the huge amounts paid to the army rendered the balance between State income and expenditure extremely precarious, leading to a real monopoly for outgoings in the budget. Thirdly, habit and collective mentalities led soldiers to hoard their money, thus immobilizing a part of the money supply and withdrawing it from economic activity. Moreover, these habits were encouraged by the State; compulsory deposits of up to 250 denarii[55] and other voluntary deposits were made in the insignia shrine which acted as a savings bank, but one that did not invest or pay interest. These deposits were the *seposita* and the *deposita* guarded by the *signiferi*.[56] Nevertheless, these salaries, inasmuch as they were spent, played a considerable economic role in the regions.

Soldiers as consumers

In fact, the camp represented an important market as the citizens realized.[57] But first, it should be made clear that contrary to received wisdom, soldiers enjoyed a varied diet.[58] Certainly it was based on cereals, as was that of all people up to the eighteenth century; in a six-day period a legion consumed a quantity of wheat that represented the production of 8ha (20 acres). But, in addition there were large quantities of fish and seafood, vegetables like beans and lentils, wine and other produce.

To feed the camp at first there was the embryo of a supply corps which was replaced by the 'military *annona*', a system still not fully understood.[59] It may have been inaugurated as early as Trajan, according to J. Guey.[60] From that period part of the salary may have been paid in supplies. According to D. van Berchem it was the idea of Septimius Severus who created a new tax.[61] Then Caracalla improved the idea and Gordian III made it standard practice.[62] Another theory can be entertained, namely that it was not an additional tax but merely part of the old *annona* that had been hived off for the benefit of the army.[63]

Weaponry represented another considerable expenditure for the soldiers,[64] as contrary to the practice today, Roman soldiers had to arm themselves, until the third century when it was supplied by the State, but its cost was deducted from pay.[65] Similarly uniforms, clothes and tents were not supplied.[66] Moreover, the army used pack animals like oxen on the *prata* (see later), and riding animals like horses and camels.[67] Finally, like any other relatively wealthy consumers, soldiers purchased various items; one from the *legio XIII Gemina* bought a Cretan slave.[68]

The rules and regulations in force actually encouraged spending. A purchase could be made either by an individual or by a unit, in the second case a commander-in-chief made the payment on the orders of the procurator (*probatio* then *signatio*), from the funds deposited in the *quaestura*.[69] Soldiers and veterans enjoyed immunities in the form of tax exemptions;[70] from the very beginning they were exempt from tribute paying or from any personal or public fiscal obligations (*munera publica*). From Domitian's time the exemption included the *portorium* and the *vectigal* (customs duty and land-tax), not only as far as the soldier himself was concerned, but also his wife, his children and parents.[71] All the privileges were recorded on the veterans' register in Egypt, at the time of the sort of census called *epikrisis*.[72] On the other hand, certain indirect taxes remained payable to the State, particularly the *munera patrimonii*, a tax that was concerned with the national patrimony.

This situation is documented in epigraphical texts; public tariffs have been found with amounts against certain products.[73] Because he was working on African documents S.J. De Laet thought that these taxes were levied in relation to the *IV Publica Africae*, but an analogous text has been discovered in Syria also (see n. 73).

Soldiers as producers

In keeping with the mentality of their time, however substantial their incomes, soldiers sought to spend as little as possible by becoming producers themselves. The camp functioned partly as an industrial firm (or more appropriately as a craft industry) and partly as the centre of a large estate. Each fortress had its own workshop (*fabrica*) that manufactured bricks and weapons as required.[75] It also possessed lands that it cultivated, or more frequently, used as pasture.[76] One inscription informs us of 'a detachment that was sent to make hay' (*vexillatio . . . ad fenum secandum*).[77]

Epigraphists have published a series of texts written on boundary stones that marked out the area over which the army had rights of ownership.[78] To designate this military estate the texts use two different words, *prata* and *territorium*. Thus between Burgos and Santander has been found an 'imperial boundary stone [which] separates the *prata* of the IV Legion from the lands of the Juliobriga'.[79] Another 'imperial boundary stone separates the *prata* of the IV Legion from the lands of Segisamo.' Elsewhere, however, the term used is *territorium*;[80] 'The Emperor Caesar Marcus Aurelius Severus Alexander, pious, blessed, August, had these baths entirely built on the *territorium* of the *legio II Adiutrix*, pious, loyal, Severan. The responsibility for these works was entrusted to the consular Flavius Marcianus.'

No less than five different theses have been evolved to distinguish *prata* and *territorium*. (1) A. Schulten thought that the two terms designated the same area, but that *prata* was used in an economic and *territorium* in an adminstrative or military context.[81] (2) P. Salway accepts the difference in use, but contends that the *prata* constitute only part of the *territorium*.[82] (3) For H. von Petrikovits the *territorium* was essentially military and can be mapped out by the places where bricks stamped with the unit's name have been found.[83] For R. MacMullen the *territorium* was purely an economic designation, and therefore logically must have been smaller than the potential sphere of activity of the legion or auxiliary force in question.[84]

(5) M. Kandler believes that the military boundary stones which gave the distance from the camp (*a castris*) covered only the *territorium*.[85]

The thesis of P. Salway seems the most satisfactory. In fact not two but three different concepts should be taken into consideration. For economic purposes concerning either legions or auxiliary units the term *prata* was used, and its general meaning suggests pastures used for rearing animals. In a military context, since only legionary *territoria* are known, we must assume that *territorium* was the word used for the area. Finally, the administrative aspect must not be forgotten; legates often acted as governors, and the history of certain regions coincided with that of certain legions, e.g. the *legio III Cyrenaica* and *Arabia*. In that case the term *provincia* should be used, but it must not be forgotten that this word needs to be used with caution. The province of Numidia was created officially only in the time of Septimius Severus, almost a century after the arrival of the *legio III Augusta* at Lambaesis, and it comprised the region of Constantine which was not occupied militarily in normal times.

Soldiers as businessmen

Stock farming on the *prata* was carried out in the name of the unit, but the profits did not go to individual soldiers. But, as has been noted, these soldiers had liquid assets, partly hoarded, partly wasted in buying exemptions from centurions,[86] but nevertheless partly available for doing business. Money could be lent with interest, or products could be bought and resold at a profit. The fiscal situation that was thus in the soldiers' favour attracted the attention of Nero who 'issued an edict ordering that the soldiers should keep their immunities except in regard to the objects which they traded [illicitly]'.[87]

Legal protection for soldiers

Thus, whether they were buyers or sellers, soldiers lived in exceptional circumstances.[88] The advantages that went with their status, however, were more widespread than merely in the fiscal context, in that they also received an important legal protection.[89] A military law was instituted in the course of the first century BC and the first AD, and then given further impetus by Hadrian. A law specifically for soldiers was set up in the second and third centuries.[90]

Obviously real legal equality did not exist, as already seen above. Each type of unit therefore had its peculiarities, as this simplified version of the facts demonstrates: Roman citizenship was a requirement for joining the garrison at Rome or the legions; it was granted at the end of service to sailors and auxiliaries who did not already possess it.

Any praetorian or legionary accused of a crime was judged at the camp[91] by his superiors (tribune for the investigation, prefect or legate for the judgement) under an accelerated procedure.[92] Furthermore, he was recognized as having possessions that came under two categories:[93] some were of military origin (*bona castrensia*) others were non-military (*peculium castrense*)[94] having been acquired in all sorts of circumstances. Into this second category, from Hadrian on, fell the possessions of the woman he called his 'wife'.[95] The 'savings' could be passed on as inheritance, with one condition, that the soldier was to be deemed to be in the power (*potestas*) of his father.[96]

The right of ownership went hand in hand with another right that was extremely important to inhabitants of the Empire, that of bequeathing by will.[97] The *ius testamenti* was derived from the *ius testamenti in procinctu*;[98] at first soldiers were allowed to write down their last wishes before leaving for war, though in Julius Caesar's time it was only occasionally granted, in Augustus' it became a standard practice before every campaign.[99] Juvenal was particularly enraged by the fact that they could do this during their father's lifetime.[100] In Trajan's time this advantage was extended to all soldiers, but it was Hadrian who drew up the largest number of regulations: from that day soldiers could make out their will like any other civilian, thus circumventing paternal authority (*patria potestas*), whether they be veterans or on active service; in the second case their sons, who were illegitimate since marriage was forbidden to their fathers, could inherit, and from 119 they were exempt from the 5 per cent inheritance tax.[101] An oral will was even instituted, but Caracalla restricted its use to soldiers on campaign.

The status of soldiers' children is problematic. Indeed, historians and legal experts disagree on the soldiers' right to get married, but some major points can be established. These unions were contrary to the law and forbidden up to the time of Claudius, and although they were condemned from then until Septimius Severus, they were tolerated. After 197 soldiers could marry and live with their wives outside the camps.[102] Thus, during the first two centuries of the Empire the title *uxor*, which is often mentioned in inscriptions, did not correspond to any legal status, and consequently if the son of a legionary and a citizen's daughter was conceived during the time of his father's active service he was considered illegitimate.[103]

Last but not least, towards the end of their period of service some soldiers could ask for certain final privileges. This leads us to discuss the problem of discharge from service and 'military diplomas'.[104] This process was in two parts. Firstly, to those soldiers who asked for and deserved it, the army chief delivered a certificate of good conduct, called 'a certificate of honourable discharge' (*tabula honestae missionis*):

In the consulship of M. Acilius Aviola and of Pansa, the day before the Nones of January [i.e. 4 January 122] T. Haterius Nepos, prefect of Egypt, granted honourable discharge to L. Valerius Noster, cavalryman of the *ala* of the

Vocontii, of the squadron of Gavius [*Gaviana*], who has finished his service [*emeritus*].[105]

Next could be issued a document traditionally called a 'military diploma',[106] or 'double object' in Greek, since it comprised two bronze tablets tied together by a wire covered by the seals of seven witnesses. The same text is found on the outside and the inside, and if it was necessary to compare the two the seven seals could be broken. The contents were stereotyped, always made up of the same elements: (1) mention of the Emperor; (2) list of the units concerned; (3) localization of garrison's province for auxiliaries; (4) name of the army's commander-in-chief; (5) statement of merits; (6) nature of privileges granted; (7) date; (8) name of beneficiary or beneficiaries; (9) place where original was displayed; (10) list of witnesses.

An example is:[107]

The Emperor Caesar Domitian, son of deified Vespasian, August, conqueror of the Germans, Supreme Pontiff, tribune for the fifteenth time, acclaimed *imperator* on twenty-two occasions, consul for the seventeenth time, permanent censor, father of the homeland, to the cavalry and infantry serving in the praetorian wing and in the cohorts [called] Ist of the Lusitanians, Ist of the Cretans, Ist of the Montani, Ist of the Cilicians, Ist 1000-strong Flavian of Spaniards, IInd Flavian of Commagenians, IVth of Raetians, Vth of Spaniards, VIth of Thracians and VIIth of Breuci, Roman citizens, in Upper Moesia under the command of Gnaius Aemilius Cicatricula Pompeius Longinus, who have been found worthy of receiving twenty-five or more years of salary, also to those who have been discharged with honourable mention after receiving their salaries, and whose names appear below, to them, to their children and to their descendants (the Emperor) has granted citizenship and the right to marry the spouses that they might be with at the time of conferment of citizenship, or for those who were bachelors with the wives they took subsequently, as long as they had only one wife; (signed) the fourth day before the Ides of July, in the consulship of T. Prifernius Paetus and of Q. Fabius Postuminus. (Beneficiaries:) Dolens, son of Sublusius, Besse, infantryman of the VIth cohort of Thracians, under the command of Claudius Alpinus, and Valens, his son. Transcribed and attested true to the bronze tablet displayed at Rome, on the wall behind the temple of deified Augustus, near the (statue?) of Minerva.

In fact these documents are only copies certified by witnesses of legislative texts (jurists say that it is an *epistula missoria* followed by a *lex data*), displayed in public on the Capitol up until 88, and behind the new temple of the deified Augustus from 90 onwards. By these decrees the emperors granted Roman citizenship or the right to marry (*conubium*), or both of these to soldiers on campaign when their service was longer than the specified period, but especially to veterans. Praetorians of course needed only the *conubium*, and the extant 'diplomas' granted to them cover the years 72–3 to 306. For the *auxilia* two separate periods need to be distinguished: Claudius granted the two above-mentioned benefits to the soldiers, their children and their descendants; but from about 140 or 145 only the soldiers themselves were eligible for the benefits. The last extant 'diploma' dates from 203. Sailors were granted the same rights as soldiers of cohorts and *alae* from the time of Claudius; in about 140 or 145 the authorities failed to make up their minds clearly and adopted a half-measure, stating that only the sailors and their children were to be granted citizenship. It has been pointed out that legionaries did not receive this sort of document, with the exception of the *I* and *II Adiutrix* which had been set up with recruits from the navy. Various explanations have been put forward for this difference in treatment. Some scholars think that these soldiers, as heirs of the Republican army, did their compulsory military service and consequently did not need any incentives to do their duty. But in fact in the Early Empire voluntary service became widespread, so some other explanation is needed. The 'diplomas' appear to have been instituted for Praetorians in the crisis of 68–9 and for the *auxilia* in time of recruitment difficulties, particular circumstances in both cases. Perhaps there was no similar sort of situation as regards legionaries. Moreover, M. Corbier[108] has shown that the rewards given at the end of military service varied with the unit's place in the hierarchy: auxiliaries and sailors received only a diploma, legionaries only the *praemia* (money and/or land), Praetorians both. Whatever the answer, the granting of these rewards was not systematic; a person had to be entitled to them through honourable discharge, or have need of them (a Roman citizen who was a bachelor did not), and had to ask for them.

It has been demonstrated that up to 73–4 the witnesses were the companions of the beneficiaries, and afterwards they were adminstrative employees, at first cited in no particular order, but from 133 or 138 in order of seniority.

From the preceding remarks it can be seen that soldiers enjoyed numerous advantages: they had the status of freemen; the right to special procedures when brought to court; the right of ownership, of making a will, and in certain cases of receiving 'diplomas' granting them, their children and their descendants Roman citizenship; as well as the right to marry. These legal advantages together with a regular salary made soldiers privileged plebeians.

Civilians with economic links with the army

The army's presence therefore created peace and prosperity, which in turn attracted civilians, the first of whom were ex-soldiers – the veterans.

Veterans[109]

Veterans remain relatively mysterious. Either they were few and far between (for Spain, for example, there are only 52 names),[110] or else the secondary literature is difficult to assemble. Under Augustus they still remained attached to the legions for a four-year period and could be recalled if need arose, in which case they formed a detachment (*vexillum*) under the orders of a *curator* or a *triarius ordo* centurion.[111] Soon afterwards, however, they broke off all links with active service on discharge and took up full citizen rights. The title was restricted to any man up to and including the rank of centurion, provided he had carried out his duties satisfactorily. He was then called *veteranus*, *missicius* or *emeritus*, 'who has served his time'. Ex-praetorians were different because of their particular status, and were sometimes called 'the Emperor's veterans' (*veterani Augusti*).

What was really crucial was the 'discharge' (*missio*).[112] It was *ignominiosa* for a bad soldier who was dismissed for lack of discipline, *causaria* (with certain rights[113]) for one invalided out through ill-health or wounds, *honesta* for one who had completed his military service to the satisfaction of his superiors. This last category made a soldier eligible for rewards, and a distinction was made between a *missio nummaria*, which conferred a sum of money,[114] and a *missio agraria*, which conferred a plot of land, granted individually (*viritim*) or to a group of veterans on a colonial estate. The soldier who had received what he deserved (*commoda* or *praemia militiae*) considered himself honoured by this grant and called himself *acceptarius*, *commodis acceptis* or *commodis honoratus*.[115]

Ex-soldiers received a sum of money paid to them by a particular treasurer in the *aerarium militare*.[116] This body was created by Augustus in 6 BC and placed in the hands of a *praefectus* (ex-praetor) in the first place, then in the hands of a person designated by the Emperor and responsible to him from the time of Claudius. This system remained in operation until the middle of the third century. The revenues were provided for by a special 5 per cent tax on inheritances, and in addition a 1 per cent sales tax. It is understandable that Augustus dealt personally with veterans. Shortly after the battle of Actium in 31 BC he found himself in charge of a considerably larger number of men than he needed or the Empire could afford. In his *Res Gestae*[117] he boasts of setting up 120,000 discharged soldiers in some twenty colonies in Italy in 31, of 100,000 in Spain and Gallia Narbonensis in 14, and 96,000 in 2 BC. Other discharges are attested in 7, 6, 4 and 3 BC. The Emperor spent 600,000,000 sesterces on them in Italy and 200,000,000 in the provinces. Each veteran received a plot of land and a sum of money, 3000 denarii for a legionary and 5000 for a Praetorian.[118] In the ensuing period a double change occurred: cash payments increased in value as a legionary received 5000 denarii under Caligula and 8250 in 212; while land gifts decreased until they were stopped completely under Hadrian. It must not be forgotten that on the day of their discharge soldiers were given back the savings they had been forced to deposit in the chapel of *insignia*, and from Septimius Severus onwards in the college funds. After the Augustan period the numbers of discharged soldiers decreased to the point where each legion lost some 250 men per year, representing an annual loss to the whole Roman army of some 15,000 men.

These veterans could return to their homeland, to their place of birth[119] or could set up home near the camp in which they had served, near their 'wife'.[120] They established links with the municipal aristocracies and were integrated into local society.[121] Even if they lived in town they became property owners. In some cases the land was actually theirs, in others, particularly when setting up on an imperial estate, they only enjoyed leasehold and were termed *possessores*.[122]

A law existed to protect veterans, granting them certain immunities,[123] the status of decurions, at least for some of them,[124] and the right to form colleges.[125] Their role was important, as their experience in war made them and their colonies an excellent defence force for the Empire. They spread urbanization in under-populated areas, as well as Romanization (see below).

Peasants, craftsmen, tradesmen . . . and others

Because they brought peace and security, soldiers attracted many civilians who worked for the army, but also for each other, leading to a knock-on effect well-known to economists. Peasants particularly were advantaged because the legionaries surveyed and registered the land, marking out properties and thoroughfares.[126] Moreover, some agricultural activities had a strategic use. Olive trees, which give good yields only a few years after planting, and stock farming, which restricts mobility, encouraged that constant source of trouble, the nomads, to settle in one place.[127] Officers, especially legates, were not indifferent to potential profits: L. Minucius Natalis had a fortress built at the Henchir Besseriani (*Ad Maiores*) in Numidia, bought the lands of the oasis of Negrina behind it, and started an olive plantation.[128] The revolt of Avidius Cassius in 175 made Marcus Aurelius adopt the prudent strategy of avoiding sending senators to rule provinces in which they were estate owners.

The existence of the market represented by the camp also encouraged the development of crafts. These could even become industries if practised on a large enough scale, as was the case of pottery and metalwork. All these products attracted both wholesale and retail merchants, and the most adventurous of these even went beyond the camps into the heart of the barbarian countries. Sometimes they acted almost as scouts before a conquest, going ahead of the soldiers, sometimes they followed on afterwards, but they even went where no Roman soldier ever ventured.[129] It would be interesting to know how many of them came from Italy and how many were more or less Romanized natives, but evidence is lacking for this information.

Finally, it is impossible not to mention what are called 'services' today, linked by economists to the 'tertiary sector', leisure activities which always played a very important role in Roman life in general, but particularly so in that of soldiers. Near the camps gradually appeared cabarets, brothels and various entertainment places in which actors, dancers, musicians, gladiators and prostitutes of both sexes performed. Professionals in the true sense of the word identified themselves with certain units to the point of calling themselves *lixa cohortis A* or *legionis B*.[130] This probably means 'licensed purveyor' to cohort A or legion B rather than 'servant in' the unit concerned. However, we should not imagine that the soldiers were greater drunkards or sex-maniacs than the civilians;[131] graffiti found in the fortresses and their correspondence show that frequenting the dives was not the real priority in their lives (see next chapter). It is necessary to note, however, that daily life varied according to the province in which the men were garrisoned, and that it was much harsher in Germany and Britain than in Syria.[132]

Towns near camps

All these civilians, along with the veterans and the soldiers' families, created a settlement around each camp.[133] Epigraphical texts show some variety of legal status, with upward mobility to the rank of *municipium* or even *colonia* being possible.[134] The most common term is that of *canabae*, used for Haltern and Mainz in Germany as early as the Augustan era. It designated an urban-type agglomeration built not far from a fortress and possessing its own collective way of life organized by *magistri*, curators and aediles. According to some historians these *canabae* always accompanied the legionary camps and could become *municipia* or *coloniae*.[135] In other situations the term *vicus* would have been used, and this necessarily designated a smaller settlement.

In Britain however *vici* contained a wide range of monuments such as temples, baths, altars etc. Archaeologists have also discovered burial grounds and observed that these agglomerations were often built to a geometrical plan.[136] At Lambaesis in Numidia there is a carefully-built road, the *via Septimiana*, joining the town to the camp in a way that symbolized their links. Sometimes only the group of Roman citizens (*consistentes* or *incolae*), attracted by the wealth of the soldiers, advertised its presence. But in the majority of cases these agglomerations have no name or title; they are visible to archaeologists but not to epigraphists. They were sometimes built at a distance from the camp, sometimes attached to a part of it, sometimes totally surrounding it. The recent work of J.-P. Laporte[137] on the site of Sour Djouab (*Rapidum*) in Mauretania can provide examples (pl.XXXVII,38): in 122 the II cohort of Sardinians built a camp 135 × 127m (440 × 415ft); in 167 an enclosure approximately 1.15km ($\frac{3}{4}$ mile) in length marked a town of 11.6ha (28 acres), built against the fortress rampart.

The military zone

Civilians and soldiers, peasants and city dwellers were all attracted by the advantages of the 'frontier'. P. Salway has studied this phenomenon very carefully in Britain.[138] In other regions scholars have used aerial photography – A. Poidebard in Syria[139] and J. Baradez in Algeria;[140] M. Euzennat in Morocco[141] and R. Rebuffat in Morocco and Tripolitania have shown that there is no real substitute for research on the ground.[142]

This 'frontier' showed a marked peculiarity in that it was a geographical zone that owed its very existence to the army. On a map this region could appear in two different forms, either more or less continuous, as in Britain where it ran alongside Hadrian's Wall, or else discontinuous, as in Syria and Numidia, where it formed a sort of lace curtain between the Roman world and that of the barbarians. It comprised three types of construction: (1) the military monuments, which were of course of prime importance; they came in the category of what have here been called individual defences (forts, small forts and towers) and are very germane to the present chapter, or of linear defences (walls in Britain, Seguia bent el-Krass, etc.); (2) the roads, or rather tracks, which were built and maintained by the soldiers for their own use, but were also used by tradesmen and other travellers (these can be termed as mixed use); (3) purely civilian constructions, which were built both near and between camps. In these regions the settlements were mixed, urban-type agglomerations, villages, hamlets and isolated farms. The land was cultivated, with small walls to prevent the soil from erosion, and efficient use of water thanks to a sophisticated system of wells, tanks, dams and canals. The agrarian economy varied according to the lifestyle of the farmers; sedentary populations everywhere produced cereals, supplemented by vines and olive trees if the climate permitted, sometimes by cattle-raising. Beyond the military zone the major nomadic peoples stayed put occasionally to grow a few crops, but they preferred grazing their cattle (camels were only used much later in any serious manner); the semi-nomads on either side of the *limes* kept goats and sheep to supplement their arable farming.

No Latin word seems to have existed to designate this geographical sector with its particular scenery and economy. We have seen above that *prata* and *territorium* are not perfectly suitable, and it is not possible either to speak of the *limes* in the strict meaning of the term. It is a very late and very technical usage. That is why it is preferable to talk of a 'military zone'.

The army was thus an important factor in economic development, even though it needed substantial finances to allow it to play its role to the full. It goes without saying that it had a significant effect on the demography of the 'military zone'.

DEMOGRAPHY

Augustus had wanted a permanent army of soldiers serving for long periods and had stationed it along the frontiers. Unintentionally he also changed the population spread in the Empire.

The problem

The problem is one of measuring the extent of these transformations,[143] and we are faced here with a debate which has implications for a study of the population in antiquity in general, concerning the value and the scarcity of the evidence. It has been known for a long time that documentation is rare, but some does exist, and the numerous epitaphs ought to be able to tell us something about mortality rates and ages. At first scholars used these inscriptions indiscriminately, then they realized their errors and dismissed the evidence they had previously cherished. One thing they had noticed was the abnormal frequency of deaths at ages which ended with the figures 0 or 5. Common sense probably dictates that we accept the figures but also that we should not consider them precise; they have in all likelihood been rounded off. Moreover, there is some evidence that cannot be seriously doubted, namely that military service lasted about twenty-five years and concerned about 300,000 men, stationed at the edges of the Empire. Finally, if we cannot have 'quantitative' demography, there is still the possibility of studying the 'qualitative' variety. Such phenomena as the rapid increase in population in areas that are garrisoned can be noted, without being able to quantify it.

Marriage, fertility and mortality

The milieu being studied here presents some peculiarities, since soldiers by definition are all adult males. These peculiar features become apparent when trying to define the characteristics of the population by the main traditional areas of demographic studies. As regards marriage it has already been seen that all unions were forbidden from Augustus to Claudius, tolerated from then to Septimius Severus, and that concubinage was authorized after that. For the *legio III Augusta* in Numidia[144] we find that 206 out of 354 epitaphs (58 per cent) of the second century mention the existence of a 'wife'. The actual marriage rate was probably higher, as it is possible that some wives entrusted to family or friends the task of providing a gravestone for their husbands. As they stepped into the background they do not appear in the inscription. The same is true of the fertility of the wives of the soldiers serving in this unit, with a rate of 1.48 children compared to 2.25 for Africa and 2.40 for veterans (according to Lassère):[145] 46 cases give 1 child; 20 > 1; 9 > 2; 3 > 3;

1 > 4; but it is probable that soldiers had more children then epigraphical texts suggest.

In mortality the case for soldiers is more like that of civilians.[146] The average age at death was about 47, compared to 45 at Lambaesis and 46–7 in Africa. However, A.R. Burn believes that soldiers in Africa died before the age of 42 more often than the civilians did, and that afterwards this situation was reversed.[147] He observed an analogous situation for the troops stationed near the Danube, but with the difference that it was not 42 but 30 that was the turning point. Deaths through combat or 'accidents at work' played little or no part in the statistics relating to the *legio III Augusta*, where we know of only six soldiers and one centurion who fell in combat. It is more than likely, however, that this cause of death was more prevalent in other provincial garrisons.

Length of service: demographic aspects

The more 'professional' question of the length of service has never been really satisfactorily studied.[148] It is sufficient here to note that the period of activity varied in inverse proportion to the prestige of the units concerned: Praetorians served a shorter time than legionaries who in turn served a shorter time than auxiliaries. Sailors were the longest serving group. Quantitatively we can say that legionaries served 25 or 26 years in the second century.

Migrations and urbanization

We have seen above how the military zone surrounding the Empire became also a zone of urbanization due to the army's needs. Unfortunately no figures can be adduced for this phenomenon.

Certain migratory movements are better known, and are of great historical importance since they highlight the existence of links between provinces, whereas ancient Roman historians emphasized the relationship between the capital and the provinces. We have seen that recruitment generally did not take place in the sector of the garrison itself in the first years of the Empire. Afterwards it did take place in that area, and finally even closer to the camp. This brought about a significant migration that gradually decreased, until it disappeared totally in the third century. The number of men involved can be estimated approximately. A legion of 5000 soldiers serving 25 years needed an annual 250 replacements for the 250 men who left. The entire Roman army needed some 10,000 to 15,000 young recruits annually, a small number when one considers the extent of the territory. Difficulties in recruitment targets only arose in special cases such as after the disaster of Varus or during the wars of the third century. The real problem was one of quality, not of quantity, as it was easier to find soldiers than it was to find good soldiers. It was probably this political choice, along with other motives, that persuaded Trajan to create a foundation whose aim was to ensure the education of orphans born in Italy (*alimenta*).[149]

While on the subject of migrations linked to the presence of the army we should not forget the many civilians, mentioned above, who were attracted by the peace and prosperity of the 'military zone'. However, it is impossible to estimate their number too.

CONCLUSION

In the regions where they were stationed the units of the Roman army played an important material role both directly and indirectly. The various sources of soldiers' revenues, particularly their salaries, created a zone that was characterized by its economic prosperity and its demographic dynamism. There were camps and towns, roads and all sorts of people who earned their living in a multitude of ways.

But the peace of this zone remained precarious since it was exposed to the attacks of barbarians and represented only a thin curtain with many gaps in it. Above all, its wealth depended on the prosperity of the Empire.

9

CULTURAL INFLUENCE

If soldiers played an important economic role, admittedly indirect since this activity was not their principal role, they also played a part in the cultural and spiritual life of their time. Historians do not agree on the extent of this part, but two main areas of contention merit attention. Firstly there is Romanization, where one point of view holds that the army was instrumental in its diffusion, particularly through recruitment (*probatio*), while another sees the soldiers as barbarians. Secondly there is religion, where one view holds that the soldiers practised local cults, because they were recruited in the sector of the garrison, while another argues that Eastern cults were more popular because they were more suited to the soldiers' spiritual aspirations.

LAY CULTURE

The previous remarks about recruitment should throw some light on the debate; a legionary and an auxiliary, especially one in a *numerus*, cannot be considered on the same level. Moreover the situation changed between the times of Augustus and Diocletian. In addition, we know that a general evolution affecting all the inhabitants of the community took place. Thus social and chronological factors are crucial in this debate.

The Latin language

The language question is a good illustration of this. Latin maintained its exclusive nature throughout the whole period since it alone could express the commands for all the units, even the *numeri*. No orders were given in Greek, Egyptian or Aramaic, the languages of defeat.

In addition we are certain that at least a few of the soldiers had some sort of elementary education, because the *probatio* tested it. There can be no doubt that some recruits had to be able to read, write[1] and count, as a few of these were immediately assigned to jobs in the administrative offices of the unit. Indeed, future *notarii* were required to show the skills necessary for taking down speeches in short-hand.

More significant was the spread of literary culture in this milieu. In Augustus' reign centurions paid large sums of money to send their sons to school.[2] Epitaphs of soldiers are sometimes written in verse;[3] admittedly they were more metrically correct at the beginning of the first century than at the end of the second, but this is also true of other social strata. Soldiers even gave their children names taken from the great Latin writers, especially Virgilian heroes,[4] which shows that they admired them even if it does not prove that they read them.

But there is the other side of the coin. In the East, Greek was still in common use, while there can be no doubt that in the *numeri* soldiers kept their own ethnic linguistic and religious identities. J. Carcopino has shown how the presence in El-kantara (Numidia) of two Syrian units recruited at Palmyra and Emesus had created a pocket of Semitic civilization to the west of the Aures.[5] Furthermore, some soldiers could speak barbarian languages,[6] a fact that enabled commanders to use translators, like the *interprex* [sic] *Dacorum* who is attested in an epigraphical text.[7] A recently discovered document mentions a soldier sent to 'the Garamantes'[8] who presumably could understand what they said. Far from being proof of open-mindedness, it is argued that this is evidence of the presence in the army of natives who have not been Romanized to any great degree.[9]

However, a study of epigraphical texts must point to a certain decline in the cultural level in various ways. The quality of the metrical epitaphs suffered,[10] and 'vulgar Latin' forms became more numerous with time. Just like any closed circle the army generated its own jargon, a military slang that is observable through inscriptions and literary texts.[11] A compatriot became a *conterraneus*, a shout was a *barritus* and to designate a miserable shack the African word *mapalia* = 'hut' was used. This spread to all the garrisons in the Empire. In the middle of the third century, between 253 and 259 the archives at the outpost at Bu Njem in Tripolitania were written in true pidgin.[12] Many ancient writers delighted in criticizing soldiers for their lack of culture, calling them barbarians, while at the same time occasionally recognizing their bravery.[13]

These contradictory views can be reconciled by taking into consideration two parameters – the type of unit and the change in recruitment patterns. Soldiers may not be intellectuals, but neither are they ignoramuses.

It is self-evident that auxiliaries must have been less Romanized than legionaries, and the *ostraca* of Bu Njem, for example, were written hastily in a simple milieu, not as literary works for posterity to read. Moreover, we have noted a drop in the quality of recruits in the reign of Septimius Severus, and this change in selection policy at the *dilectus* could not fail to have repercussions on the cultural level. As for the criticisms levelled by the ancient writers, they appear to be no more than a stock literary theme; the image of a drunken soldier was a commonplace that found particular expression in times of crisis, notably the civil wars of 68–9, 193–7 and 238.

The army does indeed appear to have followed general trends, but always at one remove. Plebeian soldiers followed fashions and when they became the elite they placed themselves one rung above the middle. This tendency can be quantified. In 1916 L.R. Dean published a study of the *cognomina* of legionaries, which is still useful despite its age, because it was based on a truly representative sample of 5700 cases.[14] At the top there are 56 names with a frequency rate of more than 20; they are all Latin names except for one (Alexander). The second most frequent category is Greek, but it reveals only 192 names for 328 men. Apart from Celtic names (80) the rest is made up of negligible quantities, mainly Thracian, Phoenician and Arabic. In short, the onomastics of the legionaries reveal that they belonged to the Roman world.

Roman law

In the Roman world complex and varied ties were established between the army and the law (law here being public law, citizenship and institutions). The points of contact were established on three levels, the individual, the city and the province.

Law and the soldier

Some facts in relation to the ordinary individual have already been mentioned in the previous chapter. The most important fact that should be emphasized, is that the army was a machine for creating Roman citizens, spreading the *civitas romana* widely, but first and foremost for its own soldiers. In times of recruitment difficulties it was granted to young men who volunteered to join the legions. At all times it was given at the end of their service to those auxiliaries who did not already have it, but it should be remembered that this system became less efficient as fewer and fewer *peregrini* joined the *alae* and the cohorts. Nevertheless, the 'military diplomas' provide evidence of this legislation that clearly represented the intentions of the political authorities.

The soldiers' families also were advantaged by this generosity. A man who was already married at the time he enlisted had his marriage suspended until the end of his service when it automatically took effect again. This regulation constituted a guarantee for the wife and the children.[15] Furthermore, foreign 'wives' and the children conceived during the father's period of service were also granted the same status as their husband/father when he completed his service. Soldiers thus generated citizens.

Finally we should mention a very original practice hiding behind the term *ius postliminii*.[16] At all times a soldier who fell into the hands of the enemy lost his status precisely because of his captivity; he was no longer recognized by the State as a Roman. But if he escaped or was freed by some means or other he recovered all his rights.

The army and municipalization

The army also played a part in the life of the cities. As we have seen, some veterans joined the order of decurions by entering the higher circles of society. At Lambaesis in Numidia a division of the political body, the 'court of veterans' (*curia*), was reserved for them.[17] Sometimes officers had to carry out civilian tasks like the *census*,[18] drawing up the lists of citizens and non-citizens, used not only for recruitment but also for municipal and fiscal purposes. Often towns sought protection from the commander of the nearest army or legion, which meant that a legate became the patron of cities in his region of authority.

But the soldiers did not intervene only in the cities and the *coloniae*. Their most striking activity in this field was in relation to the nomads, who were a constant threat to the settled population and therefore had to be closely watched. The operation of dividing the tribes into centuries and especially putting them in reserves was aimed at immobilizing the nomads.[19] This was achieved in a reasonable period of time. Moreover, some officers were appointed over certain groups of people, acting as administrators who collected taxes, ensured public order, and even recruited auxiliaries if the need arose.[20] On inscriptions they can be recognized by such titles as *praefectus gentis* or the rarer *praefectus nationis*.[21] We have seen how the *canabae* attained the status of *municipia* or even *coloniae*.[22]

The army and provincialization

On a higher level the army also played a part in the life of a province. It has been said often enough that the history of a region coincided with that of a legion, in particular of Arabia and the *legio III Cyrenaica*, Numidia and the *III Augusta*. And it is hardly possible to speak of Britain's or Germany's past without mentioning their garrisons. In fact, as a governor acted also as head of the army it is difficult to distinguish his two types of activity.

One study has attempted to show how the army had been associated with the provincialization and the municipalization of the Spanish peninsula.[23] As regards the Empire as a whole, at least in the frontier zones, the army also played a part in the promotion of ordinary individuals.

Lifestyles

Many more complex ties between civilians and soldiers can be observed than those revealed by laws and institutions. Both groups shared more or less the same lifestyle. The ordinary soldiers were plebeians and shared their tastes while their occupation led them to give greater importance to some aspects of their contemporary world, to prefer certain activities and certain ways of thinking.

These similarities and differences became clear in their choice of entertainment, an activity that was dear to the hearts of soldiers (the *lixa*, for instance). The soldiers found their pleasures where the plebeians did, though they were more impressed by the less refined and more brutal aspects of shows. Hardly any theatres were to be found near the camps, yet theatres did not only stage plays with intellectual pretentions. What legionaries appreciated most were hunts and gladiator fights, and this appreciation can be gauged by the fact that some garrison towns like *Aquincum* (Budapest) and *Carnuntum* in Pannonia had two amphitheatres.[24] It must be remembered, however, that these buildings were also used for the soldiers' professional training. Baths were another favourite way of relaxation, and each large camp eventually had *thermae* inside its walls.[25]

Collective mentalities

The similarities and differences between ordinary soldiers and plebeians are also apparent in the collective mentalities discernible in inscriptions and in the correspondence that has come down to us in legal sources like Justinian's Code or on Egyptian papyri. As was the case with many of their contemporaries, they attached great importance to their families. Like all people close to nature, they had a love of animals and could admire a marvellous horse even if they were foot-soldiers. They also appreciated food and wine. 'All my life I drank with pleasure, so drink on you living!', is the recommendation of a veteran of the *legio V Gallica* buried at Antioch in Pisidia.[27]

Obviously aspects of their professional life weighed heavily on their minds. On his grave stone an anonymous *primuspilus* summarized his life and his preoccupations:[28]

> I wanted to hold the corpses of Dacians; I did hold some.
> I wanted to sit on a seat of peace; I sat on one.
> I wanted to march in magnificent triumphal processions; I did just that.
> I wanted all the financial advantages of being a *primuspilus*; I had them.
> I wanted to see the Nymphs naked; I saw them.

In this context promotions and careers, training and discipline were of great importance, but probably less so than the money soldiers received as their salary, a constant worry for all of them. In the above inscription it is obvious that promotion to the rank of *primuspilus* was thought of only in terms of financial advantages (*commoda* in the Latin text). As promotions required the support of the commanders, whose job included making sure that duties were not being neglected, officers occupied many of their thoughts. A soldier had to learn to appreciate them and without appearing fawning, to let them know he appreciated them, as we can see from this inscription from Egypt: 'Long live the decurion Caesius! He is a brave man! We, his companions in arms who were placed under his command all wish to thank him.'[29] A brief look through a collection of epigraphic texts is sufficient to gauge the extent of the reverence felt for the supreme commander of the Roman army, the Emperor.

The soldiers then belonged to the plebeian stratum, and gradually it becomes possible to situate them in society. Slight differences, caused by differences in units, did exist. In general these relatively wealthy, salaried men were also pretty well Romanized, even if they showed a preference for the more brutal, less sophisticated features of Early Empire culture. Their daily life was marked by the Latin language, the amphitheatre and soldiering. However, it should not be forgotten that piety formed the essence of their way of thinking.

RELIGIOUS LIFE

The Romans readily asserted that they were the most pious nation in the world, and that this attitude of *pietas* was the reason for the ease with which they conquered everybody. It also justified their conquests.[30] War cannot be divorced from religion.[31] In an article that has remained a classic of its kind H. Le Bonniec demonstrated the links with great clarity,[32] but his analysis is short and is largely concerned with the Republican era. Love of weapons and sentiments for the gods, together with respect for the law and the land, formed the four best known and most important elements in the 'collective mentalities' already studied. These four elements can be traced back a very long way, possibly to the very origins of Rome itself, and they influenced each other. Roman military law was totally imbued with religion through ideas of discipline and oath-swearing.[33]

The faithful

The history of Roman religion has too often neglected the human element, the faithful, and it is only recently that M. Le Glay has drawn attention to this fact.[34] The first question to ask is: who were they?

The role of the officers

Soldiers' reactions were governed by their way of life — that is they respected the principle of hierarchy and acted as a constituent body. Individuals rarely offered dedications; the ordinary soldier did not act like a separate individual, but as part of a group, especially in the early days of the Empire (though he did change a little by the third century). An inscription that has been ignored by many scholars should be cited here as it demonstrates the sequence of events in a collective act of piety. The document, which was found in a well of the Great Camp of Lambaesis in Numidia, was initiated by a legionary: 'The pious men who wish to make a payment to Aesculapius should place it in this collection bowl and we will make some sort of offering to Aesculapius with it.'[35] This anonymous person had therefore placed this text near a bowl for a certain period of time; his colleagues individually put in a coin, and no doubt scratched their name somewhere nearby. When the bowl was full the worshipper of Aesculapius bought an altar, a statue or something else, had an inscription engraved with the names of the god and the different donors.

However, it was through the official channels that the army was best at expressing itself religiously. We have already seen that there was a whole clergy, comprising a *haruspex*, sacrificer, etc., associated with each unit. Another study has demonstrated the important role played by the *primuspilus* in this.[36] It was he who ensured the protection of the standards, which were sacred, and was responsible for having the official dedications engraved. Moreover, it is the commanders of the units who appear the most frequently on religious inscriptions, though less frequently during the third century than in the early days of the Empire.

Perceptions of the divine

The second question that needs to be answered is how the soldiers perceived the divine. After what has been said it should not be imagined that religion, which was a part of their service, had no effect on their feelings. It is certain to have moved them, but through the hierarchical structure, being perceived more as a collective than an individual duty.

The divine was perceived by soldiers just as by ordinary people at the time, through abstract entities, *numina*, and also through an anthropomorphic pantheon. Nevertheless, in view of the dangers they were exposed to in their profession they sometimes sought special protection. Perhaps more than civilians did, they turned to 'syncretism by association',[37] adding gods to gods in order to strengthen the efficacy of their prayers: 'To Jupiter almighty and good, to Juno, to Minerva, to Mars, to Victory, to Hercules, to Fortune, to Mercury, to Luck, to Health, to the Fates, to the divinities of the training ground, to Silvanus, to Apollo, to Diana, to Epona, to the Suleviae Mothers and to the Genius of the Emperor's bodyguards . . . '[38] The safest formula was to address 'all the gods and goddesses' because that way it was certain that none would be forgotten. The adjectives used to describe the gods show them to be good (*boni*), hospitable (*hospites*), and ensurers of good health (*salutares*), as civilians said, but they were also helpful (*iuvantes*), they protected (*fautores*) and preserved from harm (*conservatores*).

These numerous powers were a witness that their wielders were omnipotent, and this all-powerful aspect was revealed at all times through miracles. This is also an important aspect of Roman religion that has been badly neglected, that the activity of the divinity can be vouched for by men. Many inscriptions were engraved following a vision (*ex visu*), a command (*iussu, monitu*). The faithful addressed requests which were granted and they were consequently under the obligation of fulfilling their vow, as can be seen from the formula that is so common that epigraphists no longer pay any attention to it (*ex voto, votum solvit libens merito* or *animo* = VSLM or A). We have already quoted the anonymous *primuspilus* who was lucky enough to see the Nymphs naked.

When Hadrian arrived in Africa in 128 to inspect the troops, his very presence inspired the first 'miracle of the rain'.[39] There was a repeat of this phenomenon in dramatic circumstances during the Germanic campaigns of Marcus Aurelius, when there was an additional 'miracle of lightning'.[40] Soldiers also thought of the sacred in spatial terms: the Roman world's frontiers were placed under the protection of the gods. We are aware of this in the case of the *pomoerium*, the sacred boundary of the city in the Republican era. During the Empire this belief was transferred to the *limes*, the frontier zone that was not merely a military defence line, but which also had a legal status and religious significance. When the barbarians crossed it they committed a sacrilegious act and exposed themselves to the anger of the gods of Rome. This complexity has been highlighted by D.J. Breeze and B. Dobson.[41] The Empire was thus protected by a heavenly militia too.

Rites

To placate these powers the soldiers carried out a certain number of rites.

Civic rites

Some rites were practised by all freemen of the period. These were the civic rites for which soldiers behaved just like any plebeian, but with the two slight differences mentioned above. The offerings were often collective, the statue, altar, monument, temple, etc., being that of a unit. The salaries of the soldiers enabled the act to be performed on a fairly lavish scale. Furthermore, it was normally the top officers who officiated on behalf of everyone involved. On Trajan's Column we can see that the Emperor started every military campaign with the *suovetaurilia*, the sacrifice of a pig, a ram and a bull, accompanied by military music, and ended every one with other sacrifices.[42] The Aurelian Column provides a similar picture.[43] In the third century the tribune Terentius officiated on behalf of the twenty-three men of the XXth cohort of Palmyranians who were present at Dura-Europos; as can be seen from a painting, he had a few grains of incense burnt. A similar occurrence is attested at Messad in Numidia.[44]

Military rites

Some of the rites which were carried out during the course of a campaign were of an exclusively military nature. Although these date back to the Republic, they had undergone some changes by the end of the period under consideration.

The mobilization of an army was marked by a ceremony of swearing an oath (*sacramentum*),[45] binding the soldier to the general and the Emperor in the presence of the gods. In the early years of the Empire this rite underwent a degree of secularization (the *sacramentum* became a *iusiurandum*), but reverted to a religious nature in the third century, probably because of the crisis but possibly also because of the influence of the monotheistic competition. This reversion, however, caused problems for the consciences of Christians in the army.[46]

Before an army could enter enemy territory it had to be purified in a ceremony of *lustratio*, accompanied by a *suovetaurilia*.[47] Analogous ceremonies also marked the end of each campaign season; during the Republic a horse was sacrificed in October (*equus october*). Other rites were carried out with the specific purpose of cleansing the camp: insignia and arms in the *armilustrium*, trumpets in the *tubilustrium*.

War was declared by the *fetiales* and the gates of the Temple of Janus were opened. The actual conduct of a battle also had to follow a fixed pattern. Hostilities could not be engaged on an ill-fated day or without the blessings of the gods.[48] Taking auspices or examining the entrails of sacrificial victims ensured the latter.

If there is little evidence in the Empire of the *evocatio*, the calling to Rome of the enemy's gods, there is no doubt that the *devotio* persisted, though in a modified form. In the Republic this was the supreme sacrifice, in which a general who found that his army was in a hopeless situation threw himself into the middle of the enemy's ranks. By killing him the enemy were virtually making an offering to the gods for their own defeat. The Emperor Claudius II (268–70) is supposed to have sacrificed himself in this way for the good of the State.[49] But in the Principate the word was rarely used, and the act, which is often misunderstood by those who describe it, became more 'democratic' insofar as it was an ordinary soldier who offered his life in sacrifice thereafter. Josephus describes the act of a soldier who sacrificed himself during a siege,[50] but the Jewish historian's account of this 'unparalleled act of bravery' shows that he did not understand its religious significance:

A Syrian called Sabinus, serving in the auxiliary cohorts, stepped forward. He was remarkably strong and courageous, but anyone who had seen him previously would not even have thought that he was an ordinary soldier, to judge by his physique, as he was black-skinned, puny, mere skin and bone. But in this light body, which was too slight for the strength it contained, there was the soul of a hero. He was the first to come forward, and said: 'Caesar, it is with joy that I give you my life by being the first to climb the rampart. I hope that your good fortune will go with my strength and determination, but if fate views my act in an unfavourable light be sure that I shall not be surprised by my setback, but that I made a deliberate decision to die for you . . . ' Advancing under a hail of projectiles and buried beneath a shower of arrows, Sabinus ran without pausing until he had reached the top and routed the enemy . . . After succeeding in his venture this hero then tripped over a stone, slipped, and fell on it head-first. Riddled with wounds he let his weapon fall from his hand and died under another shower of arrows. He was a hero whose courage deserved a better end, but whose death was commensurate with his venture.

When the Roman army had finally succeeded in defeating the enemy it was right to honour the gods again. Thanks were given in a sort of 'Te Deum'.[51] Afterwards the dead were buried amid all the traditional rites; honouring the dead was an integral part of paganism.[52] Next the victors left a trophy on the battlefield.[53] This Greek practice, introduced to Rome quite late, consisted of putting a dummy in soldier's clothes on top of a heap of weapons taken from the defeated enemy (pl.XXXVII,40a). This sort of effigy could be made permanent by casting it in bronze or sculpting it in marble. From Sulla's time the deities who received thanks were Venus, Mars and Victory. Augustus emphasized the role of Victory, associated with Fortuna-Tyche, which made clear the imperial charisma, the Genius of Augustus. Trajan reverted to the Republican orthodoxy that believed that Victory was a gift of *Virtus*, devotion. During the third-century crisis the gods took a back seat in the face of imperial absolutism, and fewer trophies were consecrated. The most impressive was that erected by Trajan at Adamklissi. It is built on a circular plinth and commemorates the Emperor's revenge on the Dacians, the Roxolani and the Bastarnae. Others are depicted on the columns of Trajan and Marcus Aurelius beside Victory.[54]

In the Republic the soldiers could thank a general whose leadership had been successful by acclaiming him *imperator* in the evening after the battle. If, after due enquiry, the Senate ratified this claim, the victor was entitled to a triumph.[55] It is not clear that these procedures were always followed in the Empire, and in any case, Augustus soon claimed for himself the glory that came from this ceremony.[56] The triumph, organized by a *curator*,[57] came into the category of religious processions. The victorious general was the focal point; he incarnated Jupiter and rode in a chariot, dressed in a purple tunic under a toga embroidered with golden stars. In his hands he held a sceptre with an eagle and a laurel branch on top. On his forehead he wore a laurel crown, while behind him a little slave held a golden crown and repeated to him over and over again that he was actually only a man, so as not to make the real Jupiter jealous. The new hero was accompanied by Senators and his soldiers who had to deride their leader to prevent any feeling of envy among the gods (Julius Caesar was 'the man for all women, the woman for all men'). Behind him came the spoils and the defeated, either in person or represented by symbols, as well as the sacrificial animals. The whole procession had one end in view as it left the Campus Martius, traversed the Forum before reaching the Capitol – this was the sacrifice to the gods.

Many descriptions of triumphs are extant. Germanicus' triumph in 18 AD celebrated his humiliation of the Germans,[58] but the most interesting and perhaps the best known is the one sculpted on the Arch of Titus that rises above the Forum in Rome. It commemorates the defeat of the Jews, represented by the famous seven-branched candelabra among all the booty (pl.XXXIX,40).[59] It was taken from the Temple of Jerusalem.

The ceremony brought the hero a great deal of charisma, and a consequence of this was that after the triumph of Cornelius Balbus in 19 BC no ordinary individual was allowed to have one. Henceforth triumphs were reserved for the Emperor and his family, even if the ruler had not been present on the battlefield; it was his Genius and *Numen* that had won the war. Good generals had to be content with the trappings of triumph.[60]

The calendar

These celebrations only happened in time of war, but soldiers were not allowed to forget the gods in time of peace. The calendar of the XXth cohort of Palmyranians has been found at Dura-Europos.[61] The text of this papyrus was written between 224 and 235, probably between 225 and 227, and lacks the last three months of the year. The soldiers were concerned with three types of celebration, that of the Emperor, the State and the army.

ROMAN DATE	CHRISTIAN DATE	CELEBRATIONS AND REMARKS
Calends of January	Jan 1	?
3rd day before Nones of Jan	Jan 3	greetings
7th day before Ides of Jan	Jan 7	discharge (*missio*) and payment of salaries
6th? day before Ides of Jan	Jan 8?	birthday (*Natalis*) of anon. goddess
3rd? day before Ides of Jan	Jan 11?	birthday of L. Seius, the Emperor's father-in-law
9th day before Calends of Feb	Jan 24	birthday of *Divus* Hadrian

ROMAN DATE	CHRISTIAN DATE	CELEBRATIONS AND REMARKS
5th day before Calends of Feb	Jan 28	Victory of *Divus* Severus and coming to power (*imperium*) of *Divus* Trajan
day before Nones of Feb	Feb 4	coming to power of *Divus* Caracalla
Calends of March	Mar 1	anniversary of Victorious Mars
Nones of March	Mar 7	coming to power of *Divus* Marcus Aurelius and *Divus* L. Verus
3rd day before Ides of March	Mar 13	Alexander Severus acclaimed *Imperator*
day before Ides of March	Mar 14	Alexander Severus named Augustus, father of the homeland and supreme pontiff
14th day before Calends of April	Mar 19	*Quinquatria* in honour of Minerva
day before Nones of April	Apr 4	anniversary of *Divus* Caracalla
5th day before Ides of April	Apr 9	coming to power of *Divus* Septimius Severus
3rd day before Ides of April	Apr 11	anniversary of *Divus* Septimius Severus
11th day before Calends of May	Apr 21	anniversary of City of Rome
6th day before Calends of May	Apr 26	anniversary of *Divus* Marcus Aurelius
Nones ? of May	May 7?	anniversary of *Diva* Maesa
6th day before Ides of May	May 10	*Rosalia Signorum* (festival of the standards) see also May 31
4th day before Ides of May	May 12	circus games in honour of Mars
12th day before Calends of June	May 20	*Divus* Septimius Severus acclaimed *Imperator*
9th day before Calends of June	May 23	anniversary of Germanicus
day before Calends of June	May 31	*Rosalia Signorum*: see also May 10
5th day before Ides of June	June 9	festival of Vesta
6th day? before Calends of July	June 26?	Alexander Severus received title of Caesar and took the adult toga
Calends of July	July 1	Alexander Severus is elected to his first consulate

ROMAN DATE	CHRISTIAN DATE	CELEBRATIONS AND REMARKS
4th? day before Nones of July	July 4?	anniversary of *Diva* Matidia, niece of Trajan
6th day before Ides of July	July 10	coming to power of *Divus* Antoninus Pius
4th day before Ides of July	July 12	anniversary of *Divus* Caesar
10th day before Calends of August	July 23	festival of Neptune
Calends of August	Aug 1	anniversary of *Divus* Claudius and *Divus* Pertinax
Nones of August	Aug 5	circus games in honour of Salus
? day before Calends of Sept	Aug 14–28	anniversary of empress Mamaea
ditto	Aug 15–28	?
ditto	Aug 16–30	anniversary of *Diva* Marciana, sister of Trajan
day before Calends of Sept	Aug 31	anniversary of *Divus* Commodus
7th? day before Ides of Sept	Sept 7?	payment of salaries
14th day before Calends of Oct	Sept 18	anniversary of *Divus* Trajan (and coming to power of *Divus* Nerva ?)
13th day before Calends of Oct	Sept 19	anniversary of *Divus* Antoninus Pius
12th–10th? day before Calends of October	Sept 20–22	anniversary of *Diva* Faustina
9th day before Calends of Oct	Sept 23	anniversary of *Divus* Augustus
16th day before Calends of Jan	Dec 17	festival of Saturn

Table 42: The military calendar at Dura-Europos

The soldiers' pantheon

Whether we are talking about warrior rites or simply military celebrations, the various ceremonies honoured the official gods. The study of the deities in the soldiers' pantheon confirms this view. Soldiers were no different from their civilian contemporaries[62] in this respect except for the fact that they naturally accepted greater importance to those powers that could protect them when carrying out their military duties. The men in the *numeri* however retained a more national devotion.

Traditional Roman military gods

Soldiers expected special protection from a whole series of powers called the 'military gods', *dii militares*[63] who helped them in their daily tasks, in particular on the training ground,[64] and even more so in battle.[65] Four major groups can be distinguished: the great gods; the deified abstractions; the Genii; and the insignia.

It should be remembered that nearly all the great anthropomorphic gods exercised two main functions, bringing food and security. This is the case for the Capitoline triad at Rome, whose head, Jupiter, was given various adjectives that recalled his role: *stator*, the very ancient one in the *Urbs*, recalled that it was he who stopped the enemy; as *depulsor* he drove back the adversaries (the troops in Pannonia recognized this particular merit in him); he was also brave, *valens*, notably for the army of Africa, which assimilated him to the local Balidir; as *conservator* he defended the fatherland. If his partner, Juno Regina, received less veneration in the camps, her daughter Minerva won the approval of the accountants and the trumpet players.[66] Another god, Silvanus, was a rural deity in Italian tradition, but in Pannonia where he reminded the soldiers of Vetiri, he took on a more military aspect. The same was true for the troops in Africa. His success spread to the Praetorians who called him *castrensis*.

Some great gods are less unexpected in this list. Janus had helped the Romans from the beginning of time in combat and he was not neglected in the Early Empire. Before a conflict it was advisable to open the gates of his temple so that he could make his way to the battlefield. Only when hostilities had ceased were they closed again. In the same way Venus ensured victory, she was *Victoria*. Nevertheless, the most obvious one was Mars, the master of arms, who directed military service (*militiae potens*); he kept watch over the training ground, hence he was called *campester*.[67] In Britain, where he was imposed upon a native god, he was simply said to be *militaris*. But for everybody he was *Gradivus*, an ancient adjective that emphasized his warlike nature. However, he tended to fade into the background somewhat, especially in the third century, giving way to a demi-god, the Greco-Roman Hercules, Commodus' favourite deity and patron of Leptis Magna, the city of Septimius Severus and Caracalla. Hercules spread to the armies of Germany who assimilated him with Donar, and of the Danube and Africa. He even found favour in Rome with the Praetorians and the *equites singulares Augusti*. The *Lares*, the protectors of crossroads and of the household, were also qualified as *militares*.[68]

One of the peculiarities of Roman religion was to leave a lot of room in the pantheon to deified abstractions. Though the Greeks were familiar with this practice they did not go in for it to any considerable degree. They are often mentioned on inscriptions and coins. The most important power was *Victoria*, represented by a winged woman holding a wreath. She often has trophies on either side of her,[69] consecrated to the triad Mars-Venus-*Victoria*, as we have seen.[70] Sometimes she is represented with Mars alone.[71] On inscriptions it is necessary to distinguish the

Victoria Augusta, a deity related to the imperial person, from the *Victoria Augusti* or *Augustorum*, which emphasized the role of the Emperor(s) in a successful engagement of the Roman army. This goddess was entreated before a battle and thanked afterwards. But *Victoria* did not come alone. She could be accompanied by the Good Result (*Bonus Eventus*) and above all by Good Fortune (*Fortuna*).[72] The name of this last divinity must not be taken in its modern connotation, and particularly not that referring to money. It represents chance or destiny, highly honoured in the East Mediterranean of the Hellenistic period under the name of Tyche. Soldiers were very ready to place her statues in the camp baths.

Victoria and *Fortuna* made manifest the omnipotent nature of the gods; other abstractions emphasized the human role. We have already seen the dual meaning of *Disciplina* as both 'knowledge' and 'obedience' when dealing with training;[73] coins were struck in her honour (pl.XXXVIII,39) and altars were offered to her. This Discipline could not be acquired without *Virtus*, which was characteristic of the male sex (the *vir*, the 'virile' being), that is the service to the State in two forms, civilian and military. The latter implied courage, the other meaning of *virtus*. Soldiers also had to possess Piety (*Pietas*) in order to obtain Victory, so they did not omit it from their pantheon.

Honour (*Honos*) represented the last important abstraction worthy of note. This word too was rich in resonances; at first it designated an individual attitude, the respect for a code of conduct, as practised in seventeenth-century France. But most frequently it called to mind the glory attached either to the exercising of a function or association with a high-ranking person or divine being. Thus in the legions the *primipili* celebrated the *Honos Aquilae*, the Honour of the Eagle, which was the emblem and the sacred symbol of the unit.[74]

There was yet another category of protectors that could be added to the anthropomorphic gods and abstractions. These were the Genii, similar to the guardian angels of Catholicism, and they were of two major types. Some had a 'topographic' function, being attached to buildings, in particular the camp,[75] which was a sacred enclosure,[76] inaugurated by a sacrifice, the *suovetaurilia* performed to the sound of the double flute.[77] They were also associated with the general's residence, *praetorium* or *augural*.[78] Other Genii kept watch over the hospital, the shops, the archives, the college buildings (*scholae*) and the legate's rostrum.[79] We know of others outside the camps that protected the police stations (*stationes*) and the training grounds (*campi*), where they were associated with the *dii campestres*. The other Genii were linked to groups of men, rather than places, and foremost to soldiers in general.[80] We also know of Genii of the legion, the cohort, the century and the *principales*; for the *auxilia* there were the Genii of the *alae*, the cohort, the *numerus*, the squadron and the century, while at Rome there were the Genii of the *frumentarii* and the *equites singulares Augusti*. The list is by no means complete.

Nevertheless, to finish we should not forget a cult that is typically military, that of the insignia, the anniversaries of which were celebrated,[81] and which were placed in a shrine, the *aedes signorum* at the heart of the *principia*, the central section of the camp. There they stood next to the portrait (or portraits?) of the Emperor. The eagle of the legion was paid particular reverence on the day of its anniversary,[82] the *natalis aquilae*, and also through its *Honos*, as just noted. The *signa* were celebrated and decked with flowers at the time of the *Rosalia*. So were the *vexilla*. Each legion's eagle carried symbols which were the focus of the celebrations. The coins issued in the course of the third century demonstrate that the choice of symbols changed, but other evidence can be adduced to gain a better understanding of them.

If we add to this list the non-Roman gods (see below), for instance

Unit	First – second centuries	Gallienus	Victorinus	Carausius
I Adiutrix	Capricorn	Capricorn		
	Pegasus	Pegasus		
I Italica	boar	boar		
	bull	bull		
	Bos marinus			
I Minervia	Minerva	Minerva	ram	ram
	ram			
II Adiutrix	boar	boar		
	Pegasus	Pegasus		
II Augusta	Capricorn			Capricorn
	Pegasus			
	Mars			
II Italica	she-wolf	she-wolf+twins		
	Capricorn	Capricorn		
	stork			
II Parthica	Centaur	Centaur		Centaur
II Traiana	Hercules			Hercules
III Augusta	Capricorn			
	Pegasus			

Unit	First - second centuries	Gallienus	Victorinus	Carausius
III Gallica	bull			
III Italica	stork	stork		
IV Flavia	lion	lion	lion	lion
IV Macedonica	bull			
	Capricorn			
V Macedonica	bull	eagle	bull	
VI Victrix	bull			
VII Claudia	bull	bull		bull
	lion			
VIII Augusta	bull	bull		bull
X Fretensis	bull		bull	
	boar			
X Gemina	bull	bull		
XI Claudia	Neptune	Neptune		
XII Fulminata	lightning			
XIII Gemina	lion	lion	lion	
XIV Gemina	Capricorn	Capricorn	Capricorn	
	eagle			
XVI Flavia	lion			
XX Valeria	boar		boar	boar
	Capricorn			
XXI Rapax	Capricorn			
XXII Primigenia	Capricorn	Capricorn	Capricorn	Capricorn
	Hercules			
XXX Ulpia	Neptune	Neptune	Capricorn	Neptune
	Capricorn			
	Jupiter			

Table 43: Emblems of the legions[83]

Azizu, a sort of Arabian Mars called *Bonus Puer* in Latin, we can see that the 'professional' aspect played a major role in the religious life of the camps. But the most important point seems to me not to be this. Here, we can see confirmation of the thesis developed above: the official and traditional cults played the dominant role in the military world.

Roman traditional civilian gods

This view is reinforced when a list of civilian gods, those whose military role is secondary, is drawn up and the same classification as before, major gods, abstractions and Genii is apparent. The entire Early Empire pantheon is represented in this way, more or less satisfactorily it is true, influenced by Greek and native ways of thought to an extent we cannot quantify.

However, some sort of divine 'health service' under Apollo, with his sister Diana in a secondary role, was accorded great importance in the Early Empire. His place was taken in the hearts of legionaries by Aesculapius, to whom a huge sanctuary was dedicated at Lambaesis in Numidia. Pilgrims flocked to it in droves. Prayers were also addressed to the Good Goddess (*Bona Dea*), also called Good Health, *Hygia* or *Salus*. All the inhabitants of the Empire used the medicinal properties of water, which was also deified; at the very centre of the Great Camp at Lambaesis there was a *Nymphaeum*, while outside, but still in the city, there was a temple and other buildings dedicated to Neptune which attracted suppliants from far away.

The case of Cereus, an Italian god, adopted by the army in Africa, is rather special. His cult was celebrated by the consecration of an altar every 3 May, the last day of the *Floralia*. It was Flora[84] who gave man honey and wax (*cereus* as a common noun means 'candle'), and who gave Juno a magic plant so that she could conceive Mars without the aid of her husband Jupiter. This legend explains the link between Cereus and the army.

We also find all the deified abstractions worshipped by the civilians, including the goddess Rome, who was particularly revered under Hadrian and in the East, and various Genii attached to places through which the armies passed. As the soldiers often served far from their birthplaces they remembered to pray to their *deus patriae* who would enable them to return home. In all this there is little that should surprise us.

The imperial cult

With the imperial cult, however, some slight differences and divergences among the various units are discernible. Praetorians, who lived in the shadow of the ruler, and auxiliaries, the least Romanized corps, showed more enthusiasm for this cult than legionaries did. The latter apparently remained attached to the more reserved Italian tradition, probably because they were proud of their status as Roman citizens who had not been recruited in the *Urbs* itself. They did not go beyond wishing 'the safety of the Emperor',[85] and they prayed to Jupiter to protect their ruler (*Jupiter conservator*). Yet it was clear what the political powers wanted. There was a celebration and the swearing of an oath on the Emperor's birthday;[86] the imperial bust was to be found in the shrine of the insignia at the centre of the camp, and a soldier, the *imaginifer*, was specifically attached to its cult. The colleges that were authorized by Septimius Severus followed this practice, as did the legates on occasion. The soldiers did not become actively involved until the time of Septimius Severus. As far as the Emperor was concerned the results were fairly disappointing in the legions; only his *Genius* and his *Numen* (guardian angel and active will) were worshipped, along with the *divi* (Emperors deified after their death) and the *domus Augusta* (Emperor's family) and various Augustan gods. Only towards the year 200 did the *domus Augusta* become *domus divina*, and the Emperor get called 'master' (*dominus noster*) in any more than sporadic fashion. In the Severan dynasty the Empress became the 'mother of the camp'.

Non-Roman gods

It is understandable that there was little room left in the hearts of the soldiers for non-Roman gods. Only the most barbaric soldiers serving in the *numeri* kept their links with the cults of their ancestors. The Palmyranians, for example, worshipped Malagbel and Hierobol everywhere they went, at Dura-Europos[87] and at El-Kantara and Messad in Numidia.[88] The people of Emesus worshipped the sun wherever they were. To be sure, other types of units manifested their piety towards exotic divinities. The *equites singulares Augusti* venerated the *Matres*, the *Suleviae*, Silvanus, Apollo and Diana, described as *dii patrii*, while a Thracian inscription on the Esquiline would seem to be associated with the Praetorians. Silvanus was worshipped by the Illyrians.

For the rest, the non-Roman gods can be classified in two main groups. A few appear to have belonged to the native backgrounds of the various provinces, but it is difficult to gauge their importance with any exactitude because they are disguised by the *interpretatio romana*, a process which Latinized their names. This paucity of gods can be demonstrated in Africa where legionaries have left only one inscription honouring Saturn, another for his partner Caelestis and none for the Cereres. The *dii Mauri* were slightly more popular in Mauretania, as were British deities near Hadrian's Wall: a temple had been built in honour of Antenocitius, and several texts commemorated those like him (Veteres, Belatucadrus, Cocidius). In countries that were Celtic in tradition, Epona was worshipped, and in Pannonia Sedatus and Trasitus. The soldiers' attachment to the protectors of the countries in which they were garrisoned was a very Roman tradition. Protection always had to be sought from the local gods, and an army always did just that before entering enemy territory on campaign. On the columns of Trajan and Marcus Aurelius we can see the deified Danube watching over the Roman troops on campaign there.

A second non-Roman group is formed by the Eastern deities, who in the past have been credited with too much importance. First of all it should be said that they are also found in Anatolia, Syria and Egypt, and that in those countries they should be considered as part of the previous class of gods. Thus one morning during the civil war that followed Nero's death 'the sun was rising. As was the custom in Syria, the IIIrd legion saluted it'.[90] We are here dealing with a local cult of the worship of the Sun in Syria, whom the soldiers stationed in Syria were honouring even though they were on campaign in Italy. This is not the only example of the *legio III Gallica*'s attachment to the god of Emesus.[91] In fact, the Eastern gods were only of any real significance in the Roman army in the third century, when they first attracted the devotion of the officer class. The main one was the Iranian Mithras who became Sol Invictus, the guarantor of order in the cosmos. His cult caught on because it was like a militia; the third of the seven steps of initiation entitled the devotee to be called 'soldier (of the god)'. Soldiers built *mithraea*. The Syrian Jupiters were also popular. Jupiter Dolichenus[92] in Commagene reinforced political power, but the authorities ignored him. This Hittite Ba'al Tarz had his disciples in Rome among the *equites singulares Augusti*, on the Danube, the Rhine and even as far away as Britain. His cult was related to that of the insignia, to Apollo and Diana, to the Sun and Moon. The Jupiter of Heliopolis (Baalbek) was 'the angel, the messenger of Bel'. The Arabian Azizu (*Bonus Puer*) was reminiscent of Mars. Finally, Isis and Serapis from Egypt were often associated with the cult of water.

In conclusion, it does seem that the Eastern cults that were introduced into the West at a fairly late date concerned only a fraction of the Roman army. They were more popular obviously in the Eastern Mediterranean.

Syncretism by accumulation

It is a pity that little has been written about the very important but not widely known phenomenon of syncretism (see above). M. Le Glay has devoted a general study to the theme,[93] but only the army in Africa[94] has been the object of detailed preliminary research. Syncretism consisted of adding together a large number of gods in order to reinforce their action, as was seen in the inscription cited above.[95] Apparently the concatenation of gods was not haphazard, and two different types can be distinguished. In the first case a dominant characteristic emerges, for instance war: all the divinities mentioned have combat as their sphere of influence. The second category joins two related themes, for instance war and the garrison, war and the fatherland, war and health, etc.

The cult of the dead

It is not possible to end a study of Roman paganism without mentioning the cult of the dead, a cult that was particularly important to men whose profession exposed them to a premature demise. *Pietas* imposed on survivors the burial of their comrades killed in action and the celebration of the traditional cults. Later they would erect tombs with funerary monuments, or cenotaphs if the body had not been recovered. For soldiers who died in their beds the cult was exactly the same as for civilians. As already seen,[96] the survivors dedicated *stelae* in the first century, altars in the second and cupulas in the third (at least in Africa). The tombs were grouped together in a vast necropolis that lined the roads leading from the camp. At best a soldier's salary could enable him to have reliefs carved next to his commemorative inscription. A centurion could use his wealth to have a mausoleum built over his body.

In short, soldiers acted in the same conservative manner when dealing with the great gods or the cult of the dead, maintaining the traditions of paganism.

Christianity in the Roman army

This attitude causes problems for historians because Christian sources emphasize the ready acceptance of the new faith. As early as 174, as the pagan Cassius Dio himself believed,[97] the *legio XII Fulminata* is said to have been saved by a miraculous fall of rain sent by God. In his *Apologeticus* Tertullian frequently remarks on the presence of fellow Christians in camps, while his *De Corona* shows a Praetorian who preferred to die rather than sacrifice to the pagan gods.[98] Throughout the third century soldiers were persecuted, especially in Egypt under Decius in Judaea under Gallienus. But Diocletian and Maximian were the most energetic in this anti-Christian policy, and they may even have gone as far as exterminating the 'Theban Legion' which they considered to be completely tainted.[99]

These persecutions can be explained by several factors. From a theological viewpoint no syncretism between the gods of the army, who were essential for discipline, and the Christian God was possible; the Christians could not worship idols; a strict moral code highlighted the incompatibility of the soldier's oath (*sacramentum*) and the sacraments (also *sacramentum*), the army of the Emperor and of the army of Christ, even to the point of forbidding the spilling of blood. This has led some historians to talk of 'conscientious objectors'[100] and 'deserters'.[101] Some have even gone so far as to accuse Christianity of having caused the fall of the Roman Empire's defences that let in the invading Germans.

In fact, the Church Fathers and ancient apologists are guilty of exaggeration. Only a heretical minority, influenced by Montanism,[102] sought martyrdom. Christianity came little and late to the Roman army. The feebleness of its influence has been demonstrated for the *praetorium*,[103] for Britain[104] and for Africa.[105] The situation was possibly different in the East, but in general the soldiers were only too ready to side with the persecutors.

CONCLUSION

In the Early Empire the army had a conservative effect on society. It spread Romanization and a very traditional paganism. Admittedly a distinction must be made between the Eastern and the Western halves of the Empire. In the Eastern Mediterranean Greek often preceded, accompanied or replaced Latin, but its influence was more noticeable on the civilians than on the soldiers.

A change must also be highlighted. The policy of Romanization and traditional paganism meant that an army recruited on the basis of quality had to be strictly adhered to, but this required considerable sums of money. The old order that financed this was to be overthrown in the third-century crisis.

10

GENERAL CONCLUSION

'Battle-history' is dead and unmourned. Out of its ashes can come a new type of military history that has begun to show signs of vigour in the past few years. On the French side alone one could point to Ph. Contamine[1] for the Middle Ages, A. Corvisier[2] for the seventeenth century, and for contemporary history P. Renouvin,[3] G. Pedroncini,[4] and A. Martel.[5] A manifest lesson emerges from a comparison of their work, namely that the past cannot be pieced together without taking into account the conflicts that shook it. This observation is true of antiquity also.[6] The study of the Roman army forces one inevitably to touch on all aspects of life, political, economic, social, cultural and religious. The study of these different aspects of the topic cannot, however, come first; logic dictates that we first look at this imperial army before trying to discover what it did.

SPECIFIC CHARACTERISTICS OF THE ROMAN ARMY

This first enquiry is therefore somewhat technical and professional in nature. It shows us that for the Romans of the Early Empire, war had become a science that was studied and written about. It had found its way into libraries.[7] At first sight the complexity of this army and the operations it undertook are striking. In no way was the legion a rabble, because each man occupied a particular place in one of the many specializations.[8] Similarly, the construction of a camp needed very diverse skills,[9] while the qualities of the navy were far higher than we have been led to believe.[10]

Officers had to be familiar with evolving strategic studies,[11] which often came into play in the complex zone that is called *limes*,[12] a fairly wide strip of land comprising individual defences (camps and towers), linear obstacles (rivers and walls) and roads. Legions and *auxilia*, the bulk of the army, had been stationed on the borders; there was a garrison of the Empire's best soldiers at Rome, the 'centre of power', and even though it played a secondary role, the navy had not been neglected. Generals were more often on the defensive, but this did not prevent them from taking the offensive at times. The destruction of an enemy wherever it happened to be caused no problems for Roman consciences or Roman diplomacy.[13] The objectives of war therefore were characteristically simple and clear: security of the Empire or enemy wealth.[14]

This strategy implied the use of intelligent tactics, something that has been overlooked for some time because of the discredit into which 'battle-history' has fallen.[15] Roman officers therefore had to know how to make a bridge, build roads and camps. Marching order and battle order were based on instructions of some complexity, though not to quite the same extent as those that governed siege warfare. A military engagement in open country demanded exceptional manoeuvring qualities from everybody concerned. The Roman army was the phalanx of Alexander with added flexibility. But this military science was not fixed for all time. When studying tactics, or armour for that matter, the scholar cannot but be struck by the great qualities of adaptability of this Roman army. The impression is that after each defeat the generals drew their conclusions in order to be better prepared the next time round.

The complicated tactics could only be put into operation by men who were well-trained. Strange as it may seem, training, which was fundamental to the success of the Roman army, has never been properly studied.[16] We know that soldiers toughened their bodies by exercise, that they learned how to handle a sword and a javelin, a sling and a bow, and that they practised manoeuvres under the orders of carefully selected instructors. Some of these activities were carried out in the open air, others in gymnasia and basilicas, others on purpose-built training grounds (*campi*).

We can now appreciate that technical or professional reasons account for some part of the Roman army's successful qualities. Every victory brought its lessons which the chiefs-of-staff were quick to evaluate, but essentially the officers saw war as a science, and in their ambitious strategy they used sophisticated tactics that required daily intensive preparation to hone the skills of their men.

THE ROMAN ARMY AND SOCIETY

The complexity of the army meant the juxtaposition of people from several social strata.[17] The legions were not strong simply because they used a book of techniques, but because of their soldiers. But it would be wrong to think that the army was an image of society, as the picture it presented was distorted and incomplete.

Only a man, a *vir* with *virtus*, could be a soldier. Slaves, who were either not counted as human beings or at best only partially human, did not have access to this honour because of their lack of status.

Freeman were classified according to their legal status.[18] The least Romanized, the 'foreigners' or *peregrini* joined the auxiliary units, wings and cohorts in the first century, but thereafter formed barbarian *numeri*. Roman citizens went into the legions, but as only relatively small numbers were required (fewer than 10,000 men a year), and as military service was theoretically compulsory for everybody, the recruiting officers could choose the best from the plebeians.

It was the best of these best plebeians who became the subalterns, the cavalry decurions and infantry centurions.[19] It has often been said that the effectiveness of the Roman army was due in large part to these NCOs, but an important fact has been overlooked here. Some of them had been appointed directly to these posts without coming up through the ranks. This was the case for the sons of municipal notables and even certain Roman equestrians, the *centuriones ex equite romano*. The conclusion might therefore be drawn that recruitment based on birth rather than merit would result in weakness.

But if we examine the officer corps we can see that this practice proved successful. Equestrians provided the tribunes and prefects for the garrison at Rome, the fleet, the auxiliary units and the legions; in the last mentioned they were subordinate to the senatorial legates and the laticlavian tribunes. Thus the Empire's nobility, the Senators, and this partial or second-rank nobility, the equestrians, had the exclusive privilege of forming the officer class. Although it has been criticized for many years, this officer corps deserves to be rehabilitated.[20] Because of their physical exercise they were strong and energetic, and they acquired military science by reading the books that were part of every well-brought up young man's education, as well as by actual command, since the first months of their duty were a sort of training course or practical school.

This ideal picture is only valid, however, for the first two centuries AD. The crisis in the third century brought many changes; long, dangerous wars made noblemen avoid their duty[21] and Senators shun the camps. The best of the plebeians also tried to get out of their obligations because of the dangers involved, admittedly, but also because military service was now a real profession, and one that was becoming less and less remunerative.

Thus, Augustus clearly took the decision to go for quality in his choice of officers and soldiers, but the implementation of this policy required two conditions to be fulfilled — the spilling of the least blood possible and the outlay of considerable sums of money.

THE ARMY AND THE ROMAN WORLD

These financial requirements remind us that far from being separated from the contemporary world the army lived in symbiosis with the Empire. They were linked by many ties, the first of which was political.

The regime was defined as a military monarchy, that is to say it relied more or less openly on its soldiers. To counterbalance the pressures the Senate and the Senators exerted it had to find reinforcements in the lower levels of society. It should be remembered that Tiberius invited the Senators to witness the training of the Praetorians,[22] and the writer who retold this anecdote, Cassius Dio, did not mistake its meaning. It was clearly intended to remind his guests where power really lay. Elsewhere Tacitus wrote of 'the secret of the Empire',[23] and it is clear how this should be interpreted. The head of State was no longer chosen in Rome, and certainly not in the Curia, but in the provinces, in the provincial camps to be more precise.[24] In fact, proudly conscious of their status as Roman citizens, the legionaries regarded themselves as the heirs of the Romans, true *Quirites*. And since it was they who wielded the power it is difficult to see why they should have neglected their duty in this matter.

The soldiers carried out their political obligations in the full knowledge of what they were doing. But probably unknowingly they also played an even more important role in other domains. First of all, the influence of their mere presence on the material life of their time should be noted, creating a prosperous zone along the periphery of the Empire.[25] They kept the peace in respect of brigands and barbarians, the famous *pax Romana* which was considered to be a factor of prosperity. Their first task was to fight the enemy from without, the second to police the enemy from within.[26] Moreover, they spent their salaries in the regions in which they were garrisoned and later often lived in retirement. As these salaries were regular and reasonably large, paid in good denarii, silver coins, the soldiers' lifestyle was fairly affluent. Thus a zone of monetary economy was created separate from the rest of the world. Towns, villages and large estates grew up near the camps and attracted craftsmen, merchants, peasants and entertainment managers. The soldiers surveyed and registered the land and settled the tribes. They built bridges and roads, opened up new trade routes. This prosperous strip, however, had two weaknesses: it had gaps and in any case was reliant on the salaries which in turn depended on the prosperity of the State.

Culture was another domain in which soldiers played an important role unintentionally and probably unknowingly. They spread Romanization in the regions in which they spent their salaries. Latin was the language of command, the only one in which orders could be given. Also the army spread the Roman citizenship that was a *sine qua non* for joining the *praetorium*, the urban cohorts and the legions.[27] In the auxiliary units it was granted at the end of the period of military service. Furthermore it helped in the municipalization of the Empire: some officers governed tribes or carried out the *census*; some veterans entered the *Curia* and legates were patrons of cities. On an even higher level it intervened in the process of provincialization.[28] Army commanders were also governors. However, the concept of Romanization should not be restricted only to institutions as it also represented a lifestyle, even if the soldiers manifested in this domain their membership of the plebeian order with their less sophisticated, not to say downright vulgar tastes. They were attracted by gladiatorial contests more than by the theatre. The importance of leisure, family and service were the main characteristics of what we now call the 'collective mentalities'.

But the soldiers' psyche was even more marked by the presence of the divine. Romans shouted loud and clear without the slightest hint of self-consciousness that they were the most pious race in the world,[29] and the soldiers were Romans. Like the civilians they saw the presence of deities everywhere and in many miracles recognized their powers. Also like the civilians, though possibly to a greater degree, they prayed to a multitude of celestial powers that they joined together in many 'syncretisms' in order to increase the efficacy of their prayers.[30] The fundamental and most original characteristic of this religiosity seems to me to be the strong attachment of the legionaries to a most traditional, national paganism. Though this is not the received wisdom, I would emphasize that they were Romans. Consequently, although there was some place given to native and Eastern cults in the camps, it was very small. The same was true for Christianity, with the soldiers being far more willing to be on the side of the persecutors than of the persecuted.[31] Moreover, the authorities reinforced these tendencies by imposing official calendars of celebrations of rites and anniversaries,[32] some of which went back to the origins of Rome.

Secular culture and religiosity coincided since soldiers belonged to the civilian milieu of the plebeians. This was not something that happened fortuitously, it was the result of a clear, conscious policy of recruitment, which itself was dependent on State finance. It was predicated on the belief that substantial salaries would attract the elite of the young men from the right social class. So, the study of the army leads to a vast enquiry about civilization via society in general.

EVOLUTION AND CHANGE

The financial aspects just mentioned lead also to another aspect of history, that of evolution. Even if permanent features characterized the Early Empire, the whole period was not uniform. Augustus' reign was outstanding for the impressive effort of organization that took place, the establishing of the *limes* policy, even though the actual word did not then appear in the official vocabulary with the meaning given here. This policy had to be supported by a permanent army recruited on grounds of quality. Even more, despite an occasional setback, the Emperor was able to enlarge considerably the lands he had inherited. After him, no major campaigns were undertaken until the arrival of Trajan, who attacked the Dacians and the Parthians. On the other hand, Marcus Aurelius had to fight defensive campaigns in the East and on the Danube. Septimius Severus resembled Augustus in his actions, carrying out reforms such as allowing soldiers to live with their 'wives' and going on the last great offensive of the Principate, particularly in Mesopotamia. At the end of two centuries of history it is possible to see that the most formidable enemies were to be found on the other side of the Rhine and the Danube. First were the German peoples, then Iran and the Arsacid Parthians.

The situation became critical in the third century when these Parthians succeeded the Sassanian Persians, and the Empire was attacked on the northern and eastern fronts at the same time. Although this crisis was not quite so serious as has been claimed, it led to another transformation of the army. In response to the problems Gallienus, the third Emperor to make important reforms within the army, changed the strategy and the command structure. The Senators were a prime example of a ruling class abandoning and shirking its responsibilities; they refused to serve in the army. It is not certain that this was beneficial to the army, as the myth of the 'professionalization' of the officer class should be examined again more closely. As for strategy, pulling back the troops well behind the *limes* and using them as mobile forces seemed a better plan of action.

By their very frequency, these minor adjustments to policies and strategy represented a major change, particularly in the wake of the setbacks suffered in the third century. Their accumulation finally caused a complete change. The army of the Early Empire displayed three fundamental characteristics, the strategy of the *limes*, with the army stationed on the frontiers, an aristocratic officer class and a quality recruitment policy. The characteristics of the army of the Late Empire were diametrically opposite.[35] From the middle of the third century officers no longer came from the Senate. Diocletian then replaced quality by quantity;[36] in his reign the number of soldiers increased dramatically, though Lactantius was probably exaggerating in claiming that it quadrupled.[37] Constantine then adopted another strategy which appears to have been a modification of the ideas of Gallienus. He withdrew the majority of the fighting troops far behind the frontiers, leaving these to be guarded by troops of inferior quality. There does not appear to have been any violent transition, any revolution. The mid-third-century crisis had imposed transformations on Gallienus which in turn affected the policies of Diocletian and Constantine.

The Roman army of the Early Empire, especially of the first two centuries, was characterized by an aristocratic officer class, a recruitment policy based on quality and the choice of a strategy based on the *limes*. In the Late Empire the battle corps was moved behind the frontiers, the officers came from the ordinary people, quantity replaced quality in recruitment. These characteristics contributed towards the image of the 'Fourth-Century Renaissance'.

NOTES

Notes to *Introduction*
1 Suetonius, *Augustus* XXIII,4.
2 Y. Garlan, *La guerre dans l'Antiquité*, 1972; J. Harmand, *La guerre antique, de Sumer à Rome*, 1973.
3 G.R. Watson, *The Roman Soldier*, 1969; G. Webster, *The Roman Imperial Army*, 1969. Most recently M. Bishop and J.C.N. Coulston, *Roman Military Equipment*, 1993.
4 See Conclusion.
5 See ch. 5, pt. II.
6 P. Petit, *La paix romaine*, 1967.
7 Y. Garlan, p. 3.
8 P. Veyne, *Le pain et le cirque*, 1976.
9 In a work as general as this it is not possible to make systematic use of prosopography or onomastics; see Y. Le Bohec, *La IIIe Légion Auguste*, 1989.
10 V. Giuffre, *La letteratura 'De Re Militari'*, 1974.
11 A. Neumann, *Classical Philology* 41, 1946, 217–25.
12 *Corpus Inscriptionum Latinarum* (henceforth CIL), esp. XVI and supplement; *L'Année épigraphique*; M. Roxan, *Roman Military Diplomas*, 1978 and 1985.
13 H. Dessau, *Inscriptiones Latinae Selectae* no. 2341.
14 P. Le Roux, *L'armée romaine . . . des provinces ibériques*, 1982, p. 28.
15 J.-J. Hatt, *La tombe gallo-romaine*, 1951; M. Clauss, *Principales*, 1973, pp. 114–15 and *Epigraphica* 35, 1973, 55–95; J.-M. Lassère, *Antiquités Africa aines* 7, 1973, 7–151.
16 M. Clauss, *loc. cit.*; D.B. Saddington, *VIe Congrès international d'épigraphie*, 1973, pp. 538–40, and *Aufstieg* II,3, 1975, pp. 176–201; Y. Le Bohec op. cit.
17 R.O. Fink, *TAPA* 84, 1953, 210–15.
18a H. Mattingly and E.A. Sydenham, *Roman Imperial Coinage* I–IV, 1923–1933, and *Coins of the Roman Empire in the British Museum* I, 1923—.
18b R.O. Fink, *Roman Military Records on Papyrus*, 1971.

19 Y. Le Bohec, pp. 81–116.
20 A. Poidebard, *La trace de Rome dans le désert de Syrie*, 1934; J. Baradez, *Fossatum Africae*, 1949.
21 *La vie mystérieuse des chefs-d'oeuvre. La science au service de l'art*, 1980, p. 248 (Roman surveying around Montélimar).
22 See Pt. III, ch. 9.
23 Ch. Ardant du Picq, *Études sur le combat*, 1903, p. 1.
24 Matthew 8, 5–13, Luke 7, 1–10; Josephus, *Jewish War* IV, 8, 1 (442); *Talmud of Jerusalem*, Baba Qama III,3.
25 Pliny the Younger, *Letters* X, 74.
26 Pliny, *Letters* X, 19–20 and 77–78; CIL VIII, no. 18122; Cassius Dio, LXXVI,10; *Historia Augusta*: Septimius Severus XVIII,6.
27 *HA*: Caracalla III, IV, VIII 4 and 8.
28 Pliny X, 19–20; *Talmud*, Yebamoth XVI,5.
29 Pliny X, 21–2 and 27–8.
30 See Pt. III ch. 9.
31 Tacitus, *Annals* IV,41,3 (the official post is called *cursus publicus*).
32 *Theodosian Code* IV,14,3 (*portorium*); there is no evidence that soldiers were involved with other taxes.
33 P. Le Roux, pp. 119–21.
34 See Pt. III chs 8,9.

Notes to chapter 1: *The divisions of the army*
 1 Tacitus, *Annals* IV,4,5 and 5.
 2 M. Durry, *Les cohortes prétoriennes*, 1939; A. Passerini, *Le coorti pretorie*, 1939.
 3 Pseudo-Hyginus, *De Munitione Castrorum*, VI–VIII.
 4 Tacitus, *Annals* IV,5,5; Cassius Dio LVII,19,6.
 5 See *L'Année épigraphique* 1980, no. 24.
 6 Herodian III,13,4; Cassius Dio LXXIV,1; *HA*: Septimius Severus XVII,5; Zosimus I,8,2.
 7 H. Freis, *Die cohortes urbanae, Epigr. Stud.* II, 1967.
 8 Suetonius, *Augustus* XLIX.
 9 *Inscriptions latines d'Afrique*, no.64.
10 P.K. Baillie Reynolds, *The Vigiles of Imperial Rome*, 1926.
11 Suetonius, *Claudius* XXV,6.
12 Tacitus, *Annals* I,24,2; Suetonius, *Augustus* XLIX,1; Herodian IV,7,3 and 13,6; *HA*: Severus Alexander LXI,3 and Maximinus-Balbinus XIII,5-XIV; R. Paribeni, *Mitteilungen d. Kaiserl. d. arch. Instit.* XX, 1905, 321–9.
13 Tacitus, *Histories* I,31,1.
14 M. Speidel, *Die equites singulares Augusti*, 1965.
15 P.K. Baillie Reynolds, *JRS* 13, 1923, 152–89.
16 R. Paribeni, op. cit. 310–320; W.G. Sinningen, *Mem. Amer. Acad. Rome* XXVII, 1962, 211–24.
17 *HA*: Hadrian XI,6 and Macrinus XII,4.
18 Tacitus, *Histories* I,31,3 and 6.
19 See e.g. Tacitus, *Histories* I,31,2,6 and 7.
20 Herodian II,10,2.
21 E. Ritterling in Pauly-Wissowa XII,2,1925 *sub Legio*; H.M.D. Parker, *The Roman Legions*, 1958 (2nd ed.).

22 E. Bickel, *Rhein. Museum* 95, 1952, 97–135; E. Sander, *ibid*, 79–96; L.J.E. Keppie, *Papers Brit. School Rome* 41, 1973, 8–17.
23 Suetonius, *Nero* XIX,4.
24 Dio, LV,24; J.C. Mann, *Hermes* 91, 1963, 483–9.
25 See *Pauly-Wissowa Ala, Cohors, Numerus*; G.L. Cheesman, *The Auxilia of the Roman Imperial Army*, 1914; D.B. Saddington, *The Development of the Roman Auxiliary Forces (49 BC – AD 79)*, 1982.
26 CIL VIII, no. 2637: 'The IIIrd Legio Augusta and its auxiliaries.'
27 Tacitus, *Histories*, II,89,2.
28 Pseudo-Hyginus XVI; Arrian, *Tactical Manual* XVIII,3 (512 men in a 500-strong ala).
29 E. Birley, *Melanges E. Swoboda*, 1966, pp. 54–67.
30 Pseudo-Hyginus XXVIII.
31 Tacitus, *Annals* I,8,3 and 35,3 (*cohortes civium Romanorum* and *voluntariorum civium Romanorum*).
32 CIL X no. 4862.
33 Josephus III,4,2(67):120 cavalry and 600 infantrymen; Pseudo-Hyginus XXV–XXVII:120 cavalry and 380 infantrymen = 6 centuries and three squadrons or 240 cavalry for 760 infantrymen = 10 centuries and 6 squadrons; CIL III, no. 6627:4 decurions.
34 R.W. Davies, *Historia* 20, 1971, 751–763.
35 CIL VIII no. 18042; M. Le Glay, *XIe Congrès du limes*, 1978, pp. 545–58.
36 CIL VIII, no. 21040.
37 See n. 25; F. Vittinghoff, *Historia* 1, 1950, 389–407; J.C. Mann, *Hermes* 82, 1954, 501–6; M. Speidel, *Aufstieg* II,3, 1975, pp. 202–31. See *L'Année épigraphique* 1983 no. 767 for the exceptional *numerus* to denote a legion.
38 M. Speidel, *Guards of the Roman Army*, 1978.
39 *L'Année épigraphique* 1969–1970 no. 583.
40 W. Enslin, *Klio* 31, 1938, 365–70; *Pseudo-Hyginus*, ed. M. Lenoir, pp. 78–80, 127–33.
41 *L'Année épigraphique* 1900 no. 197.
42 E. Birley, *Ancient Society* 9, 1978, 258–73.
43 Herodian III,9,2.
44 Herodian VI,7,8; *HA: Severus Alexander* LVI,5.
45 *HA: Claudius* XI,9.
46 Zosimus I,50,3.
47 O. Fiebiger, *Leipzig. Stud.* 15, 1893, 275–461; V. Chapot, *La flotte de Misène*, 1896; D. Kienast, *Kriegsflotten d. röm. Kaiserzeit*, 1966; see n. 48.
48 M. Reddé, *Mare Nostrum*, 1986.
49 Suetonius, *Augustus* XLIX,1.
50 R. Saxer, *Vexillationen d. röm. Kaiserheeres, Epigr. Stud.* 1, 1967.
51 Tacitus, *Annals* I,38,1 (member of a *vexillatio*) and 41,1 (standard-bearer of cavalry).
52 P. Le Roux, *Zeitsch. f. Papyr. u. Epigr.* 43, 1981, 195–206.
53 CIL VIII no. 10230.
54 Pseudo-Hyginus V.
55 Suetonius, *Vespasian* VI,2; Josephus II,18,8 (494).
56 Tacitus, *Annals* XIII,36,1 and 5.
57 Tacitus, *Annals* XII,38,3 and 55,2.

58 J. Sasel, *Chiron* 4, 1974, 467–77; M. Christol, *Carrières sénatoriales*, 1986, pp. 35–9.

59 Y. Le Bohec, *XIIe Congrès du limes*, 1980, pp. 945–55 and *IIIe Congrès de Sassari*, 1986, pp. 233–41.

60 This interpretation can be supported by an inscription at Rome, where a soldier was *collat(us) in sing(ulares)* 'added to the bodyguard' (*L'Année épigraphique* 1968 no. 31.

61 R. Cagnat, *De municipalibus et provincialibus militiis in Imperio romano*, 1880; A. Stapfers, *Musée Belge* 7, 1903, 198–246.

62 *HA*: Severus Alexander LVIII,4 and Probus XIV,7.

63 D. Fishwick, *JRS* 57, 1967, 142–60.

64 M. Jaczynowska, *Les associations de la jeunesse romaine*, 1978.

65 H. Demoulin, *Musée Belge* 3, 1899, 177–192; F. Jacques, *Antiq. Afric.* 15, 1980, 217–30.

66 C. Nicolet, *MEFR* 79, 1967, 29–76.

67 ILS no. 6087, CIII.

68 *Inscr. Rom. Tripolit.* no. 880.

69 E. Birley (*Mél. Swoboda*, pp. 54ff.) estimates for the IInd century 270 *quingenariae cohortes* and 40 to 50 *milliariae*, 90 *quingenariae alae* and 10 *milliariae*.

70 Tacitus, *Annals* XIV, 58,3–4 and IV,5,6.

Notes to Chapter 2: *The men*

1 A. von Domaszewski, *Die Rangordnung des römischen Heeres*, 1967 (2nd ed. revised B. Dobson), the standard work on the subject.

2 G. Lopuszanski, *MEFR* 55, 1938, 131–83.

3 Onesandros I,13, 21–5 and XXXIII. D.C.A. Shotter, *CQ* 19, 1969, 371–3.

4 *L'Année épigraphique* 1903 no. 368.

5 *L'Année épigraphique* 1956 no. 124.

6 Zosimus I,14,2.

7 Herodian IV,12,2; V,2,5; *HA*: Gallienus XX,3 and Tr. Tyr. XXXIII; B. Campbell, *JRS* 65, 1975, 11–31.

8 *HA*: Elagabalus VI,2.

9 Dio LIII,17.

10 Pseudo-Hyginus X.

11 Herodian I,8,1; G.M. Bersanetti, *Athenaeum* 29, 1951, 151–70.

12 Herodian I,12,3.

13 Zosimus I,11,2.

14 Tacitus, *Agricola* VII,5–6.

15 CIL VIII no. 18042, Aa 11; *Bulletin Comité Tr. Hist.* 1899, p. CXCII no. 6, CCXI no. 6, CCXII no. 22; Vegetius II,9.

16 Josephus III,5,2; Pliny the Younger, *Panegyricus* X,3; Tacitus, *Agricola* VII,5–6; Vegetius II,9; R. Egger, *Sitzungs. Oesterr. Akad. Wissens. Wien* 250,4, 1966.

17 Vegetius II,9.

18 CIL VIII no. 18078 (showing the hierarchy).

19 Josephus III,5,2.

20 Pliny, *Panegyricus* XV,4; Vegetius II,12.

21 Pliny, *Panegyricus* XV,2–3; *Letters* III,20,5; VI,31,4; Suetonius, *Augustus* XXXVIII; Tacitus *Agricola* V,1,2; *L'Année épigr.* 1981 no. 495.

22 Vegetius II,10.
23 Tacitus, *Annals* XII,38,3 and 55,2; XIII,36,1.
24 Tacitus, *Annals* XIII,39,2.
25 Suetonius, *Vespasian* I.
26 Josephus VI,2,5(131).
27 CIL VIII no. 18048, Ba(?); Josephus III,5,2; Vegetius II,12; *Digesta Justitiani* XLIX, 16,12(2).
28 Pliny, *Panegyricus* X,3; XV,2.
29 See Pt I ch. 1 n. 58.
30 Pliny, *Letters* X,87; Tacitus, *Annals* XIII,36,1 and 5.
31 *HA*: Caracalla VII,1 (dubious); T. Nagy, *Acta arch. Hung.* 17, 1965, 298–307; M. Christol. *Chiron* 7, 1977, 393–408.
32 G. Jacopi, *Rend. Accad. Lincei* 6, 1951, 532–56; E. Sander, *Historia* 6, 1957, 347–67.
33 CIL X no. 3348.
34 CIL IX no. 3365.
35 *HA*: Maximinus V,1.
36 Suetonius, *Claudius* XXV,1.
37 H. Devijver, *Anc. Soc.* I, 1970, 69–81.
38 CIL II no. 2637.
39 J. Osier, *Latomus* 36, 1977, 674–87.
40 Pliny, *Letters* X,21 (*praefectus orae Ponticae*).
41 Tacitus, *Annals* I,20,2.
42 Tacitus, *Histories* 46,1.
43 Y. Le Bohec, *La IIIe Légion Auguste* p. 122.
44 P. Le Roux, *Mélanges casa Velazquez* 8, 1972, 89–147; Y. Le Bohec, *ZPE* 36, 1979, 206–7.
45 Tacitus, *Annals* I,32,3.
46 CIL VIII no. 18065.
47 See Pt I ch. 1 n. 22.
47a K. Strobel, *Tyche* 2, 1987, 203–9, challenges this view.
48 B. Dobson and D.J. Breeze, *Epigr. Stud.* 8, 1969, 101–2; P. Le Roux, *Mél. Casa Velazquez* 8, 1972, 89–147; Y. Le Bohec, *La IIIe* . . . pp. 147–84.
49 CIL II no. 4147.
50 S.J. De Laet, *Ant. Class.* 9, 1940, 13–23; B. Dobson *Die Primipilares*, 1978.
51 CIL II no. 3399.
52 CIL VI no. 1627.
53 M. Christol art. cit. n. 31.
54 CIL XI no. 5215.
55 CIL III no. 7326; V no. 8278; VI no. 3558; M. Durry, *Cohortes prétoriennes*, 1968, p. 168.
56 Tacitus, *Histories* III,22,8.
57 Tacitus, *Histories* III,49, 3–4.
58 G. Goetz, *Corpus Gloss. Lat.* II,451,29; 451,15; V,606,13; Vegetius II,7 (see Modestus VI).
59 J.F. Gilliam, *TAPA* 71, 1940, 127–48.
60 Goetz II 453,36, and 458,57; R.W. Davies, *ZPE* 20, 1976, 253–75.
61 See Pt I ch 1, n. 48.
62 See n. 1. For the whole of this chapter see also Vegetius II,7 and Y. Le Bohec,

La IIIe ... p. 185 (the complete list of sources and bibliography will not be given here).

63 See e.g. E. Birley, *Roman Britain and the Roman army*, 1953; B. Dobson, *Anc. Soc.* 3, 1972, 193–207; D.J. Breeze, *Bonner Jahrb.* 174, 1974, 245–92.

64 CIL V no. 940; VI no. 2440; IX no. 5840.

65 Pliny, *Panegyricus* X,3 (Trajan is *dux, legatus, miles*).

66 CIL V no. 896 (but rarely does one admit to being a mere *munifex*).

67 CIL IX no. 1617 and no. 5809. M. Clauss, *Principales*, 1973 (as early as the Ist c); E. Sander (not before the second century; see n. 68).

68 E. Sander, *Historia* 8, 1959, 239–47.

69 Only one *triplicarius* is known: see *L'Année épigr.* 1976 no. 495.

70 Goetz III,208,25 (*epopheles*).

71 CIL XIII no. 5093.

72 CIL XIII no. 6801.

73 Frontinus, *Strategemata* II,3,17; Goetz V,638,5.

74 A. D'Ors, *Emerita* 47, 1979, 257–9 (foals).

75 *L'Année épigr.* 1969–1970, no. 583.

76 Julius Caesar, *De Bello Gallico* VII,25,3; *De Bello Civili* II,2 *and* 9,4; *Vitruvius* X,10–16; *Josephus* III,5,2(80); *Vegetius* II,10 *and* 25; *Ammianus Marcellinus* XIX,7,6 *and* XXIII,4,7. *E.W. Marsden, Greek and Roman Artillery*, 1971.

77 Tacitus, *Annals* II,20,12; XIII,39,5 (the reading *libratores* is better than the otherwise unknown *libritores*).

78 Arrian XXVII.

79 Tacitus, *Histories* III,50,2 and 52,1.

80 Frontinus II,8,1; Arrian XIV,4.

81 Frontinus I,1,9; Josephus III,5,3(86).

82 Frontinus I,1,13; Josephus III,5,3(89,90,91).

83 Tacitus, *Annals* I,28,3.

84 Tacitus, *Annals* I,28,3 and 68,3; Trajan's Column nos 7–8 and 77–8.

85 Arrian XIV,4.

86 Vegetius II,22 (see Modestus XVI); Goetz V,50,18.

87 Goetz III,84,24; Dio LXIII,26.

88 Trajan's Column nos 37,74.

89 P. Roussel, *REG* 43, 1930, 361–371; J. and L. Robert, *Journal Savants* 1976, 206–9.

90 Tacitus, *Histories* III,43,2.

91 Tacitus, *Histories* II,34,1; III,54,4.

92 Pliny, *Panegyricus* XIII,5.

93 Goetz II,96,56; III,353,14; E. Beurlier, *Mélanges Charles Graux*, 1884, pp. 297–303.

94 CIL VIII no. 18224.

95 Aurelius Victor, *De Caesaribus* XXXIII,13.

96 CIL V no. 8275; Goetz II,228,8 (see ILS no. 2542: municipal *salariarius*).

97 Frontinus II,7,12; Pseudo-Hyginus XLVI.

98 Pliny, *Letters* X,41–42 and 61–62 (but are they really soldiers?).

99 Pliny, *Letters* X,17–18 (a civilian *mensor*).

100 Pliny, (see n. 98); CIL VI no. 2725.

101 Goetz V,168,3.

102 E. Sander, *Bonner Jahrb.* 162, 1962, 149; H. von Petrikovits, *Legio VII Gemina*, 1970, pp. 246–7.
103 J. Scarborough, *Roman Medicine*, 1969; R.W. Davies, *Epigr. Stud.* 8, 1969, 83–99 and *Saalb. Jahrb.* 27, 1970, 1–11; R.J. Rowland, *Epigraphica* 41, 1979, 66–72.
104 Trajan's Column no. 29.
105 *HA*: Elagabalus XXIII,2; Goetz II,127,26; IV,536,21. L. Robert, *Hellenica* 1, 1940, 136.
106 Aurelius Victor, *De Caesaribus* XXXIII,13.
107 *Talmud of Babylon, Moed Katan* 13a.
108 Goetz II,314,38; 90,21; etc.
109 Goetz V,566,14.
110 M. Clauss, *Principales*, p. 41.
111 Pliny, *Letters* X,31,2; Suetonius, *Vespasian* XVIII.
112 Tacitus, *Histories* I,28,1.
113 CIL V no. 3375.
114 Tacitus, *Histories* I,46,1; Dio LXXVIII,14 (a soldier becoming *procurator*).
115 Tacitus, *Histories* III,49, 3–4.
116 CIL II no. 2610.
117 Clauss, p. 80.
118 *Theodosian Code* II,27,1(2).
119 R. Marichal, *Comptes Rendus Acad. Inscr.* 1979, 436–52.
120 Tacitus, *Annals* I,34,3.
121 Tacitus, *Histories* II,80,5.
122 Josephus III,5,3(87).
123 Josephus III,5,3(85).
124 Tacitus, *Annals* XI,18,3.
125 Tacitus, *Histories* I,46, 3–6; *Annals* I,17,6.
126 Tacitus, *Histories* II,89,3 (see 2).
127 Suetonius, *Augustus* XXIV,3–5.
128 Frontinus, *Strategemata* Iv,1,21.
129 Polyaenus VIII,24,2.
130 Josephus III,5,7(103); VI,7,1(362); Tacitus, *Annals* XI,18,3; Suetonius, *Augustus* XXIV,5; Polyaenus VIII,24,1.
131 Polyaenus VIII,24,5 (probably as decorations).
132 Suetonius, *Augustus* XXV,3–4.
133 Pliny the Elder, *Naturalis Historia* XVI, 6–14; XXII, 4–7; Aulus Gellius V,6; V.A. Maxfield, *The Military Decorations of the Roman Army*, 1981.
134 CIL V no. 7495; see Josephus VII,1,3(14).
135 T. Nagy, *Acta Ant. Ac. Sc. Hung.* 16, 1968, 289–95.
136 *HA*: Severus Alexander XL,5; Aurelianus XIII,3; Probus V,1; Modestus VI.
137 Y. Le Bohec, *La IIIe . . .* , p. 542.
138 Dio LV,23.
139 Tacitus, *Annals* I,78,2.
140 Tacitus, *Annals* I,17,3.
141 Y. Le Bohec, *La IIIe.*
142 G. Alföldy, *Römische Heeresgeschichte*, 1987, pp. 51–65.

Notes to Chapter 3: *Recruitment*

1 There is an excellent summary in J. Gagé, *Les classes sociales dans l'Empire romain*, 1971, 2nd ed., pp. 82–122.
2 K. Kraft, *Zur Rekrutierung der Alen und Kohorten an Rhein und Donau*, 1951; see n. 5.
3 G. Forni, *Il reclutamento delle legioni*, 1953; see next note.
4 G. Forni, *Aufstieg* II,1,1974, pp. 339–91 and *Esercito e marina di Roma antica*, *Coll. Mavors*, 5, 1992, pp 51–65; Y. Le Bohec, *La III* ... , pp. 491–530.
5 P. Le Roux, *L'armée romaine ... des provinces ibériques*, 1982, pp. 171ff, 337ff; N. Benseddik, *Les troupes auxiliaires ... en Maurétanie Césarienne*, 1982, pp. 92–3; Y. Le Bohec, *Epigraphica* 44, 1982, 265.
6 J.-M. Lassère, *Ubique populus*, 1977, p. 94 and n. 129: the question of the origins of the African Septimii has not been settled.
7 M. Benabou, *La résistance africaine à la romanisation*, 1976, pp. 583–4.
8 Tacitus, *Histories* II,16,2 and 5; 69,4; 82,1; III,58, 3–4; *Annals* XIII,7,1; 35,4; XVI,3,5; see n. 9.
9 *Acta Maximiliani* I; P. Monceaux, *La vraie légende dorée*, 1928, p. 251.
10 Tacitus, *Annals* XIV,18,1.
11 *L'Année épigr.* 1951 no. 88.
12 G. Forni, *Il reclutamento ...* p. 30.
13 Tacitus, *Histories* II,69,4.
14 Tacitus, *Histories* II,82,1.
15 The *Acta Maximiliani* (n. 9) clearly show how the *dilectus* operated; see also Pliny, *Letters* X, 29–30; R.W. Davies, *Bonner Jahrb.* 169, 1969, 208–32.
16 Vegetius I,5.
17 Suetonius, *Augustus* XXV,2.
18 Pliny, *Letters* X,30 (see 29).
19 C.G. Starr, *Classical Philology* 37, 1942, 314–17.
20 *Digest* XLIX,16,4(7); J. Vendrand-Voyer, *Normes civiques et métier militaire à Rome*, 1983, p. 82.
21 See Pt II, ch. 4.
22 Y. Le Bohec, *La IIIe* ....
23 Pliny, *Letters* X,87.
24 Tacitus, *Histories* III,58, 3–4.
25 B. Dobson, *Die Primipilares*, 1978.
26 Y. Le Bohec, *La IIIe* ....
27 P. Le Roux, *Mél. Casa Velazquez* 8, 1972, 89–147.
28 Josephus IV,1,5(38).
29 J.-M. Lassère, *Ubique populus*, pp. 32–201.
30 Dio LII,25.
31 Th. Mommsen, *Ephemeris Epigraphica* 5, 1884, 159–249.
32 M. Rostovtzeff, *The Social and Economic History of the Roman Empire*, 1957, 2nd ed., 2 vols.
33 W. Ensslin, *Cambridge Ancient History*, 12, 1939, 72ff; L. Foucher, *Hadrumetum*, 1964, pp. 313–15 are examples.
34 P. Le Roux, *L'armée romaine ...* ; Y. Le Bohec, *La IIIe* ....
35 CIL III no. 6580.
36 Pliny, *NH* VII,XLV (149).

37 CIL III no. 6627; H.A. Sanders, *AJP* 62, 1941, 84–7.
38 P. Salway, *The Frontier People of Roman Britain*, 1965, p. 32.
39 A. Mócsy, *Acta Anc. Ac. Sc. Hung.* 13, 1965, 425–31, and 20, 1972, 133–68 (see *L'Année épigr.* 1974 no. 493.
40 F. Vittinghoff, *Chiron* I, 1971, 299–308.
41 Y. Le Bohec, *La IIIe* . . . .
42 Pliny, *Paneg.* XXVIII,3 and 5.
43 P. Veyne, *MEFR* 1957, 81–135, and 1958, 177–241.
44 *HA*: Marcus Antoninus XXI, 8–9 (see 6–7 for the auxiliaries).
45 Herodian II,9,11 (Pannonia during the civil war following the death of Commodus).
46 Cyprian, *Lib. ad Dem* III and XVII.
47 Herodian VI,3,1.
48 Herodian VII,12,1.
49 Tacitus, *Annals* XIII,7,1; 35,4.
50 Virgil, *Aeneid* VI,851; W. Seston, *Scripta Varia*, 1980, pp. 53–63.
51 Tacitus, *Annals* XVI,13,5 (65 for Illyria); Y. Le Bohec, *La IIIe* . . . .
52 Tacitus, *Histories* II,6,6; M. Speidel, *Aufstieg* II,7,2, 1980, pp. 730–46 (Asia Minor generally).
53 Tacitus, *Annals* XIV,18,1; *L'Année épigr.* 1951 no. 88.
54 A. Grenier, *Bull. Soc. Nat. Antiquaires Fr.* 1956, 35–42.
55 H. Solin, *Aufstieg* II,29,2, 1982, pp. 587–1249.
56 Y. Le Bohec, *La IIIe* . . . .
57 P. Le Roux, *L'armée romaine* . . . .
58 G. Forni and D. Manini, *Mél. L.de Regibus*, 1969, pp. 177–210.
59 J. Vendrand-Voyer, *Normes civiques* . . . pp. 69ff; p. 77.
60 Paulus, *Sententiae* XXXI.
61 Y. Le Bohec, *La IIIe* . . . .
62 e.g. Tacitus, *Annals* XLVI,1; A. Michel, *Mél. M.Durry* (REL XLVII B), 1969, 237–51.
63 Y. Le Bohec, *La IIIe* . . . .
64 *Ibid.*
65 *Ibid.*
66 *Ibid.*
67 *Ibid.*; see also P. Le Roux, *L'armée romaine* . . . .
68 P. Salway, *Frontier People*, p. 18.
69 I. Kajanto, *The Latin Cognomina*, 1965.
70 Y. Le Bohec, *La IIIe* . . . .
71 R. Syme, *Historia* 27, 1978, 75–81.
72 J.-J. Hatt, *Rev. arch. Est* 15, 1964, 327–9.
73 Y. Le Bohec, *La IIIe* . . . .
74 H. Solin, *Beiträge zur Kenntnis der griechischen Person-namen in Rom*, 1971.
75 P. Leveau, *Bull. arch. Alger.* 5, 1971–4, 22 and *Revue des études anciennes* LXXVI, 1974, 296.
76 P. Huttunen, *The Social Strata in the Imperial City of Rome*, 1974.
77 Y. Le Bohec, *La IIIe* . . . .
78 J. Vendrand-Voyer, *Normes civiques* pp. 77 and 99.
79 K. Kraft, *Zur Rekrutierung* . . . ; H.T. Rowell, *JRS* 43, 1953, 175–9.
80 G.L. Cheesman, *The Auxilia of the Roman Army*, 1914.

81 P. Holder, *The Auxilia from Augustus to Trajan*, 1980 (partial updating of our knowledge).
82 For an understanding of this question see CIL XVI and Supplement; *L'Année epigr.*; M. Roxan, *Roman Military Diplomas*, 1978 and 1985.
83 D.B. Saddington, *XIIe Congrès du limes*, 1980, p. 1072:3 *alae* and 12 cohorts in the Early Empire.
84 P. Le Roux, *L'armée romaine* . . . to which should be added the *Lemavi* and the *Lungones*.
85 L. Van de Weerd, *Ant. Class.* 5, 1936, 341–72:1 *ala* of Nervii, 2 of Tungri, 3 cohorts of Belgae, 1 of Menapii, 1 of Morini, 11 of Nervii and 2 of Tungri (3/18); see n. 86.
86 G. Drioux, *Rev. Ét. Anc.* 48, 1946, 80–90:6 cohorts in Britain.
87 J. Smeesters, *Xe Congrès du limes*, 1977, pp. 175–86:2 *alae*, 4 cohorts.
88 E. Ritterling, *Klio* 21, 1926–7, 82–91.
89 C.C. Petolescu, *Revista de Istorie* 33, 1980, 1043–1061: some 12 units, mainly cohorts.
90 M.G. Jarrett, *Israel Explor. Journal* 19, 1969, 215–24:9 *alae* and 28 cohorts.
91 A. Merlin, *Rev. Arch.* 17, 1941, 37–9:7 *alae* of Phrygians.
92 G. Cantacuzène, *Musée Belge* 31, 1927, 157–172; I.I. Russu, *Acta Musei Napoc.* 6, 1969, 167–86.
93 D.L. Kennedy, *XIe Congrès du limes*, 1977, pp. 521–31:8 units, mainly *alae*.
94 J. Carcopino, *Rev. Ét. Anc.* 1922, 215 and 218–19: men with Egyptian status could only serve in the auxilia or the fleet.
95 Y. Le Bohec, *La IIIe* . . . , pp. 512–15: approx. 13,000 men, i.e. 5 *alae* and 21 cohorts.
96 The Afri, a small tribe from the north of modern Tunisia, should not be confused with the Africans as a general term.
97 K. Kraft, *Zur Rekrutierung* . . . , pp. 64–8.
98 N. Benseddik, *Les troupes auxiliaires* . . . ; Y. Le Bohec, *Epigraphica* 44, 1982, 265.
99 Josephus II,13,7 (268).
100 G. Cantacuzène, art. cit.
101 See n. 98.
102 K. Kraft, pp. 80–1.
103 Tacitus, *Annals* III,42,1.
104 *Ibid*. III,33,5.
105 Tacitus, *Histories* II,22,2.
106 Tacitus, *Agricola* XXVIII and XXXII,3.
107 *HA*: Marcus Antoninus XXI, 6–7; XXIII,5.
108 Tacitus, *Annals* IV,5,5; J. Sasel, *Historia* 21, 1972, 474–80.
109 M. Durry, *Les cohortes* . . . , pp. 239–57.
110 A. Passerini, *Le coorti* . . . , pp. 141–89.
111 Tacitus, *Annals* IV,5,5; A. Pagnoni, *Epigraphica* 4, 1942, 23–40.
112 F.C. Mench, *The Cohortes Urbanae*, 1968, pp. 495–7 and 501–5.
113 H. Freis, *Die cohortes urbanae, Epigr. Stud.* II, 1967, 50–62.
114 N. Duval, S. Lancel and Y. Le Bohec, *Bull. Com. Tr. Hist.* 1984, 33–89.
115 P.K. Baillie Reynolds, *The Vigiles* . . . , p. 64.

116 M. Speidel, *Die equites singulares Augusti*, 1962, p. 18; also *Riding for Caesar*, 1994.
117 F. Grosso, *Latomus* 25, 1966, 900–9.
118 L. Wickert, *Die Flotte d. röm. Kaiserzeit*, *Wurzb. Jahrb. f. Alt.* IV, 1949–50, 105–13; M. Reddé, *Mare nostrum*, 1986.
119 Th. Mommsen and J. Marquardt, *Manuel des antiquités romaines*, transl. J. Brissaud, XI, 1891, p. 242.
120 S. Panciera, *Rend. Accad. Lincei* 29, 1964, 316–27.
121 C.G. Starr, *The Roman Imperial navy*, 1941, pp. 66ff.
122 W. Seston, *Rev. Philol.* 7, 1933, 383–84.
123 V. Chapot, *La flotte de Misène*, 1896, pp. 180–1.
124 Y. Le Bohec, *La Sardaigne et l'armée romaine*, 1991.

Notes to Chapter 4: *Training*
   1 E.g. Ch. Ardant du Picq, *Études sur le combat*, 1903, pp. 16 and 79.
   2 A. Neumann, *Class. Philol.* 31, 1936, 1ff.; 41, 1946, 217–25; 43, 1948, 157–73, and *Klio* 26, 1933, 360ff.
   3 R. Davies, *Latomus* 27, 1968, 75–95; *CJ* 125, 1968, 73–100; *Aufstieg* II,1, 1974, pp. 299–338.
   4 Y. Le Bohec, *Cahiers Groupe Rech. Armée rom.* 1, 1977, 71–85 and pls XLV–XLVII.
   5 TLL V,2, 1938, col. 1379–83 and 1384–7.
   6 Varro, *De lingua latina* V,87: *exercitus quod exercitando fit melior*.
   7 Cicero, *Tusculan Disputations* II,16,37.
   8 See n. 5 particularly and also other notes in this chapter.
   9 Onesandros IX–X.
  10 Josephus II,20,7 (577); III,5,1 (72–75); 10,2 (476).
  11 Dio LXIX,9 (also LVII,24); *HA*: Hadrianus X,2; XXVI,2.
  12 M. Le Glay, *XIe Congrès du limes*, 1978, pp. 545–58.
  13 Arrian, *Black Sea Journey*.
  14 CIL III no. 3676.
  15 Fronto, *Hist. Princ.* VIII–IX (introduction to the Parthian War of Lucius Verus).
  16 Vegetius I and II *passim*.
  17 Frontinus, *Strategemata* III,1,2 (Gaius Duilius).
  18 Herodian II,10,8.
  19 Josephus III,5,7 (102); see also III,10,2 (476). Herodian (n. 18) is of the same opinion.
  20 Cicero, *Tusc.* II,16,38.
  21 Frontinus, *Strateg.* III,1,1.
  22 Josephus II,20,7 (577 and 580–581); III,5,1 and 6–7; V,1,71; Tacitus, *Histories* II,77,7; 87,2; 93,1; III,2,5; V,21,5; *Annals* II, 18–19; Suetonius, *Galba* VI.
  23 Frontinus IV,1; Pliny, *Letters* X, 29–30; Goetz II,51,2.
  24 Tacitus, *Histories* II,76,12; 93,1; III,42,1: *disciplina militiaque nostra*.
  25 Frontinus IV, 1–2 and 5–6.
  26 Tacitus, *Histories* IV,71, 6–9.
  27 Arrian *Tactics* V.
  28 Dio LXXX,4; LXXXVIII,3.
  29 Plutarch, *Pompey* XLI,4–5.

30 Suetonius, *Tiberius* XIII,1.
31 Tacitus, *Histories* XXXVI,1.
32 Pliny, *Paneg.* XIII,1.
33 *HA*: Severus Alexander III,1.
34 Herodian VII,1,6.
35 Suetonius, *Augustus* LXXXIII,1.
36 Dio LVII,24.
37 M. Rambaud, *Mel. R. Schilling*, 1983, pp. 515–24 (on Caesar).
38 Tacitus, *Annals* II,55,6; III,33,3; CIL VIII no. 2535 = 18042 (with M. Le Glay n. 12); Vegetius I and II *passim*.
39 Josephus V,3,4 (123–6).
40 Dio LXIX,9; J. Vendrand-Voyer, *Normes civiques . . .* , p. 313ff.
41 Justinian, *Institutiones* IV,3,4.
42 Josephus III,5,1 (73); *HA*: Maximini Duo X,4.
43 Arrian, *Journey* III,1; Goetz II,64,30 etc.
44 Frontinus IV,1,1; Tacitus *Annals* II,55,6; III,33,3; XI,18,2; Aulus Gellius VI,3,52; Vegetius I,9; II,33.
45 Vegetius I,9; II,33.
46 *ibid*; Porphyrio on Horace *Odes*, I,8,8, II,7,25 and 12,2.
47 Josephus III,5,1 (73); Vegetius I,26; II,33.
48 Juvenal VI,247; Vegetius I,11; II,23.
49 Pliny, *Paneg.* XIII,1,2; Arrian, *Journey* III,1; Vegetius I,14.
50 H. Russell Robinson, *The Armour of Imperial Rome*, 1975, p. 107.
51 Plutarch, *Pompey* XLI, 4–5; Suetonius, *Augustus* LXXXIII,1 and *Tiberius* XIII,1; Vegetius I,18.
52 CIL VIII no. 2728 = 18122; Y. Le Bohec, *La IIIe . . .* p.378.
53 Tacitus, *Annals* XI,18,2; XVI,3,2 (see 1,1); Suetonius, *Augustus* XVIII,2; *HA*: Probus IX, 3–4.
54 J. Lassus, *Timgad* 1969.
55 Frontinus IV,2,1.
56 CIL VIII no. 2532 = 18042 Bb.
57 Pseudo-Hyginus XLIX: *causa disciplinae*.
58 J. Fitz, *Oikumene* 1, 1976, 215–24 and *Acta Arch. Slov.* XXVIII, 1977, 393–7; Y. Le Bohec, *Epigraphica* 43, 1981, 127–60.
59 *L'Année épigr.* 1973 no. 359.
60 *L'Année épigr.* 1975 no. 729.
61 Onesandros X,1–6; Josephus III,5,1 (74–75); Pliny, *Paneg.* XIII; Tacitus, *Histories* II,55,6; Vegetius I,11–3 and III; *HA*: Maximini duo VI,2.
62 Pliny, *Paneg.* XIII,5.
63 Tacitus, *Annals* II,55,6; III,33,3.
64 Vegetius III,2.
65 There is no proof that CIL III no. 6025 (ILS no. 2615) mentions a training basilica, although it does mention a basilica built in 140 at Syene (Assouan) in Egypt by the first cohort of Cilicians.
66 *JRS* 50, 1960, 213.
67 R.G. Collingwood and R.P. Wright, *The Roman Inscriptions of Britain*, I, 1965, no. 978 (ILS no. 2619).
68 Collingwood and Wright no. 1091 (ILS no. 2620; CIL VII no. 445).
69 *L'Année épigr.* 1971 no. 364.

70 TLL III, 1912, col. 212ff.
71 Pliny, *Paneg.* XIII,1: *meditatio campestris*; *HA*: Maximini duo III,1; Justinian IV,3,4. For the inscriptions see below.
72 CIL VIII no. 2532 = 18042 (see n. 12).
73 S. Gsell, *Inscr. Lat. Algérie* 1, 1922, no. 3596; Y. Le Bohec, *La IIIe . . .* , p. 362.
74 *L'Année épigr.* 1933 no, 214; *Cahiers Groupe Rech. Armée rom.* 1, 1977, 78.
75 *L'Année épigr.* 1931 no. 113.
76 *L'Année épigr.* 1972 no. 636.
77 R. Davies, *Archaeological Journal* 125, 1968, 73–100.
78 H. Mattingley and E.A. Sydenham, *The Roman Imperial Coinage* II, 1926, p. 331ff. and p. 436 no. 739.
79 Speech of Hadrian in Africa (n. 12 and 72); Herodian II,10,1; VI,9,3; VII,8,3.
80 *HA*: Probus X,4.
81 Suetonius, *Augustus* XXIV,2; XXV,1.
82 Tacitus, *Annals* I,4,3 and 12,5.
83 Aurelius Victor, *De Caes.* IV,2.
84 Tacitus, *Annals* XI,19.
85 Tacitus, *Histories* I,5,3.
86 *ibid*; Suetonius, *Galba* VI,3; Dio LXIV,3.
87 Tacitus, *Histories* III,56,3: Vitellius is *ignarus militiae*.
88 Tacitus, *Histories* V,21,5.
89 Suetonius, *Vespasian* VIII, 3–5.
90 Pliny, *Paneg.* VI,2.
91 Pliny, *Paneg.* IX,3; XIII; XVIII. Fronto *Princ. Hist.* VIII–IX is of the same opinion.
92 Fronto VIII–IX.
93 *HA*: Pertinax III,10.
94 *HA*: Pescennius Niger VII,7 and X.
95 Aurelius victor, *De Caes.* XX,21; *HA*: Pescennius Niger III,9–12.
96 Herodian II,10,8.
97 Herodian III,8,5.
98 Herodian IV,14,7.
99 Aurelius Victor XXIV,3; *HA*: Severus Alexander LII–LIV; LXIV,3.
100 *HA*: Maximini duo VIII,7.
101 *HA*: Gallieni duo XVIII,1.
102 *HA*: Claudius XI,6ff.
103 *HA*: Aurelianus VI,2; VII,3ff; VIII.
104 Aurelius Victor XXXVII,2.
105 I.A. Richmond, *Bull. John Rylands Library* 45, 1962, 185–97.
106 e.g. ILS no. 3810.
107 ILS no. 2604.
108 Collingwood and Wright I, 1965, no. 1334, translate as 'the three Mother Goddesses of the Parade-Ground'.
109 CIL II no. 4083.
110 CIL VI no. 533.
111 Dio LXIX,3; LXXVII,13.

Notes to Chapter 5: *Tactics*

1 Ch. Ardant du Picq, *Études sur le combat* p. 5. A myth about peace did exist at Rome (cf. the Ara Pacis), but only as a consequence of Victory.

2 On this point see, e.g., P. Petit, *Histoire générale de l'Empire romain*, 1974, p. 158.

3 Arrian *Tactics* cites Pling the Younger, Clearchus, Pausanias, Polybius, etc.

4 P. Couissin, *Les armes romaines*, 1926; for a well-illustrated book see H. Russell Robinson *The Armour of Imperial Rome*, 1975; P. Salama, *Bull. Soc. Ant. Fr.* 1984, 130–142 (parade weapons); M. Bishop and J.C.N. Coulston *Roman Military Equipment*, 1993.

5 G. Waurick, *XIIe Congrès du limes* 1980, pp. 1091–8.

6 Russell Robinson p. 9.

7 Josephus III,5,5 (94–97).

8 Herodian III,4,9.

9 Tacitus, *Annals* XII,35,5; Aurelian column pl.III, XVI, XXXI–XXXII (ed. C. Caprino *et al.*, 1955).

10 Aurelian Column pl.III.

11 *ibid.*. Many articulated breastplates figure on Trajan's Column.

12 *Ibid.* XXXI–XXXII.

13 *Ibid.* XVI.

14 *Ibid.* XVI; XXXI–XXXII.

15 Herodian IV,10,3; 14,3.

16 Tacitus, *Annals* XII,35,5.

17 Russell Robinson pp. 86–7.

18 Arrian XXXIII.

19 Trajan's Column XV.

20 Arrian IV.

21 Josephus III,7,18 (211).

22 H. Stein, *Archers d'autrefois, archers d'aujourd'hui*, 1925; H. Van de Weerd and P. Lambrechts, *Diss. Pann.* 10, 1938, 229–42: 6 *alae*, 28 cohorts and 10 *numeri*.

23 Aurelian Column XXXIX.

24 Herodian III,9,2 (Septimius Severus against the Parthians).

25 P. Medinger, *Revue Archéol.* 1933, 227–34.

26 T. Sulimirski, *Rev. Intern. d'Hist. Milit.* 1952 447–61.

27 Arrian IV; J.W. Eadie, *JRS* 57, 1967, 167.

28 *Talmud of Jerusalem, Taanith* XII,8; the same *Talmud, Berakoth* IX,1, speaks of *essedarii*, soldiers in chariots in the Roman army, but this is probably an anachronism.

29 R. Heuberger, *Klio* 31, 1938, 60–80.

30 Trajan's Column XVII; XLIX.

31 *ibid.* XLIII–XLIV.

32 Herodian I,15,5.

33 CIL XI no. 5632.

34 M. Clauss, *Principales*, pp. 78, 97.

35 F. Magi, *I rilievi flavi del Palazzo della Cancellaria*, 1945 (these reliefs are probably slightly more recent than Magi thought).

36 M. Durry, *Les cohortes . . .* pp. 195–236.

37 M. Durry, *Revue Archéologique* 1928, 303–8.

38 Russell Robinson, p. 136ff, 147ff.
39 E. Sander, *Historia* 12, 1963, 144–66; R. MacMullen, *Soldier and Civilian*, 1967, pp. 179–180; M. Speidel, *Bonner Jahrb.* 176, 1976, 123–63.
40 Gaius, *Institutiones* II,101; Goetz V,576,43 (and 137,25); Y. Le Bohec, *La IIIè* . . . p. 163.
41 G. Ville, *Africa* 2, 1967–8, 139–82 (more analysis is needed on this).
42 M. Reddé, *Mare nostrum*.
43 ILS no. 2833.
44 S. Panciera, *Epigraphica* 18, 1956, 130–56; the *liburna* was a huge boat according to the *Talmud of Babylon, Baba Mezia*, 80 b.
45 See following notes, not forgetting the Columns of Trajan and Marcus Aurelius.
46 Julius Caesar, *De Bello Gallico* II, 19, 2–3.
47 Onesandros VII; see Aurelian Column pl.XIV.
48 Josephus V,2,1 (47–49).
49 Tacitus, *Annals* I,51, 5–6.
50 Onesandros VI.
51 Onesandros X,7.
52 Arrian XI, XIII, XVI (Alans *passim*).
53 G. Ch. Picard, *Castellum Dimmidi*, 1947, p. 45ff.
54 Pseudo-Hyginus XXIV.
55 P. Davin, *Bull. Com. Trav. Hist.* 1928–1929, 665–682; Y. Le Bohec, *La IIIe* . . . ; see also Trajan's Column.
56 Aurelian Column XIII, XXX, LXXXI.
57 Trajan's Column, no. 4–5, and 34.
58 Aurelian Column III, LXXVIII, LXXXIV, CVIII; Dio LXVIII,13.
59 Trajan's Column no. 74.
60 Apollodorus of Damascus IX.
61 Frontinus I,5,3.
62 Polybius VI, 27–42 (Republican era); Onesandros VIII–IX; Joesphus III,5,1 (76–78); Pseudo-Hyginus.
63 Trajan's Column nos 1–3, 9–12, 29, 36, 41, 45, 48, 53, 69, 78–79, 90, 98; Aurelian Column LXXXII, XCIV.
64 Frontinus IV,1,14.
65 J. Le Gall, *MEFR* 87, 1975, 287–320.
66 Livy XXXI,34,8.
67 Pseudo-Hyginus LVI.
68 Pseudo-Hyginus LVII.
69 Pseudo-Hyginus XXVI–XXVII, LVII; Vegetius III,8.
70 Josephus III,5,1 (77).
71 Josephus III,5,1 (79,84); Pseudo-Hyginus XLVIII.
72 Trajan's Column nos 46, 55 etc.; Pseudo-Hyginus L.
73 Josephus III,5,1 (80); Pseudo-Hyginus LVIII.
74 Josephus III,5,1 (81).
75 Pseudo-Hyginus XLIX.
76 Pseudo-Hyginus LV; M. Lenoir, *MEFR* 89, 1977, 699–722.
77 Pseudo-Hyginus LI (M. Lenoir translates as 'stags').
78 Pseudo-Hyginus XLVIII.
79 Polybius VI, 27–42.

80 Josephus III,5,1 (76–78); 9.7 (477); 10,1 (462).
81 Pseudo-Hyginus XXI.
82 Pseudo-Hyginus XVIII.
83 Pseudo-Hyginus XII.
84 Josephus III,5,1 (79).
85 Josephus III,5,1 (82); 9.2 (447); 10,1 (462).
86 Pseudo-Hyginus XI.
87 Josephus III,5,1 (83); Pseudo-Hyginus XI.
88 Josephus *passim*; Pseudo-Hyginus IV, XXXV.
89 Pseudo-Hyginus IV, XXXV.
90 Josephus III,5,1 (83).
91 M. Reddé, *Mare nostrum*.
92 Trajan's Column nos 3, 23–25, 34, 59.
93 C.G. Starr, *The Roman Imperial Navy* pp. 191–2.
94 CIL VIII no. 1322 = 14854; B. Dobson, *Die Primipilares*, p. 301, no. 205.
95 M. Reddé, op. cit.; E.W. Marsden, *Greek and Roman Artillery*, 1969, p. 164ff.
96 Onesandros XLII; Vitruvius X,13ff.; Apollodorus of Damascus.
97 E.g. Josephus and Tacitus (see below for refs).
98 Trajan's Column nos 86–7.
99 Trajan's Column nos 46, 87–88, 101–2.
100 R. Rebuffat, *Latomus* 43, 1984, 3–26.
101 Tacitus, *Histories* II,22; Trajan's Column nos 46, 87–88, 101–2.
102 Josephus III,7,28 (271–5) gives a detailed description of the effects of boiling oil; Apollodorus of Damascus VIII,2 of water.
103 Trajan's Column nos 46, 101–2.
104 Josephus III,7,13 (186); V,10,3; Frontinus III,4 and III,7.
105 Josephus V,13,4 (550–6).
106 Tacitus, *Histories* III,84,2.
107 Josephus III,7,4 (146).
108 J. Le Gall, *Alésia*, 1963, p. 85 (based on excavations done in the time of Napoleon III); J. Harmand, *Une campagne césarienne: Alésia*, 1967.
109 Josephus V,2,3 (72); 3,5 (133–4); 7,2 (303); 12,1 (499).
110 Josephus VII,8.
111 A. Schulten, *Zeitschrift d. deutsch Palästina Vereins* 56, 1933, 1–185; C. Hawkes, *Antiquity* 3, 1929, 195–213; I.A. Richmond, *JRS* 52, 1962, 142–55.
112 Tacitus, *Histories* II, 19ff.
113 Tacitus, *Histories* III,26,2.
114 Tacitus, *Histories* III,84,2.
115 Josephus III,7, 8–9.
116 Josephus V,12,1 (499).
117 Josephus VII,8,2 (276–7).
118 Trajan's Column no. 90 (before Sarmizegethusa).
119 Julius Caesar, *De Bello Gallico* VII,84,1 and *De Bello Civili* II,10; Apollodorus of Damascus I.
120 Josephus V,3,2(107); 9,2(358); 11,4(467); VI,2,7(149); 8,1(374).
121 Josephus VII,8,5 (304).
122 Josephus VII,9,2 (402).

123 Apollodorus of Damascus III,5; IV, 1–2.
124 Vitruvius X,16; Frontinus III,8,1; Josephus VI,4,1 (222); Apollodorus of Damascus II.
125 *Excavations at Dura-Europos: Preliminary Reports* and *Final Reports*, 1, 1929 etc.
126 Vitruvius X,15; Josephus III,7,30 (284); V,7,1 (291); VII,8,5 (309); Apollodorus of Damascus VI–VII.
127 Collingwood and Wright, I, no. 722 (unless we should add *aquam* as in CIL IX no. 3018); R. Saxer, *Die Vexillationen, Epigr. Stud.* 1, 1967, p. 73, no. 188. See n. 128.
128 Livy IV,9,14. Numerous references, especially to the Caesarean corpus, in TLL II, 1900, col. 2160.
129 Livy XXXI,26,8; see also XXII,52,1 (Hannibal 216 BCE).
130 Frontinus III,17,5.
131 Trajan's Column no. 72.
132 Vitruvius X,13ff; Apollodorus of Damascus I.
133 Frontinus IV,7,2.
134 Josephus III,7,5 (151).
135 E.W. Marsden, *Greek and Roman Artillery*.
136 Tacitus, *Histories* III,23,4; 84,2 (see 33,4).
137 Josephus III,7,5 (151); 7,9 (167–168); *Talmud of Jerusalem, Horaioth* III,2.
138 Tacitus, *Histories* III,84,2.
139 G. Ch. Picard, *Dimmidi*, p. 95: balls of 300/400 grams in the fourth century.
140 Julius Caesar, *De Bello Civili* II,2 and 9,4.
141 Tacitus, *Histories* II,22,3 (siege of Piacenza).
142 Vitruvius X,16; Josephus V,11,5 (473); VI,1,3 (26).
143 Vitruvius X,13; Josephus III,7,19 (214–17): Jotapata; VII,8,5 (310): Masada; Apollodorus of Damascus V.
144 Josephus III,7,24 (254–6).
145 Tacitus, *Histories* III,31,1 and 84,2; Arrian XI; Trajan's Column no. 50; Aurelian Column LIV.
146 Josephus III,7,21 (252); Apollodorus VIII,2; Trajan's Column no. 86.
147 Josephus III,7,34 (329–31) and 36.
148 Tacitus, *Histories* III,33.
149 Julius Caesar, *De Bello Gallico* III,24,1 and IV,14,1; Onesandros XV–XXI; Josephus III,10, 3–5 (fundamental); Tacitus, *Agricola* XXXV and *Annals* XIII, 38,6; Arrian, *Alans*, XI–XXX; Dio LXII,8,3; Vegetius II,20.
150 Trajan's Column *passim* (e.g. nos 17–18); monument of Adamklissi (F.B. Florescu, *Monumentul de la Adam-Klissi*, 1959; M. Speidel, *Revue Archéol.* 1971, 75–8).
151 J. Kromayer and G. Veith, *Heerwesen und Kriegsführung* in I. von Muller, *Handbuch* IV,3,2, 1928, p. 249ff; J. Thouvenot, *Mél. J. Carcopino*, 1966, pp. 905–16.
152 Frontinus I,5, 1–8.
153 Frontinus II,1,15.
154 Frontinus II,1,17.
155 Josephus III,5,6 (98–100).
156 Frontinus II,3, 17–18.
157 Frontinus II,3.

158 Onesandros XV–XXI; Dio LI,10.
159 Tacitus, *Agricola* XXXV, 2–3 and XXXVII,1 (formation recommended by Onesandros: see previous note).
160 Arrian, *Marching and Battle Orders against the Alans.*
161 Tacitus, *Annals* XIII,40, 3–4.
162 Phalanx: Tacitus, *Histories* IV,78,4; V,18,8; Dio LXII,8; Arrian (see n. 160). Cohorts and maniples: Tacitus, *Histories* IV,78,2; J. Harmand, *L'armée*, pp. 236–7 (Republic); H.M.D. Parker, *Legions*, 1928, p. 31; Kromayer and Veith, *Handbuch* IV,3,2, pp. 550–2; H. Delbruck, *The Art of War* I, 1975, pp. 415–6; E. Wheeler, *Chiron* 9, 1979, 303–18; M. Speidel, *Epigr. Stud.* 13, 1983, 50, unlike Parker, believes in tactical role of cohorts and centuries.
163 Onesandros I,13; Tacitus, *Agricola*, XXXIII–XXXIV; Aurelian Column IV,LV,LXXXIII,XCVI,C.
164 Tacitus, *Histories* III,23,4.
165 Josephus VI,1,7 (75); Arrian, *Alans* XXV.
166 Josephus III,7,25 (259); Arrian *passim.*
167 Arrian, *Alans* XXVI–XXX.
168 Frontinus, II,3.
169 Tacitus, *Agricola* XXXVI,1; *Histories* II,22,1ff.
170 See n. 169.
171 Arrian, *Tactics* XII; *Alans* XV,XXV; Ch. Ardant du Picq, *Études*, pp. 19–20, 72.
172 *Talmud of Babylon, Nazir*, 66 b.
173 Frontinus II,3,15; Trajan's Column nos 50–1.
174 Tacitus, *Histories* II,41,7; 43,2; *Talmud of Jerusalem, Sota*, VIII,1.
175 Tacitus, *Agricola* XXXVI,3; Arrian, *Tactics* II,2; XVI; du Picq, pp. 73–5; P. Vigneron, *Le cheval dans l'Antiquité*, 1968, p. 238, seems to believe that the absence of stirrups did not necessarily entail absence of force.
176 Josephus VI,2,8 (161–163); see also e.g. V,7,3 (313).
177 Josephus VI,1,7 (75).
178 Tacitus, *Agricola* XXXVI, XXXVII,1.
179 Tacitus, *Agricola* XXXVII,3.
180 Onesandros VI,11; XI; Tacitus, *Agricola* XXXVII,6; Frontinus II,9,7.
181 Tacitus, *Histories* III,54,4; Frontinus I,2.
182 Trajan's Column nos 106–108; Aurelian Column LXXII.
183 *L'Année épigr.* 1968–1970 no. 583; M. Speidel, *Rev. Archéol.* 1971, 75–78; see n. 182 for Trajan's Column.
184 Josephus VI,1,5 (46); CIL XIII no. 7323.
185 ILS no. 2244.
186 F.B. Florescu, *Monumentul* . . . .
187 Tacitus, *Annals* III,19.

Notes to Chapter 6: *Strategy*
1 G. Forni, *Dizionario epigr.* IV, 34ff. *sub 'limes'*, is an excellent start to the problem.
2 H. von Petrikovits, *Die Innenbauten römischer Legionslager wahrend der Prinzipatszeit*, 1975, a remarkable book that should be translated to give it a wider readership.

 3 J. Szilagyi, *Acta Ant. Acad. Sc. Hung.* 2, 1953–4, 117–219: an important study but based solely on epigraphic material.
 4 Y. Garlan, *La Guerre dans l'Antiquité*, 1972, p. 103.
 5 W. Seston, *Scripta Varia*, 1980, 53–63.
 6 Virgil, *Aeneid* VI, 852–3.
 7 E.N. Luttwak, *The Grand Strategy of the Roman Empire*, 1976, 2nd ed.; P. Le Roux, *L'armée romaine* . . . ; see also Y. Le Bohec, *La IIIe* . . . .
 8 Frontinus II,11,1; Tacitus, *Annals* XI,19,2; Josephus VI,6,4 (357); Pliny, *Paneg.* XII,2.
 9 M. Le Glay, *XIe Congrès du limes*, 1978, 545–58.
10 Arrian, *Journey* VI, 1–2; X,3.
11 A. Poidebard, *La trace de Rome dans le désert de Syrie*; J. Baradez, *Fossatum Africae*.
12 Tacitus, *Annals* XV,3,4.
13 P. Leveau, *Bull. Com. Trav. Hist.* 1972, 17; N. Benseddik, *XIIe Congrès du limes*, 1980, pp. 977–98.
14 Cicero, *De lege agraria* II,73.
15 Tacitus, *Agricola* XVI,1; *Annals* XIV,31,5.
16 R. Rebuffat, *Bull. Arch. Maroc* 9, 1973–5, 317–408.
17 R. Rebuffat, *MEFR* 90, 1978, 829–61.
18 Frontinus II,11,7.
19 R. Rebuffat, *Comptes Rendus Acad. Inscr.*, 1969, 189–212; 1972, 319–39; 1975, 495–505; P. Trousset, *Limes tripolitanus*, 1974, pp. 149–50.
20 G. Ch. Picard, *Castellum Dimmidi*, 1947.
20b P. Arnaud, *MEFR (Mod)* 96, 1981, 537–602.
21 Pliny, *NH* VI,35.
22 CIL VIII no. 21567.
23 J. Desanges, *L'activité des Méditerranéens aux confins de l'Afrique*, 1978, p. 189ff.
24 G. Forni, *IXe Congrès du limes*, 1974, pp. 285–9.
25 Y. Le Bohec, *La IIIe* . . . .
26 *Esse in procinctu* simply means 'to be in battle dress', and not 'to be near the theatre of war' nor 'to be in the war zone'; *ora* denotes the shoreline, with a very occasional defensive connotation: ILS nos 2672, 2714, 2714a, 2715–2717; Pliny, *Letters* X,21.
27 Goetz II,158,15.
28 CIL VIII no. 22602 notably.
29 H.G. Pflaum, *Inscr. Lat. Algérie*, II,2, 1976, no. 4681.
30 ILS nos 2709, 2737.
31 Tacitus, *Histories* III,46,4; *Annals* I,36,2; XV,3,3.
32 J.F. Gilliam, *TAPA* 72, 1941, 157–75.
33 D.J. Breeze and B. Dobson, *Hadrian's Wall*, 1976, pp. 233–4.
34 One should avoid using the terms *clausura* and *fossatum*, the exact meaning of which is difficult to establish when one does not have an inscription that is explicit.
35 Y. Le Bohec, *La IIIe* . . . .
36 Tacitus, *Annals* III,26,2; CIL VIII nos 2546, 2548.
37 The difference is clear in Tacitus, *Histories* III,46,4; *Annals* I,16,2 and 30,3.
38 Tacitus, *Agricola* XIV,3; XVI,1; XX,3; XXV,3.

39 Goetz II,426,26.
40 CIL VIII nos 2494, 2495.
41 *Talmud of Jerusalem, Eroubin*, V,1.
42 *Talmud of Jerusalem, Aboda Zara*, IV,1.
43 Tacitus, *Histories* I,28,1.
44 Suetonius, *Augustus* XXXII,3.
45 H. Lieb, *Mel. E. Birley*, 1965, pp. 139–44; J. Sasel, *Xe Congrès du limes*, 1977, pp. 234–44.
46 A. von Domaszewski, *Westd. Zeitschr. f. Gesch. u. Kunst* 21, 1902, 158–211.
47 Y. Le Bohec, *Bull. Com. Trav. Hist.*, 1984, 54ff.
48 W. Schleiermacher, *Mél. F. Wagner*, 1962, pp. 195–204; D.J. Smith, *Libya in History*, 1968, pp. 299–311, 317–18.
49 *The Inscriptions of Tripolitania*, no. 880.
50 Tacitus, *Agricola* XIV,5; XVI,1; XX,3; *Talmud of Babylon, Mo'ed Katan*, 28b.
51 Trajan's Column no. 2.
52 Arrian, *Journey* IX,3.
53 R. Cagnat, *Manuel d'archéologie romaine*, 1, 1917, 250–67; H. von Petrikovits, *Die Innenbauten* . . . ; J. Lander, *Roman Stone Fortifications*, 1983; for the Late Empire see S. Johnson, *Late Roman Fortifications*, 1983; M. Reddé *et al.*, *Le camp romain de Louqsor*, 1986.
54 T. Bechert, *Bonner Jahrb.* 171, 1971, 201–87.
55 H. von Petrikovits, *JRS* 61, 1971, 178ff.
56 *L'Année epigr.* 1974 no. 723; H.G. Kolbe, *Rom. Mitteil.* 81, 1974, 281–300.
57 E.g. ILS no. 9176.
58 Picard, *Castellum Dimmidi*, pp. 127–31.
59 E.g. ILS no. 2375.
60 R. Rebuffat, *Libya Antiqua* 11–13, 1974–5, 204–7.
61 Tacitus, *Histories* I,38,6; Goetz II,25,21; 502,46; 528,59; ILS no. 9178.
62 J.M. Carrie, *MEFR* 86, 1974, 819–50.
63 R. Schultze, *Bonner Jahrb.* 139, 1934, 54–63; ILS no. 9174.
64 E. Sander, *Bonner Jahrb.* 162, 1962, 139–61; H. von Petrikovits, *IXe Congrès du limes*, 1974, pp. 399–407.
65 G. Rickman, *Roman Granaries and Store Buildings*, 1971; A.P. Gentry, *Roman Military Stone-Built Granaries in Britain*, 1976.
66 E.g. ILS no. 2620.
67 Suetonius, *Domitian* VII,4.
68 Herodian III,8,5.
69 Picard, *Castellum Dimmidi* p. 87; G.C. Boon, *Segontiacum*, 1963, p. 15; R. Rebuffat, *Thamusida* 1, 1965, p. 185; G. Webster, *Roman Imperial Army*, p. 206; Y. Le Bohec, *La IIIe* . . . ; M. Reddé, *Gallia* 43, 1985, pp. 72,76.
70 CIL III no. 13796.
71 B.E. Thomasson, *Opuscula Romana* 9, 1973, 61–6 (a list of provinces with legions).
72 Tacitus, *Annals* IV,5,2.
73 Herodian II,9,1.

74 Tacitus, *Annals* IV,5,5.
75 M. Reddé, *Mare nostrum*.
76 Trajan's Column no. 3.
77 G. Jacopi, *Rendic. Accad. Lincei* 6, 1951, 533.
78 E. Ritterling, *JRS* 17, 1927, 28–32.
79 Suetonius, *Vespasian* VIII,5.
80 Suetonius, *Claudius* XXV,6; ILS no. 2155 (*castra* at Ostia).
81 Strabo XVII,3,3.
82 N. Duval, S. Lancel and Y. Le Bohec, *Bull. Com. Trav. Hist.* 1984, 33–89.
83 Tacitus, *Histories* IV,48; Dio LIX,20,7.
84 Tacitus, *Annals* IV,5,1.
85 P. Fabia, *La garnison romaine de Lyon*, 1918.
86 M. Reddé, *Cahiers Groupe Rech. armée rom.* 1, 1977, 35–70; 3, 1984, 103–137, and *Gallia* 43, 1985, 49–79.
87 D. and F. Tassaux, *Travaux militaires en Gaule romaine*, II, *Caesarodunum*, 1978, 354–72.
88 R. Goguey, *ibid.*, 329–33.
89 G. Alföldy, *Acta arch. Hung.* 14, 1962, 259–96.
90 Herodian II,8,10.
91 R.K. Sherk, *AJP* 78, 1957, 52–62.
92 Pliny, *Letters* X, 21–22; E. Ritterling, *JRS* 17, 1927, 28–32; W.M. and A.M. Ramsay, *ibid.* 18, 1928, 181–90; R.K. Sherk, *AJP* 76, 1955, 400–13.
93 D.J. Breeze and B. Dobson, *Hadrian's Wall*; P. Holder, *The Roman Army in Britain*, 1982.
94 R. Syme, *JRS* 18, 1928, 41–25; E. Stein, *Die kaiserlichen Beamten und Truppenkorper im röm Deutschland*, 1932; K. Kraft, *Zur Rekrutierung . . .* ; G. Alföldy, *Die Hilfstruppen d. rom. Provinz Germania Inferior, Epigr. Stud.* 6, 1968; D. Baatz, *Der röm. Limes*, 1932.
95 W. Wagner, *Die Dislokation der rom. Auxiliarformationen in der Prov. Noricum. Pannonia. Moesia. Dacia*, 1938; *IIIe Congrès du limes*, 1959. See n. 94 and *L'Année épigr.* 1981, no. 845.
96 Herodian II,9,1 underscores its importance for the end of the second century.
97 J. Fitz, *Der röm. Limes in Ungarn*, 1976. See notes 94 and 95.
98 B. Gerov, *Acta Antiqua* 1967, 87–105. See notes 94 and 95.
99 V. Vaschide, *Histoire de la conquête romaine de la Dacie*, 1903; V. Christescu, *Istoria militara a Daciei romane*, 1937. See notes 94 and 95.
100 Arrian, *Journey*.
101 V. Chapot, *La frontière romaine de l'Euphrate*, 1907; A Poidebard, *La trace de Rome . . .* ; B. Isaac, *The Limits of Empire*, 1990.
102 V. Chapot, p. 250.
103 S.T. Parker, *XIIe Congrès du limes*, 1980, 865–78; D.L. Kennedy, *Roman Frontier in North East Jordan*, 1982; G.W. Bowerstock, *Roman Arabia*, 1983; see n. 104.
104 M. Speidel, *Latomus* 33, 1974, 934–9; M. Sartre, *Trois Études sur l'Arabie*, 1982.
105 J. Lesquier, *L'armée romaine d'Egypte*, 1918; R. Cavenaile, *Aegyptus* 50, 1970, 213–320; N. Criniti, *Aegyptus* 53, 1973, 93–158 and 59, 1979, 190–261.

106 R.G. Goodchild, *Libyan Studies*, 1976, 195–209; *L'Année épigr.* 1983, nos 940–2.

107 Y. Le Bohec, *La IIIe Légion Auguste*, 1989 and *Les unites auxiliaires en Afrique et Numidie*, 1989.

108 G. Ch. Picard, *Castellum Dimmidi*.

109 J. Baradez, *Fossatum Africae*.

110 P. Trousset, *Recherches sur le limes tripolitanus*, 1974.

111 Several articles by R. Rebuffat, e.g. in *Armées et Fiscalité*, 1977, pp. 395–419.

112 N. Bensaddik, *Les troupes auxiliaires de l'armée romaine en Maurétanie Césarienne*, 1982; Y. Le Bohec, *Cahiers Groupe Rech. Armée rom.* 2, 1979, 20–3 and *Epigraphica* 44, 1982, 216–67.

113 H. Nesselhauf, *Epigraphica* 12, 1950, 34–48; M. Roxan, *Latomus* 32, 1973, 838–55; Y. Le Bohec, *Cahiers*, 20–1 and 23–4. See n. 114.

114 M. Euzennat, *Le limes de Tingitane*, 1989.

115 P. Le Roux, *L'Armée romaine* . . . (see A. Tranoy, *La Galice romaine*, 1981, pp. 167–8).

Notes to Chapter 7: *History of the Roman army*

1 For each reign there is a supplementary bibliography in Y. Le Bohec, *La IIIe Légion Auguste*, 1989.

2 Tacitus, *Histories* I,4,1.

3 P. Le Roux, *L'armée romaine* . . . , p. 127ff.

4 For the main chronological changes see P. Le Roux op. cit. and E.N. Luttwak, *The Grand Strategy of the Roman Empire*, 1976.

5a L. Keppie, *The Making of the Roman Army*, 1984.

5b P. Le Roux, op. cit., pp. 83 and 127.

6 E.g. A. Piganiol, *Histoire de Rome*, 1962, 5th ed., p. 225: 'Augustus had few talents as a general'; P. Petit, *Histoire générale de l'Empire romain*, 1974, p. 32: 'Augustus had none of the qualities of a war leader'.

7 Aurelius Victor, *De Caes.* I,1.

8 Suetonius, *Augustus* XXIV–XXVI and XLIX; Herodian II,11,5; Dio LIV,25, 5–6 (important).

9 Tacitus, *Annals* I,4,3, recognizes this despite his aversion for Tiberius; Suetonius, *Tiberius* XXI,5.

10 Tacitus, *Annals* I,16ff; 31ff; 50ff.

11 Tacitus, *Annals* III,39.

12 Tacitus, *Annals* II,52; III, 20–21, 32, 35; IV,13,3 and 23–26.

13 Tacitus, *Annals* III,40ff.

14 Tacitus, *Annals* XII,31ff.; CIL V no. 7003.

15 Aurelius Victor, *De Caes.* III,4 and 17.

16 Suetonius, *Claudius* XXV,1 (see also XXII,1).

17 Tacitus, *Annals* XI,18–19.

18 Tacitus, *Annals* XII,28.

19 Tacitus, *Annals* XIII,6ff.

20 Tacitus, *Annals* XIV,29ff.

21 Josephus, *Jewish War*.

22 Dio LXIV,3.

23 Suetonius, *Vitellius* VIII,2.

24 Tacitus, *Histories* IV,78,3.

25 Suetonius, *Vespasian* VI,4; VIII; Aurelius Victor, *De Caes*. VIII, 2–3.
26 Suetonius, *Domitian* II,5.
27 P. Le Roux, *L'armée romaine* ... p. 169; see also E.N. Luttwak, *Grand Strategy*, p. 51ff. ('territorial Empire': forward defence).
30 Pliny, *Paneg*. XIV; Aurelius Victor, *De Caes*. XII,1; CIL V no. 7425.
31 J. Carcopino, *La vie quotidienne à Rome*, 1939, p. 16.
32 P. Petit, *Histoire générale de l'Empire romain*, 1974, p. 156.
33 Pliny, *Paneg*. V,7 and *Letters* X,106; Dio LXVIII,8.
34 M. Gervasio, *Mél. G. Beloch*, 1910, pp. 353–64.
35 F.B. Florescu, *Monumentul*; I.A. Richmond, *Papers Brit. School Rome* 35, 1967, 29–39.
36 CIL II no. 4461 (career of a centurion decorated during the Dacian War and again in the Parthian War).
37 J. Guey, *Essai sur la Guerre Parthique de Trajan*, 1937; F.A. Lepper, *Trajan's Parthian War*, 1948.
38 Aurelius Victor XIV,1; Mattingly and Sydenham, *Roman Imperial Coinage* II, 1926, pp. 458–62.
39 Dio LXIX,9.
40 *HA*: Hadrian XII,6.
41 Aurelius Victor XVI,2.
42 *L'Année épigr*. 1960 no. 28.
43 Herodian I,2,5 and 4,8.
44 Herodian I,8,1 (Perennis).
45 *Nouveaux choix d'inscriptions grecques*, 1971, pp. 85–94.
46 CIL VI no. 31856.
47 Dio LXXI,1.
48 W. Zwikker, *Studien zur Markussaule*, 1941; J. Guey, *Rev. Ét. Anc.* 50, 1948, 185–189; J. Morris, *JWCI* 15, 1952, 33–47.
49 Aurelius Victor XVII,2.
50 J. Fritz, *Klio* 39, 1961, 199–214 (fight against the *latrunculi*).
51 Herodian I,17,2; *HA*: Pertinax VI,6.
52 Herodian II,1,4; 2,7; 3,1; 9,9; *HA*: Pertinax VI,3.
53 *HA*: Pertinax IX,6.
54 Herodian III,8,8 and 15,2 (with a restriction for discipline); Aurelius Victor XX,14; Zosimus I,8,2; Mattingley and Sydenham, *Roman Imp. Coins*, IV,1, 1936, pp. 92–3.
55 Herodian II,6,4 and 10; 11,7; *HA*: Didius Iulianus III.
56 Herodian II,7,7; 8,1; *HA*: Pescennius Niger II,4; III, 6–8; IV; VI,10; VII,7; X.
57 *HA*: Clodius Albinus V, 1–2; XI,6; XIII,2.
58 The only other important conflict during this reign (in Britain) started in 206 (see below).
59 In fact as early as 193.
60 Herodian II,11,2.
61 Herodian III,8,5 (previous increase under Domitian; see next chapter).
62 Dio LXXVIII,34,3; *HA*: Severus Alexander XV,45,2 and 47,1.
63 Huge bibliography: J.-P. Waltzing, *Étude historique sur les corporations professionelles chez les Romains*, 4 vols, 1895–1900; Y. Le Bohec, *La IIIe* ... , p. 394.

64 J. Carcopino, *Mel. P. Dussaud*, 1939, pp. 209–16.
65 M. Christol, *Carrières sénatorialles*, pp. 35–9.
66 R.E. Smith, *Historia* 21, 1972, 481–500.
67 Dio LXXVII,3,9, 16 and 24.
68 *HA*: Elagabalus IX.
69 *ibid*. VI,2.
70 Herodian VI,3,1 and 5,9; *HA*: Severus Alexander L, LV-LVI.
71 Herodian VI,7,2; VII,2,1; *HA*: Severus Alexander LIX.
72 H. Pavis d'Escurac, *Mél. A. Piganiol*, II, 1966, pp. 1191–204.
73 *HA*: Severus Alexander LVIII,1.
74 *Ibid*. XXVII,10; Zosimus I,11,2.
75 Herodian VI,1,4.
76 *HA*: Elagabalus XIII,3; XIV,2; Severus Alexander I, 6–7; II,3; XXI,6.
77 *HA*: Severus Alexander XXIII,1.
78 *HA*: Tacitus VII,3.
79 P. Le Roux, *L'armée romaine* . . . , pp. 169, 361: from the 'army of peace' to the 'stationary army'.
80 Herodian VII,1,6.
81 Herodian VII,1,4.
82 Zosimus I,14,2.
83 *HA*: Gordiani tres XXVIII, 3–4.
84 *Ibid*. XXIV,3.
85 *Ibid*. XXII,2; XXIII,1.
86 *Ibid*. XXIII,6; XXVI,3ff.
87 *Ibid*. XXX.
88 Zosimus I,21,3; Mattingly and Sydenham, *Roman Imp. Coinage* IV,3, 1959, pp. 112, 114, 134 etc.
89 *HA*: Aurelianus XLII,4 (but see Carus III,5).
90 Zosimus I,36,2.
91 J. Guey, *Rev. Ét. Anc.* 57, 1955, 113–22.
92 J. Fitz, *Mél. J. Carcopino*, 1966, pp. 353–65, and *Ingenuus et Regalien, Collection Latomus* 81, 1966.
93 H.-G. Pflaum, *Historia* 25, 1976, 110–17; L. de Blois, *The Policy of the Emperor Gallienus*, 1976.
94 Aurelius Victor XXXIII,6; see also *HA*: Gallieni duo XVII,4ff; XXI,3.
95 M. Christol, *Bull. Soc. Franc. Numismat.* 27, 1972, 250–4; Mattingly and Sydenham, V,1, 1927, 92–7.
96 Zosimus I,30,2 and 37,2 (in favour of Gallienus).
97 Aurelius Victor XXXIII,34 (see XXXVII,6); M. Christol, *Carrières sénatorialles*, pp. 39–48 (262?).
98 *HA*: Gallieni duo XV,1.
99 *HA*: Aurelianus XXII,1ff.
100 *ibid*. XXX,4.
101 *HA*: Tacitus XIV,3 and Probus IV.
102 *HA*: Probus VIII,1; X,9.
103 *ibid*. XI,9.
104 Aurelius Victor, *De Caes.* XXXIII,3; *Panegyrics* IV,18,3; Zosimus I,71,2.
105 *HA*: Carus V,4; VII,1.
106 *ibid*. VIII,1.

107 Zosimus I,72,1 (Carinus).
108 Suetonius, *Titus* V,3.
109 Josephus VI,6,1 (316).
110 Pliny, *Paneg.* XII,2.
111 CIL IX no. 1558.
112 R. Cagnat, *Epigraphie latine*, 1914, 4th ed., pp. 177–231.
113 The sobriquet 'Germanicus' was given to the grandson of Livia, wife of Augustus.
114 Copying Caligula, Claudius took 'Germanicus' more as a personal name than a victory sobriquet. The son of Claudius and Messalina, better known as Britannicus, was called Germanicus at first (Suetonius, *Claudius* XXVII,1).
115 Dio LV,23.
116 G.M. Bersanetti, *Athenaeum* 18, 1940, 105–35 and 21, 1943, 79–91.
117 Note that one writes *legio* VII *Gemina Antoniniana* but *ala Parthorum Antoninianorum*.
118 J. Fitz, *Oikumene* 1, 1976, 215–24 and *Acta Arch. Slov.* 28, 1977, 393–7.
119 Y. Le Bohec, *Epigraphica* 43, 1981, 127–60.
120 E. Ritterling, *Realencyclopädie* XII, 2, 1925, *s.v. Legio*; J.C. Mann, *Legionary Recruitment*, 1982.

Notes to Chapter 8: *The practical role*
1 J. Gagé, *Les classes sociales dans l'Empire romain*, 1971, 2nd ed., pp. 133–8, 249–72.
2 Juvenal XVI, 1–2.
3 P. Salway, *The Frontier People of Roman Britain*, 1965.
4 Expression used by Seneca, *De Clementia* I,4,2 (see *De Providentia* IV,14); the same idea is found in Tacitus, *Agricola* XXX,7 (peace and dominion).
5 Petronius, *Satyricon*: the narrative is often set in the milieu of lawbreakers; Apuleius, *Metamorphoses* IV, 1–27; Dio LXXV,2; CIL III no. 3385; VI no. 234; VIII no. 2728 = 18122, 13–17; XI no. 6107; J. Gage, op. cit. pp. 143–52; R. MacMullen, *Enemies of the Roman Order*, 1966, pp. 255–66.
6 CIL VIII no. 17626; H. Lieb in *Britain and Rome*, 1965, pp. 139–44.
7 M. Cary and B.H. Warmington, *Les explorateurs de l'Antiquité*, 1932, esp. p. 11 and p. 109.
8 Strabo XVI,4; XVII,54; Pliny, *NH* VI,35; E. Bernand, *Inscr. Philae*, II, 1969, no. 128; J. Desanges, *Les Méditerranéens*, pp. 307–21.
9 Seneca, *NQ* VI,8 3–5 and Pliny, *NH* VI,35; J. Desanges, p. 323ff.
10 C.M. Daniels, *The Garamantes of Southern Libya*, 1970, pp. 24–5.
11 CIL VIII no. 2728 = 18122 and S. Gsell, *Monuments antiques de l'Algérie*, I, 1901, p. 249ff.
12 Translation by J.-P. Martin, *Le siècle des Antonins*, 1977, 90–1 and P.-A. Février, *Les dossiers de l'archéologie* 38, 1979, 88–9.
13 Tacitus, *Annals* I,17,6; Dio LIX, 15 (centurions).
14 *Talmud of Jerusalem, Scheqalim* V, 1; *Baba Mecia'* II,5; *Aboda Zara* I.
15 Arrian, *Journey* VI, 1–2; X,3.
16 R.W. Davies, *Historia* 16, 1967, 115–18.
17 Pt I, ch. II *passim*.
18 Tacitus, *Annals* I,17,6.
19 Suetonius, *Domitian* VII,5; XII,1.
20 Herodian III,8,5; *HA*: Septimius Severus XVII,1.

21 Y. Le Bohec, *La IIIe* . . . , pp. 534–5. This table has been greatly modified due to a recent discovery, as seen in M. Speidel, 'Roman Army pay Scales', *JRS* 82, 1992, pp. 87–106.

22 Herodian IV,4,7.

23 R. Duncan-Jones, *Chiron* 8, 1978, 541–60.

24 *HA*: Claudius XIV (tribune) and XV (*dux*), but these late passages may well be pure fictions.

25 M. Christol in *Armées et fiscalité*, 1977, pp. 235–77.

26 G.R. Watson, *Historia* 8, 1959, 372ff.

27 A.C. Johnson, *Roman Egypt*, 1936, p. 670ff; A. Passerini, *Acme* 1, 1948, 366; A. Brunt, *Papers Brit. School Rome* 18, 1950, 264–5.

28 M. Speidel, *JRS* 63, 1973, 141–7, from a new reading of *Pap. Gen. Lat.* 1.

29 R. Marichal, *Mel. I. Levy*, 1955, 399–421, using *Pap. Gen. Lat.* 1 and 4, and *Pap. Berl.*, 6866, confirms the intuition of Domaszewski (see next note).

30 A. von Domaszewski, *Neue Heidelb. Jhb* 10, 1900, 218ff. Inscription no. 661 in *L'Année épigr.* 1969–1970 reveals a legionary cavalryman promoted *duplicarius* in an *ala*.

31 E. Sander, *Historia* 6, 1957, 365–6.

32 CIL XIII no. 3162, left side, 1.13–16; H.-G. Pflaum, *Le marbre de Thorigny*, 1948, p. 26.

33 B. Dobson, *Anc. Soc.*, 3, 1972, 193–207 and *Aufstieg* II,1, 1974, p. 408. See n. 21.

34 H.-G. Pflaum, *Abrégé des procurateurs equestres* (adapted by N. Duval and S. Ducrous), 1974, pp. 17–18.

35 *HA*: Marcus Aurelius XVII, 4–5.

36 Dio LXXVIII,36,3 (see 28).

37 Gaius, *Institutiones* IV,27.

38 Tacitus, *Histories* III,50,6; Suetonius, *Vespasian* VIII,5.

39 Suetonius, *Vespasian* VIII,5.

40 M. Corbier in *Armées et fiscalité*, 1977, pp. 209–12.

41 G. Forni, *Reclutamento*, pp. 34–8 and 49; S. Daris, *Epigraphica* 17, 1955, 162–3.

42 *HA*: Pescennius Niger III,6; F. Girard, *Textes de droit romain*, 1918, 4th ed., pp. 205, 207.

43 CIL III no. 12336.

44 Gaius, *Inst.* II,69.

45 Tacitus, *Histories* III,19,6 (see 33).

46 Onesandros VI,11; XXXV; Tacitus, *Agricola* XXXVIII,1 and *Histories* III,26,5; see n. 47.

47 Josephus VI,5,1 (271) and 6,1 (317).

48 Trajan's Column nos 96, 103.

49 Aurelian Column LXIV, LXXIII, LXXXV, CIV, CXVI.

50 *HA*: Septimius Severus XVI,5.

51 Suetonius, *Augustus* CI,3.

52 *HA*: Severus Alexander XL,5.

53 Suetonius, *Galba* XVI.

54 Y. Le Bohec, *Bull. Com. Trav. Hist.* 1984, p. 50.

55 Suetonius, *Domitian* VII,4.

56 R.W. Davies, *Bonner Jahrb.* 168, 1968, 161–5.

57 Tacitus, *Annals* I,17,6.
58 R.W. Davies, *Britannia* 2, 1971, 122–42.
59 *HA*: Severus Alexander XV,5 and Gordiani tres XXIX,2; Vegetius II,7.
60 J. Guey, *MEFR* 55, 1938, 56–77.
61 D. van Berchem, *Bull. Soc. Ant. Fr.* 1937, 137–202 and in *Armées et fiscalité*, 1977, p. 332; N. Baynes, *JRS* 29, 1939, 116–18.
62 *HA*: Severus Alexander XV,5 mentions the military *annona* in the time of the last ruler of the Severan dynasty.
63 See M. Corbier in *Armées et fiscalité* p. 337 and J.-M. Carrie in *Les dévaluations à Rome*, 1978, pp. 237–8.
64 Tacitus, *Annals* I,17,6 (under Tiberius).
65 R. MacMullen, *Amer. Journ. Arch.* 1960, 23–40, and *Soldier and Civilian*, 1967, pp. 179–80; H.U. Nuber, *Chiron* 2, 1972, 483–507.
66 Tacitus (n. 64) and *HA* (n. 52).
67 Tacitus, *Histories* IV,60,2.
68 F. Girard, *Textes* p. 845.
69 R.W. Davies, *Latomus* 28, 1969, 435–49.
70 Gaius, *Inst.* I,57.
71 Tacitus, *Annals* XIII,35,2 and 51,1; F. Girard, *Textes*, p. 193.
72 J. Lesquier, *Armée romaine d'Egypte*, 1918, p. 163.
73 CIL VIII no. 4508 = 18653 and 18352; *L'Année épigr.* 1914 no. 234. (Numidia); H. Seyrig, *Syria* 22, 1941, 155 (Syria).
74 S.J. de Laet, *Portorium*, 1949, pp. 263–71.
75 Tacitus, *Histories* II,82,1 (arms were made in the cities).
76 Tacitus, *Annals* XIII,54, 2–3.
77 CIL VIII no. 4322 = 18527.
78 A. Mocsy, *VIe Congrès du limes*, 1967, pp. 211–14.
79 ILS nos 2454, 2455.
80 ILS no. 2456; see n. 81.
81 A. Schulten, *Hermes* 29, 1889, 481–516, approved by A. Mocsy, *Acta Arch. Hung.* 3, 1953, 179–200 and by A. Garcia Y. Bellido, *Arch. Esp. Arqu.* 34, 1961, 118–19.
82 P. Salway, *Frontier People* p. 188, followed by J.M. Roldan, *Hispania y el ejercito romano*, 1974, pp. 196–7, by F. Vittinghoff, *Acc. Naz. Linc.* 194, 1974, 109–24, and by P. Le Roux in *Armées et fiscalité*, pp. 350–3.
83 H. von Petrikovits, *Realencyclopädie* VIII A,2, 1958, col. 1825.
84 R. MacMullen, *Soldier and Civilian*, pp. 7–11.
85 M. Kandler, *XIe Congrès du limes*, 1977, 145–54.
86 Tacitus, *Histories* I,46, 3–6 and *Annals* I,17,6.
87 Tacitus, *Annals* XIII,51,1 (see 35,2).
88 A. Segré, *Rend. Pont. Acc. Rom.* 17, 1941, p. 181 (it is possible that the Aurelii of 212 did not enjoy all the advantages of military status).
89 J. Vendrand-Voyer, *Normes civiques et métier militaire à Rome*, 1983.
90 Vendrand-Voyer, pp. 147, 211, 316.
91 Juvenal XVI, 13–17; Tertullian, *De Corona Militis* I.
92 Juvenal XVI,50.
93 Vendrand-Voyer, pp. 185, 248ff.
94 F. Girard, *Textes*, pp. 373, 407, 496 (Papinianus and Paulus); Vendrand-Voyer, p. 184ff.

95 A. Guarino, *Boll. Ist. Diritto Rom.* 7, 1941, 61 and 64.
96 Justinian, *Inst.* I,12,4.
97 Gaius, *Inst.* II,101,114; Ulpian XXIII,10; Justinian, *Inst.* II, 11–12; Vendrand-Voyer, p. 212ff.
98 Gaius (see n. 97).
99 J. Carcopino, *Rev. Ét. Anc.* 24, 1922, 110.
100 Juvenal XVI, 51–2.
101 F. Girard, *Textes*, p. 195.
102 J. Carcopino, *Mel. P. Thomas*, 1930, p. 97–8; P. Tassistro, *St. Doc. St. Dir.* 22, 1901, 3–82; R.O. Fink, *Trans. Proc. Amer. Phil. Assoc.* 72, 1941, 109–24; E. Sander, *Rhein. Mus.* 101, 1958, 164–5; P. Garnsey, *California St. Class. Ant.* 3, 1970, 43–53; B. Campbell, *JRS* 68, 1978, 299–333.
103 Vendrand-Voyer, pp. 109–10.
104 M. Absil and Y. Le Bohec, *Latomus* 44, 1985, 855–70.
105 CIL XVI, App. no. 1; see *L'Année épigr.* 1980 no. 647.
106 A bibliography can be found on pp. 869–70 in article cited in n. 104.
107 M. Roxan, *Diplomas*, 1978, no. 6.
108 M. Corbier in *Armées et fiscalité*, 1977, p. 208.
109 A.R. Neumann, *Realencyclopädie*, Suppl. IX,2, 1962, col. 1597–1609; J.C. Mann, *Legionary Recruitment and Veteran Settlement*, 1982.
110 P. Le Roux, *L'armée des provinces ibériques*, 1982, pp. 344–7.
111 See Pt I, ch. 1, n. 21.
112 A. Segré, *Rend. Pont. Acc. Rom.* 17, 1941, 167–82, esp. p. 171; E. Sander, *Rhein. Mus.* 101, 1958, 166–9.
113 Suetonius, *Vespasian* I,3.
114 ILS no. 9085.
115 M. Speidel, *AJP* 104, 1983, 282–6 (see Le Bohec, *Epigraphica* 43, 1981, 132–4).
116 M. Corbier, *L'aerarium Saturni et l'aerarium militare*, 1974, and in *Armées et fiscalité*, pp. 197–234.
117 Dio Li,4 and 17; A. Muller, *Neue Jhrb. f. d. klass. Altertum*, 29, 1912, 267–84; E.G. Hardy, *CQ* 14, 1920, 187–94; L. Keppie, *Colonisation and Veteran Settlement in Italy*, 1983, and *Papers Brit. School Rome* 52, 1984, 77–114; J.C. Mann, *Legionary Recruitment*.
118 Tacitus, *Annals* XIV,27 and 31, 4–5 (see also the *Res Gestae*).
119 CIL VIII no. 4800.
120 Suetonius, *Nero* IX, Tacitus, *Annals* XIV, 27 and 31, 4–5; ILS nos 2460, 2574.
121 P. Le Roux (see n. 110).
122 H. Pavis d'Escurac, *Mél. A. Grenier* II, 1962, pp. 571–83.
123 ILS no. 9059.
124 *Digest* XLIX, 18,3.
125 A.R. Neumann, *Realencyclopädie*, Suppl. IX,2, 1962, col. 1608–9.
126 Survey of 29–30 in Africa: CIL VIII nos 22786 and 22789, and *Inscr. Lat. Tun.* nos 71, 73, and 74; limits under the Flavians, in Africa: CIL VIII nos 14882, 23084, 25967; *Inscr. Lat. Tun.* no. 263; *Inscr. Lat. Alg.*, II, nos 4343, 6252; *Rom. Inscr. Trip.* no. 854; *L'Année épigr.* 1912 nos 148–51; 1935 no. 28; 1939 no. 31; 1942–1943 no. 35; *Bull. Com. Trav. Hist.* 1932–1933, p. 152 (just one example!).

127 J.-M. Lassère, *Ubique populus*, 1977, pp. 356–8, for example; similar practices could be found in Syria, Egypt, etc.
128 Compare CIL VIII no. 2478 = 17969 and X no. 8045,12.
129 Tacitus, *Annals*, II,62,4.
130 Suetonius, *Augustus* XIX,4; Tacitus, *Histories* II,87,2 where soldiers' 'valets' (*calones*) are cited; H. von Petrikovits, *XIIe Congrès du limes*, III, 1980, pp. 1027–35.
131 Nevertheless see curious graffito: *L'Année épigr.* 1980 no. 262, and P. Le Roux, *Epigraphica* 45, 1983, 66–73.
132 Tacitus, *Histories* II,80,5.
133 F. Vittinghoff, *Chiron* 1, 1971, 299–318.
134 *L'Année épigr.* 1983 no. 858 (Porolissum in Dacia); A. Schulten, *Hermes* 29, 1894, p. 500, is perhaps a little too systematic.
135 P. Salway, *Frontier People*, pp. 9–11, 117; A. Mocsy, *Acta Arch. Hung.* 3, 1953, 179–200; *Acta Ant. Ac. Sc. Hung.* 13, 1965, 425–31, and *Acta Ant. Hung.* 20, 1972, pp, 159, 168.
136 E. Birley, *Roman Britain and the Roman Army*, 1953, pp. 71–80.
137 J.P. Laporte, *Rapidum*, 1989.
138 P. Salway (see n. 135).
139 A. Poidebard, *La trace de Rome.*
140 J. Baradez, *Fossatum Africae.*
141 M. Euzennat, *Le limes de Tingitane*, 1989.
142 R. Rebuffat, see Pt II, ch. 6, n. 111.
143 On this point see the *Acta* of the 1985 Caen conference *La mort, les morts et l'au dela*, 1987.
144 Y. Le Bohec, *La IIIe . . .* , p. 543, and notes 143, 144.
145 J.-M. Lassère, *Ubique populus*, p. 519ff.
146 Y. Le Bohec, 'Peut-on "compter la mort" des soldats de la IIIe Légion Auguste', *Colloque de Caen*, 1987, 53–64.
147 A.R. Burn, *Past and Present* 4, 1953, 1–31.
148 See n. 144.
149 Pliny, *Paneg.* XXVIII,5; CIL XI no. 1147.

Notes to Chapter 9, *Cultural influence*

1 Tacitus, *Annals* IV,67,7; Vegetius II,19.
2 Horace, *Satires* I,6,70–5.
3 CIL III no. 2835; VI no. 2489; VIII no. 702 = 12128; ILS no. 2167 (by no means an exhaustive list!).
4 L. Vidman, *Anc. Soc.* 2, 1971, 162–73; it is probable that other writers were mined for names, particularly Ovid and Catullus.
5 J. Carcopino, *Syria* 6, 1925, p. 148; H.I. Marrou, *MEFR* 50, 1933, pp. 55, 60 (a more nuanced view); Y. Le Bohec, *Les unités auxiliaires en Afrique et Numidie*, 1989.
6 Tacitus, *Histories* III,33,5.
7 *L'Année épigr.* 1947 no,35; CIL III no. 10505: *interpres Germanorum.*
8 *L'Année épigr.* 1975 no. 869b.
9 J.-M. Lassère, *XIIe Congrès du limes*, 3, 1980, p. 967 and p. 972, n. 54.
10 H. Bianchi, *Studi Ital. Filol. Class.* 18, 1910, 41–76; M. Clauss, *Epigraphica* 35, 1973, p. 90; D. Pikhaus, *Ant. Class.* 50, 1981, 637–54.

11 W. Heraus, *Archiv. Lat. Lexik. Gram.* 12, 1900, 255–80.
12 R. Marichal, *Les Ostraca de Bu Njem, Libya Antiqua*, Suppl. 7, 1992.
13 Juvenal XVI; Tacitus, *Histories* III,33,5 and *Agricola* XXXII; *HA*: Didius Julianus VI,5.
14 L.R. Dean, *Cognomina of Soldiers in Roman Legions*, 1916.
15 R.O. Fink, *Trans. Proc. Amer. Phil. Assoc.* 72, 1941, 109–124, speaks of *engagements*.
16 E. Sander, *Rhein. Mus.* 101, 1958, 175–9.
17 CIL VIII no. 18214 (see no. 18234).
18 CIL III nos 388, 6687; XIV no. 3955.
19 See Pt III, ch. 8, n. 126.
20 P. Collart, *Bull. Corr. Hél.* 57, 1933, 321–4.
21 CIL V no. 5267; IX no. 5363; *L'Année épigr.* 1931 no. 36.
22 See previous chapter.
23 P. Le Roux, *L'armée des provinces ibériques*, 1982.
24 J.-Cl. Golvin and M. Janon, *Bull. Com. Trav. Hist.* 1976–8, 169–93.
25 H. von Petrikovits, *Die Innenbauten* pp. 102–4.
26 CIL VIII no. 17978; M. Mondini, *Atene e Roma* 1915, 241–58; G.B. Pighi, *Lettere latine d'un soldato di Traiano*, 1964; L. Huchthausen, *Mél. W. Hartkes*, 1973, pp. 19–51.
27 CIL III nos 6824, 6825.
28 *Bull. Com. Trav. Hist.* 1928–9, p. 94, no. 2.
29 ILS no. 2609.
30 Onesandros IV.
31 A. von Domaszewski, *Aufsätze zur röm. Heeresgeschichte*, 1972, pp. 81–209; E. Birley, *Aufstieg* II,16,2, 1978, pp. 1506–41; J. Helgeland, *ibid.*, 1470–1505; Y. Le Bohec, *La IIIe . . .* , pp. 548–72.
32 H. Le Bonniec in J.-P. Brisson, *Problèmes de la guerre à Rome*, 1969, 101–15.
33 J. Vendrand-Voyer, *Normes civiques*, pp. 28–42.
34 M. Le Glay, *Saturne africain*, 1966, p. VI.
35 *Bull. Com. Trav. Hist.* 1907, p. 255.
36 J. Kolendo, *Archeologia* 31, 1980, 49–60.
37 M. Le Glay in *Syncrétismes dans l'Antiquité*, 1975, pp. 148–9.
38 ILS no. 2181.
39 Compare CIL VIII nos 2609, 2610 with *HA*: Hadrian XXII,14.
40 Aurelian Column XI and XVI; Dio LXXI, 9–10 (see also LX,9).
41 D.J. Breeze and B. Dobson, *Hadrian's Wall*, 1976, pp. 5, 233–4.
42 Trajan's Column nos 74, 77 and 77–8.
43 Aurelian Column XIII, XXX, LXXV.
44 F. Cumont, *Mon. Mem. Acad. Inscr.* 26, 1923; G.-Ch. Picard, *Castellum Dimmidi*, p. 167.
45 Frontinus IV,1,4; S. Tondo, *St. Doc. Hist. Iur* 29, 1963; 34, 1968, 376–96; D. Gaspar, *Acta Arch. Hung.* 28, 1976, 197–203.
46 E. de Backer, *Sacramentum*, 1911; Ch. Pietri, *MEFR* 74, 1962, 649–64; D. Michaelides, *Sacramentum*, 1970; C. Mohrmann, *Mél. J.H. Waszink*, 1973, pp. 233–42.
47 Onesandros V; Trajan's Column no. 7; Aurelian Column VI.
48 Onesandros X, 25–8.

49 Aurelius Victor XXXIV, 3–6. See also Frontinus IV,5,4 (abortive attempt at *devotio*), and n. 50.
50 Josephus VI,1,6 (54–66).
51 Onesandros XXXIV.
52 Onesandros XXXVI.
53 G.-Ch. Picard, *Les trophées romains*, 1957.
54 Trajan's Column no. 58; Aurelian Column LV.
55 Dio, *Fragments* VIII; H.S. Versnel, *Triumphus*, 1970; V.A. Maxfield, *Military Decorations*, 1981, pp. 101–9.
56 Suetonius, *Augustus* XXV,4.
57 CIL XIV no. 2922.
58 Tacitus, *Annals* II,41, 2–4.
59 Josephus VI,8,3 (387–388) and 9,2 (417).
60 Suetonius, *Tiberius* IX,4; *Claudius* XXIV,5 and XXVI,3; Tacitus, *Annals* IV,26 and 46; XI,20.
61 R.O. Fink, A.S. Hoey and W.F. Snyder, *Feriale Duranum, Yale Class. Stud.* 8, 1940; A.D. Nock, *Harvard Theol Rev.* 45, 1952, 187–252.
62 Dio LXXVII,16; M. Henig, *Britannia* 1, 1970, 249–65.
63 CIL III no. 7591 (A. von Domaszewski, *Aufsätze* p. 99); ILS no. 2320.
64 See Pt II, ch. 4.
65 Trajan's Column nos 18, 27.
66 ILS no. 2584.
67 CIL II no. 4083.
68 CIL III no. 3460.
69 See n. 54.
70 G.-Ch. Picard, *Les trophées romains*.
71 ILS no. 2585.
72 Onesandros *Pr.* 6.
73 Pt II, ch. 4.
74 P. Herz, *Zeitschr. Papyr. Epigr.* 17, 1975, 181–97.
75 CIL VI no. 230.
76 Tacitus, *Histories* IV,58,13.
77 Trajan's Column nos 7, 37.
78 Tacitus, *Annals* II,13,1.
79 CIL II no. 2634; III no. 1019; *L'Année épigr.* 1898 no. 12a (just some examples).
80 CIL II no. 5083; III nos 1646, 15208; VI nos 227, 234; ILS no. 2180 (also as some examples among many).
81 CIL II no. 2556.
82 *Talmud of Babylon, Pesahim* 87b; CIL II no. 2552.
83 Ch. Renel, *Cultes militaires*, 1903, p. 212; A. von Domaszewski, *Aufsätze*, p. 55; H.M.D. Parker, *Legions*, 1980, pp. 261–3.
84 Ovid, *Fasti* V,20ff.
85 Pliny, *Letters* XX, 100 (at the beginning of the year).
86 Pliny, *Letters* X,52 and 102.
87 F. Cumont, *Mon. Mem. Acad. Inscr.* 26, 1923.
88 Picard, *Dimmidi*, pp. 159–72.
89 Trajan's Column no. 4; Aurelian Column III.
90 Tacitus, *Histories* III,24,6; Dio LXV,14.

91 Herodian V,3,9 and 12.
92 M. Speidel, *The Religion of Iuppiter Dolichenus in the Roman Army*, 1978.
93 M. Le Glay in *Syncrétismes*, 1975, 123–51.
94 Y. Le Bohec, *La IIIe . . .* , p. 570.
95 See n. 38.
96 Introduction and pl. I,1.
97 Dio LXXI, 9–10.
98 Y. Le Bohec, *Bull. Com. Trav. Hist.* 1984, p. 50.
99 L. Dupraz, *Les passions de saint Maurice d'Agaune*, 1961.
100 P. Siniscalco, *Massimiliano: un obiettore di coscienza*, 1984.
101 E. Beurlier, *Les chrétiens et le service militaire*, 1892; see n. 31 (J. Helgeland).
102 L. de Regibus, *Didaskaleion* 2, 1924, 41–69.
103 M. Durry, *Mél. J. Bidez*, 1956, pp. 85–90.
104 G.R. Watson in *Christianity in Britain*, 1968, pp. 51–4.
105 Y. Le Bohec, *La IIIe . . .* , p. 571.

Notes on Chapter 10: *General conclusion*

1 Ph. Contamine is best known for his work on the Hundred Years' War and the end of the Middle Ages.
2 A. Corvisier has made a particular study of *L'armée française de la fin du XVIIe siècle au Ministère de Choiseul* (1964, 2 vols).
3 P. Renouvin has done a lot of work on World War I.
4 G. Pedroncini, who wrote a remarkable book on the mutinies of 1917, has organized the teaching of history at the military school of Saint-Cyr.
5 A. Martel has set up a centre of military studies in the University of Montpellier. Mention could also be made of G. Bouthoul and his reflections on the 'polemology'.
6 Y. Garlan, *La guerre dans l'Antiquité*, 1972 and J. Harmand, *La guerre antique*, 1973, illustrate this point.
7 See above.
8 A. von Domaszewski, *Rangordnung* (2nd ed. by B. Dobson); Y. Le Bohec, *La IIIe . . .* , pp. 185–95.
9 H. von Petrikovits, *Die Innenbauten*, 1975; J. Lander, *Roman Stone Fortifications*, 1983.
10 M. Reddé, *Mare Nostrum*, 1986.
11 E.N. Luttwak, *The Grand Strategy of the Roman Empire*, 1979, 3rd ed.
12 G. Forni, *s.v. limes* in E. de Ruggiero, *Dizionario epigrafico*, IV, 1959, p. 1074ff.
13 Rome did have a diplomatic service but this has been rarely studied.
14 E.N. Luttwak (n. 11) insists on this clearness of vision, influenced perhaps by contemporary preoccupations.
15 J. Kromayer and G. Veith, *Heerwesen und Kriegsführung* in I. von Muller, Handbuch IV,3,2, 1928; H. Delbrück, *Art of War*, I, *Antiquity*, 1975.
16 See bibliography.
17 J. Gagé, *Les classes sociales dans l'Empire romain*, 1971, 2nd ed., p. 249ff.
18 K. Kraft, *Zur Rekrutierung der Alen und Kohorten*, 1951; G. Forni, *Il reclutamento delle legioni*, 1953 (this classification is very important for the understanding of ancient mentalities).

19 See Pt III, ch. 8.
20 E. Birley, *Durham University Journal* 1949, 8–19 and J. Gagé, were the first to undertake this revision.
21 M. Christol, *Carrières senatorialles*, 1986.
22 Dio LVII,24.
23 Tacitus, *Histories* I,4,2.
24 P. Le Roux, *L'armée romaine des provinces ibériques*, 1982, p. 127ff.
25 P. Salway, *The Frontier People of Britain*, 1965.
26 R. MacMullen, *Enemies of the Roman Order*, 1966.
27 See n. 18.
28 P. Le Roux op. cit. n. 24.
29 E. Birley and J. Helgeland in *Aufstieg* II,16,2, 1978.
30 M. Le Glay in *Syncrétismes*, 1975, pp. 123–51.
31 M. Durry, *Mél. J. Bidez*, 1956, pp. 85–90; G.R. Watson in *Christianity in Britain*, 1968, pp. 51–54; Y. Le Bohec, *La IIIe Légion Auguste*, 1989, p. 572.
32 R.O. Fink, A.S. Hoey, and W.F. Snyder, *Feriale Duranum, Yale Classical Studies*, VII, 1940.
33 The importance of Augustus' conquests has often been played down by scholars.
34 M. Christol, op. cit. n. 21.
35 D. van Berchem, *L'armée de Diocletien et la réforme constantinienne*, 1952; R. MacMullen, *Soldier and Civilian in the Later Roman Empire*, 1967; D. Hoffman, *Spätröm. Bewegungsheer, Epigr. Stud.* VII, 1 and 2, 1969 and 1970; E. Gabba, *Per la storia dell'esercito romano*, 1974; see also n. 36.
36 W. Seston, *Dioclétien et la Tétrarchie*, 1946.
37 Lactantius, *De Mortibus Persecutorum* VII.
38 This interpretation of the facts has been emphasized by E. Stein, *Histoire du Bas-Empire*, 1959, 2 vols.

SUMMARY
BIBLIOGRAPHY

The author is preparing a complete bibliography on the Roman army; only the most important and most recent works are listed here.

GENERAL WORKS

General Histories
WATSON, G.R., *The Roman Soldier*, New York, 1969 (1981).
WEBSTER, G., *The Roman Imperial Army*, London, 1969 (1974).

Dictionary
MARIN Y PENA, M., *Instituciones militares romanas*, Madrid, 1956.

Special problems
CAMPBELL, J.B., *The Emperor and the Roman Army*, Oxford, 1984.
DELBRUCK, H., *History of the Art of War, I, Antiquity*, Westport, 1975.
GIUFFRE, V., *La letteratura 'De re militari'*, Naples, 1974.
KEPPIE, L., *The Making of the Roman Army*, London, 1984.
MANN, J.C., *Legionary Recruitment and Veteran Settlement*, London, 1982.

COLLECTIONS OF ARTICLES

Congrès du limes
(Only those colloquia actually cited in the footnotes are listed here.)
  9. *Actes du 9e Congrès international d'études sur les frontières romaines*, Bucharest, 1974

10. *Studien zu den Militärgrenzen Roms*, Bonn, 1977
11. *Akten des 11. internationalen Limeskongresses*, Budapest, 1977
12. *Roman Frontier Studies*, Oxford, 1980
13. *Studien zu den Militärgrenzen Roms*, Stuttgart, 1986

Aufstieg und Niedergang der römischen Welt, Berlin and New York
(Only the articles most often cited in the book are listed here.)

BIRLEY, E., 'The religion of the Roman army (1895–1977)', II, 16, 2, 1978, pp. 1506–41.

DOBSON, B., 'The significance of the centurion and the primipilaris in the Roman army and administration', II, 1, 1974, pp. 392–434.

FORNI, G., 'Estrazione etnica a sociale dei soldati delle legioni', II, 1, 1974, pp. 339–91.

HELGELAND, J., 'Roman army religion', II, 16, 2, 1978, pp. 1470–1505.

SADDINGTON, D.B., 'The development of the Roman army auxiliary forces from Augustus to Trajan', II, 3, 1975, pp. 176–201.

SPEIDEL, M., 'The rise of ethnic units in the Roman imperial army', II, 7, 2, 1980, pp. 730–46.

Collection MAVORS Amsterdam

ALFÖLDY, G., *Geschichte des römischen Heeres*, 1986 (MAVORS III).

FORNI, G., *Esercito e marina di Roma antica*.

GILLIAM, J.F., *Roman Army Papers*, 1985 (MAVORS II).

SPEIDEL, M., *Roman Army Studies, I*, 1984 (MAVORS I) and *II*, 1989.

Varia

BIRLEY, E., *Roman Britain and the Roman Army*, London, 1953.

DAVIES, R., *Service in the Roman Army.*

GABBA, E., *Per la storia dell'esercito romano in età imperiale*, Bologna, 1974

KRAFT, K., *Gesammelte Aufsätze zur Militärgeschichte*, Darmstadt, 1973

VON DOMASZEWSKI, A., *Aufsätze zur römische Heeresgeschichte*, Cologne, 1972

ARMY ORGANIZATION

BAILLIE REYNOLDS, P.K., *The Vigiles of Imperial Rome*, Oxford, 1926.

CHEESMAN, G.L., *The Auxilia of the Roman Imperial Army*, 1914 and Hildesheim and New York, 1971.

CICHORIUS, C., 'Ala' and 'Cohors' in *Realencyclopädie*, I, 1894 and II, 1900.

DURRY, M., *Les cohortes prétoriennes*, Paris, 1939 and 1968.

FREIS, H., *Die cohortes urbanae, Epigraphische Studien*, II, 1967.

KEINAST, D., *Untersuchungen zu den Kriegsflotten der römischen Kaiserzeit*, Bonn, 1966.

PARKER, H.M.D., *The Roman Legions*, Chicago, 1958 and 1980.

PASSERINI, A., *Le coorti pretorie*, Rome, 1939.

REDDÉ, M., *Mare Nostrum*, Rome and Paris, 1986.

RITTERLING, E., 'Legio' in *Realencyclopädie*, XII, 2, 1925.

SAXER, R., *Die Vexillationen des römischen Kaiserheeres, Epigraphische Studien*, I, 1967.

SPEIDEL, M., *Die equites singulares Augusti*, Bonn, 1965.
SPEIDEL, M., *Riding for Caesar*, 1994.
STARR, C.G., *The Roman Imperial Navy*, Westport, 1941 and 1975.

OFFICERS AND MEN

CLAUSS, M., *Untersuchungen zu den principales des römischen Heeres*, Bochum, 1973.
DEVIJVER, H., *Prosopographia militiarum equestrium*, 4 vols, Louvain, 1976–1987.
DOBSON, B., *Die primipilares*, Bonn, 1978.
MAXFIELD, V.A., *The Military Decorations of the Roman Army*, London, 1981.
PICARD, G.-CH., and LE BONNIEC H., 'Du nombre et des titres des centurions légionnaires', *Revue Philologique*, 1937, 112–24.
SPEIDEL, M., *Guards of the Roman Army*, Bonn, 1978.
VON DOMASZEWSKI, A., *Die Rangordnung des römischen Heeres*, revised by B. Dobson, Bonn, 1967.

RECRUITMENT

FORNI, G., *Il reclutamento delle legioni da Augusto a Diocleziano*, Milan and Rome, 1953 (see *Aufstieg und Niedergang*, II, 1, 1974).
KRAFT, K., *Zur Rekrutierung der Alen und Kohorten an Rhein und Donau*, Bern, 1951.

TRAINING

DAVIES, R., 'The training grounds of Roman cavalry', *Archaeological Journal*, CXXV, 1968, 73–100.
LE BOHEC, Y., 'Le pseudo "camp des auxiliaires" à Lambèse', *Cahiers du groupe de recherches sur l'armée romaine et les provinces*, 1, 1977, 71–85.
NEUMANN, A., 'Militärhandbuch', *Klio*, 8, 1928, 360 ff.
NEUMANN, A., 'Heeresreglement', *Classical Philology*, 1946, 217ff.
NEUMANN, A., 'Rekrutenausbildung', *Classical Philology*, 1948, 148ff.
NEUMANN, A., 'Heeresdiziplin', *Klio*, 28, 1934, 297ff.

TACTICS

COUISSIN, P., *Les armes romaines*, Paris, 1926.
KROMAYER, J. and VEITH G., *Heerwesen und Kriegsfuhrung*, in VON MULLER

I., *Handbuch der klassischen Altertums-wissenschaft*, IV, 3, 2, Munich, 1928.

MARSDEN, E., *Greek and Roman Artillery*, Oxford, 1971.

STRATEGY

ALFÖLDY, G., *Die Hilfstruppen der Germania Inferior, Epigraphische Studien*, VI, Bonn, 1968.

BAATZ, D., *Der römische Limes zwischen Rhein und Donau*, Berlin, 1975.

BREEZE, D.J. and DOBSON, B., *Hadrian's Wall*, London, 1980.

FITZ, J., *Der römische Limes in Ungarn*, Budapest, 1976.

FORNI, G., 'Limes' in DE RUGGIERO E., *Dizionario epigrafico*, IV, 1959, pp. 1074ff.

KENNEDY, D.L., *Archaeological Explorations on the Roman Frontier in North-East Jordan*, Oxford, 1982.

LE BOHEC, Y., *La IIIe Légion Auguste*, Aix-Marseille-Paris, 1989.

LE BOHEC, Y., *Les unités auxiliaires de l'armée romaine en Afrique proconsulaire et Numidie*, Aix-Marseille-Paris, 1989.

LE ROUX, P., *L'armée romaine et l'organisation des provinces ibériques*, Paris, 1982.

LESQUIER, J., *L'armée romaine d'Egypte*, Cairo, 1918.

LUTTWAK, E.N., *The Grand Strategy of the Roman Empire*, 1974, Baltimore and London, 1979.

POIDEBARD, A., *La trace de Rome dans le désert de Syrie*, 2 vols, Paris, 1934.

RICKMAN, G., *Roman Granaries and Store Buildings*, Cambridge, 1971.

STEIN, E., *Die kaiserlichen Beamten und Truppenkorper im römischen Deutschland unter dem Prinzipat*, Vienna, 1932.

SZILAGYI, J., 'Les variations des centres de prépondérance militaire dans les provinces frontières de l'Empire romain', *Acta Antiqua Academiae Scientiarum Hungaricae*, 2, 1953–1954, 117–219.

VON PETRIKOVITS, H., *Die Innenbauten römischer Legionslager*, Opladen, 1975.

WAGNER, W., *Die Dislokation der römischen Auxiliarformationen in den Provinzen Noricum, Pannonia, Moesia und Dacia*, Göttingen, 1938.

HISTORY

GUEY, J., *Essai sur la guerre parthique de Trajan*, Bucarest, 1937.

LEPPER, F.A., *Trajan's Parthian War*, Oxford, 1948.

PRACTICAL ROLE

SALWAY, P., *The Frontier People of Roman Britain*, Cambridge, 1965.

VENDRAND-VOYER, J., *Normes civiques et métier militaire à Rome sous le Principat*, Clermont-Ferrand, 1983.

CULTURAL INFLUENCE

FINK, R.O., HOEY, A.S. and SNYDER, W.F., 'Feriale Duranum', *Yale Classical Studies*, 7, 1940.

LE BONNIEC, H., in BRISSON J.-P., *Problèmes de la guerre à Rome*, Paris, 1969, pp. 101–15.

PICARD, G.-CH. *Les trophées romains*, Paris, 1957.

PIGHI, G.B., *Lettere latine d'un soldato di Traiano*, Bologna, 1964.

SPEIDEL, M., *The Religion of Juppiter Dolichenus in the Roman Army*, Leiden, 1978.

See also *Aufstieg und Niedergang*, II, 16, 2, 1978 (BIRLEY and HELGELAND).

INDEX OF NAMES

INDEX OF SUBJECTS